Iterations of Loss

Iterations of Loss

MUTILATION AND AESTHETIC FORM, AL-SHIDYAQ TO DARWISH

Jeffrey Sacks

FORDHAM UNIVERSITY PRESS *New York* 2015

the modern language initiative

THIS BOOK IS MADE POSSIBLE BY A COLLABORATIVE GRANT
FROM THE ANDREW W. MELLON FOUNDATION.

Visit us online at www.fordhampress.com.

The image of the painting by Ahmed Cherkaoui that appears as a frontispiece to this book and on its cover is reproduced with the permission of Hassan Ezzaim, Director of Fondation ONA (Rabat).

Passages that appear in Chapters 1, 2, and 3 of this book have been published in *diacritics* 37.4 (2007) and are reproduced here with the permission of Johns Hopkins University Press. Portions of Chapter 3 have been published in an article, "Falling into Pieces, Or Ahmad Faris al-Shidyaq and Literary History: A Love Letter" (*Middle Eastern Literatures* 16.3 [2013]), and are reproduced here with the permission of © Taylor and Francis. The article may be accessed on line at the following address: http://www.tandfonline.com/doi/full/10.1080/1475262X.2013.891392#.U77w2UDPYZQ.

Library of Congress Cataloging-in-Publication Data

Sacks, Jeffrey.
Iterations of loss : mutilation and aesthetic form, Al-Shidyaq to Darwish / Jeffrey Sacks. — First edition.
pages cm
Includes bibliographical references and index.
ISBN 978-0-8232-6494-0 (cloth : alk. paper)
ISBN 978-0-8232-6495-7 (pbk. : alk. paper)
1. Psychic trauma in literature. 2. Violence in literature. 3. Arab-Israeli conflict—Literature and the conflict. 4. Arabic literature—19th century—History and criticism. 5. Arabic literature—20th century—History and criticism. 6. Hebrew literature—20th century—History and criticism. I. Title.
PJ7519.P78S33 2014
892.7'09—dc23

2014030502

Printed in the United States of America

17 16 15 5 4 3 2 1

First edition

for Leah, Leila, Bella

CONTENTS

ABBREVIATIONS

A Mahmoud Darwish. *Ahada 'ashara kawkaban*. Beirut: Dar al-Jadid, 1992.

AB Mahmoud Darwish. *'Abirun fi kalam 'abir*. Beirut: Dar al-'Awda, 1994.

AF Mahmoud Darwish. *Athar al-farasha*. Beirut: Riyad al-Rayyes, 2008.

B Elias Khoury. *Bab al-shams*. Beirut: Dar al-Adab, 1998. Tr. Humphry Davies as *Gate of the Sun*. New York: Archipelago, 2006.

F Taha Husayn. *Fi al-shi'r al-jahili*. Susa, Tunis: Dar al-Ma'arif, [1926] 1998.

FH Mahmoud Darwish. *Fi hadrat al-ghiyab*. Beirut: Riyad al-Rayyes, 2006.

FS Ahmad Faris al-Shidyaq. *Kitab al-saq 'ala al-saq fi ma huwwa al-Fariyaq, aw ayam wa shuhur wa a'wam fi 'ajam al-'Arab wa al-a'jam*. Paris: Benjamin Duprat, 1855.

G Jacques Derrida. *Glas*. Paris: Galilée, 1974. Tr. John P. Leavey and Richard Rand as *Glas*. Lincoln: University of Nebraska Press, 1986.

H Mahmoud Darwish. *Hisar li mada'ih al-bahr*. Beirut: Dar al-'Awda, 1984.

I Shimon Ballas. *Iya*. In *Otot stav*, 9–50. Tel Aviv: Zmora-Bitan, 1992. Tr. Susan Einbinder as *Iya*. In *Keys to the Garden: New Israeli Writing*, ed. Ammiel Alcalay, 69–99. San Francisco: City Lights, 1996.

IK Taha Husayn. *Falsafat Ibn Khaldun al-ijtima'iyya*. Tr. Muhammad 'Inan. Cairo: Matba'at al-I'timad, 1925.

J Mahmoud Darwish. *Jidariyya*. Beirut: Riyad al-Rayyes, 2000.

K Mahmoud Darwish. *Ka zahr al-lawz aw ab'ad*. Beirut: Riyad al-Rayyes, 2005.

L Mahmoud Darwish. *Limadha tarakta al-hisana wahidan?* Beirut: Riyad al-Rayyes, 1995. Tr. J. Sacks as *Why Did You Leave the Horse Alone?* New York: Archipelago, 2006.

LT Mahmoud Darwish. *La ta'tadhir 'amma fa'alta*. Beirut: Riyad al-Rayyes, 2004.

M Theodor Adorno. *Minima Moralia: Reflexionen aus dem beschädigten Leben*. Frankfurt am Main: Suhrkamp, [1951] 1969. Tr. E. F. N. Jephcott as *Minima Moralia: Reflections from Damaged Life*. London and New York: Verso, 1974.

MA Edmond Amran El Maleh. *Mille ans, un jour*. Paris: La Pensée Sauvage, 1986.

P Jacques Derrida. *La carte postal: De Socrate à Freud et au-delà*. Paris: Flammarion, 1980. Tr. Alan Bass as *The Post Card: From Socrates to Freud and Beyond*. Chicago: University of Chicago Press, 1987.

SG Mahmoud Darwish. *Sarir al-ghariba*. Beirut: Riyad al-Rayyes, 1999.

SL Ahmad Faris al-Shidyaq. *Sirr al-layali fi al-qalb wa al-ibdali*. Ed. and introd. Muhammad al-Hadi bin al-Tahir al-Mutawwi. Beirut: Dar al-Gharb al-Islami, [1867] 2006.

SM Jacques Derrida. *Spectres de Marx: L'état de la dette, le travail de deuil at la nouvelle Internationale*. Paris: Galilée, 1993. Tr. Peggy Kamuf as *Specters of Marx: The State of the Debt, the Work of Mourning, and the New International*. New York: Routledge, 1994.

Y Mahmoud Darwish. *Yawmiyyat al-huzn al-'adi*. Beirut: Dar al-'Awda, [1973] 2007.

ACKNOWLEDGMENTS

Writing is a solitary act, and yet it will never have been one's own. Avital Ronell opened a door many years ago, and I thank her for her generosity and the gift of her teaching, and for her continued support and kindness. Ammiel Alcalay taught me the place and force of translation, and of declining to translate, and has steadfastly supported my work. Elias Khoury has given more than I can possibly ask. His writing and teaching remain a gift. Muhsin al-Musawi has been a giving mentor and teacher. His wealth of knowledge of Arabic letters continues to be humbling. Hamid Dabashi welcomed me as a graduate student to the Department of Middle East and Asian Languages and Cultures at Columbia University (now the Department of Middle East, South Asian, and African Studies), and I thank him for his support. Prior to her untimely death, Magda al-Nowaihi, with whom I had been privileged to study, was a giving adviser. I thank Gil Anidjar for a difficult question he asked many years ago, and to which I hope to have responded, if belatedly, here. The late Olfat Kamal al-Rubi, of Cairo University, taught me to read Arabic poetry, and I remain indebted to her teaching. The Center (now Institute) for Comparative Literature and Society at Columbia University formed an important institutional site for the work on what was to become this book. Since my time at Columbia several individuals have supported my work in ways the importance of which it is difficult to overstate. I thank Judith Butler for her interest in and support of this book. Her integrity and writing have shaped it in more than one way. Ali Behdad and Ed Dimendberg were unfailingly giving and generous, and I thank them. Elliott Colla and Stephen Sheehi read early drafts of this manuscript, and I thank them for their questions and critique. Najat Rahman and

David Lloyd read the manuscript for Fordham University Press, and I hope to have responded to their questions adequately in the pages that follow. Parts of this book have been presented at Cairo University, the American University of Beirut, Columbia University, Brown University, Harvard University, the University of California, Los Angeles, Tufts University, New York University, Penn State University, Princeton University, and the University of California, Riverside. The engagement and conversation on those occasions pressed my work in new ways. Ramzi Baalbaki hosted me at the Department of Arabic at the American University of Beirut in 2003–4, and Muhammad Ali Khalidi arranged for me to have access to the library of the Institute for Palestine Studies in Beirut during that time, and I thank each of them. In California, time in residence at the Center for Ideas and Society at the University of California, Riverside, and the Humanities Research Institute at the University of California, Irvine, provided support at distinct moments to write portions of this book and to complete it. Subventions from the College of Humanities, Arts, and Social Sciences, and the Department of Comparative Literature at the University of California, Riverside, supported the publication of this book. I thank Stephen Cullenberg and Tom Scanlon for their generosity. Hassan Ezzaim, Director of the Fondation ONA in Rabat, generously agreed to allow me to publish the image of the painting by Ahmed Cherkaoui that appears in this book and on its cover. Najah Azzouzi, who kindly helped me to contact him, deserves all the thanks in the world. Over the years, in Beirut, Cairo, New York, Ann Arbor, Austin, and Riverside, teachers, colleagues, and friends taught me, in different ways. I thank Sinan Antoon, Shiko Behar, Taoufiq ben Amor, April Durham, Khaled Abou El-Fadl, Alex Elinson, Nergis Ertürk, Nouri Gana, John Ganim, William Granara, Walid Hamarneh, Michelle Hartman, Barbara Harlow, Annemarie Jacir, Emily Jacir, Elizabeth Johnston, Fady Joudah, Chad Kia, Sharon Kinoshita, Brian Lennon, Joseph Massad, Sofian Merabet, Aamir Mufti, Mara Naaman, Tsolin Nalbantian, Noha Radwan, Najat Rahman, Dina Ramadan, Kamran Rastegar, Teofilo Ruiz, Jill Schoolman, Sherene Seikaly, Samah Selim, Anton Shammas, Stephen Sheehi, Setsu Shigematsu, Shaden Tageldin, Nader Uthman, and Veli Yashin. My colleagues in the Department of Comparative Literature and the Program in Middle East and Islamic Studies at the University of California, Riverside, have been supportive and giving. Helen Tartar, at Fordham

University Press, expediently supported the publication of this book. It will never have come to be what it is without the gift of her interest and generosity. Her sudden death points to the urgency of thinking loss without leaving it behind. Thomas Lay, before and following Helen's death, has been supportive and giving. The debts I owe to my wife, Leah, and, differently, to my daughters, Leila and Bella, far exceed whatever I may have been able to give.

NOTE ON TRANSLATION AND TRANSLITERATION

Translations in what follows are my own unless an existing English-language translation is indicated in the bibliography, and existing translations have on occasion been silently modified. A simplified version of the *International Journal of Middle East Studies* system has been followed in the transliteration of Arabic and Hebrew words. The only diacritics included are the hamza and the ʿayn, which are indicated with a closed and open apostrophe, respectively. The former is not transcribed when it occurs at the beginning of a word but is when it occurs elsewhere. In certain instances personal names with spellings that have become conventional in English are transliterated according to that convention (e.g., Mahmoud Darwish, Elias Khoury). Certain inseparable prepositions and conjunctions are not connected to what follows with a hyphen, and the letter *alif* in the definite article is not rendered in writing as elided when followed by these prepositions or conjunctions (e.g., *wa al-shiʿr* and not *wa-l-shiʿr*).

A wound of the tongue is like a wound of the hand.

IBN JINNI, quoting Imru' al-Qays

But mourning is without limits and without representation.
It is tears and ashes.

JEAN-LUC NANCY

Introduction: Loss

I think
And there is neither fault in my doing so
Nor delusion
That I shall
Cut through the steel with a silk thread
And
Build distant tents with a woolen one
And flee from them, from her
And from me
Because I . . .
As if I

MAHMOUD DARWISH, *Athar al-farasha*

This is a book about loss. But to speak of loss is already to do so in relation to "the long familiar idea of time as that which passes away" and the destruction this idea and its proliferation impart.[1] Loss, and with the dividing expansion of capital and the asymmetrical force of colonial, juridical violence, is to be left behind, the archaic debris of a time said to be no longer.[2] *Iterations of Loss* turns to nineteenth- through twenty-first-century Arabic and Arab Jewish writing to read the time of loss, between and within languages, and to read the aporetical dimension of language, which loss gives. Already bereaved, loss disrupts the privileging of figures of sovereignty and autonomy in language, to gesture to a temporal excess, where language, in order to be itself, becomes something other than what it is.[3] And language, like loss, stalls its mournful appropriation into the state and the figures it privileges. It forms the occasion for an ethical or political disruption of sense, to give place to ways of being and of being with others that occur as interrupted, interruptive events of form.

§

This book reads the relation of language, and languages, to the devastating events of loss that took place in the destruction of Palestine in 1948, and in relation to colonizing acts of violence that preceded, occasioned, and followed it.[4] The loss of Palestine imparts a destruction of world and a violent rupture with ways of being and living, and yet this rupture will never simply have ended, having been located, finally, within a historical past. Remaining with unfinished ruptures and the iterated incursion of loss into the time of life, this book considers texts said to be separated by period, language, literary institution, and genre—Mahmoud Darwish's late lyric poetry and his *Limadha tarakta al-hisana wahidan?* (Beirut, 1995), Ahmad Faris al-Shidyaq's *al-Saq 'ala al-saq* (Paris, 1855), Taha Husayn's *Fi al-shi'r al-jahili* (Cairo, 1926), Edmond Amran El Maleh's *Mille ans, un jour* (Paris, 1986), Elias Khoury's *Bab al-shams* (Beirut, 1998), and Shimon Ballas's *Iya* (Tel Aviv, 1992). In what follows I read the shared and divided legacies of events of loss imparted to language and poetic statement, to consider those legacies in relation to reading and form. Rather than privilege sharp temporal distinctions (between the modern and premodern, colonial and precolonial, Ottoman and post-Ottoman), I remain with the bereaved time of language, where language is already in loss. Attention to this quality of language, where language parts from itself, teaches a placing in question of the asymmetrical destruction and degradation of life and lives, and the institutional separation of Jews from Arabs, Hebrew from Arabic, life from death, the past from the present, and language from loss, pointed to in the date, 1948, I have underlined.[5] The texts under consideration here give these distinctions to be read—the texts I consider teach us to read, and they teach us to do so differently—even as these distinctions remain sites to which acts of reading return, and it is for this reason that I attend closely to language and form in this book.

Iterations of Loss remains with the unreadability of language, where the desire to mournfully gather language into recognizable, monadic bits of sense is interrupted, where the readability of language will already have been lost. I point in the subtitle of this book to a temporal coherency or literary history ("al-Shidyaq to Darwish"), but this coherency and history are interrupted in relation to loss, tradition, and death. I retain this sequence because the languages of criticism will never have mourned the comprehending force of literary history or the institutions and languages that give place to it. And I do so to recall that this sequence also asks us to read and understand history differently, because language takes place as an event that will already have been sent, from al-Shidyaq to Darwish, a gift which teaches us that language already points elsewhere and to another, to other languages and sites, to other words and events, recalling us to a responsibility in reading. In drawing attention to older, nineteenth-century and other legacies in relation to post-1948 literary and poetic writing, I ask how literature studies may linger with colonial and older and other forms of violence, where this violence forms a condition for language. This condition points to a bereaved quality of language, where language is already in loss, and where, in the words of the poet Adunis (b. 1930), "languages break upon languages/ and speech/ leans toward the remains of speech [tankasir al-lughat 'ala al-lughat/ wa yanhani/ qawlun 'ala talal al-maqul]."[6] Language, one is given to read in this passage, is already languages, it is already more than one, and I read this excess to argue that literature, Arabic and others, is already a comparative literature. Literature, I argue, implies a comparability—a capacity for comparison, an event of language solicited where language is at once more and less than itself—where comparison does not privilege a renewed giving of sense but gives place to a new sense of relation.[7]

THE FORM OF LOSS

> When there is a general change of conditions it is as if the ground of creation has changed and the entire world been altered. It is as if there were a new creation and a new life, a world brought into being anew.
>
> IBN KHALDUN, *al-Muqaddima*

Acts or events of language are said to be grounded in a subject, but the one who speaks is already in loss, touched upon by death and tradition, in mutilation. To open a reading of this anteriority I turn here to a poem by the Palestinian poet Mahmoud Darwish (1942–2008), which I have placed as the epigraph to this introduction. The poem appears in a volume titled *Athar al-farasha* (Beirut, 2008), and in it Darwish writes of a subject—"I"—that speaks to offer a poetic word. This subject already takes place in relation to the events of violence the poem metonymically gestures. From the moment at which there is "I," and at which there is thought or supposition ("I think/ And there is neither fault in my doing so/ Nor delusion [azunnu/ wa la ithma li fi mithla dhalika/ wa la wahma]" [*AF*, 233]), there is a relation to a destruction of world and a devastation in language. The word of the poet is already given in, while still never reducible to, loss. The steel to which Darwish gestures points to the barbed wire fencing surrounding the refugee camps of the West Bank, Gaza, Lebanon, and elsewhere, and the dispossession of the Palestinian people from their lands and homes in 1948, if also earlier and later. These events are not represented in the poem but are repeated there, as they are displaced onto a future. "That I shall cut through the steel with a silk thread [anni/ bi khayti haririn aqussu al-hadid]/ And/ build distant tents/ with a woolen one." These tents point to ones that served as makeshift homes in the fallout of 1948, yet they will never have retained a place solely in the past. They will never simply have belonged to another time, because in Darwish distance, *bu'd* ("wa anni/ bi khatin min al-suf/ abni khiyam al-ba'id"), is complicated and retained. In the understanding of time one is given to read in the poem, the future, a building of tents that does not leave the past behind, will never have occasioned the mourning of the losses, including the loss of Palestine, finally, and once and for all, in what Sigmund Freud has called "the mourning work [die Trauerarbeit]."[8]

The poetic subject, in Darwish, is a figure of excess, and this excess compels a reflection on the way in which language becomes an event that is also an occasion for thought. "I"—the subject of language in the poem—is already given in relation to more than one event of destruction and loss, said now to belong to a past. The poem does not gesture to a subject of ontological consistency or self-mastery but one that occurs as the partially opaque relation to language that is remarked, at once given and repeated, in the poem: the poetic subject is already in flight. "And flee from them, from her/ And from me/ Because I/ As if I [wa ahribu minha/ wa minni/ li'anni/ ka'anni]." The pronoun *ha* (it, she, they) is discreetly imprecise: it refers to the woolen tents the poet will have built, to "her," perhaps an unnamed woman, to language, *al-lugha* (fem. sing.), languages (*al-lughat*, pl.), or to the Arabic language. The referential dimensions of language are indeterminate. This indeterminacy anticipates the final words of the poem, which offer an interruptive moment of the suspension of sense, an anacoluthon of sorts. Those final words are given through a category of the sentence, *jumlat inna wa akhawatiha*, that solicits closure: *ism inna wa khabar inna*. Ending the poem in this way—"as if I [ka'anni]"—the Darwishian sentence iterates the mournful dimension of words as it points to a placing in question of the privileging of closure with the giving of sense in language. To speak of a poetic subject in Darwish is, then, to speak of the Arabic language and of a violent, repeated reorganization of the terms for the giving of sense, a colonization of language, which takes place in the Arabic nineteenth century, where an older practice of language is displaced in relation to a colonial, European conception and practice of form. Poetic statement, in Darwish, points to and confounds this displacement. The poem shares in an event of destruction it also repeats, if never simply or solely, and which one is given to read through this belated repetition.

Attention to the imperatives of language and form, which the reading of Darwish compels, requires considerable elaboration. I pursue this elaboration in chapter 1 through a consideration of Adunis's theoretical work, *al-Thabit wa al-mutahawwil* (Beirut, 1974–78), and his discussion of the death of the prophet Muhammad (d. 632), and through other writing in and on Arabic letters, which I read and learn from in different ways (Muhammad 'Abid al-Jabri, Nasr Hamid Abu Zayd, Faysal Darraj, Abdallah Laroui, Abdelkabir Khatibi, Abdelfattah Kilito, Sayyed al-Bahrawi, Radwa 'Ashour, Jurj Tarabishi, and Muhsin Jasim al-Musawi). I offer these readings to articulate a set of proximate, if distinct questions, which the word "I" in Darwish also compels. If in Darwish reading occurs as something that may not be taken for granted, and if this points to and places in question form as a figure of coherency, in "the aesthetic unity of manner and substance," then his text compels a reading of literary institutions, those institutions that desire to read literature in order to form it into bits of consumable, interiorizable, temporally coherent linguistic sense.[9] To reflect on reading in this way is to read the institution of a literary object in the Arabic language and to consider its relation to the formation of states, and it is to reflect on the problems of literary comparison and the legacies that give place to it. I pursue the first of these in chapter 2 through a reading of Taha Husayn's *Fi al-shi'r al-jahili* (Cairo, 1926), which I read in relation to older, nineteenth-century texts. And I pursue the second through a consideration of loss and literary comparison, which is approached, in detailed readings, in each chapter of this book. To study the relations between loss and reading is not to mute the historicity of language but to recall it, because the historical, rather than an event that belongs in time, already points to a relation to loss, as if the time of history were that of a stalled, catachrestic event of language.

§

Loss confounds the belonging of language to time, to point to the urgency of declining to secure loss on the far side of a harsh line of separation between the living and the dead.[10] Language cites the words of more than one other who has died "as soon as we open our mouths" ("It's always the same thing that comes back, the same wound, it speaks in my place as soon as I open the lips, my own, however [*P*, 134/122]," Jacques Derrida has written), to point to disarticulations of a subject in mutilation.[11] Yet it is not that this return gestures to an identity—a sameness that will have persisted through what returns ("It's always the same thing that comes back, the same wound [C'est toujours la même chose qui revient, la même plaie]")—but that the being of "I" is already, irreparably confounded, without consolation. What comes back, a "thing" (*chose*) that is also a "wound" (*plaie*), speaks in my place to give place to "me." "I" take place as an effect of this speech ("it speaks in my place as soon as I open the lips [elle parle à ma place dès que j'ouvre les lèvres]"), where "my place" is already a displacement, never and no longer my own, and where a coherent subject of language is given only through a metalepsis. "My place" is the place of an originary return or a repetition, a ghost or *revenant* ("la même chose qui revient"), and language, if also being, is given to be read as an event where everything begins by coming back. "I" take place as the being that I am "as soon as I open the lips, my own, however [dès que j'ouvre les lèvres, les miennes pourtant]," and this "as soon as" is what the time of "I" is. In *The Post Card* (Paris, 1980), and if also elsewhere, Derrida gives us to read the form of a subject of language—"I"—through this aporetical temporality. Its time will never simply have belonged to itself, and "I," then, already takes place in mutilation. And language occurs as the iteration of loss.

In this book I follow Derrida's intervention to ask how a privileging of specific, European, aesthetic and temporal categories imparts a destruction to language and world. This intervention has solicited, in different ways, readings from which I learn in this book, in the discussion of stuttering, stunted modes of being in Avital Ronell's *Stupidity*,[12] of the subject's "turning back" on itself in Judith Butler's *Psychic Life of Power*,[13] the reflection on "looking away" in Rei Terada,[14] and the "dance of death and mutilation" in the "disarticulation of words themselves" in Paul de Man's reading of Heinrich von Kleist.[15] Walter Benjamin's *Origin of German Tragic Drama* is, and not solely, a book about aesthetic form. "Tirelessly thought makes new beginnings, returning in a roundabout way to the thing itself. This continual pausing for breath is the most proper *form of being* [my emphasis] of the process of contemplation [Dies unablässige Atemholen ist die eigenste Daseinsform der Kontemplation]."[16] The continual pausing for breath Benjamin underlines is mournful ("Pensiveness is characteristic above all of the mournful" [318/139–40]), pointing to the bereaved dimension of thought. Thought interrupts itself to be itself, and loss, then, does not come later to thought but interruptively gives place to it. Thought, if also language, already takes place in relation to more than one other said to be no longer, as it keeps returning to a site of loss to become a melancholic event of commemoration ("The persistence which is expressed in the intention of mourning is born of its loyalty to the world of things" [334/157]). This intention points to an anterior relation to loss, where a loyalty to "the world of things" gives place to what language is and does, where language already occurs through this intention, unsettling an anthropocentric privilege imparted through institutions of reading. Language, Arabic and others, will never have grounded itself in a being that practices it but becomes an occasion for a practice of relation where relation ceases to confirm identity but interrupts it, stalling a political and a social order of relations.[17]

§

The privileging of a new understanding and practice of language in the Arabic nineteenth century, and which is the subject of chapter 2, points to an epistemic, linguistic violence.[18] This violence is discussed in Timothy Mitchell's pathbreaking *Colonising Egypt* (1988) as a "breakdown of a textual authority," where writing comes to appear as if it were "a vehicle of communication" in relation to a new understanding of language and world.[19] This understanding is, for Mitchell, starkly new ("Colonial or modern politics will seek to create for this subject a continuous theatre of certainty, unknown to premodern politics" [178]), and it forms the occasion for the imparting of a European, theological understanding of language, which privileges "a realm of 'meaning' that is believed to exist quite apart from words themselves under the theological name of 'language' or 'truth' or 'mind' or 'culture'" (149). Mitchell reads this understanding as opposed to that of Husayn al-Marsafi (d. 1890), a lecturer at the state-sponsored teacher's training college Dar al-'Ulum, which was founded in Egypt in 1872, and who "shared a belief in no such metaphysical realm" (142). In al-Marsafi, Mitchell writes, and in his *al-Kalim al-thamin* (Eight Words), "the questions of meaning and the play of difference remained problematised" (146), declining to cohere into a univocal giving of sense. I remain indebted to Mitchell's intervention, because it underlines language as a site for the enactment of colonial violence. But the privileging of an oppositional understanding of the Arabic language in relation to "European languages" (149), and the expansion of this opposition in historical terms, obscures the violence of which Mitchell also offers a critique.[20] One may ask, then, whether, in recognizing the past as the past—Mitchell writes that the Arabic nineteenth century, like Descartes, if differently, "breaks" with the past—and whether in doing so through a particular grid of terms, *Colonising Egypt* repeats those terms, historical and other, which it has also taught us to read.[21]

The critique Mitchell offers has opened a reading of language, and institutions, in relation to colonial violence, and in relation to the Arabic nineteenth century and its legacies. This violence has been read and elaborated, differently, in subsequent scholarship in Arabic studies, in relation to the totalizing sociality of the novel form in Samah Selim's *The Novel and the Rural Imaginary in Egypt*, practices of epistemic self-colonization in Stephen Sheehi's *Foundations of Modern Arab Identity* and Joseph Massad's *Desiring Arabs*, the institution of historicizing legibility in Elliott Colla's *Conflicted Antiquities*, the formation of disciplinary objects in Omnia El Shakry's *The Great Social Laboratory* and state-bounded fields of reading in Kamran Rastegar's *Literary Modernity between the Middle East and Europe*, the privileging of a colonial form of the body in Wilson Chacko Jacob's *Working Out Egypt* and the confounded staging of this form in Tarek El-Ariss's *Trials of Arab Modernity*, and the institution of sovereignty in language in Shaden M. Tageldin's *Disarming Words* and of juridical categories of humanist privilege in Samera Esmeir's *Juridical Humanity*. In the pages that follow I learn, in different ways, from this scholarship, to argue that the event of violence I study in the nineteenth- and early-twentieth-century texts I consider is already repeated in "later" events of citation and acts of linguistic performance. This violence enacts a temporal rupture that gives place to a sense of time and being in language, where the past is compelled to appear as if it belonged to another time, as if it were on the side of stillness and death, of "religion" and the "theological."[22]

The mournful terms that mediate this rupture are both aesthetic and philological, and I discuss them in greater detail below in this introduction. I underline here only that language, insofar as it declines to belong to the simplicity of a temporal period or epoch, and insofar as it will never have been its own, stalls the terms that are called upon to read it. This stalling, I argue, points to an eventfulness of language, where the form of loss takes place as an interruption.

I approach this interruption through a reading of Darwish, and I address it, differently, in relation to al-Shidyaq and his *al-Saq 'ala al-saq fi ma huwwa al-Fariyaq* (Paris, 1855). If in Darwish poetic utterance is already given in relation to death and loss, in al-Shidyaq language is solicited to become recognizable in relation to an anthropocentric privilege. "Al-Saq 'ala al-saq," which may be rendered in the English language as "One Leg over Another," promises, while it still never presents, the body of "man" as a coherent figure. Two legs crossed, one over the other, point metonymically to a whole, complete body, and yet this body remains in pieces, a corpus cut into. The writing of the body in *al-Saq 'ala al-saq* repeats this double movement, as do the words that form the name "al-Fariyaq." "Fariyaq" gathers together, it cuts into, divides, and joins the words *Faris* and *al-Shidyaq*, just as it encrypts a relation to the words *farq* (difference), *fariq* (distinction), and *firaq* (group). "Man," in al-Shidyaq, is already a group, a plurality that declines to come down to one, pointing to the excess in language I study. The second section of the title, "fi ma huwwa al-Fariyaq," implies a relation to being—*ma huwwa* is a gloss on "what is"—and the title of this text may then be translated, if awkwardly, as "One Leg over Another, in Relation to What al-Fariyaq Is." Rendering the title, differently, as "Being al-Fariyaq: One Leg over Another," might, and if with a certain violence, underline the question of being and its relation to language, which al-Shidyaq asks us to read in the words *ma huwwa*. Below, in chapter 2, I follow the title of the work, *al-Saq 'ala al-saq fi ma huwwa al-Fariyaq*, to read language in al-Shidyaq in relation to the form of the body and the grounding of world. In *al-Saq 'ala al-saq* "man" is both promised and interrupted as the subject and the ground of language, as an older understanding and practice of language—one indexed in the Arabic word *adab*, a word that has come to be translated in Arabic and in the European languages as "literature"—is displaced and relocated, compelling the reading of form I offer in this book.

§

In the persisting and proliferating wars of the United States against Iraq, Afghanistan, and elsewhere, legibility is privileged in what Natalie Melas has called the "normalizing and generalizing activity" reading is solicited to perform in the disciplines of the humanities, in literature studies and comparative literature, where older, Hegelian, Pauline legacies are repeated ("For we write you nothing but what you can read and understand" [2 Corinthians 1:13]).[23] To read this privileging in relation to the institution of literature in Arabic is a principal burden of this book. I underline that this institution is formed, and repeatedly instituted, in relation to the legacies of Orientalism and the juridical violence of the colonial state. What is said to have been a "purification and simplification"[24] of language in the nineteenth century, its "modernization,"[25] occasions language's dislodging from older Arabic-Islamic practices, in the asymmetrical proliferation of capital, and with the conscription of language into a new understanding of form and a European philological and aesthetic inheritance.[26] The terms of this inheritance are repeated and interrupted in Immanuel Kant's *Critique of the Power of Judgment* (1790), and I turn to read this text below in this introduction. I underline here only that these terms do not come to the Arabic language from an outside but are imparted through acts of writing and translation, between and within languages, which redesignate the terms of more than one inside and outside. There is no exteriority with respect to this violence—in relation to language and in relation to forms of being and life—even as it is neither total nor undifferentiated. It is a violence that forms the occasion for who or what "I" am, because language is already mediated through this violence, where "I am, as it were, dispossessed by the language that I offer."[27] And it is a violence that sets the terms of temporal and social intelligibility, if never finally, imparting a particular understanding of time, which obscures the conditions of sociality and the unequal, asymmetrical imparting of violence, that also give place to that understanding. A reading of the past as exterior to this violence, as what Aamir R. Mufti has compellingly discussed as "undifferentiated," is given to be read in relation to the epistemic and linguistic forms that condition and sanction it.[28] Declining simply to belong to time, even as it is not atemporal—there is no recourse to a beyond here, no transcendental shelter—language interrupts the identitarian privilege that it also promises in reading institutions.[29]

THE PHILOLOGICAL-POLEMICAL SUBLIME

For though reason's prospect of proportionately greater employment in a practical respect has come to compensate it for the mentioned loss, still it seems that reason cannot help being pained as it tries to part with those hopes and to sever its old attachment.

IMMANUEL KANT, *Kritik der Urteilskraft*

Iterations of loss point to events of loss and destruction, which are repeated, as if for the first time, in subsequent acts and events of language. And iterations of loss point to a relation to citation and death that is occasioned in language, and in poetic statement in general, to point to what Derrida has called "iterability."[30] I turn in greater detail to Derrida's discussion of iterability below, in chapter 4, and I underline here only that it is in this sense that I repeat in this book, in its title and elsewhere, the argument that loss "already" touches upon language and that language is already "in" loss. In this book I speak of "iterations of loss" because loss does not come to language as if it were an accident—as if it came later to language—but points to an essential dimension of what language is. In the chapters that follow this argument is at once intensified, in detailed readings of texts, and broadened, through a reading of the institution of a literary object in the Arabic language. This instituting event, I argue, bears a relation to loss and destruction, to a reorganization of the tongue of language in the Arabic nineteenth century, an event of violence that is generalized in language, if however differentially and asymmetrically, in relation to the form of a social and political body and the institution of historical categories. The historical understanding of language I study is privileged in the institution of a literary object in Arabic, and yet this event is not simply "historical," but occasions a violence that is repeated—already—in "later" and "subsequent" texts and events of language. This violence is, then, not historicizable. It does not take place "in" time. And the time of this violence is, then, catachrestic—it is, if you will, poetic—and it is, if in part, for this reason that the work of Mahmoud Darwish is privileged in this book.

The institution of a new privileging of formal coherency in language, in the Arabic nineteenth century, is occasioned in events of translation and textual inscription to which I have gestured, and which I study in chapter 2 in detail. These events of language are given through the categories privileged in the "Analytic of the Sublime" in Kant's third *Critique*—they are the categories to which language is conscripted, and which are both aesthetic (an understanding of totality in language and political and social form is promised) and philological (a new, colonial understanding of language, religion, and history is privileged).[31] The texts of the Arabic nineteenth century have and continue to be read—more or less explicitly or implicitly—in the aftermath of the third *Critique*, where these texts are said to be more (or less) modern, and more (or less) secular, against a historicist, anthropocentric, philological backdrop. I turn to Kant here not to reiterate these comparisons but because the violence imparted to language in the nineteenth century, through the inheritance remarked in Kant, gives place to the historicity of language.[32] This violence is not one that may be interpreted and mourned in its turn but compels close textual explication. It compels a reading. Such reading may begin, here, with Kant's third *Critique*, a text that does not install identity but imparts the stalled reorganization of difference, and differences, between and within.[33] The third *Critique* is to articulate the gap opened between the first two—*Critique of Pure Reason* and *Critique of Practical Reason*—a gap between the conditions of knowledge and freedom, the theoretical and the practical. But this articulation, in the promise of the aesthetic, is given in philological terms. Derrida has underlined that both Kant and G. W. F. Hegel "consider a certain Judaism as the historical figure of the sublime irruption," and this consideration—to solicit "man" Kant must speak of "a certain Judaism," if also, as Gil Anidjar has taught us, Islam—points to a desire to manage difference in a being whose death is to fulfill and complete the time of life.[34] In the third *Critique* "man" appears as "a finite, sensory being,"[35] and this finitude, in the institution of a world, is to transform "loss into knowledge of loss," to give "man" to appear as "an entity capable of universalizing its own mortality."[36] The aesthetic—as the subordination of time to the time of the life and death of man—sets the terms for the philological categories Kant privileges. The aesthetic is solicited to exemplify what a relation is—it *is* relation as articulation—even as language interrupts this articulation, giving an unsettled, disrupted sense of relation.

In Kant, "man," "the only subject of this *Critique* of judgment,"[37] is privileged, but it is immediately stalled as it gestures to "modern philosophy's effort to discover a ground for itself in the activity of the judging subject."[38] The subject of judgment is already bereaved, and the terms of this bereavement are given through Kant's reading of the mathematical and dynamic sublime.[39] The mathematical sublime is linked to an experience of judging the size of something "absolutely large."[40] What is absolutely large is incomparable ("The latter is what is large beyond all comparison" [110/103]), and the sublime is not the attribute of an object "but must be sought solely in our ideas" (113/105). In judgment the mind demands totality, manically recuperating the losses—Kant underlines that the sublime occasions a feeling of inadequacy on the part of the judging subject (115/107)—through "our intuition of the world" (119/111). Gayatri Chakravorty Spivak has underlined, in *A Critique of Postcolonial Reason* (1999), that the dynamic sublime elaborates judgment in the figure of man over against "the person who is uncultivated." "It is a fact that what is called sublime by us having been prepared through culture comes across as merely repellent to a person who is uncultivated [dem rohen Menschen] and lacks the development of moral ideas," Kant writes.[41] Spivak translates *dem rohen Menschen* as "man in the raw," which "can, in its signifying reach, accommodate the savage and the primitive," to show that Kant includes by violently excluding this figure to and from the figure of man.[42] The subject of the third *Critique* is fated to commit a subreption in calling nature sublime, misrecognizing object for affect, but "man in the raw" calls nature "repellant," pointing to its exclusion from and subordination within Kant's terms.[43] They are terms—the savage, the primitive—that are invented philologically, and that impose more than one harsh opposition, between life and death, and between what ought to exist and what ought not ("He is not only not the subject as such; he also does not quite make it as an example of the thing or its species as a natural product. If you happen to think of him, your determinant judgment cannot prove to itself that he, or a species of him, need exist" [25]). Asymetrically imparting itself, giving itself to the world, the aesthetic in Kant—an "itinerary of recognition through assimilation of the Other" (281)—is already polemical.[44]

But it is in this distinction that true enlightenment consists.

IMMANUEL KANT, *Religion*

All language is signification of thought and, on the other hand, the best way of signifying thought is through language, the greatest instrument for understanding ourselves and others.

IMMANUEL KANT, *Anthropology*

This I learned from Carl Schmitt, that formulas aren't neutral, but polemical.

JACOB TAUBES, *The Political Theology of Paul*

The sense of relation given, and given to be read, in the fallout of Kant compels the readings pursued here. The cultural politics of *Bildung* in the colonies—where language, "the greatest instrument for understanding ourselves and others," is to become a medium for the comprehension of a self in the time of its life and death—is given, in Kant, through the aesthetic and philological terms I have underlined.[45] These terms—the savage and the primitive, in the reading Spivak pursues—are given in the third *Critique* through Kant's discussion of religion. Religion, in Kant, and like the sublime, divides: religion (in the singular) from religions (in the plural), a division one is given to read in the "General Comment" that follows the discussion of the dynamic sublime in paragraph 29 of the third *Critique*. Kant: "Perhaps the most sublime passage in the Jewish law is the commandment: thou shalt not make unto thee any graven image, or any likeness of any thing that is in heaven or on earth, or under the earth, etc."[46] To privilege this commandment Kant describes scripture as something that will have been left behind, as religions morph to become religion, or, in Kant, Christianity. Kant gestures to "the Jewish people [das jüdische Volk]" and "the pride Islam [der Mohammedanism] inspires" (147/135), placing each on the side of the sublime, toward which the judging subject feels repulsion. The divisions staged in this passage—the judging subject, if also the subject of language, is given as itself through its division of itself at once from "the Jewish people" and "Islam"—translate the terms of *Die Religion innerhalb der Grenzen der bloßen Vernunft* (1798) into those of the third *Critique*, and I turn to this translation presently.

In Kant natural religion is Christianity, and Christianity is the idea of religion and its divided explication. To read this explication I underline the passage in *Religion* in which Christianity and its origin appear as a "total revolution." "Inasmuch as this history is to constitute a system, we cannot begin the universal history of the Church anywhere but from the origin of Christianity which, as a total abandonment of the Judaism in which it originated, grounded on an entirely new principle, effected a total revolution in doctrines of faith."[47] If the origin of Christianity is the "total abandonment" of

Judaism, to write of this abandonment Kant divides: Christianity—"pure moral religion unencumbered by statutes" (223/187)—from historical, ecclesiastical faith. Yet Christianity, "the one and only religion, valid for all worlds" (112/123), is also parasited by its relation to religions. The origin of Christianity implies its history, and the history of Christianity is its generalization of itself as the world history of religions. The religions Kant names, for example, Judaism ("Judaism as such, taken in its purity, entails absolutely no religious faith" [171/155]), are already their becoming Christianity. The interpretation of scripture in relation to "the highest concepts and grounds of reason," *zu den höchsten Vernunftbegriffen und Gründen* (147/142), has and is to give place to "all types of faith" becoming, and if only, Kant underlines, in the future, "religion." "We shall also find that this is how all types of faith—ancient and new, some written down in holy books—have always been treated, and that rational and thoughtful teachers of the people have kept on interpreting them until, gradually, they brought them, as regards their essential content, in agreement with the universal principles of moral faith" (148–49/143). To isolate the content of "moral faith," Kant names more than one example.

"Late Judaism, and Christianity itself, consist of such in part highly forced interpretations, yet directed to ends undoubtedly good and necessary to every human being. The Mohammedans know very well (as Reland shows) how to inject a spiritual meaning in the description of their paradise, otherwise dedicated to every sensuality, and the Indians do the same with the interpretation of their *Vedas*, at least for the more enlightened part of their people" (149/143), Kant writes, naming more than one "religion." The "poetic fabrications" of such writing point to "the predisposition to moral religion [die Anlage zur moralischen Religion]" (149/143), where religions—in the plural—are already their becoming religion, or, Christianity—what remained, in Kant, and if also elsewhere, the only religion. To speak of religion and its being freed from history and empirical grounds of determination, Kant must therefore speak of late Judaism, Mohammedans, *die Muhammedaner*, Indians, *die Inder*, and Christianity itself, *selbst das Christentum*. It is as if the propensity of which Kant speaks already describes what takes place with religion: it cannot separate or stop separating itself from religions. It gestures to the becoming religion of Jews, Mohammedans, Indians, and others, as it also points to their becoming literature. What Kant calls "sacred narrative" harbors a relation to presentation, *Darstellung*, "to make the extent of

God's love comprehensible to us" (84/107). Just as religion must have recourse to literature, so too it must not dispense with Judaism, Islam, or others, none of which may be, in Kant's terms, a religion, even as each is staged as its becoming the single and only one: Christianity.

The "Analytic of the Sublime" in the third *Critique* points to the terms elaborated and disarticulated in *Religion*. Religions are to religion as the "uncultured" is to its becoming human in the figure of "man." "But the fact that a judgment about the sublime in nature requires culture (more so than a judgment about the beautiful) still in no way implies that it was initially produced by culture and then introduced to society by way of (say) mere convention. Rather, it has its foundation in human nature: in something that, along with common sense, we may require and demand of everyone, namely, the predisposition to the feeling for (practical) ideas, i.e., to moral feeling."[48] The "savage" and "religions" are incorporated into "man" and "human nature" as excluded from it, as Kant desires to mournfully leave "metaphysics" behind. The desire to recuperate an immanence of sense through a privileging of the figure of man is generalized and interrupted. War is not one moment among others in this privileging ("Though war is an unintentional human endeavor [incited by our unbridled passions], yet it is also a deeply hidden and perhaps intentional endeavor of the supreme wisdom, if not to establish, then at least to prepare the way for lawfulness along with the freedom of states, and thereby for a unified system of them with a moral basis" [357/320]) but structures it. "Man" already imposes itself, asymmetrically and unequally. The subject of aesthetic judgment is installed and confounded in the repetition of a divided anthropocentrism, to remark the proliferation and domestication of difference, and differences, on a global scale. The explication of the aesthetic in Kant occurs as a lexicographical machine for the institution of names. The sublime remarks the extension of a European, Christian, and older legacy in the stalled, compulsive practice of colonial violence. It is not a violence—I repeat—that comes to its object from an outside but already extends itself to the world's languages, an extension I consider below through a reading of the Arabic nineteenth century.

§

The linguistic violence I study in this book is gestured in the institution of world in Kant. The first *Critique* solicits a comprehension of world in relation to a self's understanding of its interiority ("Pure reason is in fact occupied with nothing but itself, and it can have no other vocation"), and it does so to treat God, self, and world as fictions.[49] "It is only by way of its [God's] relation to the world that we can attempt to establish the necessity of this supposition; and it then becomes evident that the idea of such a being, like all speculative ideas, seeks only to formulate the command of reason, that all connection in the world be viewed in accordance with the principles of a systematic unity—*as if* all such connection had its source in one single all-embracing being, as the supreme and all-sufficient cause" (A 686/B 714). This fiction points to the distinction between knowing and thinking ("But our further contention must also be duly born in mind, that though we cannot know these objects as things in themselves, we must yet be in a position to think them as things in themselves" [B xxvi]) to solicit an imperative ("we must yet be") that compels a law of mourning. "I cannot even assume God, freedom, and immortality, for the sake of the necessary practical use of my reason, if I do not at the same time deprive speculative reason of its pretensions to transcendent insight" (B xxx). This loss is also that of the knowledge of man (objective and subjective genitive) in relation to its finitude. The gift of man is a Christian one, where, as Cathy Caruth has written, "the sacrifice is a loss suffered in the service of a gain,"[50] what Kant called "the benefit the world has thus far obtained from the teachings of pure reason."[51] Imparting itself to the world, and doing so into the future, critique generates a difference it cannot stop imposing ("Criticism, Kant suggests, permits a different way of representing God, which is not an attempt to know the supersensible, but only a relation to it").[52] In the giving of place of Christian, theological knowledge to knowledge of relations, a figure "which had thought to establish itself in the transparency of self-contemplation" (18)—"man"—is installed and interrupted. It is not that the inheritance remarked in Kant may be avoided; it may not, and in whichever language. This book reads the divided and dividing proliferation of this inheritance, and the political-theological and aesthetic form of the body it privileges, in writings of the Arabic nineteenth century and traces its divided legacies, between and within languages, in the twentieth and twenty-first.[53] To recall this proliferation is not to confirm identity but to read the aporetical force of juridical, colonial violence in relation to the privileging of identitarian categories. I remain with this proliferation because it points to the historicity of language and of institutions. And I do so because, in the texts under consideration here, language exceeds the orbit of those categories, giving place to new—if still not absolutely other, and if however old and ancient—ways of being and events of language in social and political form.

LITERARIA MORALIA

The thing of language is that if it is there to be given, it is to be given away.

AVITAL RONELL, *The Telephone Book*

Literary comparison "begins in bereavement."[54] The translation of non-European texts under asymmetrical conditions of colonial domination occasions what Edward W. Said called "a lexicographical police action," an event that shares in a desire to domesticate that bereavement, to render it legible in particular, European, philological terms.[55] In this book I follow Said in *Orientalism* (1978), to place an emphasis on German romance philology, because it sets the terms for the installation of new divisions through the reorganization of older ones, where "race, color, origin, temperament, character, and types overwhelmed the distinction between Christians and everyone else" (120).[56] This inheritance gestures to what Said also called "the great transformation in culture and learning that took place at the end of the eighteenth century and the beginning of the nineteenth," with "the metamorphosis in knowledge about language from being a religious issue to being a linguistic, scientific, and even a racial one," and it occasions, as Said made clear, dimensions of repetition.[57] What is said to have been left behind ("the distinction between Christians and everyone else") is reformulated in new terms. Said elsewhere reads this event in relation to Kant. "Cultural experience or indeed every cultural form is radically, quintessentially hybrid, and if it has been the practice in the West since Immanuel Kant to isolate cultural and aesthetic realms from the worldly domain, it is now time to rejoin them."[58] But, if "since" Kant domains are isolated, in Kant oppositions are multiplied. In Kant the aesthetic is not dissociated from the worldly, or the world, but gives place to it. The aesthetic points to a reorganization of an understanding of world and that being, "man," said now only to think and no longer know self, world, or God.[59] This reorganization shares in the divided, dividing legacies of colonialism, which are remarked in Said, pointing to a passivity in writing that compels sustained attention. "In many ways my study of Orientalism has been an attempt to inventory the traces upon me, the Oriental subject, of the culture whose domination has been so powerful a factor in the life of all Orientals," Said wrote.[60] In this passage "I" is given place to, "I" may be said to be who or what I am, only in relation to my being an "Oriental subject"—a subject "constituted" (26) in relation to the event of cultural "domination" Said studied. In what follows I read this anteriority in relation to the violence imparted to language in the Arabic nineteenth century, one among other consequences of what Said called Orientalism. And I consider iterations of this event, its bereaved repetition in "later," post-1948 writing, as the confounding of the divisions said to hold between and within languages.

In a late volume in which the voice of the poet addresses Said, Mahmoud Darwish asks what remains for poetry to say in a time of catastrophe. To do so he appeals to the figure of the reader as a figure of futurity. "Neither I, nor he/ but a reader who asks about what/ poetry says to us in the time of catastrophe [fi zaman al-karitha]" (*K*, 191–92). In Darwish this time is generalized in language. Language is already in the time of loss. And the poet, in the passages I read in the opening pages of this introduction, and in others I read in chapter 1, occurs as a belated figure. The poet comes after, only and already in the fallout of loss. In Darwish poetry is one name for this belatedness. "I walk lightly, lightly, as if I/ have evaporated from my body, and as if I have an appointment/ with one of my poems" (105). Just as the poet is belated, pointing to what Said, following Adorno, called "late style," so too is the poem.[61] This lateness gestures to the loss of the poem, an anterior interruption in language, and poetic statement becomes a site at which the reflection on reading in literary comparison is solicited.[62] Pursuing this reflection, *Iterations of Loss* is offered to contribute to the reading of the formation of literary institutions in the fallout of philology—and Orientalism—in the colonies.[63] Adorno writes in *Minima Moralia*, "The division which makes everything objects must itself become an object of thought [muß selber zum Objekt des Gedankens werden], instead of guiding it" (*M*, 163/125), and this imperative compels attention to the damaged condition of writing in relation to more than one colonial legacy. This imperative schools us in a refusal to read the pain and suffering imparted in colonialism in a way that "has no sooner grasped the particular than it reduces it to a through-station, and finally comes all too quickly to terms with suffering and death for the sake of a reconciliation occurring merely in reflection" (90/74). To read otherwise would be to decline such reconciliation in the reading, and in the social and political forms and "facts on the ground" reading is called upon to sanction.[64] "No other hope is left to the past than that, exposed defenselessly to disaster, it shall emerge from it as something different" (*M*, 219/167), Adorno also wrote. This difference is solicited in language, if also in the lyric poem, and it will never have emerged from disaster as if untouched by it.[65] It will already have taken place in disaster's wake. To read would be to do so in relation to this anteriority, where one would decline to leave the losses behind, including those of this writing, in "the complicity that enfolds all those who, in the face of unspeakable collective events, speak of individual matters at all" (*M*, 11/18).

§

This is a book about loss, but it is equally a book about philology and the legacies it imparts in relation to literary comparison. Philology is the invention and proliferation of historical—if also linguistic, racial, and religious—categories, yet it immediately forms an occasion for language's discombobulation of the terms of hermeneutic and historical understanding. "Philology would then be attention to that which interpunctuates, brings to a hold, creates caesuras," Werner Hamacher has written.[66] In remaining with this philological attention and this bringing to a hold, this book is offered, finally, to contribute to the critique of the domesticating force of legibility in the disciplines of the humanities in the university.[67] If acts of reading in literary scholarship will no longer have occasioned the bringing of an object from darkness into the light in acts of discriminating clarification, this does not point to a privation but teaches us to remain in what Emily Apter has called "the aporia of comparison."[68] To remain in this way would be to refuse what Ronell has discussed as "the new civic readability" and its targeted installation of sense in the field of language.[69] The dislodging of this readability is pursued by Spivak in the reflection she offers on the discipline of comparative literature, which recalls the translation of non-European languages into the idioms of literature studies in Euro-America, an event that would "transmute the literatures of the global South to an undifferentiated space of English" as it hierarchically reorganizes the differences.[70] Spivak's intervention, *Death of a Discipline*, points to the relation to time death occasions in the division of the mother tongue. "The mother tongue is actively divided" (20), and this division remarks more than one alterity at work in language, interrupting literature's time. The object of literature studies is ruined as it is given, disrupting a privileging of legibility to give place to "a permanent from-below interruption of a Comparative Literature to come" (16), an interruption without end. This interruption is taught in the texts under consideration in this book, in each instance through the singularity of its idiom, where language, from al-Shidyaq to Darwish, already points to another, still yet another other said to be no longer. And this understanding of language gives an understanding of relation, where relation becomes relations—and where relations give place to a politics and a sociality that declines to ground itself in temporally monadic forms—to gesture to the popular and collective struggles of our time.[71]

CHAPTER ONE

Citation

Fa-l-tahfaz layl al-alam hadha ‘an zahri qalb

MAHMOUD DARWISH, *Fi hadrat al-ghiyab*

“Retain this night of pain in your memory” (*FH*, 38), Mahmoud Darwish wrote. But to speak of pain is to speak of the ways in which pain may not be overcome or left behind. The imperative with which this passage opens repeats the pain of which it speaks (“retain this night”), pointing to the singularity of a night and of more than one night, and of more than one event of loss and inscription of pain, in relation to poetic utterance. If the coherency of a poetic subject is promised in reading and in “the ceaseless war against pain,” attention to language, and its imperatives, compels us to remain with the words of the poet, declining to leave them behind.[1] To open the reading of Darwish I pursue here, I retain the Arabic of this passage, transliterating it into Latin characters in the epigraph to this chapter. The words *tahfaz ‘an zahri qalb*, which form a part of this passage, gesture to memory.[2] Yet to speak of memory, in Darwish, is to do so in relation to time and the practice of writing. Poetry, in Darwish, is a “literary textual practice,” an event of language that implies the time of writing in relation to poetic statement.[3] The poem does not leave the temporal event of writing, its vocation, *mihna*, behind but is given in an unfinished relation to it.[4] The relation of writing to the poem may be compared to the time of the colonization of Palestine and its destruction and loss, from before and in the wake of 1948. Just as the time of the poem does not finish, so too the time of the destruction and loss of Palestine—if also that of the institution of the state of Israel, a state erected through the appropriation and destruction of the homes and lives of others, of more than one place and of the times and places of other's lives and languages—does not end or close. This is not only because the colonial, military, and juridical practice of that state continues, and it does, but because to consign the loss of Palestine to a past would be to seal it within history, in another time, said to have passed. If the desire of the Israeli state has been to close the past into the past, if only, and not solely, by recognizing it as being no longer, Darwish declines to close the time of loss. He declines to close the time of language, the eventfulness and temporal nonbelonging to which language points, and which is named, in Darwish, poetry.

§

Poetic statement, in Darwish, is an event of form. The passage with which I open this chapter points to the retention of the text of the Qur'an in memory, and this retention becomes a way of reading form, and of reading a relation to loss, death, and tradition, in Darwish. The lexicographer Ibn Manzur (1230–1311) writes in *Lisan al-'arab*, "It is said: someone bears the Qur'an on the back of his tongue, as it is said: he preserves it on the back of his heart [hafizahu 'an zahri qalbihi]."[5] "You say," Ibn Manzur further explains, "I recited the Qur'an from the back of my heart, that is to say, I recited [qara'tuhu] it from memory" (606). The movement of the tongue, and the inscription of language in relation to the time of that movement and its bearing of words ("It is said: someone bears the Qur'an on the back of his tongue [yuqal: hamala fulanun al-qur'ana 'ala zahri lisanihi]"), has come to be muted through a translation within the Arabic language, one that renders the Arabic words *tahfaz 'an zahri qalb* as "you shall learn by heart" or "you shall memorize." The translation of a textual enactment of memory—of a retention, inscription, and preservation of language upon the tongue—would participate in effacing the act or event of remembering which that translation sought to convey. The reorganization of the tongue of language is the subject of the second chapter of this book, and I underline this event here because if in Darwish language is something new, it is a newness that remarks an older poetic, rhetorical, and linguistic tradition.[6] It is not that language in Darwish points to what has been called "the liberation of words from their lexicographical stagnation and their general or stable meaning" but that it teaches a way of remaining with tradition during the time of its loss and devastation.[7] This devastation points to the loss and destruction of Palestine in 1948, and it reaches into the nineteenth century, to another place and another time, to gesture to the loss of language and an ode. Such losses are not set aside, transcended, or overcome in poetic statement. Neither are they mourned or left behind, if only, and not solely, because they form a condition for language. What one is given in Darwish is a reflection on a responsibility in reading, a responsibility to loss and death in which one is schooled in poetic utterance.

To consider the relation of poetic utterance to loss in Darwish I turn to a single word as it appears in a volume of poetry titled *Limadha tarakta al-hisana wahidan?* (Why Did You Leave the Horse Alone?) (Beirut, 1995), which I read in relation to the epigraph to this chapter and the inheritance to which that epigraph points. The word I read is *here* ("Here is a present that yesterday doesn't touch . . . [hahuna hadirun la yulamisuhu al-ams . . .]" [*L*, 28/22]), and it forms the occasion, I argue, for an event of citation in relation to the destruction and loss of Palestine.[8] If poetry, in Darwish, is an "act of freedom" (*FH*, 64), this is only insofar as language is already touched upon by another, where "one word rubs against another, and rhythym gives way" (*AB*, 149), and where language is a name for the interruption of the free act of a poetic subject.[9] Najat Rahman has compellingly written that in Darwish poetic statement is a "discontinuity," where loss guards the poem ("Loss here is protected, guarding the lyric").[10] This discontinuity does not follow upon a continuity, but it points to the bereaved time of poetic statement. Time and homeland, Rahman underlines, are "mediated already through loss" (61). This mediation involves a relation to the force of the imperative: the commanding gesture of the opening words of the jahili ode, a poetic form that preceded the institution of Islam, and the imperatives given in the Qur'an. The qur'anic injunction is an injunction to recite—"Recite: In the Name of thy Lord who created, created Man of a blood clot [iqra' bi ismi rabbika alladhi khalaka, khalaqa al-insan min 'alaq]" (Qur'an 96:1–2)—and it already touches upon the tongue of the poet.[11] Poetry in Darwish, and as Muhsin J. al-Musawi has underlined, "means recitation."[12] This anteriority teaches an attention to the words Darwish cites and the legacy to which they point, as it gives those words to be read through their iteration in a time of loss. If in the fallout of colonialism and with the formation of literary institutions language is to be recognized historically, in historical, and not solely historicist terms, in Darwish, what is said to belong to the past is already touched upon by language. Poetry is formed and displaced through this anteriority, and it occurs, in Darwish, as something other than itself, where "language doesn't settle down."[13]

MOURNING THE POEM

Whenever I looked for myself I found others.

MAHMOUD DARWISH, *Jidariyya*

In reading the passage in Darwish I have underlined ("Here is a present that yesterday doesn't touch"), I draw widely upon his poetic and prose writing. Rather than underscore a division of his poetic corpus into phases (early and late, before and after Beirut, the political and the aesthetic), I ask how his poetry confounds these temporal and other forms of designation. I do so because in his poetic text language is already bereaved. "You, from now on, are another" (*AF*, 275), Darwish writes, suggesting this bereavement in a relation to an alterity which touches upon "you" not only "from now on" but already. "Now," in Darwish, is already in relation to another time, it speaks to us of a past and of what belongs to a time and a place that are no more. And language holds the words of others to give place to poetic statement, an event that is its own because it repeats and iterates, cites and recites. Darwish's poetry is said to belong to what Shakir al-Nabulsi has called the "modernity of language."[14] Language is said to occasion a movement "in itself" (607), and this movement is to point to the future. "Whether the verb is perfect, imperfect, or a command, each one bears in its womb a seed of the future" (608). But to read language in genetic terms—in terms of an understanding of language as an entity that grows and develops in time, to give place to a future—is to mute the movement the critic underlines. Movement is not something that comes from itself—language in Darwish is not autonomous and what takes place with it is not a sovereign, anthropocentric event—but something that already takes place in relation to others. "Although the subject surely speaks, and there is no speaking without a subject, the subject does not exercise sovereign power over what it says," Judith Butler has written.[15] Already "the lines and borders that separate life from death" break apart.[16] This temporal relation does not impinge upon language but gives place to it, to become a condition for the future. A future is solicited in poetic statement ("What will happen . . . What will happen after the ashes?" [*L*, 14/6]), but time is not thought based upon a present that grounds a relation to a past and a future. Time is already a mode of division. Like language, it parts from itself to be itself ("We shall only meet parting at the crossroads of speech [lan naltaqiya ila wida'an 'inda muftaraq al-hadith]," Darwish writes [80/86]). This event, a coming apart that is immediately a departing, in the offering of a word of farewell, is an event of language which, in Darwish, is what a poem is.

> I am you in words. A single book
> binds us. I bear the ashes you bear, while
> we were, in the shade, two witnesses, two victims
> two
> short
> poems
> about nature
> waiting for the destruction to end its feast. (*L*, 56/56)

The passage I cite here appears in a poem titled "Hibr al-ghurab" (The Raven's Ink). It is the third poem in the second cycle of poems in *Limadha tarakta al-hisana wahidan?*, and in it the poetic subject, "I" ("I am you in words"), speaks in the first person. The words are addressed to the raven, which in the Qur'an, in *Surat al-Ma'ida*, had been sent to search for a site so that Cain might bury the body of his brother, Abel. But the voice of the poet is also the voice of the latter. "Be my second brother/ I am Abel, the earth returns me/ to you as a carob tree, so that you may sit on my branch, oh raven" (56/56). The poetic subject is a voice that speaks as the voice of a brother who has died. And it is only later, belatedly, that in reading this poem one must return to its opening lines and read them again. "You find solitude in the desolate carob tree, oh/ dark-voiced bell of sunset! What/ do they demand of you now? You searched in/ the garden of Adam, so that a casual killer could conceal his brother,/ and you locked yourself in your blackness/ when the victim opened onto its expanse,/ and you withdrew into your affairs like absence withdrew/ into its own" (54/54). The movement of reading compelled in this passage—to read the poem one must return to its first words and reread—points to the corpus of texts I have begun to underline. It points to the trope of the return of the poet to a site of loss, to the remains of an encampment and the loss of a beloved, in the opening section of the jahili ode, the *nasib*.[17] In Darwish poetic voice is not given through an unmediated relation to tradition, as if this voice, and if also the past, were "outside of the world, outside of time (*AB*, 122). Voice is not given in a way that locates it within or outside of tradition, because tradition, in Darwish, is not given in advance but occurs only through a relation to poetic statement: it is already temporal. The poem, as Sinan Antoon has underlined, "has arrived late," it occurs in the fallout of more than one loss.[18] And it is for this reason that poetic statement opens onto a future: pointing to another, it gestures toward a time to come.

The opening sentence of this poem points to a relation to solitude: "You find solitude in the desolate carob tree." But this solitude is already ruined by the mode of address staged in the poem, where the poet addresses the raven. You are alone and absolutely solitary *and* a subject of address, ruining that solitude, because "you" is already related to another. I'tidal Uthman has read address and voice in Darwish in relation to what she calls a "fusion."[19] For Uthman difference is resolved into unity to compensate for the losses of the past and the dispersion and dispossession of the present. In Darwish poetic statement "is built upon intertwining, coherence, and connection, and it is formed in its entirety as a substitute for and parallel to the division, fragmentation, and separation in the present Arab condition" (121). But the poem, in Darwish, is not a totality ("it is formed in its entirety") but an event of language that draws away. "The poem draws away from me" (*L*, 101/110), Darwish writes. Like the city of 'Akka, the poem withholds resolution: "This was my first experience of 'Akka. I always look there for things I don't find. I looked for my mother, but she had already returned to the village. Years later I searched for my lover, but she had married someone else. I looked there for work, but poverty kept up with me. I looked for my people, and I found a prison, a shameless police officer. It was the farthest place away in the world, my first attempts and disappointments. And its walls were being worn away by time" (*Y*, 12).[20] The poem becomes what Ammiel Alcalay has called a "fundamental fact," interrupting the exteriority of what is "fundamental" from the excess of poetic statement.[21] This excess is gestured to in what Darwish calls "love" ("Of course, I wish to be a love poet, or I wish that my historical circumstances would allow me to be a love poet, because love poetry is the most beautiful poetry that one can write. And love does not end"), as it is in the use of the dual, a grammatical form that points to two beings rather than one (the singular) or three or more (the plural).[22] And each of these is remarked in the voice of the poet—of Abel—in the poem we are considering here, where this voice, a voice that is solely one, already bears within it the voice of another. And where this voice—these two voices that do not become one, and which complicate the notion or understanding of "one"—is staged through a poetic address to a raven that had been called upon by God.

Yet if "I am you in words," then the binding of two—of the poetic voice, which has taken on the voice of Abel, and the raven—is immediately a coming apart. The word *book* ("a single book [kitab]/ binds us" [*L*, 56/56]), points to the Qur'an, which is cited in the closing lines of the poem. The unsettled joining together staged in the poem articulates the relation of language to the qur'anic text. "We" are our binding in and through a single book, but that binding already takes place through the ashes that each of us bears ("I bear the ashes you bear"). The Qur'an does not stand outside the scene staged in the poem, but the poem gives the Qur'an, and the legacies it imparts, to be read in relation to that scene. Already language is routed through destruction, *kharab*, where "we" fall into two: two witnesses, two victims, two poems. Language, then, is bereaved, and it imparts a "poetic injunction" to read, and to read tradition, through that bereavement.[23] "Poetry," Darwish has also offered, "must say something that may only be said poetically," and this imperative points to the urgency of reading this bereavement in Darwish.[24] As the poem closes the poet tells the raven that the Qur'an will light its way, that it will illumine the darkness: "The Qur'an illuminates you:/ And God sent forth a raven, scratching into the earth/ to show him how he might conceal his brother's corpse. He said:/ Woe is me! Am I unable to be like this raven?" (*L*, 56–57/56–58).[25] Yet if the raven, at the close of this poem, is to remain hovering—"the Qur'an will illumine you/ So search for our resurrection, and hover, oh raven!" (57/58)—the movement from darkness to light is not completed. One does not move from obscurity to illumination but remains in a partially opaque, unsettled relation to language. Like the words of the poem, which compel the reader to return to its opening lines, the words of the Qur'an illumine insofar as they refuse to draw a clear line between darkness and light. This refusal is pointed to in the events of repetition remarked at the poem's opening and closure. The event of citation at the close of the poem repeats the confounding of voice in its first words. The relation of poetic voice to Abel may be compared to the relation of the poem to the Qur'an. In the beginning one will have been haunted by the words of another said to be no longer. The poem iterates this anteriority. It closes by repeating—the citation points to the poet's assuming the voice of Abel—as it recalls the poem's title, "The Raven's Ink." And the title repeats the poem in advance, to point to a writing that is a departure that will never have left the past behind. "So get out/ of Cain's new home/ like the mirage drew away/ from your feather's ink oh raven" (55/54).

§

The poem, in Darwish, words "that fall upon you like droplets of dew" (*FH*, 106), interruptively performs the citation of tradition it asks us to read. Uthman has written that Darwish's poetry entails a "mixture of narrative and the lyric," but this mixture does not give place to "a historical continuity, which flows from the speaking self and its relations to the world," but points to where the poetic word cites—where it repeats—more than one event of destruction from which it never will have separated itself.[26] In this chapter I read citation in Darwish in relation to form. To read this relation I focus on the citation of the jahili ode in Darwish, and in *Limadha tarakta al-hisana wahidan?*, to consider this event of citation as a way of declining, while still not securing, or desiring to secure, a place outside of the understanding of time and loss privileged in colonial modernity. I read this citation, then, not because Darwish's text may be said to master the words of others—it does not—but because it allows itself to receive them as one receives a gift: not in an economy that would affirm the being of the one who gives and the one who receives, but in the unsettled receipt or nonreceipt language occasions. That the word of another is not mastered in an economy means that the poem will already have been lost, and in Darwish this involves "a historical loss of a native place," and the loss of the ode of Imru' al-Qays.[27] This ode shares in the corpus of texts, *al-shi'r al-jahili*, the jahili poetry, to which I have pointed, and what Mohammed Bamyeh has called "the first constitutive element of what we call tradition."[28] To read the loss of this "first constitutive element" is not to read something that comes to touch upon language belatedly. From the beginning, and before, the beginning will have been lost. This loss, like the others considered throughout this book, is one which is "not ours to move on from," and which points to the urgency of remaining with loss in reading poetic statement.[29]

The ode of Imru' al-Qays opens with an unreadable utterance and a command in the dual ("Qifa nabki min dhikra habibin wa manzili, bi siqt al-liwa, bayna al-dakhuli fa hawmali [Halt, let us weep, recalling the memory of a lover and an abode, by the rim of the twisted sands, between Dakhul and Hawmal]"), and Darwish's text keeps us trained upon the force of that imperative.[30] Here language, in the words of the poet Selim Barakat (b. 1951), "tears, between your hands, the hope of words,"[31] and one is invited to read this tear, to "linger at the words of an ode" (*L*, 104/114), in the texts we have begun to read and shall consider in what follows in this chapter. To linger in this way is not to leave behind the political engagements of Darwish's early poetry and prose, and "resistance literature," but to read the political in Darwish anew.[32] It is not that in the late poems politics is "raised up" to a "pure existential, aesthetic" level but that language becomes a site of reflection on form in relation to, and in the wake of, historical and political, individual and collective losses.[33] In an early essay published in *Yawmiyyat al-huzn al-'adi* (Journal of Ordinary Grief) (Beirut, 1973), Darwish underlines that the difference between a nostalgic reflection on loss and the reflection compelled in relation to the loss of Palestine is one that "resembles death" ("But I mean that the Palestinian is not able to treat his homeland in these terms, the way the Arabs thought of al-Andalus, and as the believers await their reward. Between Palestine and al-Andalus is a difference that resembles death" [*Y*, 14]). To think loss in nostalgic terms—to think that what has been lost once was, and that it may be recuperated through an overcoming of time—would be to think loss on the side of death. Loss is retained in Darwish, and this retention becomes a name for poetic form. "Is poetry not," Darwish wrote, "a certain attempt to correct a mistake?" (*FH*, 100). Already in relation to something or someone that has been lost—already belated, having lost itself—the poem takes place as a way of writing the form of loss.

Arabic poetic modernity has privileged a newness, a "revolution in form," which gestures to a desire to have left the past behind.[34] Darwish declines that newness, and what he called "a certain break," to remain with the interruptive force of words.[35] In a late interview Darwish explains that he read Ibn Manzur's *Lisan al-'arab*, each morning: "I don't hide from you that I read a lot. And perhaps this is the first time in my life that I am revealing this: I have a daily exercise. I open *Lisan al-'arab* each morning, at a random spot, and read about a word, its history, its origin, and the other words that are derived from it. And I learn, always, that I do not know the Arabic language very well."[36] Language and its history are approached through a relation to repetition, a practice of reading. The title of the the lexicon Darwish reads points to the physical organ, the tongue, that gives place to language. The tongue is also the organ that gives place to the designation of meaning and sense through the articulation of sound. I discuss this further in chapter 2 and underline here only that in Darwish language comes to us already routed through the act or event that the writing of poetry is. Sound occupies a privileged place in Darwish, and this place is not one of the poet's mastery over language but points to "the task of his song" (*AB*, 147). "The sea," a word which also means a verse of poetry, "is rhythms" (*FH*, 76). Giving place to poetry, rhythm also becomes poetry's "source" ("The sea is rhythm's first source" [30]). Darwish speaks of the poetic task in the following terms. "The problem is that the poet thinks that he controls language. This is not true. Language has a greater command over the poet, because it has its memory, place, order, history, and heritage."[37] This command is related to music. "I begin, then, from the musical moment" (81). This moment is linked to rhythm, and it is one to which poetic writing yields, where the poem is given place to through a yielding to sound. "So, rhythm is what leads me to writing. However many thoughts, intuitions, or images I have, as long as these do not transform into a musical vibration, if there is not a rhythm, I am not able to write" (81). The ability of the poet to write—the ability of "I"—is a passivity, an inability not to yield to rhythm. In Darwish "I" ("So, rhythm is what leads me to writing") may be said to be this inability, an event of language that takes place in relation to a persisting refusal of sound to disappear.

Sound, in Darwish, mirrors the retention of names. "I pass by your name when I am alone/ like a Damascene passing through al-Andalus" (*L*, 148/170). To speak of a single name Darwish speaks of others—Damascus, al-Andalus—suggesting that language imparts a condition of unfreedom in poetic statement, where the name shelters a relation to loss ("That night, you didn't understand anything. You asked your father, but he refused your question, because you were young. They put you in a neighboring village and left. The history professor tells you that they didn't expel anyone. In southern Lebanon you become a refugee, eating from a relief agency, and waiting to return. There you know, for the first time, what the homeland is. It is this thing that has been lost. And it is this awaited return" [*Y*, 35]). The colonization of Palestine occasions the appropriation of the Palestinian past through a practice of naming, and not solely in that way. "No trace," Darwish writes, "remains of al-Birwe," the village in which the poet was born (*FH*, 158).[38] And poetry becomes a name for language ("Poetry is your language" [*Y*, 119]), to decline the sealing of the past into the past. The implication of the past in the present may be compared to the interruption of poetic voice in the citation of tradition. Names are retained, "the names of Jerusalem" ("Numbers are shed like blood, eyes, dates, shoes, elegies, thrones, nails, poems . . . They are shed and they kill me, to increase the numbers of the dead, of lovers, and of the names of Jerusalem" [126]) and the name "qasida." "The question that remains is: How is a poetics achieved in the form of a poem [fi qiwam qasida]?"[39] Form presses a question of politics ("The intentions of the political poem have been depleted, in my opinion, except for in important states of emergency. Perhaps I'll scream angrily tomorrow, to express something, but the political poem is no longer a part of my different understanding of poetry" [67]), to give Darwish to ask, "But what is poetic and what is not? That is also a question. Politics may not be removed entirely from the margins or the cells of the poem. The question is how to express this politics" (67). Politics, in the late lyric poems, becomes a question of form. And form occurs as a relation to loss and death—as a relation of the poem to something else, as the poem's becoming something other than what it is, and as its declining to belong solely to the present—in the persisting devastation of our shared and divided time.

PLACES OF BEREAVEMENT

Were it mine to do so, I would return to my rose, to my footstep
But I will not return to Cordoba . . .

MAHMOUD DARWISH, *Ward aqall*

In Darwish there is already a relation to sound and the ways in which sound touches upon poetic statement. This relation gestures to the belated time of the poem and its rapport with tradition. ("Now, after you . . . and a well-wrought rhyme/ and exile, the trees change their stance and laugh./ It is summer in fall . . . like a vacation at the wrong/ time, like a hole in time, like a break in a song" [*K*, 99]). This break does not come later to the poem but gives place to it. It remarks more than one date, each of which is gestured in the time of poetic utterance. "Where is your body? Beneath my clothes. What are its limits? Dates: South—15 May 1948. East—November 1956. West—5 June 1967. North—September 1970. These are the limits of my body" (*Y*, 148). The time of the poem is the time of its dates. The remarking of loss does not give the poem to be read in time but dislodges the poem from temporal belonging, opening the poem to an understanding of history in excess of empirical, postivist, historicist, or archival understandings of this term. The poem does not record an event exterior to it but repeats it, placing in question the category of history, and if also of experience, that is called upon to make sense of language in reading. In this repetition language points to the singularity of a place and a time, even as this singularity is divided, remarking "a cut or an incision that the poem bears in its body like a memory, sometimes several memories in one, the mark of a provenance, of a place and of a time."[40] This pluralized inscription in memory ("sometimes several memories in one") gives a relation to time that will not have been founded upon an understanding of the present as temporal plenitude, or the future and past as derivative modes of it. The time of the poem is already several. In this multiplicity the poem withdraws, where each word is "a word that is entered into, wounded in order to be what it is, a word that is cut into, written because cut into, caesuraed in its origin, with the poem" (110/62). The wounded dimension of words is generalized in poetic statement, and it points to the retention of the word *qasida* and its legacies in Darwish. Its place, I argue, is "here."

The word *here* appears in the following stanza.

> Here is a present that yesterday doesn't touch . . .
> When we reached
> the last of the trees we noticed that we
> were no longer able to notice. When
> we turned toward the trucks we saw absence
> heaping up its selected things and pouring
> its eternal tent around us . . . (*L*, 28/22)

The poem is titled "Laylat al-bawm" (The Owl's Night), and the word *here* points to the act and event of expulsion and flight of those Palestinians who did not remain inside the portions of Palestine colonized in 1948. This word also opens each of the poem's six stanzas, pointing to an event of repetition and citation in language. The poem is an event citation ("I'll gather the Cordoban love poems scattered/ by the wind, and complete *Tawq al-Hamama* [*The Ring of the Dove* of Ibn Hazm al-Andalusi]," Darwish writes [*K*, 140–41]), and it gives itself to be read as a citational event. I have underlined that this poem appears in a text titled *Why Did You Leave the Horse Alone?*, which Darwish has called "the echoes of a personal-collective autobiography" (*FH*, 142), and it teaches us to read language in relation to loss.[41] Palestine, and its loss, is not "an axis for his [Darwish's] poetry," because in Darwish poetry is a name for the relation of language to loss.[42] In loss, the poem appeals to a poetic tradition through the ear, and through a practice of listening, "the possibility that opens toward language."[43] Listening is an anterior sensibility, a passivity with respect to language. "I kept nothing but the rhythm/ I listen to it/ I follow it/ I lift it, like doves/ on the path to the sky/ the sky of my song" (*L*, 110–11/124), Darwish writes. The words I have rendered as "I kept nothing but the rhythm" may be transliterated as *lam ahfaz siwa al-iyqa'*. The verb is *hafiza*, the same verb that appears in the passage with which I opened this chapter. It renders to keep or to preserve, guard, or retain. It is not that in Darwish "I" keeps a rhythm, or that it preserves the rhythematicity of rhythm, but that I am given place to as who or what I am only in relation to the keeping of rhythm, to my listening to and following it, to my heeding it and the legacy toward which it gestures. The relation given here is not simply receptive (if one may be said to receive language) but also, I have underlined, interruptive, as if the poem were "a hand that breaks the azure with a single gesture/ and gives the horses to dance upon the nahawand" (*K*, 77). "Identity," Darwish also writes, "is what we give to be inherited not what we inherit" (*AF*, 270), to give the thought that inheritance is neither passive nor given in advance, but an event of reading which compels attention to language's interrupted—and interruptive—dimensions.

Sound becomes, in Darwish, "the poem/ of this poem" (*K*, 95). The word *here* in "Laylat al-bawm" cites the ancient poetic practice of the giving of names in the *nasib*, with the loss of the beloved. This loss is one that will already have taken place, and this belatedness is mirrored in the opening of the poem at a distance from the site of loss. "Indeed, the first line of Imru' al-Qays's ode does not yet speak of an actual arrival at the place called *siqt al-liwa*,"[44] Jaroslav Stetkevych has written. The designation "here" as the place of the poem remarks the relation of the poem to a tradition it repeats and will never simply have displaced. This designation is iterated throughout Darwish's poetic corpus, in the citation of names of place: Damascus, al-Andalus, Cordoba, Jerusalem ("In al-Quds, I mean, within its ancient wall/ I walk from time to time, without being struck by/ a memory" [*LT*, 47]), and others. The citation of these and other names points to the enunciation of names of place that marks the opening lines of the jahili ode: "Tudih and al-Miqrat, their traces have not been erased by the north and south winds which have blown across them."[45] Four sites are named—al-Dhakul, Hawmal, Tudih, al-Miqrat—and the rim of the twisted sands, *siqt al-liwa*, lies among them.[46] It is not only that the word of the poet opens as a response to the call of what has come to appear as tradition, "the silk of ancient words" (*A*, 97), but that there will have been no poetry, and no song, without that call. The poem relates itself to tradition by citing it, and it relates itself to itself in that act of citation, ruining the place of a poetic past as one that would stand, starkly, outside of the poem. It is not that the citation of the ode is nostalgic—it is not—but that it appeals to a time said to be no longer, another time. This appeal repeats the call in the dual at the opening of the ode, to invite a thought of the origin as something that repeats and divides. One may consider this division, in Darwish, in terms of the figure of the father.

> My father
> would draw water from his well and say to it
> Don't dry up.
> He would take me by my hand
> to see how I would grow like rose moss . . .
> I would walk at the edge of the well: I have two moons
> one in the sky
> and another in the water, swimming . . . I have two moons
> each certain, like their forefathers, of what is true
> of the law . . . (*L*, 21–22/13–14)

To speak of "my father" the moon divides in two: one in the sky, another in the water. This division repeats—it is enunciated in the poem twice—to point to forefathers and a relation to the law. The doubling of the moon mirrors that of the poem's falling into two in "The Raven's Ink." In Darwish tradition already occurs in relation to time and death. It is already touched upon by tears and pain, the pain one is called to read in the passage I cited as an epigraph to this chapter ("Retain this night of pain in your memory" [*FH*, 38]), and in what Darwish calls the "tear of the pigeon's coo": "A tear of the pigeons' coo in the/ tale of eternal pain sheds us" (*L*, 26/18). "The category of the root, of the origin itself, is a category of domination [Die Kategorie der Wurtzel, des Ursprungs selbst ist herrschaftlich]," Theodor Adorno wrote, and the force of iteration in Darwish compels attention to this dimension of this category and its persistence in the ideology and practice that colonized portions of Palestine in 1948, giving place to the dates Darwish asks us to read in *Yawmiyyat al-huzn al-'adi*.[47] This ideology and practice, Zionism, and however important it would be to recall all of the internal divisions, remarks, as Abraham

Serfaty has written, "a logic of death," which, as Amnon Raz-Krakotzkin has further underlined, points to the linkages between Orientalism, colonialism, and secularization, through the notions of the negation of exile and the return to history (Hebrew, *shlilat ha galut, shiva la historia*).[48] The privileging of what Ella Shohat has called a "return to origins" reads Jewish and Palestinian existence through these terms, asymmetrically imparting a distinction between life and death, and between the living and the dead.[49] "Zionism sees in the notion of exile only the absence of Jewish sovereignty and residence outside of the land of Israel," Raz Krakotzkin has written, and this understanding of time, death, and sovereignty points to the colonization, differently, of more than one past and present.[50] Language, in Darwish, confounds its belonging to the understanding of time privileged here, iterating a relation to more than one loss said to belong, finally, to the past.

I have underlined that Darwish retains and remarks the word *qasida* to gesture to a relation to an older inheritance. The retention of this word mirrors the retention and proliferation of names Darwish asks us to read. *Why Did You Leave the Horse Alone?* was written in Paris,[51] where Darwish had come to live after moving to Tunis following the Israeli bombardment of Beirut and the massacres at Sabra and Shatila and the departure of the Palestine Liberation Organization from Lebanon in 1982 (Fawwaz Traboulsi: "Each cluster bomb shot out a single piece of shrapnel so that there would be one for each pair of civilians in West Beirut during the siege [June–August 1982]. A piece of shrapnel that hits the head or the chest kills instantly").[52] In the text he published about Beirut, Darwish wrote, "We are no longer able to form complete sentences, and yet we are asked to reformulate the elements of an experience exposed, in the open, to destruction."[53] If the late lyric poems may be said to attend to the imperative offered here—How may one write sentences after Beirut?—this attention does not leave that destruction behind but writes in its persisting fallout. "The Owl's Night" is, then, a linguistic event that takes place in the wake of Beirut, a taking place that does not point to a firm break between the present and the past but complicates the time of the poem. Poetic statement interrupts the belonging of the poem to time, "where autonomy and heteronomy lose their distinctness," and language becomes a form of "displacement," giving place to the poem in relation to its loss.[54] This displacement does not confirm the being of the poem but interrupts it, discombobulating the legacies called upon to read the poem and domesticate it as a legible object. The difference between the poem and itself mirrors the relation between a dove and a farewell. "You wonder, Is it the right of someone like you to ponder a painting?/ To ask about the origin of God/ Or to name the difference between a dove and a mother's kerchief, as she says farewell?" (*H*, 53). And the poem will already have bid farewell to itself, it will already have departed, as it repeats a relation to an event of devastation in language and with its loss.

In "Laylat al-bawm" "we" retracts into "I."

> Here is a present that yesterday doesn't touch . . .
> When we reached
> the last of the trees we noticed that we
> were no longer able to notice. When
> we turned toward the trucks we saw absence
> heaping up its selected things and pouring
> its eternal tent around us . . .
>
> Here is a present
> that yesterday doesn't touch
> A silk thread slips between the mulberry trees
> letters upon the night's notebook. Only
> the butterflies light our way
> descending to the hollow of strange words:
> Was this miserable man my father?
> Perhaps I'll look after myself here [huna]. Perhaps
> I'll give birth to myself, with myself
> and choose for my name vertical letters . . . (*L*, 28–29/22)

The retraction of "we" into "I" remarks the bereaved time of the poem. If the second line of the poem points to a collective subject ("When we reached"), the singularity of "I" interrupts that collectivity, to inscribe the poem in a singular relation to loss. The poem speaks of a collective experience of expulsion, even as in the poem this expulsion has already taken place. The poem does not write of the expulsion from a place outside of it and its legacies—it does not speak in an unmediated fashion of the loss of Palestine—but only after, later, in its wake. In Darwish "Palestine transforms into a language, more so than it does into a poetic subject," and the poem cyphers an event of loss in relation to language and poetic form.[55] Loss is at once recalled and repeated, in poetic form, and as "the poem itself" (*AF*, 109), in the irruption of "I" into the poem. A singular event of loss is already its repetition in the poetic act that bears witness to it. This singularity is given to be read and is effaced in the poetic act that speaks of it. The poem that speaks of the loss of Palestine relates itself to that loss as exterior to it. It is in a certain sense other than it, through its repeating and reciting its relation to it. "A date marks itself and becomes readable only in freeing itself from the singularity it nonetheless recalls,"[56] Derrida has written. The poem recalls an event whose time it also disrupts, teaching us to read the verb *to be* in relation to the imperatives of sound and loss in Darwish. I underline here only that this relation—the relation of sound and loss to language and colonial violence—already points to what a sentence in Darwish is ("So how will almond flowers scatter in my language/ if I am their echo?/ They are translucent like watery laughter that grew/ upon the branches from the dew's shyness . . . / They are light like a white, musical sentence . . . " [*K*, 47]). Already "I" ("if I am their echo") occasions an interruption of temporal belonging and the borders installed to secure the division of more than one inside from outside. The poem appears as a sentence, *jumla*, which interrupts the giving of sense and of legibility in language.

HERE, OR, ANDALUSIAN SEQUENCES

And how could one, here, speak of arrival or departure?

EDMOND JABÈS, *Le livre des questions*

"To break the rhythm, from time to time, is rhythm's necessity" (*AF*, 257), and this interruption and its necessity teaches what a poem, in Darwish, is. This interruption may be considered in the retraction of "we" into "I" in the passage I am reading in "The Owl's Night." This retraction points to the poet's father ("Was this miserable man my father?"), and it elicits the name as a matter of letters ("Perhaps/ I'll give birth to myself, with myself/ and choose for my name vertical letters . . . [*L*, 29/22]). The poet gives birth to himself through a relation to language, and through a relation to the materiality of language and its vertical, divided letters. Birth, in Darwish, is not an event of patriarchical order, or of the giving of place of what is or what has been to what is to come in time, but an event that confounds patrimony in relation to language. Already, in Darwish, the father is more than one, it is already "poetry's first rhythms" (*AF*, 75), in the plural, and it is already divided, distended, and exposed. Language, in Darwish, is finite, it is the coming apart of language in the material event of written letters. "Parting is the silence that divides a sound from its echo" (*FH*, 176), and parting, then, in Darwish, never comes to an end. Relation, including the relation to poetry to sound, does not cease but points to other relations. In the closing pages of this chapter I turn to a passage in which Darwish spells his name in *Jidariyya* (Mural) (Beirut, 1999), an event staged in relation to the city of 'Akka and its name, "the oldest of the beautiful cities, the most beautiful of the ancient ones" (*J*, 98–99). The misery of the father points to the loss and destruction of a poetic tradition I have been reading thus far. Yet if what is gestured to in Darwish, and in relation to rhythm, is "the deep essential music, which is hidden in the structure of language, before poetry and after it," this essence is already touched upon by its devastation in the time of loss.[57] Such loss is pointed to in the name, and names gesture to a sheltering and a breaking up of language: "Upon which bridge have the songs thrown you/ killed, to light up this sky?" (*H*, 23), Darwish wrote in relation to Beirut, 1982. I listen here to the enunciation and repetition of names as it is recalled for us through the word and the name "Samarkand."

> Samarkand is a tent of my fugitive spirit
> and five directions for my mother's tear
> Samarkand is a thread of silk
> that suspends the bank of a riverbed upon a mare carrying the rain
> and a voice that descends from God
> and breaks up
> Samarkand is a river that bends
> Samarkand is a tent for my fugitive spirit. (*H*, 22)

This passage anticipates a second, which I translate as follows.

> Samarkand is what roses leave for the wind
> What a nightingale leaves
> upon a fleeting moon in the poem [fi al-qasida]
> Samarkand is what kisses leave
> upon a withered passion . . .
> Samarkand is a carpet for a distant prayer
> Samarkand is a minaret for the dew
> and a compass for the echo.
> Samarkand is a hasty description of what falls apart of our love when we depart
> When a heart breaks, it screams: Samarkand
> like a partridge . . .
> Do you remember how I entered the city?
> I smashed my final ribs
> one arch
> another

> And when I bent down to see my heart's image
> I saw Samarkand in a tomb. (*H*, 26–27)

The passage cites the word *poem* ("Samarkand is what roses leave for the wind/ What a nightingale leaves/ upon a fleeting moon in the poem" [*H*, 26]). Darwish has pointed to his retention of this word, and to listen to the legacies in which it shares I translate its glossing in *Lisan al-'arab*. Ibn Manzur writes that *qasida* is derived from *qasd*, "the straightness or soundness of a path."[58] In Arabic poetics *qasid* is "that whose verses have been partitioned," and "it is named in this way because of its completeness and the correctness of its meter" (435). The definition of *qasida* offered here points to an older, rhetorical tradition, where language is understood in relation to what has appeared, at least since al-Jahiz (d. 868), as the communicative intention of a speaker.[59] "It is called *qasid*," Ibn Manzur continues, "because the one who utters it attends to it and cares for it with a well formed word and a well chosen meaning [or image] [bi al-lafz al-jayyid wa al-ma'na al-mukhtar]."[60] *Qasida*, then, points to an elaboration of an ancient meaning of the word: *qasd*, Ibn Manzur explains, is also "the opposite of excess" (434).[61] Darwish's text retains the economy of this gesture—his text, one might argue, is an economy of division—even as it iterates division through its attention to, and repetition of, the paths of the ode. This repetition is staged in Darwish's late poems through the legacy of al-Andalus. The *nasib* is repeated in that later poetic tradition—which extends from Ibn Zaydun (1001–71) to the poets Ibn Khafaja (1058–1138), Ibn al-Farid (1181–1235), Ibn Hazm (994–1064), and, elsewhere, Abu Tammam (805–45), whose "La anti anti, wa la al-diyar diyar [You are not you/ nor are the abodes abodes]" is cited as an epigraph to *La ta'tadhir 'amma fa'alta* (Do Not Apologize for What You Have Done) (Beirut, 2005)—and it is approached, in the late lyric poems of Darwish, through this repetition.[62] The devastation remarked in poetic statement is, then, twice belated. It repeats the loss of two: al-Andalus and Palestine. The opening of the ode of Imru' al-Qays in the dual and the imperative is routed, in Darwish, through its repetition in al-Andalus. Its citation in Darwish is already in translation, already belated. The ode does not appear as a poetic ground for language or tradition but as a ground that will already have been lost, that is already displaced, partitioned, divided: in two.

In Darwish, Beirut, "a gazelle slaughtered by a sparrow's wing" (*H*, 137), is already touched upon by language. "I turn the city like

I turn the pages of a book/ I carry this small earth like a bag of clouds" (124–25). But if the city may be likened to the pages of a book, one will never have been able to leave language behind. Like the departure of the poet, seeing the other off will have remained impossible, if however necessary, because the poem already parts from itself. Aristotle described the task of the poet as "to speak of what sort of things would come to be, i.e., of what is possible [Arabic, mumkin] according to the likely or the necessary" (*Poetics*, 1451a37–38), but the poem, in Darwish, may not be read in these terms.[63] A distinction between what comes into being and perishes and what does not, and the proliferation of this legacy in the practices of reading I underline in this book, is ruined in poetic statement. It is not that in Darwish language "accumulates in a particular, organic way"[64] but that poetic statement is already given in the fallout of "the words that have died out in *Lisan al-'arab*" (*L*, 13/4). The word I have translated here as "to die out," *inqarada*, implies extinction and perishing. But it also encrypts a relation to *qarid*, a synonym for the word *poem*.[65] The poem writes the devastation in language it also describes, to iterate a relation to tradition, and it gives tradition to be read differently, without its circumscription in relation to an identitarian privilege.

> We are the leaves of a tree
> words of the broken time. We are
> the flute, when the house draws away from the flute. We are
> the field, when it extends in the painting . . . We are
> We are a sonata upon the moon's light
> We only demand of our mirror
> what resembles us
> We do not demand of the earth
> a foothold for the spirit
> We are water in the voice that will call out to us
> and which we don't hear. We are the other bank of a river
>   between a voice and a stone
> We are what the land, which is not ours, produces
> We are what we produce in the land that was ours
> We are the trace we leave in exile and in us
> We are the grasses of the broken vessel
> We are what we are and who we are—so what is the use of place?
> We must, now, circle this earth, which is pregnant with those
>   who resemble us
> and those who give it to fall from its high throne
> So that we may be buried anywhere [fi ayy makan]. (*H*, 72–73)

The collective and individual losses to which Darwish points in this passage gesture to the topography of states and statelessness installed in the nineteenth and the early twentieth century, in the creation of the state of Israel and the destruction of Palestine and what followed, and which belongs to what Hannah Arendt has called "the damage suffered by the very structure of the legal national institutions when a growing number of residents had to live outside the jurisdiction of these laws [the laws of the nation-state and the minority treaties] without being protected by any other."[66] These events point to the formation of monolingual states and literary institutions, in the discriminating transformation in language that took place during the nineteenth and early twentieth century. "The authority and self-identity of the nation-state, like that of the city and the colonial world, are not stable, circumscribed conceptions but internal boundaries of hierarchical separation which must be constantly policed," Timothy Mitchell has written.[67] This interiority and the distinction of inside from outside it repeats is persistingly collapsed in Darwish. Already, the poem, like language, draws away ("We are the leaves of a tree/ Words of the broken time. We are/ the flute, when the house draws away from the flute" [*H*, 72]). The word I have rendered as "house," *bayt*, also gestures to a verse of poetry. Its being remarked in this passage points to the intertwining of a poetic and a political idiom, an intertwining that gestures to politics as a matter of form. The drawing away of the house from the flute is also the drawing away of the poem from sound. The event of destruction, the damage inflicted and suffered, is spoken, given to be read as a condition of poetry, as the past declines to be left, finally, in the past ("Perhaps," Darwish writes, "the ghosts converse/ like spirits" [*AF*, 170]).

One name for this drawing away is love ("Samarkand is a hasty description of what falls apart of our love/ when we depart" [*H*, 26]). This departure is written through the repetition of the staging of the *nasib* in the poetry of al-Andalus. Darwish repeats the poet Ibn Khafaja, and the tradition of *ritha' al-mudun*, citing the passage of Abu Tammam he placed as an epigraph to *Do Not Apologize for What You Have Done*.[68] "A land whose people were expelled by calamities, death shaken by its destruction," Ibn Khafaja writes, "Written in its abandoned courtyards one reads, 'You are not you, nor are the abodes abodes.'"[69] Repeating this repetition, citing this event of citation, Darwish opens a reading of language in relation to its loss. Here, poetry welcomes and shelters loss ("He said: The poem might receive loss as a guest/ a thread of light that shines in the heart of the guitar" [*K*, 194]), giving language to decline the harsh imposition of temporal boundaries, which the state form, if also institutions for reading, compels. Reading the Andalusi tradition of the rewriting of the *nasib*, Jaroslav Stetkevych has emphasized, "As echoes, these old things sound different now, and they sound only as echoes. Nothing is simple and direct," and so, too, already, in Darwish.[70] In the poem simplicity will have been ruined by the time of repetition. The belated dimension of the poem points to a beginning, to an origin or provenance that opens, as did the ode of Imru' al-Qays, in citation. "I said: Where are you taking me? He said: toward the beginning, where you were born/ here, you and your name" (*K*, 154). Already accompanied by another, divided in two, the beginning parts from itself. It is a departure that is also an event of iteration. The new takes place only in relation to the citation of more than one old name, it already relates itself to itself as itself through its loss.

§

"Darwish requests of his language—his poem—that it welcome the stranger," yet this welcome does not secure the being of the poem but points to an excess in poetic statement.[71] If in this excess Darwish figures language as a shelter ("And a little bit of the speech of God for the trees/ is enough for me to build, with words/ a safe shelter/ for the cranes the hunters missed . . . " [*L*, 160/186]), it is already touched upon by the loss of an ode. In the fallout of that loss, and with what remains of words, Darwish tells the story of 1948, as he tells what Elias Khoury has called "his shattered story."[72] This telling points to more than one event of colonial violence that, as Sherene Seikaly writes, "did not begin in 1948, nor did it end there."[73] The story of 1948, in Darwish, involves the village of al-Birwe, "a village that stood upon a rocky hill, which descended toward the plain of 'Akka, and whose inhabitants lived by growing wheat, barley, corn, sesame, watermelon, and olives," which "was destroyed and erased from existence" and on the ruins of which stands the Kibbutz Yas'ur.[74] The destruction of al-Birwe compelled the poet and his family, upon returning to Palestine in 1949, "to live temporarily in the village Dayr al-Asad, before moving to live permanently in the village al-Jadida" (126), and to tell this story forms a part of what is at stake in poetic statement in Darwish, even as this story is not a single one and even as its telling remains impossible. Its "protagonist is not the 'I' but its image" (138), and its rendering in language occasions a split or division: *infisam* or *inqisam*. This rendering does not point to "a return to the distant past," and its telling does not offer "a history which has never ruptured or followed a winding path" (*AB*, 45). This story "has divided upon itself," and it may not be understood as an effect of "a single event: expulsion and the seeking of refuge."[75] In poetic statement, "language becomes a name," and "the division of the self in two is the opening of the story" (133, 138). "The wound is deep, it is deep, and, perhaps, it will never mend" (*AB*, 20), Darwish writes, declining to seal loss, and the loss of language, in the past. To speak of loss the poet repeats the words of others. "There is no possibility of *not* repeating," in the iteration of a command in the dual, which cites the idiom of more than one other, as it rewrites, differently, and anew, the tradition of the ode.[76]

> I saw April over the sea
> I said: I forgot the glance of your hands
> I forgot your hymns over my wounds
> How many times will you be able to be born in my sleep
> How many times will you be able to kill me so that I may
>   scream: I love you
> so you can rest?
> I call out to you before speech
> I fly at your hip before arriving to you
> How many times will you be able to place in the beaks of doves
> the addresses of my spirit
> and disappear like the distance in the mountain slopes
> so that I'll know you're Babylon, Egypt, Damascus (*H*, 97–98)

INTERRUPTION I

What, then, is reading? Undoubtedly it is something philological.

FRIEDRICH SCHLEGEL, *Zur Philologie*

To read Darwish, and to read literature, is to do so in relation to "the aftermath of Jena" and its continuing effects.[77] The writings of the *Athenäum* (1798–1800) point to "the inauguration of the *theoretical* project in literature" (9/2), as they promise a theory of literature that solicits the realization of literature as work. This is what Philippe Lacoue-Labarthe and Jean-Luc Nancy call the "literary absolute" as they cite Friedrich Schlegel: "not 'this or that genre, content to attain some formation or other by chance, but rather literature itself [die

Literatur selbst] that would be a great, thoroughly connected and organized Whole, comprehending many worlds of art in its unity, and being at the same time a unitary work of art'" (277/91).[78] The connected, organized, unitary work is an aesthetic figure of wholeness ("a unitary work of art"), and this figure is, equally, a figure for the interconnected comprehension of works ("comprehending many worlds of art in its unity"). Literature, as the literary absolute, promises a completion as it forms the occasion for "an entirely new, infinitely new Work," and this infinite newness gestures to the excess, which Lacoue-Labarthe and Nancy also ask us to read.[79] "The process of absolutization or infintization, the Process as such, *exceeds*—in every way—the general theoretical (or philosophical) power of which it is nonetheless the completion" (278/92). The uneasy solicitation of "completion" points to a text adjacent to the *Athenäum* writings—"The Oldest System Program of German Idealism," a text the authorship of which remains undetermined, even as this absence of determination recalls us to the imperative this text gives, and the "infintization" the literary absolute promises. Forming philosophical statement into an aesthetic act ("I am now convinced that the highest act of reason, the one through which it encompasses all ideas, is an aesthetic act, and that truth and goodness only become sisters in beauty—the philosopher must possess just as much aesthetic power as the poet"), a privileging of totality in relation to form is called for—it is called out to—as it is stalled.[80] Form, as philosophical or literary exposition, is to be aesthetic (it is to be a form that "encompasses all ideas") and familial ("truth and goodness only become sisters in beauty"), and yet this aesthetic organization of relations is interrupted through the "must" that articulates it. It is a "must" ("the philosopher must possess") that cannot stop. "Philosophy must effectuate itself—complete, fulfill, and realize itself—as poetry," Lacoue-Labarthe and Nancy write, to point to a completion of never ceasing incompletion.[81] "For the romantics, the work never ceases to imply the fundamental motif of completion" (67/46), and the economy of terms given in this unceasing implication impart a legacy to more than one language and literary institution.

§

The promise of the work is given—and interrupted—in Schlegel through his writing in *Über die Sprache und Weisheit der Indier* (Heidelberg, 1808). If there, as we shall consider below, new divisions are installed in order to capture the infintizing imperatives of langauge, elsewhere in Schlegel language relates to what he called "irony." Paul de Man wrote of "the act of irony" in terms of a temporality that "relates to its source only in terms of distance and difference and allows for no end, for no totality."[82] He elaborates, "The technical term for this in rhetoric, the term that Schlegel uses, is *parabasis*. Parabasis is the interruption of a discourse by a shift in the rhetorical register."[83] De Man cites Schlegel, who writes, "Die Ironie ist eine permanente Parekbase.—" (179). Parabasis is permanent because it takes place constantly and everywhere. It is generalized in relation to language and world. "A great part of the incomprehensibility of the *Athenäum* is unquestionably due to the *irony* that to a greater or lesser extent is to be found everywhere in it."[84] "Irony," Schlegel writes, "is to be found everywhere," and there is therefore no shelter from irony or from the interruptive force of parabasis. This absence of shelter means that language is already finite—it is already temporal. And this temporality gives language to mean in more ways than one. "Generally speaking," Schlegel wrote in "On Incomprehensibility," "the most fundamental irony of irony probably is that even it becomes tiresome if we are always being confronted with it. But what we want this irony to mean in the first place is something that happens in more ways than one" (369/267). The foundational pluralization of the first ("in the first place") and of the "one" ("something that happens in more ways than one") means that irony confounds the "articulation of mind and body, intellect and life," interrupting the form of aesthetic coherency and genetic, familial relation, for which "The Oldest System Program" calls.[85] While one would not wish to set the *Athenäum* writings off starkly from the later writing on "Indian" languages—the interruptive dimensions of language are already present in each, as is the compulsive pull toward a totalization of form—the later text does address itself, decisively, to the philological reorganization of languages into "families" (Aryan and Semitic, for example, as Edward W. Said and Maurice Olender have taught us). The terms of this reorganization come to be imparted to the Arabic langauge in the nineteenth century, and through the institution of a literary object in the Arabic language (a matter I discuss in detail in chapter 2), and I turn here to Schlegel's 1808 text to read those terms as they give place to a new understanding of relation in relation to languages.

To capture the interruption Schlegel named parabasis, *Über die Sprache* opens new linguistic and temporal divisions with the invention of "comparative grammar."[86] Heinrich Nüsse explains of this text, comparing it to the writings of Wilhelm von Humboldt and Franz Bopp, "In it Schlegel sketched the *plan* of a new science; he did not construct its first *foundation*. It is only in this sense that he may be called a founder. His real achievement in the science of language may not be compared to those of his aforementioned contemporaries. It indisputably remains that he first formulated the methodological ideas which in research proved to be so fruitful; the history of the science of language was given with Friedrich Schlegel to begin a new epoch" (40). Schlegel, like irony, the Orient, and literature, must be managed. He is incorporated into and excluded from the science of language and its history, just as the Orient, in Schlegel, is to take the place of Greece as Europe's source. This event is already at work in the *Athenäum* writings ("In the Orient we must search for the most sublime form of the Romantic") and is restated in an 1803 letter to Tieck[87]: "Here is the real source of all languages, all thought, and all poetry of the human spirit; everything, everything, without exception, originates in India."[88] The excess the Orient commands stalls the originarity of the source for which Schlegel wishes to search. This interruption is mirrored in *Über die Sprache*, which was to have been "an Indian Chrestomathie in Latin and in the original characters," yet the hand copied versions of the texts Schlegel wished to include were cut from the manuscript.[89] The economy is sacrificial, and it points to a pain. "The sacrifice of an advantage in the aim of science has its own reward. But if that aim is of the kind that it may not be reached without outside assistance, it is painful to have to remain still, half way to the desired goal" (109/427). The cut remarked here—the work of the philologer pauses halfway—gestures to an interruptive relation to loss. It asks us to read a date inscribed in the labor of philological, linguistic, and familial explication, around the name "Charles August Schlegel, who died in Madras on the 9th of September, 1789," whose work and writing "was prematurely broken off by his death" (111/428). The mourning work forces the installation of clarity, separating Sanskrit from Greek and Latin only to link it to them. Differences are reorganized and put in their place, as if something or someone had to be buried, in the division of internal and external, originary and derivative, essential and accidental, in what Schlegel called "comparison [Vergleichung]."[90]

The oppositions at work in this passage install and manage difference by deriving it from simplicity. "We shall not repeat what earlier has been casually said about similar points of agreement, passing over much that may be quite important for others. Admittedly with this substantial agreement in essence and as a whole there remains considerable variety in detail and accident. In principal however the distinction consists in this: the grammar of the Indian language is of the same kind as the Greek and Roman but more regular, its structure of the same law, if I might say so, but truer and even more simple and more artistic than they are" (147/444). But Schlegel must repeat, inscribing a relation to idiom as he tells us he is not repeating himself ("We shall not repeat what earlier has been casually said"). Difference is managed by deciding which single difference is the most decisive, and this privileging gives place to Asia as a site of historical and originary import. Asia is the provenance of Europe, and this inclusion works to domesticate the former by making it Europe's origin. This domestication compels the formation of a family and its organization into an undivided whole—a figure that mirrors the philosophical-poetic wholeness promised in "The Oldest System Program." "As in popular history, the Asians and Europeans form only one great family, Asia and Europe one indivisible whole [ein unzertrennbares Ganzes], so one should try to view the literature of all cultivated people as a progressive development and a single intimately joined building and shape, as a great whole, where each one-sided and limited view would disappear in itself, where many in their connections with others would first appear understandable, and where all would appear in this light new" (315/526). The installation of comprehensibility through a political-theological anthropocentrism is the controlling gesture of comparison in *Über die Sprache*, but this theologism interrupts itself; like philology, it is already in incomprehensibility. This interruption gestures to an excess as Schlegel repeats the division of the simple from the complex and the originary from the derivative. "It may hardly be remembered that all of these observations should do no more than to only roughly open the prospect of how fruitful Indian studies may be in drawing historical inferences. When more abundant resources are obtained many details in the earliest history of the people of Asia will first be soundly determined, and a complete image of the whole will then first be able to be traced" (291/513). The promise of the whole keeps positing itself, it remains to come as it repeats, to give and interrupt itself again, without end.

This promise is the promise of philology. "The end of φλ remains undetermined. It is unendingly determinable," Schlegel writes.[91]

Philology's unending determination does not point to a determinability that will one day have arrived but one that arrives in not arriving. Schlegel calls this nonarrival "history." "*The end of philology is history.* A single sentence. This has almost never happened. There is still no history. Here again the so called history of humanity" (37). This passage points to Herder's *Ideen zur Philosophie der Geschichte der Menschheit* (1784–91), yet unlike Winckelmann ("The most important part of a philosophy of philology is a theory of historical critique.—Winckelmann's historicism" [35]) and Wolf ("Wolf's *Prolegomena* perhaps the best φσ ραψ [philosophical rapsody] that exists.—"), Herder lacks rigor.[92] "*Heyne* and *Herder*—out of laziness—against grammatical and critical *rigor*, which is the essence of φλ [philology] as an art. φλ is not a science. <As a science it is a part of history. φλ [philological] grammar is also not a science, it cannot be one>."[93] Philology as a science would be its morphing into Herderian history, in the loss of precision ("What is *precision* at all—and in φλ?—Without precision there is no real classical φλ"), and it is for this reason that philology is, for Schlegel, ironic.[94] "There is a φλ irony, which only *Wolf* had" (79). Responding already to an imperative, philology interrupts itself ("Here the mere necessity of the *philological imperative*" [64]), implying that history is given in this interruption, where language "speaks as absolute ex-position: as *ekbasis*, as excess, interruption, opening up."[95] This excess and interruption is what philology is, even as philology must recognize itself in relation to religion ("The spirit of religion is antiφλ") and place itself on the side of Christianity. "The spirit of Christianity is φλ."[96] "Religion" is on the side of "die Araber" (the "philology of the Arabs," Schlegel writes, is "quite poor, absolute, standstill, uncritical" [49]), if also on the side of Islam and Herder, neither Winckelmann nor Wolf. If Schlegel gives us to read language as excess, his text also shares in the installation of religion, and religions, as a philological category. This event, what one might call the permanent parabasis of philology, implies an imperative for reading in the humanities. "The question, why is φλ called *Humaniora*?, must from *here* be answered" (49).

§

"The romantic theory of the work of art is the theory of its form," Walter Benjamin writes, and he situates this theory in relation to

Schlegel.[97] "The idea of art during the period of the *Athenäum* is a—and outside of the concept of history perhaps the sole—legitimate fulfillment of the systematic intention of Friedrich Schlegel" (44). In "The Concept of Irony" de Man reads Benjamin's reading of Schlegel, and to do so he considers Benjamin's discussion of destruction. Benjamin writes, "The ironization of form consists in a deliberate destruction of the form," and destruction is the task of the objective moment in art and criticism.[98] "Far from being a subjective whim of the author [weit entfernt, eine subjective Velleität des Autors darzustellen] this destruction of the form is the task of the objective moment in art, in criticism" (85/183). To read Benjamin, de Man translates *Darstellung* (*darzustellen*) as "being" ("far from *being* [my emphasis] a subjective whim of the author"). This rendering does not mute the resonances of the theatrical and of language *Darstellung* implies.[99] It generalizes *Darstellung* in relation to being. This privileging of language points to what Benjamin calls "allegory" (Samuel Weber has crucially underlined that in Benjamin "whatever is represented allegorically has no being apart from its being represented"), to imply the bereaved sadness of the ruin.[100] "As with so many signs of rupture, the break was merely a repetition of prior, more sullen breaks and could not be limited to one moment," and so too the desire to separate being from language is confounded, even as the disciplines of reading in the humanities reiterate this separation.[101] It is not that these disciplines leave religion behind ("The history of languages and their philosophy ceased to be a matter of religion," Raymond Schwab wrote in his monumental *La renaissance orientale* [Paris, 1950]) but that to read them, and if they are readable, is to attend to the ways in which older, Christian and other legacies remain at stake.[102] If in the fallout of Jena the world will have become a site of colonizing designation, and if world is shattered and obsolesced in that designation, this event interrupts itself to open a relation to a future. "Irony suspends the infinite project, its work of appropriating meaning to itself—permanently, which is to say: time and again."[103] The texts I consider here, then, are also a condition for the future, including the future of the word *adab*. To approach a reading of this word, which I elaborate in chapter 2 and what follows, I return to Darwish and the reading of language his text compels us to pursue.

WORDS, OR, THE QUR'AN WITH THE POEM

Here, there—a clear furrow to the desert.

MAHMOUD DARWISH, *Ara ma urid*

In the poetic statement of Mahmoud Darwish language is already routed through a relation to loss. The legacies that attach to the word *qasida* are retained to suggest that poetic statement points to the ancient hermeneutic relation between the Qur'an and Arabic poetry. "But I think: It was only the prophet Muhammad/ who spoke the Arabic language [al-lugha al-'arabiyya al-fusha]./ 'And what after that?'/ What after that?" (*LT*, 48). In the Arabic rhetorical and poetic traditions, *fasaha* exemplifies clarity of expression, and its most perfect exposition takes place in the Qur'an. The Qur'an is defined by Ibn Khaldun (1332–1406) as follows: "The Qur'an is the word of God which has been sent down to his prophet, and which has been written between the two covers of the book."[104] But if the being of the Qur'an is its division into the word of God that has been sent down and that may not be said to partake in time, *kalam Allah al-munzal 'ala nabihi*, and the writing of that word and its collection between the covers of a book and its textual materiality, *al-maktub bayna daffatay al-mushaf*, this division points to the formation of disciplines for reading the Arabic language in the wake of the Prophet's death. The question of language and its relation to the future is the question of the negotiation of this inheritance, and poetic utterance in Darwish compels engagement with it, to teach us to read language in relation to an anterior interruption. The poem, in Darwish, points to a rhythm, to a call from another ("Poems," Darwish writes, "come from a distance" [*FH*, 114]), remarking the call in the dual that opens poetic tradition in the ode. To read language in Darwish is to read this remarking, and to do so I turn to Adunis and to his *al-Thabit wa al-mutahawwil* (The Stable and the Changing) (Beirut, 1974–78).

In each great Arabic poem there is a second one, language.

ADUNIS, *Diwan al-shi'r al-'arabi*

Trees lean down to say farewell. Flowers open, blossom, and draw their petals back, to say farewell. Roads are like interludes, between a breath and a word, they say farewell. A sandy body falls into its desert, to say farewell. Paper that loves ink, and the alphabet, and poets, say farewell. And the poem said farewell.

ADUNIS, *Kitab al-hisar*

Each of us sits upon piles of ash.

ADUNIS, *Muqaddima li al-shi'r al-'arabi*

I wish to focus attention on the discussion of language that appears in the second volume of *al-Thabit wa al-mutahawwil*, which is titled *Ta'sil al-usul*. This title foregrounds the questions of repetition and retention, and of names and their iteration, which we are reading throughout. It occasions this question because, to address what it calls *al-thabit* (the stable) and *al-mutahawwil* (the changing), and to place itself on the side of the latter, it must set to work to translate a word—*asl*—that belongs to a rhetorical, juridical, and philosophical lexicon. The exposition of the aporia Adunis considers—if the Qur'an is inimitable and therefore uncreated, *ghayr makhluq*, or eternal, *qadim*, if "the eternal, in philosophico-theological terminology, is that which does not have a beginning, or which is its own cause," and if the Arabic language is the language in which the Qur'an is given expression, how may one think or write the new in language?—already entails the repetition of that vocabulary which contributes to making that aporia recognizable as aporetical.[105] The eternity of the Qur'an entails its inimitability because one may not produce something like it, and this gesture communicates with a set of relations among juridical decision, *hukm*, and interpretation, *ta'wil*. "For the Qur'an is eternal insofar as it is something inimitable [mu'jaz], of which the 'created' human being is incapable of bringing a likeness, insofar as it is the speech of God and his revelation, and insofar as it contains that which only God knows how to interpret; and the secret of the prohibition of the human being's use of his opinion in the interpretation of the Qur'an lies in this final point" (138). That the Qur'an is *mu'jaz* and *qadim* means that it is *asl*. It means that it is an atemporal ground. "The eternal is then the ground upon which that which is other than itself is built, or, it is that which is needed, as opposed to the derivative [far'] which is that which needs something other than itself" (141).

Ta'sil al-usul opens with a discussion of the jurist al-Shafi'i (d. 820) and his *al-Risala*.[106] Adunis's exposition of the juridical institution in which al-Shafi'i shares begins with a discussion of the Qur'an and its revelation. "For the Qur'an is the negation of what preceded it, and it is a new institution. It envelops everything: what was and what shall be [ma kana wa ma yakun]. It knows everything: what was and what shall be."[107] The institution of jurisprudence, *fiqh*, requires a knowledge of the Arabic language, the language in which the Qur'an was revealed, and the understandability of language turns on the reading and comprehension of poetry and its lexicon. Poetry retains a decisive hermeneutic function because, as Ibn Khaldun writes, "the Qur'an was sent down in the language of the Arabs using their forms of speech and eloquence ['ala asalib balaghatihim]," and they were therefore able to understand it.[108] "So they all understood it and recognized its meanings in its vocabulary and expressions" (469). It is not, as al-Suyuti (1445–1505) explains, that poetry became a ground for the Qur'an, *wa laysa al-amr kama za'amu min anna ja'alna al-shi'r aslan li al-Qur'an*, but that poetry was used to clarify what remained unrecognizable in it.[109] The tradition remarked in these passages in Ibn Khaldun and al-Suyuti return to Ibn 'Abbas (d. 687), a figure whose authority is cited in the poetic, rhetorical, and lexicographical traditions in Arabic.[110] "Ibn Abbas said: Poetry is the register of the Arabs; if a letter of the Qur'an, which God sent down in the language of the Arabs, is hidden from us, we return to its register, and we take our knowledge of that from it."[111] Following the death of the Prophet the proliferation of readings of the Qur'an compelled its canonization, and poetry, through its preservation of the language of the bedouin, was called upon to secure legibility.[112] If poetry was to clarify the meaning to which the materiality of words points, the belonging of the Qur'an to language signals not only the institution of a division within language, the division of what Ibn Khaldun called the "word of God" from its inscription in writing, but also a division between meaning, *ma'na*, and the linguistic utterance, *lafz*.[113] It is not that the Qur'an may be said to belong or not to this institution but that its canonization and written inscription as *mushaf* occasioned the formation of the latter.

It is at this moment that Adunis opens a discussion of language in the second chapter of the third part of *Ta'sil al-usul*. The stakes of Adunis's discussion of language turn on the crisis of reading occasioned in the death of the Prophet. In the fallout of the Prophet's death, a mournful, bereaved relation to language is installed. The loss of sense occasioned in this relation gives place to an ontology of language as belated, as devastated. One writes only after, following this loss, and poetic statement in Arabic retains the legacies imparted in this event. It is an event of loss—in the words of Hichem Djaït, "The death of the prophet made the companions orphans of God"—that occasioned a proliferation of divisions.[114] "It was natural after the death of the prophet and his companions, the spreading out of the Islamic lands, the growth of the scientific movement, the multiplication of divisions and the sharpness of the disagreement among them, that a disagreement would arise regarding the understanding of texts and, following from that, regarding opinions and judgments."[115] In the field of language, this gave place to the disciplines of *nahu* (grammar), *lugha* (lexicography), *bayan* (rhetoric), *adab*, and, later, jurisprudence, *fiqh*. "In this way, a disagreement arose regarding the understanding of the Qur'an, the originariness of the *sunna* (Is it a source [asl] that completes the Qur'an, and how may one rely upon it?), the position of the companions of the prophet with respect to the sources, juridical decision, and what it entails regarding opinion, analogy, juristic preference, and public interest, and regarding consensus" (152). Jurisprudence, Adunis suggests, is instituted to manage the lexical strife, *fitna*, that followed upon the death of the Prophet and that attended the call for the canonization of the qur'anic text. Death threatened those who had placed the Qur'an in memory. "It was not at all a matter of an act of government wishing to provide an expanding community with a unifying code or written reference. Simply, they tell us, at 'Aqraba, the greatest of the battles of *ridda*, most of the reciters were killed," Djaït underlines, and it was this relation to death that led Abu Bakr to collect the text of the Qur'an.[116] "Abu Bakr assembled the scattered fragments and made them into a *corpus*, and he kept them, not wanting to distribute them. 'Umar inherited it from him and upon his death he gave it to his daughter Hafsa, the widow of the prophet" (131). Djaït explains that the stakes occasioned in the preservation of the qur'anic text were "politicio-religious" (136–37), and those stakes entailed the management of poetic statement and language in relation to the Qur'an. "The Qur'an took the place of poetry, it was substituted for the anthropological culture of the Arabs which issued from the period of Jahiliyya" (134), and it was this relation—the relation between poetry and the Qur'an—that had to be secured.[117]

If the formation of the *mushaf*—which Djaït translates with the Latinate word *vulgate* (135), and which Ibn Manzur explains is "the collection of written pages gathered between two covers [al-jami' li al-suhuf al-maktuba bayna al-daffatayn]"—was undertaken to preserve the written text of the Qur'an and to manage social strife by securing the place of the Qur'an with respect to poetry, it was also undertaken to manage language.[118] As Ibn Khaldun explains regarding the account of the codification of the text of the Qur'an that he presents in *Kitab al-'ibar*, what the call for the codification of the text entailed was Sa'id bin al-'As's informing Hudhayfa bin al-Yaman of "the disagreements which he saw among people regarding the Qur'an."[119] He further explains that after Hudhayfa had sent Uthman to get the text that had been collected during the time of Abu Bakr ("He commanded Zayd bin Thabit to collect it from pieces of cloth, palm branches, and from the memories of men. He wrote it on paper and it was in the possession of Abu Bakr, and then 'Umar, and then Hafsa" [2:557]), he ordered that it be copied and that any disagreement in language be resolved according to the language of Quraysh, the tribe of the prophet. "He commanded Zayd bin Thabit, 'Abd Allah bin Zubayr, Sa'id bin al-'As, and Abd al-Rahman bin al-Harith bin Hisham to copy it in codices [an yansakhuha fi al-masahif [sing. *mushaf*]). He said: if you disagree write it in the language of Quraysh, and they did. They copied the codices and sent in each direction a single one upon which to rely, and they burned whatever remained" (557).[120] The copies of the Qur'an were sent, Djaït writes, "to Mecca, Syria, Yemen, Bahrayn, Basra, Kufa, and one remained in Madina."[121] What is at stake in these passages is not only the safeguarding of the qur'anic text in relation to time ("It is a matter of unifying the text, of safeguarding it, of giving an official and definitive version of it" [135]), but a reorganization of language in the institution of reading in Arabic in relation to the social and political order.

The poem means more than what language is able to say.

ADUNIS, *Zaman al-shi'r*

Adunis underlines four moments in what he calls the thought, *fikr*, that, in his reading, became hegemonic in the fallout of the canonization of the Qur'an. This thought is theological, *lahutani*, because "it makes the religious conception [al-tasawwur al-dini] of God the source, axis, and end,"[122] oriented toward the past (58) ("Arabic thought became standardized, by which I mean that it takes the measure of the present and the future according to the past, without consideration of experiment or development" [114]), logocentric ("Speech imitates more closely the spoken divine word, or revelation, which is to say meaning, than writing. Writing is nothing but speech that has fallen into time" [60]), and in contradiction with modernity (62). Adunis underscores *fiqh* because with it, and with the formation of the disciplines of *balagha* (eloquence), *kalam* (theology), and *naqd* (criticism), "Arabic thought became juridical" (112). *Fiqh* requires the readability of language, and knowledge of the law requires knowledge of the Arabic language, because the sources of the law are Arabic ones. "In this way al-Shafi'i restricts the source of legislation to the text, that is to say, to the Book [the Qur'an] and the *sunna*," and juridical interpretation is to take place "based upon an analogy with the text" (13). "Juridical interpretation is a means of discovering the will of the eternal lawgiver with respect to the new event, and not a means of discovering what the human being who encounters this event wants" (13). Opinion, for al-Shafi'i, in Adunis's reading, had therefore to derive from what Adunis calls a "religious ground." "And this means that opinion must be derived, and by necessity, from a religious ground [min asl dini]: the Qur'an, the *sunna*, or consensus" (10). In this reading, opinion is subsumed into *qiyas*, analogy, the fourth source of the law. These sources—the Qur'an, the *sunna*, and *ijma'* (consensus) and *qiyas*—remain for Adunis textual, and above all religious. The religious, in Adunis, is *asl*, and it is for this reason that the inheritance of which he writes is given to appear in his text as religious and juridico-theological. I turn to consider this translation here.

Religion, in Adunis, is textual and not rational, still and not in motion. In religion, "work is something secondary with respect to thought, and the quality of movement [al-harakiyya] is neither in nature nor reality, but it is in the will of God. History is produced from the will of God, not of the human being. This means that reality, and individual and collective behavior, must conform to religious thought" (25). The "idea of religion itself" (89) is compelled to appear as conformity, "chatter" (127), "explication [sharh]" (131), mere abstraction (132), and the immobility of the dead letter, *al-harf al-mayyit* (98). It is not only that a European, Christian notion of religion becomes generalized in these passages (Adunis writes of Ibn al-Muqaffa' that "he rejected religion [al-din] setting out from a rational measure" and explains that this points to "his critical stance with respect to religion in general, and Islam in particular" [75]), but that his text partakes in and repeats the translation of this notion within the Arabic language. The word *din* in Arabic is linked to the taking on of debt ("I lent him something, so he is indebted [madin wa madyun]."[123] *Dayn* is the debt one takes on ("He borrowed something and so he took on a debt [dayn] and became indebted [da'in]" [203]) and one is therefore *muddan* "someone who still owes a debt" (204). It is linked to punishment, *al-jaza'* (204), to a taking of account, *al-hisab* (205), and to shame and humility, *al-dhull* (206). If the word *din* registers a relation to an alterity, to a temporal relation to difference, in Adunis it appears as what will have to have been and must be transcended in revolution, just as the Zanj and Karmathian movements of the third hijra century were attempts to "transcend one's race and one's tribe to reach the human as a human, insofar as he is a social being."[124]

What must be transcended and left behind is the bookishness of books, the "dead letter" of writing, in order that reason, *al-'aql*, and experiment or experience, *al-tajriba*, may take its place. "Thus the Companions [of the Prophet], and in particular 'Umar and 'Ali, instituted the path of juridical interpretation using one's opinion and welfare [al-maslaha], but it remained a juridical opinion based upon transmission and on the Qur'an and the *sunna*, not upon reason or from experience" (151). This imperative bears on the use of figural language. "What is particular about metaphor, in other words, is that it draws one's attention away from the letter [al-harf] and from what is apparent to the spirit and what is hidden" (132). This drawing away from the letter is to give the self-sufficient movement of poetry: poetry is its own beginning. "Abu Tammam creates in language an independent vitality, and his poetry moves beginning from itself, from its self-sufficiency and not from its subject or from an exterior component" (128). Adunis's earlier *Diwan al-shi'r al-'arabi* (Beirut, 1964–68) had remarked itself in relation to *Diwan al-hamasa*, the poetic anthology of the 'Abbasid poet Abu Tammam (d. 845 or 846).[125] *Al-Thabit wa al-mutahawwil* encrypts a relation to this remarking, to elaborate a newness and vitality in language through an appeal to a human being that is to be its own origin. Language, then, and like poetry, exceeds itself, it bids farewell to itself, to confound the understanding of origination Adunis wishes to have secured. Through the readings pursued in *al-Thabit wa al-mutahawwil*, Adunis recalls us to the historicity of language, in relation to the prophet Muhammad's death, as he reinscribes this death in relation to the terms privileged in the Arabic nineteenth century. To read this reinscription is not to do so in relation to a linguistic voluntarism, where one will have decided in relation to language. It is, rather, to read "the small room in which the alphabet was born," where language already occurs in relation to the iterated, asymmetrical force of colonial violence.[126]

INTERRUPTION II

We have then to take a further step out into the desert of comparative precision.

J. L. AUSTIN, *How to Do Things with Words*

G. W. F. Hegel writes in *Phaenomenologie des Geistes* (1807) that rhythm designates the speculative proposition. "Formally what has been said can be expressed thus: the general nature of the judgment or proposition, which involves the distinction of Subject and Predicate, is destroyed by the speculative proposition, and the proposition of identity which the former becomes contains the counter-thrust against that subject-predicate relationship.—This conflict between the general form of proposition and the unity of the Notion which destroys it is similar to the conflict that occurs in rhythm between meter and accent."[127] Poetic statement is solicited, in philosophical speculation, to resolve conflict and to install peace. The consuming practice of the Hegelian text must relate itself to poetry—and to the dead letter of literature—to be what it is.[128] To speak of itself, and to present itself as new, this text must reach out to—and domesticate—an alterity, if one from which it will never have been able to distinguish itself, finally, and once and for all. The formal presentation of the speculative proposition remains indebted to poetry—the conflict between "the general nature of the judgment or proposition" and "the speculative proposition" is like, "it is similar to," "the conflict that occurs in rhythm between meter and accent."[129] This indebtedness points to the labor of the negative and its "suffering," and the speculative proposition already, then, arhythmically, interrupts itself.[130] If rhythm points to a unification ("Rhythm results from the floating centre and the unification of the two" [46/38])—and in Hegel, unity and identity retain, with and against the reading pursued in Adorno, a certain privilege—it is immediately interrupted.[131] The project of speculative philosophy in Hegel is to have been starkly new—he writes in the *Encyclopaedia Logic,* "The present exposition is not like that; on the contrary, it sets out a new elaboration of philosophy, according to a method that will, I hope, be recognized eventually as the only genuine one, the only method that is identical with its content"—but this newness is interrupted by an indebtedness it will never simply have reconciled.[132]

Alterity remains a restless matter for thought. Hegel cannot finish with it. If "language is the work of thought," the Hegelian text will never simply have domesticated language, or poetic statement, into its interior.[133] Mournfully lodging it at its inside, this text of philosophical speculation speaks as if it were poetry.

Who would dare to say that the phantasm of the IC has not succeeded? Two thousand years, at least, of Europe, from Christ to *Sa*, without speaking of retroactive effects, of representations, of edging and de-bordering effects, of all that could be called the imperialism or the colonialisms and neocolonialisms of the IC.

JACQUES DERRIDA, *Glas*

For sound, the last external material which poetry keeps, is in poetry no longer the feeling of sonority itself, but a *sign*, by itself void of significance, a sign of the idea which has become concrete in itself, and not merely of indefinite feeling and its nuances and gradations. Sound in this way becomes a *word* as a voice inherently articulated, the meaning of which is to indicate ideas and thoughts.

G. W. F. HEGEL, *Aesthetics*

And so, as she begins to act in language, she also departs from herself.

JUDITH BUTLER, *Antigone's Claim*

Hegel opens the dialectical registers of thought to domesticate the interruptive valance of poetic statement. Yet this domestication is mournful. It is the containing interiorization of the dead as lifeless abstraction, and it is the repetition, without end, of this containment. What this occasions is the institution of writing ("nothing but a mechanical, hollow *repetition*") and what Hegel calls "formulae which are not even an immediate expression of thought" and "schemata."[134] The *Phenomenology* must then be an exposition of life, and it must appropriate the dead in order that what remains of the past be neither the mute abstraction of letters ("dead words and letters [toter Worte und Buchstaben]") nor the scattering of lifeless, cut-off body parts.[135] "A hand which has been cut off still looks like a hand and exists," Hegel writes, "but it has no actuality."[136] The transition from the rational to the actual and from substance to subject is also the interrupted management of death. Hegel writes in the preface to the *Phenomenology*, as in the *Encyclopaedia*, that the work to follow breaks with tradition and with a past. It is not only that what is most crucial is that philosophy separate itself from the past to tell us that it is new, modern, and Christian ("The right of the subject's particularity to find satisfaction, or—to put it differently—the right of subjective freedom, is the pivotal and focal point in the difference between antiquity and the modern age. This right, in its infinity, is expressed in Christianity, and it has become the universal and actual principle of a new form of the world"), but that this separation responds to an injunction: one must separate.[137] Philosophy, then, in Hegel, is a way of doing away with the dead. This doing away is a form of temporal domestication (as Timothy Bahti underlines, "to say goodbye to death, the grave, loss, temporality, is to have them all *within* one"), and it is one that may not simply come to an end.[138] This injunction is also the punctuating force of a "syncope" (*G*, 215/192), and it participates in the interruptive gesture that gives the rhythm of the text of philosophy and the speculative sentence. "A plurality of continuous jerks, of uninterrupted jolts—such would be the rhythm" (121/105). In Hegel, philosophy must exclude writing and the mechanical to make itself into poetry. It generates the former, "empty, ineffectual words which lift up the heart but leave reason unsatisfied, which edify, but raise no edifice," in order that literature may be excluded from and contained within the speculative economy.[139]

This containment points to what is perhaps the function to which reading is solicited in the disciplines of literature studies: language, the "object" of reading, is to be raised up and conserved in the event of writing to which literary criticism, in its most general and particular senses, is conscripted. This event—*Aufhebung*—labors to domesticate language, but it is also, again, an event of interruption. The *Phenomenology*, after everything, had abruptly to stop at its "end," cutting itself off and appending to itself the reworded word of the poet (the editors of the Felix Meiner edition write that "Hegel formuliert den Schluß von Schillers Gedicht Die Freundschaft" [620]): "from the chalice of this realm of spirits/ foams forth for him his own infinitude" (531/493). Unable to cease ending, this text stalls, as Hegel calls upon the poetic word to cosign the speculative proposition.[140] The pages we have considered in Hegel are mournful, routing a reflection on loss Hegel receives from Paul, where the law is not overthrown but retained (Hegel: "Memory alone then still preserves the dead form of the Spirit's previous shape as a vanished history, vanished one knows not how" [360/332]), and where the past is raised up and conserved as a dead form. Yet this interiorized exclusion must keep happening. It will never have finished, once and for all. If philosophy imparts a rhythm ("the essential thing for Reason is that conflict be resolved" [395/367–68]), it is one that Hegel repeats and disforms, where rhythm becomes arhythmic. And if the *Phenomenology* is to secure being from time through the explication of philosophical truth ("What is not rational has no *truth*, or, what is not grasped conceptually, *is not* [was nicht begriffen ist, ist nicht]" (361/333), and however historicist this text is, the force of the verb *to be*, which Hegel underlines here, is interrupted. It is not only that Hegel's text becomes the subordinated thing—literature—it will never have failed to name, but that it tells us that language may not separate itself out from its "own" interruptive time. The historiographical privilege in reading—a privilege remarked perhaps most insistently in Hegel—becomes a site at which a declining to affirm the interiority, or exteriority, of language with respect to time appears as perhaps the decisive imperative for literature studies, where the time of language is already the time of another.[141]

Hegel himself situates Judaism and Islam within a theologico-political history of subjection.

GIL ANIDJAR, *The Jew, the Arab*

In Hegel philosophical exposition is sacrificial, "self-consciousness through its sacrifice brings forth substance as Subject," but it keeps stumbling over the bones of the dead.[142] If spirit is to leave these bones behind ("Of course, the intention here is not to state that Spirit, which is represented by a skull, is a Thing; there is not meant to be any materialism, as it is called, in this idea; rather, Spirit must be something more and other than these bones" [320/208]), it must keep remarking its relation to them.[143] The dead stillness of bones mirrors "indigestible, excremental writing," and the figure of the Jew, and, as Anidjar has shown, the inseparable, if hardly distinct, figure of the Arab.[144] If in Kant the aesthetic is a philological polemology, in Hegel philosophy is a philological—racial and religious—historiography. "Just so, it may be said of the Jewish people that it is precisely because they stand before the portal of salvation that they are, and have been, the most reprobate and rejected: what that people should be in and for it self, this essential nature of its own self, is not explicitly present to it; on the contrary, it places it beyond itself. By this alienation it creates for itself the *possibility* of a higher existence, if only it could take back again into itself its alienated object, than if it had remained undisturbed within the immediacy of being—because Spirit is all the greater, the greater the opposition from which it has returned into itself; but it creates this opposition for itself by setting aside its immediate unity, and by alienating its being-for self."[145] Already on the side of death, the Jew points to the Oriental ("hostile peoples" subject to "a caste-system which gives the semblance of organization of a completed order, but in which the universal freedom of the individuals is lacking" [459/425]), to the Chinese, and Kant.[146] "Those who say God is jealous are liars, Greeks, Jews, or Kantians" (*G*, 239/214). "Kant is the Jew; Hegel, Christ," and philosophy occurs as the hierarchical imposition of discriminating separations.[147] If the non-Christian is unsublatable refuse, "the Christian religion, however, is the religion of freedom—although it may come about that this freedom is perverted into unfreedom under the influence of superstition."[148] Soliciting the non-Christian to its freedom—"The Greeks were to be equal because all were free, self-subsistent; the Jews equal because all were incapable of self-subsistence"—Hegel's text stages speculative philosophy in polemical terms.[149] If an end is promised—if philosophy will finally have domesticated poetry, if also all of the others, "a host of separate antagonistic national Spirits who hate and fight each other to the death"—this text, one may repeat, fails to end.[150] "Hegel's texts wish to be an omnipresent, omnipotent, reconciling nurse—and, finally, to be the mother herself, for whom the nurse is only a stand-in and a helper, a complement."[151] This finality must never come. "It must repeat itself, because it could not avoid originally losing itself" (9), as it comes to a close, and if always, yet again. "*Sa* always ends by being full, heavy, pregnant with itself" (*G*, 259/232).

BETWEEN TWO

Here is a present that yesterday doesn't touch . . .
When we reached
the last of the trees we noticed that we
were no longer able to notice. When
we turned toward the trucks we saw absence
heaping up its selected things and pouring
its eternal tent around us . . .

Here is a present
that yesterday doesn't touch
A silk thread slips between the mulberry trees
letters upon the night's notebook. Only
the butterflies light our way
descending to the hollow of strange words:
Was this miserable man my father?
Perhaps I'll look after myself here [huna]. Perhaps
I'll give birth to myself, with myself
and choose for my name vertical letters . . .

Here is a present
sitting in time's emptiness staring
at the trace of those who pass on the river's reeds
polishing their flutes with wind . . . Perhaps speech
will become transparent and we'll see windows in it, open
Perhaps time will hurry, with us
carrying our tomorrow in its luggage . . .

Here is a present
without place.
No one here found anyone who remembered
how we left the door, a gust of wind. Or anyone who remembered
when we fell off of yesterday. Yesterday
shattered across the floor, shards gathered together
by others, mirrors for their image, after us . . .

Here is a present
without place.
Perhaps I'll look after myself and scream at
the Owl's night: Was this miserable man
my father, who would have me carry the burden of his history?
Perhaps I'll change within my name, and choose
my mother's words and habits as it should
be: She'll be able to joke with me
whenever salt touches my blood. She'll be able
to comfort me whenever a nightingale bites my mouth!

> Here is a present
> fleeting
> Here strangers hung their guns over
> the branches of an olive tree, prepared dinner
> quickly from tin cans, and left
> hurrying to their trucks . . .
>
> MAHMOUD DARWISH, "Laylat al-bawm"

The poem, in Darwish, gestures to "a postponement of the end," to decline the closure of time in the totalizing form of the work.[152] The traces of the abandoned camp site in the *nasib* "bear a metonymic relation to the lost beloved," suggesting that in Darwish, and like in the loss of the beloved, bereavement will never have finished.[153] The loss of the finality of loss interrupts the desire to finish, and to take account of the losses, and it is for this reason that to speak of the *nakba*—to speak of the loss of Palestine in 1948—is also to speak of something that has been left behind: *Why Did You Leave the Horse Alone?* The clean break said to be occasioned in mourning is parasited by remains. The foundation of the Israeli state occasioned an event of naming ("With one massacre, or with two, the name of the country, our country, became another," Darwish writes [*FH*, 47]). In the stark newness the Israeli state is said to have been, a colonial settler theology, and, if more precisely, a Christian, colonial theology, is installed as a political form: the state will have to have appeared as if it had been created from nothing. That such breaks will already have been ruined means that the loss of Palestine and its destruction are not consigned to a past. In the remarking of the loss of Palestine as having been lost, the death imparted in 1948 and "the destruction of an entire society" "is something that lives on" in and as poetic statement and its form, interrupting the historicization of that destruction.[154] If in Darwish "the historical remains the referent that makes reading possible," this would be so only insofar as the historical is an eventfulness that places in question the finality of loss and the possibility of reading it, to interrupt the colonial idiom and practice called upon to securely close the time of the state.[155]

The word *here* is repeated in each of this poem's six stanzas, and it points to the first line of the poem that opens *Why Did You Leave the Horse Alone*?, "I look out, like a balcony, one what I want" (*L*, 11/2]). As in "The Raven's Ink" the beginning gestures to another, the opening points outward and elsewhere. "Perhaps I'll change within my name" (30/24), and this alteration, perhaps, takes place as the repetition of the names of others and of other places. This event is staged in *Ahad 'ashar kawkaban* (Eleven Planets) (Beirut, 1992), a text published three years prior to the one that is my focus in this chapter, in relation to the colonization of the "new world" beginning in the fifteenth century. Darwish underlines there a relation to language ("the white man will not understand the ancient words/ here, in the souls tossed between the sky and the trees" [*A*, 38]), to point to what Kadhim Jihad has called the "hermeneutic violence" that the event Darwish is reading, and those other events Darwish gives us to read, occasions.[156] The reflection on the destruction and loss of Palestine is geographically and temporally expanded to point to the repetition of a European, Christian idiom in the colonization of the Americas and through its persistence in the American invasion of Iraq in 1991.[157] The poetic word takes place in the wake of such violence, "since the Tartars returned upon our horses" (*A*, 91), and "after Iraq" ("There is no longer, on the earth, space for the poem, my companion/ So is there, in the poem, still space for the earth, after Iraq?" [92]). The time of the poem is then that of autumn, to remark "the anteriority of loss," even as its names are more than one, giving the confounding of the work of mourning in the stalled limpidity of lyric iteration.[158]

> If this autumn were the last one, we'd apologize
> for the ebb and flow of the sea and of memories . . . and for
> what we did
> to our brothers before the copper age: We've wounded
> many creatures
> with weapons made of our brothers' skeletons, so that we would be
> their descendants, near the spring's water. And we'd apologize to the
> gazelle's family for what we did to it there. When
> a thread of purple burst upon the water, we didn't notice
> that it was our blood writing our history in the anemone of the
> beautiful place. (*A*, 65)

The belated time of the poem, like the poem's drawing away, points to a relation to love. In "Shita' Rita al-akhir" (Rita's Last Winter), the fifth of the six poems included in *Ahada 'ashara kawkaban*, the breath of the lover mirrors the rhythm of poetic statement. "A wave of majestic wheat falls asleep upon her slow breath/ A red rose falls asleep in the hall/ A short night falls asleep/ The sea falls asleep in front of my window to her rhythm/ It rises and falls in the lines upon her bare chest" (78). Love points to the relation of rhythm to the poetic word, to "a sense of problematic, yet indispensible, otherness,"[159] an "exile from place," which gives place to the poem as the coming apart of language.[160] Language is the distancing of the poem from itself ("But the sky is distant/ from its earth, and I from my language" [*A*, 58]), and this distance is reinscribed and pluralized, to give a longing without recuperation ("Longing," Darwish also writes, "is the sound of the wind" [*FH*, 119]). In the volume I am considering here Darwish directs us to Ibn Hazm (994-1064), whose name I have cited Darwish recalling in *Ka zahr al-lawz aw ab'ad* ("Nothing of me remains/ other than a manuscript of Ibn Rushd, and *Tawq al-hamama*, and the translations" [*A*, 17]).[161] In Ibn Hazm the separation of the lover from the beloved is on the side of death. "Separation is the brother of death."[162] And to die parting is better than to have survived what takes place in the fallout of loss ("Were one to die at the moment of parting, he would be forgiven, if you consider what would have happened to him an hour after the severance of his hopes, his being overtaken by dread, with sadness taking the place of his happiness" [209]). To have survived is to be on the side of dread and sadness, and to have missed the moment of parting is to be on the side of death. "I know someone who came to say farewell to his beloved, on the day of their separation, to find that he had already gone. So he stood for an hour where the traces of his beloved remained, returning over and over again to the place where he had been, and then he left, sorrowful, grieved, his mood having changed. After only a few days he grew ill and died, may God have mercy on him" (211). What is solicited in Darwish, through this citation, is neither a union nor an understanding of absolute loss—where one will have missed the loss of the beloved, as in this passage in *Tawq al-hamama*—but a lingering with loss in relation to language, where poetry points to a finitude gestured in love.

History is a name for this finite relation.

> Our shadow speaks to us in the south, and wild animals howl
> at a red moon over us. We'll touch the shepherds' bread
> and wear the linen of their garments in order to surprise our-
> selves . . .
> Those are our days
> They pass, opposite us, in slow, ordered steps . . .
> Those are our days
> They pass upon the soldiers' vehicles and toss their greeting to the
> light mountain slopes
> "Peace to the land of Can'an, the land of the gazelle, and of purple"
> Those, our days . . .
> They slip away, one thread, another. And we are the ones who
> wove their cloak. The goddess had no role
> except to speak to us, and pour for us her wine . . .
> Those are our days

> They look out over us so that we'll thirst, more . . . We didn't recognize our wound in
> the crowd of old wounds. But this place—this shedding of blood
> is called by our names. (*A*, 72–73)

The names that are called repeat and encrypt a relation to loss. Repetition has been called "one prominent site among others of the harmony of the poetic text" in Darwish, but this "harmony" is an event of interruption.[163] In Darwish al-Andalus "appears as a poetic site of a certain sort"[164] to point to "that dimension of language that is the opening of language's place," and it is one among other names by which Darwish recalls and calls upon poetry and tradition.[165] Loss is mimed in the giving of names of place ("But Granada is of gold/ it is formed from the silk of words, embroidered in almonds, the silver of tears in/ the string of an 'oud" [*A*, 11]), and the repetition of the ancient practice of the recitation of names inscribes the poem in relation to the ode and its form, and in relation to love. In Darwish "the writing of love poetry is itself a kind of love," and this love asks us to read a relation to loss inscribed in language, and in the practice for the giving of sense in the tongue.[166] This practice points to the citation of names in the mouth to remark an excess in language, which fractures the desire to "transcend the unhappiness of the enigmatic."[167] Even as more than one linguistic legacy is retained. "There is a name for what you want to write, and you are going to write poetry [shi'r] in the end."[168]

> As for speech, its task is to light, with a single word—
> I love you—the night of a traveler between two odes
> and the two faces of a palm leaf.
>
> MAHMOUD DARWISH, *Sarir al-ghariba*

> Know that it is possible to do in poetry what it is not possible to do in speech.
>
> SIBAWAYH, *al-Kitab*

"Here I measure the distance/ with the odes of the jahili poets" (*LT*, 49), and the distances measured point to the ancient understanding of the relation between poetry and the Qur'an. Already the poem takes place in the fallout of losses remarked in this relation, and to speak of the loss of Palestine has meant to do so through this loss ("'And what after that?'/ What after that?" [48]). If "The Owl's Night" routes one to the opening of *Why Did You Leave the Horse Alone?*, that opening points to a doubling: the opening of the volume in which it appears and the opening of poetic tradition in the Arabic language. Just as the loss of Palestine will never have been left behind, language in Darwish retains a melancholic relation to loss. "My last ode fell from my date palm/ I am a traveler inside me/ I am besieged by doubles" (J, 36), and to be besieged by doubles is to be besieged by an ode: by a single ode that is more and less than one, "a chapter of Dante, and half of an ode" (*AF*, 48), and by what Darwish underscores is "my last ode." Just as to return to the beginning is to have done so again, so too the beginning may not be separated from this repetition. The loss of the immanent sense of language, in the interpretive function ascribed to the ode in relation to the Qur'an, becomes a site of repeated return. The last ode will never have been the final one because it repeats an excess in poetic statement, interrupting the desire to appropriate "the death of the other" in what the poem still promises as a coherency of form.[169]

> One day I'll become a bird, and draw my existence from
> my nothingness. Whenever the two wings burn
> I draw near to the truth, and rise from
> the ashes. I am a dialogue between two dreamers. I played
> upon my body and upon my soul in order to complete
> my first journey to meaning. So it burns me
> and disappears. I am absent. I am the azure
> expelled. (*J*, 12–13)

The end is confounded in the names Darwish repeats. "We/ are those who people the beautiful land between/ the Tigris and the Euphrates/ and who safeguard the names [wa nahfaz al-asma']" (*J*, 82). Like the opening lines of the ode, this confounding, something already more than one, speaks to us of losses, of the remains—*atlal*—of an abandoned site.

> One of the people of this plain . . .
> On the barley festival I visit my radiant
> ruins [atlali al-bahiyya] like a mark [washm] upon my identity
> the winds don't disperse them nor do they harden them . . . / (*J*, 75)

> What I said to ruins [al-talal]: Farewell. For I only was
> what I was once. I only was one
> time, which sufficed to know how time breaks apart
> like a bedouin's tent in the northern wind
> and how place splits and wears the past

fragments of an abandoned temple. (47)

As if I were not as if I . . . /
Whenever I listened to my heart I was filled
with what absence said, and the trees
lifted me. From one dream to another
I fly without a final intention
I was born thousands of poetic years
ago in a darkness white like linen
I didn't know, entirely, who in us was me, and who
my dream. I am my dream
As if I were not as if I . . .
My language only bids farewell to its pastoral accent
departing to the north. Our dogs
became calm. Our goats were dressed in fog upon
the hills. A reckless arrow split the face of
certainty. I've grown tired of my language speaking and not
speaking upon the backs of horses. What has the past done
with the days of Imru' al-Qays, divided
between Caesar and a rhyme . . . / (70–72)

The weariness of the poet entails a relation to the days of Imru' al-Qays and his language. It is a language that is already divided ("divided/ between Caesar and a rhyme"), and it points to an excess of sense, what Ferial Ghazoul has called "a surplus of significance," and which I have tried to read here.[170] It is a reflection on memory that divides ("We didn't inherit anything except for our two names" [*J*, 39]), to inscribe the name of the poet—Mahmoud—into the poetic word. The letters to which Darwish appeals in "The Owl's Night" ("Perhaps/ I'll give birth to myself with myself/ and choose for my name vertical letters" [*L*, 29/22]), confound the belonging of the poem to time, to point to the writing of the poet's name in *Jidariyya*. Language, in Darwish, implies "a break with the horizon of subjectivity," where the poem points to a relation to justice ("But surely justice, like reading, involves some exposure to language and its difficulties," Thomas Keenan has compellingly written).[171] In this solicitation of justice, the poetic writing of the name is not an act that belongs to itself but one where the poet already offers a reply in the dual, between two.

And as Christ walked upon the lake
I walked in my dream. But I came down from
the cross because I am afraid of heights, and because
I don't bring news of resurrection. I only changed
my rhythm to hear the sound of my heart clearly . . .
Epic heroes have eagles, I have only *The Ring*

of the Dove, a deserted star over the roofs
and a street that leads to the port . . .
This sea is mine
This humid air is mine
This sidewalk and my steps upon it and my semen . . .
are mine. The old bus station
is mine. My ghost and his companion
are mine. The copper pot,
the verse of the Throne, and the key are mine
The door and the watchmen and the bells are mine
The shoe of the mare that
flew over the walls . . . is mine. What was mine
is mine. The shreds of paper that were
torn from the Gospels are mine
The salt, traces of tears upon
the wall of the house, is mine . . .
And my name—even if I mispronounce
its five horizontal letters—is mine:
mim / infatuated, orphaned, what's finished with what's passed
ha' / a garden and a lover, each perplexed and bereaved
mim / foolhardy, ready and prepared for his
promised
death in exile, ill from desire
waw / farewell, the middle rose
loyalty to birth wherever it takes place, and the parents' promise
dal / the guide, the path, the tear
of a small castle that's worn away, a sparrow that pampers me
and bleeds me /
This name is mine . . .
and my friends', wherever they are. My provisional
body is mine, present or absent . . .
Two meters of this dirt would suffice, now . . .
I have a single meter and seventy-five centimeters . . .
And what remains belongs to the chaotic colored flowers
that drink me slowly. What was mine
is mine: my yesterday. And what will be is mine
my distant tomorrow, and the return of the fugitive spirit
It is as if it something that was, wasn't
It is as if it had never taken place
A light wound on the forearm of the vain present . . .
History is sarcastic with its victims
and its heroes . . .
It glances at them and leaves . . .
This sea is mine
This humid air is mine
And my name—
even were I to mispell it upon my coffin—

is mine.
As for me—and I've filled
with all of the reasons for my departure—
I am not mine
I am not mine
I am not mine . . . (*J*, 100–105)

Poetry occasions a parting and a coming apart, as it recalls an intimacy in relation to place. Rather than a return to a place, the serene belonging of self or a language in place, Darwish's text scripts returns that come back under one name and then another. If Darwish in a certain sense possesses his name ("This humid air is mine/ and my name—/ even were I to make a mistake spelling it upon my coffin—/ is mine"), this possession becomes a form of repetition and nonbelonging ("I am not mine/ I am not mine/ I am not mine..."). What takes place in the poetic word is what occurs where an intention to do something with or in relation to language will already have been touched upon by the words of more than one other. If in Darwish there is division, it is not that it "generates two from one," so that the poet may "enter the image of the other in its history in order to be able to take hold of that history," but that it points to an event of language where the poem already divides.[172] This anteriority gives the poem to draw away and disappear, recalling more then one event and more than one time, as it becomes what it will already have been: something other than itself. The place of this disappearance is "here," where poetic statement recalls us to a responsibility in relation to loss.

§

Poetic statement, in Darwish, points to "those killed, those whose names are not known" (*LT*, 61), and to others. Rhythm, then, becomes a name for the historicity of language ("The rhythm chooses me, it chokes on me," Darwish writes. "I am the response to the violin. I am not its player/ memory is before me/ an echo of things which speak me/ so I speak . . . " [15]). Language appeals to something other than itself, it rivets our attention to "the primary dependency that any speaking being has by virtue of the interpellative or constitutive address of the Other," and the temporal excess this dependency remarks.[173] "Autonomy in speech," Butler also writes, "to the extent that it exists, is conditioned by a radical and originary dependency on a language whose historicity exceeds in all directions the history of the speaking subject" (28). That one is chosen by rhythm means that poetry occasions an inaugurative call ("The mark interpellation makes is not descriptive, but inaugurative" [33]), which commands the reading of poetry and the legacies that form literary institutions. To respond to this command is to open a relation to "a future of language" (140) given with the promise of repetition, where the poem bears itself out toward others. And the poetic word closes, again, signing a name. Writing of Tunis, the site to which the Palestine Liberation Organization took refuge following the devastating Israeli bombardment and occupation of Beirut in 1982, Darwish writes of a wound, and offers the North African city thanks. "And thus I wish her farewell/ for the air of the sea wounds me . . . the scent of the night wounds me,/ a necklace of jasmine upon the words of people wounds me,/ it wounds me to think of the spiral path which leads to the outskirts/ of al-Andalus . . . " (*LT*, 114).

I disappeared to bring all of the gifts of language/ to you

MAHMOUD DARWISH, *Hiyya ughniya, hiyya ughniya*

The poem, in Darwish, draws away. This drawing away sets, like the notes of guitar, the unsettling, lyrical tempo of Darwish's language. The poem is a word offered to a stranger, to "Imru' al-Qays and the others" (*SG*, 32) ("Perhaps my imagination is clearer than my reality/ The winds are northern. I wouldn't love you more/ if you weren't with me/ here, now, between two icons/ and a guitar that's opened its wound to the moon" [95]). To read the poem, then, is "to let oneself be greeted by its word," to relinquish "our acquired habits of mastery" in relation to language.[174] In the poem, the coherence of the past is already shattered, as in the fourth stanza of "The Owl's Night" ("Yesterday/ shattered across the floor, shards gathered together by others/ mirrors for their image, after us . . . " [*L*, 30/24]). If the shards of "yesterday" will have been gathered by others, formed and shaped through the reflection of the image of the other in the mirror—formed and shaped through the way in which the other forms an image of herself or himself—then Darwish, in this passage, gives us to read another way through which one may think the act of formation and shaping. This other way amounts to a way of shaping and forming—a way of giving form, a poetic resource that reaches back to an ancient understanding of the Greek verb *poiein*—that does not discount the "others" but gives form to be read in relation to a temporal excess.[175]

Words, in Darwish, always point elsewhere, teaching a relation to alterity in language. The "others" to whom Darwish gestures in "The Owl's Night," and in relation to whose image the shards of the past are gathered, are those who colonized his homeland ("Here is a present/ fleeting/ Here strangers hung their guns over/ the branches of an olive tree, prepared dinner/ quickly from tin cans, and left/ hurrying to their trucks," Darwish writes in the poem's final stanza [*L*, 31/26]), and what Darwish offers, then, is a reflection on form that is also a reflection on history. If Walter Benjamin recalls us to read history and time through "the tradition of the oppressed"—a reading of history that relates to Benjamin's understanding of aesthetic form and of interruption, an understanding where interruption gives place to further interruptive and gestural acts, "For the more frequently we interrupt someone in the act of acting, the more gestures result," Benjamin also wrote—Darwish, here, offers an understanding of history which declines the recuperation or domestication of the past, of death, and of loss.[176] In "The Owl's Night" the poetic word is called upon to "gather" language—in relation to names and naming, legacy and inheritance, time and history, and death and mourning—through this declining. If the "shards" to which Darwish gestures in the poem I am reading here promise a wholeness (and one may consider Darwish's use of this word elsewhere as "shrapnel"—"The victims are shrapnel/ upon the streets and in words/ their names are torn apart/ letters, mutilated, like their bodies," Darwish writes of Iraq [*AF*, 190], and, in *Ahada 'ashara kawkaban*, "My language is shrapnel" [*A*, 79]), language is immediately recalled to the iterative density of poetic statement. The poem, in Darwish, and like history, is given to "exceed itself"—the historical is thought differently, through and in relation to a poetic or catachrestic excess—and this excess is cyphered in poetic form.[177] "Unintentionally," Darwish writes, "the small stones become a language or an echo" (*SG*, 97). The poem promises an end—"The Owl's Night" closes staging the drawing away of those "others" of whom Darwish writes—but it is an end that never arrives, finally, and that never gives place to a domestic closure of time. It arrives, and if it does, "on the last night of winter."

> After your night, the last night of winter
> the sea road emptied of the night's guard
> No shadow follows me after your night dried up
> in the sun of my song. Who will say to me
> now: Let go of yesterday, and dream, freely, without
> constraint

> My freedom sits, now, near me, with me, on
> my knee, like a house cat. It stares at me, and at what
> you've left me of yesterday: your lilac
> shawl, video cassettes about dancing among wolves, and a necklace of
> jasmine on your heart's moss . . .
>
> What will come of my freedom, after your night,
> the last night of winter?
> "A cloud went from Sodom to Babylon,"
> hundreds of years ago. But its poet, Paul
> Celan, committed suicide, today, in Paris's river.
> You won't take me to the river again. I won't be questioned by
> a guard. What's your name, today? We won't curse
> the war. We won't curse peace. We won't climb the walls
> of the garden searching for the night between two willows
> or two windows. You won't ask me: When will peace
> open the gates of our citadel to the doves?
>
> After your night, the last night of winter
> the soldiers erected their encampment in a distant place
> And a white moon set upon my balcony
> And I sat with my freedom quietly staring staring into the night
> Who am I? Who am I after your night,
> the last night of winter? (*SG*, 38–40)

The belatedness of language asks us to read "responsibility of the poem in Mahmoud Darwish."[178] It is a responsibility to time, death, and loss, to those losses said to belong to the past, and to those that remain to come. The passage I have sought to read in this chapter ("Here is a present that yesterday doesn't touch . . . ") calls out to and is recalled in the epigraph with which this chapter opens ("Retain this night of pain in your memory"). If the former points to the latter—and to those other writings of Darwish's upon which I have drawn in these pages—this relation is neither a joining nor a Hegelian *Aufhebung*. The former, what is said to have been "earlier," is not sublated, it is not raised up and conserved, in the latter. The relation between these two is citational, to give poetic utterance to be read as what Darwish has called "this untimely event about which we know neither how it will happen nor when."[179] And the poem, as an event, Darwish writes, interrupts its domestication in relation to an understanding of what *is*, to become an event of form. "Poetry . . . What is it? It is that which, when we hear it or read it we say, without any need for demonstration: this is poetry!" (*AF*, 226). If the poem is what calls for language, and if it is what compels a statement guided by the force of the copula—"This is poetry"—it immediately interrupts the time of ontological—and if also historical—designation. The poem is what interrupts the domestication of time, it retains a bereaved relation to the past, declining to leave it behind.

> There's no wounded honey for the stranger
> Here or there. So what time is it now?
> What is the name of this place that we are in? What
> is the difference between my sky and your earth? Tell me
> what Adam said secretly. Was he liberated
> when he remembered? Tell me anything that will change the ashen
> color of the sky. Tell me a few simple
> words, words that a woman desires
> that one say to her from time to time. Say:
> two people, you and I, for example, are able
> to bear all of this resemblance between the fog
> and the mirage, and return, safe and sound. My sky
> is ashen. So what do you think about when the sky is
> ashen? (*SG*, 77–78)

The name, in Darwish ("We didn't inherit anything except for our two names" [*J*, 39]), is cut into by the letters of the alphabet, pointing to a sky of ash as it repeats the losses. The poem teaches us to read those losses in relation to the giving of language ("Tell me/ what Adam said secretly. Was he liberated/ when he remembered" [*SG*, 77]). The origin of language is already in destruction and loss ("And he taught Adam all of the names [wa 'allama Adama al-asma'a kullaha]" [Qur'an 2:31]), an event I turn to read in its textual details in chapter 2, in relation language's reorganization as an object and as a new kind of practice. And poetic statement occurs, if it may be said to do so, as if it were in mourning. "What would I do," Darwish writes, "without the roses of Samarkand?" (*SG*, 113). This "without" would be what a poem "is," its finite and still not solely negative condition.

> Nothing
> is more distant from my mare than the ode of the jahili poet
> and nothing is more distant from my language than the prince
> of Damascus.
>
> *La shay'*
> *ab'ad min farasi 'an mu'allaqat al-jahiliyy*
> *wa la shay' ab'ad min lughati 'an amir*
> *Dimashq.* (*SG*, 124)

CHAPTER TWO

Philologies

This poetry is gone and all that remains of it is memory.

TAHA HUSAYN, *Fi al-shi'r al-jahili*

"I am confident that even if this research angers some and troubles others, it will satisfy this small group of enlightened people who are in reality the promise of the future, the basis of the modern renaissance [al-nahda al-haditha], and the storehouse of the new culture [adab]" (*F*, 13), Taha Husayn wrote in *Fi al-shi'r al-jahili* (Cairo, 1926).[1] An appeal to the future, through a practice of historicist, philological, text-critical reading, remarks the temporal aporia that gives place to Husayn's writing. Philological practice is to render "the knowledge of the ancients in its entirety as an object of research ['ilm al-mutaqadd-imin kullahu mawd' al-bahth]" (14). The appropriation of the words *adab* and *'ilm* in Husayn gestures to a differentiated event of devastation and reorganization in language in the Arabic nineteenth century, a violence imparted in relation to the terms of the giving of sense, where an older understanding of language suddenly appears in the perspective of a new series of terms installed in relation to the juridical violence of the colonial state.[2] A series of philological categories is generalized, pointing to the destruction of the terms of language in an older, Arabic-Islamic logocentrism, if one that is already interrupted in the iterated movement of the tongue in the practice of language.[3] Philology, as one is given to read it through the Arabic texts I consider in this chapter, is, then, an aporetical event. It is a generalization and proliferation of European terms within the Arabic language, pointing to a linguistic, epistemic violence, and it remarks a nonbelonging and an interruptive force of language. Philology, on the one hand, occasions the installation of a series of colonial, Orientalist categories in language, where the distinctions between and within languages are displaced, reinscribed, renamed, and restaged. Yet philology confounds the subordination of language to being—and to history, understood as a practice for the recognition of language in time—as it also repeats and reinscribes this subordination. And philology is, then, already more than one. It is philologies.

The proliferation of philological categories in the Arabic language imparts the destruction and loss of *adab*, a word I have rendered in the sentence that opens this chapter as "culture," and which has come to be translated in the Arabic language as "literature."[4] This translation points to the legacies indexed in Kant and Jena Romanticism, which we read in the introduction and chapter 1, to generalize a privileging of the figure of "man" as a temporally coherent ground of language. This chapter reads this translation in Ahmad Faris al-Shidyaq's *al-Saq 'ala al-saq fi ma huwwa al-Fariyaq* (Paris, 1855) and, differently, in the institution of a literary object in Husayn's *Fi al-shi'r al-jahili*, in relation to the divided totality of the social body. The imparting of the legacies I gesture to here enacts a violence inscribed upon the Arabic word *adab* and the terms for the giving of sense in language through the tongue. The entry in Butrus al-Bustani's dictionary, *Muhit al-muhit* (Beirut, 1867–70), under the word *adab* points to one register of this reorganization: *adab* entails a relation to ethical comportment, it is "a disposition that restrains one from carrying out what would disgrace [also, "disfigure"] him," and its meaning includes "to teach well mannered and composed comportment and good morals ['allamahu riyadat al-nafs wa mahasin al-akhlaq]."[5] Al-Bustani's entry cites sections of *Lisan al-'arab* ("It is called *adab* because it calls people [ya'dibu al-nas] to what is good and not to what is ugly," "The origin of *adab* is invocation" [du'a', also "call"]) and al-Fayruzabadi's fourteenth-century lexicon *Qamus al-muhit*.[6] Yet this citation and relocation inscribe *adab*, and the legacies to which it points, in relation to form. It is to be a language event that is communicable, formally monadic, temporally coherent, and legible. This inscription is displaced and remarked in al-Shidyaq. It gives place in Husayn to the formation of a discipline for reading, literature studies, where literature, the newly translated event of language *adab* will have become, is, finally, to belong to the time of the life and death of man.

ENLIGHTENMENT IN THE FIELD OF LANGUAGE

If only the destruction were to come to an end, and set a limit to these misfortunes and losses, so that we may take a final accounting of them.

BUTRUS AL-BUSTANI, *Nafir Suriyya*

But the question of the philological question may be understood in yet another way.

WERNER HAMACHER, *Für die Philologie*

Philology compels a reflection on form, and form is rendered, in the writings of Butrus al-Bustani I turn to here, as *qalib*, "mold."[7] This rendering points to a new understanding of language, which was solicited in relation to the juridical violence of the Ottoman state.[8] In 1839 the Ottoman Empire issued a decree, the *Hatt-i Şerif-i Gülhane*, which, with a later decree in 1856, granted "freedom of religion" to Ottoman subjects.[9] The expansion of capital, and capitalist relations, loosens and devastates language, as language is recaptured in relation to "the juridical equality of all subjects," an equality for which the violence of the law calls.[10] The privileging of this equality, as Ussama Makdisi has shown, gives place to a reorganization of the social and political order in Mount Lebanon. In the wake of the Egyptian occupation of 1831–40, the communal violence of 1841, and, later, of the civil war of 1860, "religion was detached from its social environment and treated as a cohesive, exclusivist, and organic force; neighbors suddenly became potential enemies."[11] This detachment and redefinition of "religion" is inscribed upon language, tearing it from its past and compelling its relocation in relation to a new series of terms. A linguistic anthropocentrism restages language, in the institution of *Bildung* in the colonies, and this restaging is an event that is iterative, differential, and proliferating, constantly stalling and reproducing itself, and giving place to itself differently. It is repeated in the work of Butrus al-Bustani—in his own writings, in his work as an editor, lexicographer, and translator, and in the encyclopedic edifice that is *Da'irat al-ma'arif.* In al-Bustani language translates itself through a series of philological, at once linguistic, racial, historical, and religious distinctions, to reorder language, where language is given to appear as if it were "Encyclopedie Arabe."[12]

To approach al-Shidyaq, and what I underlined in the introduction to this book is a privileging and an interruption of the figure of "man" in *al-Saq 'ala al-saq*, and, then, to approach Husayn, I turn to al-Bustani's reflection on language in his *Khutba fi adab al-'arab* (Beirut, 1859), a historicizing text of Enlightenment pedagogy. This text is divided into four sections, an introduction, followed by three periodizing divisions: "The State of Knowledge among the Arabs before Islam," "The State of Knowledge among the Arabs after Islam," and "On the *Adab* of the Arabs Today." It was presented extemporaneously, *irtijalan*, as a lecture "before a gathering of Europeans and Arabs in Beirut, on the fifteenth day of February, 1859," and it works as a program statement for Enlightenment in the field of language.[13] This text is an Enlightenment one because it generalizes a conception of autonomy in language—"we are able," he writes, now, "these days" to "raise our heads" (113)—and it does so through the institution of historical categories. This thinking of loss and language lays the ground for a literary history, the terms of which are repeated, appropriated, and reinstalled in Jurji Zaydan (1861–1914), Taha Husayn, and others, imparting a legacy to Arabic critical and theoretical writing with which this book is engaged. But the privileging of autonomy in *Khutba fi adab al-'arab*—from the American missionaries with whom al-Bustani worked, and with whom he wished to break, and from more than one past he wished to have left behind—repeats the autonomy he desired to gain for his time, his generation, and the future. "Had I been asked to stand before you to speak about this topic thirty years ago, I would have been embarrassed," he writes. "As for now there are many things which strengthen our hopes for the future."[14] If, in this and other texts, including his 1860 edition of the *Diwan* of the 'Abbasid poet al-Mutanabbi, al-Bustani wishes to link his project to the Ottoman political and social order and its "civilizing mission"[15] rather than to the missionaries or the Europeans ("He had by now become independent of the mission, and showed ample evidence of his disapproval of their sectarian approach," the historian A. L. Tibawi writes), the terms that articulate this break and "independence" are given through the event of translation his work remarks.[16] Here and elsewhere, one will never have left the past behind, and the break al-Bustani wishes to have installed ruins the division between the present and the past his text solicits and desires to secure. The division between the present and the past communicates with others—death and life, childhood and adulthood, poetry and philosophy—to repeat itself as it repeats the words of those others al-Bustani wishes to have left behind, finally, on the far side of "life."

The project of Enlightenment in al-Bustani—the project of *nahda* as *tanwir*—is a project for reading elaborated through the categories of life and death. If, as George Antonius wrote of the nineteenth century, repeating, in part, al-Bustani's understanding, "The [Arabic] language itself had degenerated," "life" is appealed to in order to exit this time of decay and decline.[17] In al-Bustani life, like language, grows and changes in time, and this historicism is to expand and generalize itself by expanding the means of gaining what al-Bustani calls "civilization." Such means include the printing press, the journal, the library, and the school, each of which is to educate the masses into an Enlightenment pedagogy of literacy. "There is no doubt that journals are one of the greatest means for civilizing the masses [li tamaddun al-jumhur] and for increasing the number of readers, if they are used correctly."[18] But the installation of reading as a practice violently reorganizes an understanding of language in Arabic. It subordinates and retains an older, Arabic-Islamic, juridical-logocentric one, and it does so in relation to a new series of divisions, and in a context of Ottoman juridical reform and the expansion of capital, and their devastating effects in the present: the civil war of 1860. *Khutba fi adab al-'arab* and the broadsheets titled *Nafir Suriyya* (Beirut, 1860–61) work to reorganize the relation of language to such violence. If what is at stake in al-Bustani is the installation of a new understanding of reading and language, his text imparts an anthropocentrism to install peace (as A. L. Tibawi also underlines, "Bustani was for law and order under the legitimate government").[19] This anthropocentrism requires that reading be made simple. It must not take time. Synonomy, al-Bustani writes, gesturing to "those protruding, dead words in the dictionaries of the Arabic language, which are of no use to the Arabs other than their weighing down on the Arab mind [al-dhihn al-'arabi] and the Eastern pen," makes language poorer.[20] What he calls for is not an abandonment of language but its "reform [islah]" (109), and this "reform" is to entail language's reorganization according to a privileging of use. Language is a means, and it is to be subordinated to the figure now said to use it, "man." "Does it suit the human being [al-insan], for whom language has become a means and a door to knowledge, to make it an end in itself, so that he spends his entire life standing before that door, peering at its inscriptions and external ornament, knowing that behind it there are old and new rarities, which steal his heart, and claw at his chest?" (110).

In what al-Bustani calls "reform," *nahu* (grammar), like language, is to be made communicable. The "method of the ancients in setting down the rules of this language and its order [minhaj al-aqdamiyyin fi wad' qawa'id hadhihi al-lugha wa nizamiha]" and "their long, drawn out explications" are no longer "to distract the people of our time from attending to real matters, and from attaining useful skills" (110). The privileging of use is pointed to in the book on *nahu* al-Bustani composed, *Kitab misbah al-talib fi bahth al-matalib: Mutawwalun fi al-sarf wa al-nahu wa 'ilm al-'arud wa al-qawafi* (Beirut, 1854), if also in those of Ahmad Faris al-Shidyaq, Nasif al-Yaziji (1800–1871) and Rifa' Rafi' al-Tahtawi (1801–73).[21] It is the distraction of language that has led to the decline of the present ("There is no doubt that this is among the causes for the loss of the sciences [or, knowledge] among the Arabs"), and to recuperate this loss, and to absorb the losses in time, new dictionaries are to be written.[22] "Among those things of which there is no doubt, is that one must compose a dictionary of the Arabic language, and the ways of knowing that are particular to it, in a form [qalib] that makes its acquisition within the period of one year easy for those who speak it, whose renown for learning foreign languages within that period of time means that they will not have to spend more than that in learning the fundaments of a language at which they have nursed" (110). In this new understanding of form, what has been given to appear as long, drawn out explication is reorganized into the simplicity of communicable writing. In this transformation, time is to move quickly. What al-Bustani calls the reform of the Arabic language is to contract time, so that the experience of time in the present overcomes the debilitated, stalled experience of time in the past. European knowledge is to be quickly acquirable. Through the Bulaq press, a state printing office founded in Egypt during the rule of the viceroy Mehmed 'Ali (1769–1849), al-Bustani writes, the former "adorned his Arabic language with all of the Arab and European arts and crafts, so that it will be impossible for his sons and grandsons to imitate him. So you see the European arts and sciences, which are built upon real foundations, coming to us from all directions. What took the Europeans many years, and extended periods of time, the Arabs will be able to acquire in a shorter period of time, with the greatest skill and mastery" (112).

The acquisition of knowledge, which al-Bustani describes in the pages I am reading here, is an event that is to complete history. It is to bring time full circle. "So knowledge, then, has completed its journey, with its arrival to the Arabs by way of Alexandria, Istanbul, India, and Beirut" (112). Here al-Bustani gestures to the reading of the present as a time of decline over against an earlier "golden age," and in relation to the "dark ages [al-ajyal al-muzlima]" of Europe. "While the sciences and culture were in danger of loss and destruction because of wars, conflicts, and civil strife in the Western world, they found a refuge for themselves in the schools of the Arabs, for the Arabs preserved the middle link of the chain of knowledge, which binds the ancient sciences to the modern ones. Were it not for this link, you would see a wide empty space between the ancient and modern knowledge, which there would be no way to fill" (107). The link said to have been provided by the "schools of the Arabs" repeats the one that is to have completed the circular journey al-Bustani's elaboration of language reform solicits. Yet the desire to be or have been this link, in the present or the past, is interrupted by the stalled time of al-Bustani's text. If this text promises a time of completion—when adulthood would fulfill childhood, death life, the present the past, and a new, "reformed" language an older one—this fulfillment, and the completion to which it points, is stalled without end. And if this completion calls for the figure of "man" as the ground of language, it keeps repeating that call and the promise of completion it implies, a completion also pointed to in the reading of the history of medicine al-Bustani offers, a field that, in al-Bustani's reading, remained "lacking [naqisan]" in Hippocrates and Galen until it was "completed" (106) by the philosopher Ibn Sina (980–1037). The telling of the story of decline in the present, in *Khutba fi adab al-'arab*, repeats the event it wishes only to have described. The text of Enlightenment encrypts a relation to a past it wishes to have left behind, stalling the telling of the story of the self it wishes to have carried out. If the writing of al-Bustani is to fulfill the life of al-Bustani the writer, it may hardly be said to have done so, because it gives place to a scene of reading, which instead of confirming the subject as an autonomous being, marks its subjection in relation to language.

All missionaries in all parts of the world complain about the difficulty of communicating Christian concepts to savages in their own languages.

JOHANN GOTTFRIED HERDER, *Abhandlung über den Ursprung der Sprache*

Of course, we must avoid explaining everything by coercion.

ACHILLE MBEMBE, *On the Postcolony*

Perhaps the most influential reading of al-Bustani is offered in Albert Hourani's *Arabic Thought in the Liberal Age* (1962). Hourani writes that the work he considers gave way to "questions about how men and women identified themselves and what they could believe about human life," yet in the texts he reads "human life" comes to appear newly as an effect of the discourse on it and the juridical practice in discussion of it.[23] Hourani privileges al-Bustani's relation to language, to read his writing as a work of "modernization." "To revive the knowledge and love of the Arabic language was indeed half his life's work: his Arabic dictionary, *al-Muhit*, his Arabic encyclopaedia, *Da'irat al-ma'arif*, the periodicals which he edited, all contributed to the creation of modern Arabic expository prose, a language true to its past in grammar and idiom, but made capable of expressing simply, precisely, and directly the concepts of modern thought. From the circle which gathered around him—his sons and relations, his friends and pupils—there came the modern novel and drama in Arabic as well as modern Arabic journalism" (99–100). But if "al-Bustani laid the true foundations for the modern Arabic language," this is so only insofar as his text occasions a destruction and reorganization of the terms for the giving of sense.[24] This event is discussed in relation to the conditions of knowledge, and in foundational terms, in the work of Stephen Sheehi. "Throughout his life," Sheehi writes, "al-Bustani systematically laid down the fundamental tropes and equations that are found in virtually all Arab reform discourses in later decades and, therefore, demarcated the epistemological boundaries of subsequent debates and theories."[25] In al-Bustani, in Sheehi's reading, knowledge is related to the ability of a subject ("the ability of the subject to possess and command knowledge," "a willing subject actively pursuing knowledge" [30]), and this subject, and the way it knows things, is modern (73). Sheehi points to the ways in which the "tropes and equations" he describes became "inscribed in the Arabic language itself" (42), to underline that al-Bustani iterates "a Hegelian concept of universal history" (31) and a "dialectic of recognition" (68), yet the "indeterminacy" (50) of language Sheehi importantly teaches us to read is recuperated, in the reading he offers, in the activity of an autonomous "subject."[26] If in the Arabic, Ottoman nineteenth century, "intellectuals were re-creating new historical narratives based on new regimes of knowledge rather than passively inheriting historical facts, traditions, or paradigms," I remain with the stalled, iterative dimensions of language, which give language to exceed both itself and its time, in the reading I offer here.[27]

Al-Bustani's text remarks a relation to a European, if also Hegelian, inheritance, and I trace this relation through al-Bustani's rendering of the relation between poetry and philosophy. "The Arabs before the appearance of Islam, that is to say, during the days of jahiliyya, were an illiterate people, only a small number of whom knew how to read or write. The way of knowing of which they would boast was therefore that of their language, and their knowledge of it, and the composition of poetry and speeches."[28] Yet "although God did not grant them any knowledge of philosophy, and did not dispose their nature toward an interest in it, the attentiveness of their thought, clarity of their speech, and speed of their minds were at the highest level, to the extent that they came spontaneously to what others were unable to do after reflection and preparation" (102). In the beginning, "before the appearance of Islam," the "Arabs" are on the side of spoken language and poetry. But al-Bustani immediately underlines that they did not know philosophy: "God did not grant them any knowledge of philosophy." Prior to and outside of philosophy, the "Arabs" are on the side of poetry and language—not philosophy—and this understanding is elaborated in al-Bustani's text as its explication of itself and its relation to time.[29] In chapter 1 I considered the relation between philosophical speculation and poetry in Hegel—Hegel had to subordinate poetry to philosophy *and* close his text by citing a poem—and in al-Bustani the reflection on time is given through this division. It is not only that the reflection on time in *Khutba fi adab al-'arab* is historical, and historicist, but that this text recognizes itself, through its reading of the past as belonging to another time, and through its staging of its relation to Europe, in particular kinds of ways. The past, then, has passed—both an older and other time and a more recent time of decline and loss—and historical reflection is installed through this and other divisions: the past from the present, philosophy from poetry, language from time. And this text performs this new recognition of itself as it understands and identifies itself as at once historical *and* philosophical. To recognize "the Arabs before the appearance of Islam" as nonphilosophical, to recognize them as not recognizing philosophy, al-Bustani places himself on the side of philosophy. He has to speak philosophically in order to recognize his past as not belonging to philosophy, even as this past must already be philosophical: the "Arabs" came to philosophy "spontaneously." "The Arabs before the appearance of Islam" must already have a relation to philosophy, they must be recognizable in philosophical terms, even as these terms render their exclusion and subordinated inclusion: they are included, as a margin, to be themselves.

The time of this margin is elaborated through al-Bustani's reading of Europe's "dark ages." "The Arabs at the origin of Islam did not devote themselves to any knowledge other than that of language and the law, except for medicine." "But their distaste for scientific matters gradually decreased with the expansion of their religion and power" (103). Al-Bustani's narration of this expansion compels him to gesture to Europe and deposit the birth of a spirit of civility and civilization. "Their advancement in this matter was fast and surprising, as it had been in the fields of war. Just as ignorance and barbarism were quickly overwhelming each part of the European countries, and that, because of the raging wars and deep-seated conflicts among its kings and their subjects, so that there was left neither a market nor an advocate for culture and knowledge, they found a refuge to seek protection, frightened from the treachery of those days, and the stupidity [ghabawat] of those dark ages" (103). War, in al-Bustani, is opposed to culture, knowledge, and civilization (he wrote earlier, "It is clear that the preoccupation of the Arabs, in those days, with wars and with conquering countries and regions, and the strength of their inclination toward raiding and attacking, and the excess of their intention to expand the area of their rule, distracted them from paying attention to the matter of culture and knowledge" [103]), an opposition that led him to oppose the 'Urabi revolt in Egypt, in 1881, and which gave place to the broadsheets he wrote following the 1860 civil war in Lebanon.[30] The repeated gestures to unity in these texts point to the circular, figural reading I have been considering in *Khutba fi adab al-'arab*. If this text is to become itself by becoming historical—it relates the philosophical recognition of "the Arabs" as philosophical in historical terms, it becomes itself by becoming itself historically—it closes the history it opens by fulfilling the history of "the Arabs before the appearance of Islam." "History," al-Bustani writes, "does not help us very much to examine the reality of their situation, because of the time that has passed, and because of the lack of interest in this refined art."[31] And this fulfillment keeps repeating. It is a fulfillment that can never close, finally, once and for all. The place of this impossibility is the place of language, and of the colonization of language, which I study in this book. It is rearticulated in terms of the relation of language—*al-lugha*—to world—*al-'alam*—as follows:

> There is no way to doubt that the Arabic language is among the oldest, most complete, and most noble languages in the world, and were it not for the fear that you would demand of me a proof, I would have claimed that it was the language that descended upon the heart of our father Adam on the heavenly earth. What I do wish to claim, at the least, is that it, along with its two sisters, the Syriac and Hebrew languages, are the dividing-out branches or leftover remains of that divine Adamic language [al-lugha al-Adamiyya al-munzala]. (108)

§

If *Khutba fi adab al-'arab* privileges an understanding of the origin of language in relation to an originary, divine language, a language that is a ground, *asl*, and of which the Arabic, Syriac, and Hebrew languages are the temporal remnants, *Nafir Suriyya* privileges the body as a figure of unity in the interest of settling the past into the past. Each promises the figure of the family, *al-'a'ila*, as does *Khitab fi al-hay'a al-ijtima'iyya* (Beirut, 1869), as a political-theological figure for the grounding of language through a violent relocation of the word *adab* and the legacies to which it points.[32] If *Nafir Suriyya* shares in a "secular renewal," this is so because it translates a European, philological idiom in relation to the material event of language in Arabic.[33] It is not that this event comes later to language but that it is a condition for it, as language is reorganized in relation to an obscure future. "The future is, until now, obscure. Yes, dark and obscure for us," al-Bustani writes.[34] If *Nafir Suriyya* gives place to itself in relation to these terms, it stages itself as an experience of writing in relation to loss. "The losses and damage that overtook the homeland this year, because of the recent movement, are overbearing, oppressive, making it difficult for an acute intellect to imagine them [tasawwuraha; also, "to represent them"]. To grasp them requires an intelligent, skilled pen, so that they may be accounted for and apprehended" (29). With the loss of representation, language becomes writing. It privileges the grasping or thinking, *idrak*, of the damage and the losses, *al-khasa'ir wa al-adrar*, in the labor of the pen. If this text dislodges an order of comprehension, it does so to reorganize that order into more than one figure of unity, in relation to the body, the family, and the world. This text remarks its relation to loss—it repeats the losses, by telling us that it has lost the capacity to represent them—and it recalls its readers to the iterative dimension of the unity it expounds. The unity it privileges and desires also repeats, in relation to language and loss, proliferating and dividing to be itself. Let us now read this division.

The Imperial Firman of July 8, 1860, had charged the Ottoman diplomat Fu'ad Pasha "to put an immediate stop to all discord between Maronites and Druzes, and bring back rest and tranquility to the populations," and upon the departure for Beirut of French troops under the command of General Charles de Beaufort d'Hautpoul on August 7, Napolean III figured the intervention in historical, Orientalist, humanist terms:[35] "Soldiers, you are departing for Syria, and France happily salutes an expedition which has one purpose only, that of making the rights of justice and humanity triumph. For you are not going to wage war against any nation but to help the Sultan bring back to obedience subjects blinded by a fanaticism from another century" (115). *Nafir Suriyya* desires—if differently, and if still in relation to the legacies pointed to in these documents and the juridical, colonial violence they impart—to install order and unity through a generalization and reorganization of terms. A complicity in language and in relation to form and an understanding of time is remarked. Yet it is not that this complicity stalls this writing—it already stalls and interrupts itself—but that attention to it allows one to read the anthropocentrism and historicism generalized in colonialism, each of which al-Bustani privileges. I will return to this privilege in *Khutba fi adab al-'arab* below but wish to underline here that *Nafir Suriyya* installs unity and love by dividing—religion from politics, the human from the animal, civilization from barbarism, and Europe from Africa.[36]

> It is clear that the human being, in this world [fi hadha al-'alam], is in one of two states: a state of crude roughness or barbarism, and a state of civilization or grace. The state of crude roughness is the natural state into which the human being is born, and which, were he to remain in it, there would not be a great difference between him and incoherent animals [al-hayawanat al-'ajam], and the damage he would impart to the world would be greater than that imparted by them. As for the state of civilization, it is that condition which happens to the human being following his refinement in being and morals, which he acquires slowly, by means of imitation, diligence, and

> effort, until he arrives at its highest levels. Those below it, who are by nature different from it, or are not prepared to receive it, are incapable of doing so. To attribute the quality of being a civilized human being to a rough, coarse one is like attributing knowledge to the ignorant, humanity to an animal [hayawan], light to darkness, or sight to the blind. It is like attributing to the demons of the farthest reaches of Africa, who eat each other, the qualities of the great and noble men of Paris and England. Or it is like attributing to the Arabs of the desert the qualities of the inhabitants of Beirut for example.[37]

To install world in relation to the distinctions remarked here is to do so as an event in simplicity ("My hope is that you consider what I said in this publication and the one that preceded it, in a spirit of love, sincerity, and simplicity" [15]), and in relation to a body politic. This body is to be formed in relation to religion. "Living, wakeful religions [adyan] reflect and teach their children to look upon those who are different from them in relation to religious belonging [madhhab], with neither disdain nor scorn," al-Bustani writes, "but with care and love, like the members of a single family, the father of which is the homeland, its mother the earth, its single creator, God, and all of its members of a single substance [min tin wahid]" (37–38). Children are to be raised and grow to maturity in the family, and "religious intention" is on the side of war. "The worst of what is found beneath the dome of the heavens is war, and the worst, the most ugly, and the most disgraceful are civil wars, which take place between the inhabitants of a single country, and which result, for the most part, from insignificant causes, and for the sake of religious intentions" (25). To do away with war one must separate religion from politics, one must "place a barrier between religion, or, spiritual authority [al-ri'asa ayy al-sulta al-ruhiyya] and politics [al-siyasa], or, civil authority [al-sulta al-madaniyya].[38] That is because the former is linked, in relation to the self and nature, to interior, permanent matters, which do not change with time or condition, as opposed to the latter, which is linked to external matters, which are not permanent, and are able to change or be reformed according to time, place, and condition."[39] To manage the losses is to divide, the interior from the exterior, what is permanent from what is temporal, so that "din" may be reconfigured through a separation of "religion" from "politics," a reading that enacts and obscures the linguistic, epistemic violence I study in this book. This reconfiguration gives place to a politics of *Bildung* in the colonies—to which I shall turn below in greater detail in reading al-Shidyaq and Husayn—to install a politics of the sovereign body, the members of which, al-Bustani writes, are to be "of a single substance."

Al-Bustani underlines that the losses of 1860 were without precedent. The radical break this date points to solicits a futural closure. "Our hope is that this time affairs will not be resolved through the judgment, 'what has passed has passed,' as happened in the past," but that with the arrival of Fu'ad Pasha, "the remedies will be stronger and more effective, and the final seal better and more firm" (37). "Man," a figure of autonomous action, is to effect this seal. "For as long as the Arabs are content with imitation and blind transmission, without tiring themselves with examination and scrutiny, there is no hope for their progress in the sciences and arts."[40] Yet this figure, "Man as a secular subject of knowledge, a producer of history, and a creator of culture," is installed in language through a complex event of translation.[41] It is solicited as the ground of language only to be, and if immediately, interrupted. Neither an acceptance nor a rejection of the European idiom I have underlined, what takes place in al-Bustani is a complex event of language, one that privileges the figure of "man" through a specific colonial, aesthetic, and political figuration. The differential institution of "man"—through the distinction between the human and the animal, civilization and barbarism, Europe and Africa, and the present and the past—is to be grounded in God. "God alone is the father of the orphan, a ruler for the widow, an aid for the weak, a support for the distressed. He, alone, is able to soothe the grief of the hearts of the miserable and console them, to comfort their broken hearts and put a balsam on their incurable wounds."[42] Yet the privileging of this ground is stalled in the finite event language is. The reading I offer of al-Bustani, and, differently, of al-Shidyaq and Husayn, does not privilege Europe or its languages over against Arabic but recalls only that the material event of language, which *Khutba fi adab al-'arab* and *Nafir Suriyya* are, compels attention to the ways in which the reading of the word *adab* in Arabic had to articulate itself, if it did so, through the former.

§

In al-Bustani the reflection on *adab* occurs as a stutter. It halts as soon as it starts, recalling the vocative that precedes its opening sentence: *ayyuha sada*, gentleman! *Khutba fi adab al-'arab* addresses itself to men, and this text's masculinist dimension mirrors the temporal and other divisions it installs and interrupts.[43] If the vocative partakes in a relation to an older, Arabic-Islamic understanding and practice of *adab*, to speak, al-Bustani repeats that understanding as he inscribes it in relation to a new set of terms and a new understanding of life and death. Al-Bustani may only be said to have been *mu'addab*—a word that includes within it the word *adab*, and which may be rendered as "mannered" and "eloquent"—insofar as he repeats this new setting of terms, and its burial of the past, as he performs it. Al-Bustani's text offers itself as a translation machine, where the form of language is to yield its communicability in the time of life. If *Khutba fi adab al-'arab* functions as a program statement that informs the three dimensions of al-Bustani's work—the dictionary, the encyclopedia, and translation—the interruptive quality of his text stalls the form it wishes to have generalized. The necessity of external means or tools, "tools without which the senses may not arrive to what is demanded," interrupts the "reform" of language al-Bustani desires to explicate and the communicability he wishes to secure.[44] His address interrupts itself in advance, and the subject of which he desires to speak and about which he wishes to have issued a communication—*adab*—remains incommunicable. The incommunicability of *adab* mirrors its loss: it repeats the divided paradigm of decline in relation to a pervasive juridical violence. Al-Bustani's address is not able to present itself, nor may it be represented by the pen of the scholar—neither that of the Orientalist nor "the Eastern pen" al-Bustani holds in his hand and which bears a weight he desires to have left behind—as it repeats and confounds the historical divisions he deposited at the opening of his *Khutba fi adab al-'arab*.[45]

FALLING INTO PIECES

So this created being must love some person, some thing, or some meaning.

AHMAD FARIS AL-SHIDYAQ, *al-Saq 'ala al-saq*

If al-Bustani offers a reflection on the origin of language in terms of a relation between fallen, earthly languages and a single, divine one, in the lexicographical writings of Ahmad Faris al-Shidyaq this origin is thought in relation to sound. And if in al-Bustani language is compelled to appear through a privileging of totality in relation to form and the body, in *al-Saq 'ala al-saq fi ma huwwa al-Fariyaq, aw ayam wa shuhur wa a'wam fi 'ajam al-'Arab wa al-a'jam* (Paris, 1855), language falls into pieces. It already points to more than one other in order to be itself, and the story language tells, in al-Shidyaq, is, then, a love story. "If the ancients have worked on this noble language, I've loved it passionately. I've fallen madly in love with it, and have become its slave. I've lit my candles for it and stayed up all night [sahirtu al-layali] reflecting on it, searching for what is hidden and concealed in it" (*SL*, 111), al-Shidyaq writes in *Sirr al-layali fi al-qalb wa al-ibdali* (Istanbul, 1867).[46] This passage opens with a division. It compares by dividing: the ancients, who worked on language, from "I," who have loved it, and stayed up all night with it. Insomnia points to a relation to exhaustion that is also a form of temporal discombobulation, and this discombobulation is reiterated and remarked in the excessive dimensions of his love for language. "I've fallen madly in love with it, and become its slave." The excess of this second sentence points back to the first, asking us to read it again. If al-Shidyaq's relation to language gestures to an excess—he has become its slave—this excess points to the division that the first sentence I am reading underlines, and that it underlines to give place to "I": "If the ancients have worked on this noble language, I've loved it passionately." In this passage "I" is perhaps nothing more or less than this division, the division of the past, the time of the ancients, from the present, a time that takes place as an experience of love. If this passage solicits a figure—"I"—this figure is already given in relation to time. The privileging of "man" as a figure of sovereignty and autonomy in language is promised and interrupted. And language in al-Shidyaq—and *al-Saq 'ala al-saq*—takes place as an event that both calls for and stalls the totalizing form of the literary work.

Yet the sentence I am reading—one that begins with a division and then remarks and repeats that division by pointing to an excess—also repeats, by homonymy, the title of the text of which it is a part, and it does so as it describes and points to al-Shidyaq's insomnia. We shall see that in this text al-Shidyaq links meaning, *ma'na*, to sound, and thereby links lexicography to time. But if sound is what gives place to the meaning of words, then one must attend to sound in the reading of al-Shidyaq's text, a text that is both about and of language. When al-Shidyaq says "I stayed up all night" he says "sahirtu al-layali," a passage that repeats ("sirr al-layali") and rhymes ("al-qalb wa al-ibdali") with the title of the book I am reading here, *Sirr al-layali fi al-qalb wa al-ibdali*. The figure of the reader solicited in these passages may not be separated from the reflection on language they offer. The triangulation of words one may underline here—"sahirtu" (I remained awake), "sirr" (secret), and "qalb" (the inversion of letters in a word, but also the heart, and the site of thought and philosophical reflection in Arabic philosophy)—compels sustained attention. If "I" am a being who divides myself from a past, and if this division gives place to a historical, temporal understanding of language, this understanding passes through, and is given place to through, my insomnia. This understanding of language is, then, an open secret, not something hidden, but something in which one is schooled through an experience of time. And this experience is located in the heart, *al-qalb*, a site both of love—which al-Shidyaq explicitly links to language—and of intellection, of the labor of thought. The reflection on and practice of language, then, is subordinated to the being who offers that reflection, "man," which al-Shidyaq calls a "created being" ("So this created being [hadha al-makhluq al-adamiyy] must love some person, some thing, or some meaning" [*FS*, 371]). Language comes to appear newly as if it were the effect of "man" and its historical experience, just as "man" appears as that being who is to offer a historical reflection on language. Language, finally, is understood as if it were an instrument through which intention in the giving of sense is implied. And the reader—a figure that al-Shidyaq underlines at several points in *al-Saq 'ala al-saq*—is privileged as a figure for the historical comprehension of language in time.

"It is no exaggeration to say that we are indebted to him [Ahmad Faris al-Shidyaq] in most of what is living and new in our language and literature in the nineteenth century," Fawwaz Traboulsi and 'Aziz al-'Azmeh have written, and the relation of al-Shidyaq to the reflection on him in Arabic letters points to, and repeats, an indebtedness in language, which the text on language we are reading here, *Sirr al-layali*, performs.[47] *Sirr al-layali*—like *al-Saq 'ala al-saq*—will never simply have been new. Each will have compelled attention to the iterative density of language, to the dimensions of indebtedness language gives, and in which one is schooled in al-Shidyaq. If scholarship on al-Shidyaq has underlined, in different ways, an understanding of al-Shidyaq and his text as pointing to a change in an order of language and an understanding of world—Nadia al-Baghdadi has written, in relation to al-Shidyaq, of a transformation "from a theocentric to an anthropocentric understanding" of language and time—this change is already interrupted in al-Shidyaq's text.[48] *Al-Saq 'ala al-saq* is said to have "a unity of its own," but this unity is promised and confounded in what Mohammed Bakir Alwan has called al-Shidyaq's "uncontrollable tongue."[49] This uncontrollability and its relation to language (and one may hear in Alwan's reading a reference to the word *lisan*, "language" and "tongue," and to the Arabic lexicographical tradition) suggest a reading of *al-Saq ʿala al-saq* as a poetic text ("it throbs with the poetry of life" [187]), as an event of language that falls into pieces.[50] This falling into pieces—into parts that point to no whole, and which both solicit and confound the form of the body al-Bustani wished to install—is dramatized in the second of the scenes of dream interpretation in *al-Saq ʿala al-saq*, to which I turn below. And it teaches us how to read this text, even as the reflection on language in al-Shidyaq divides as it tells us that it is modern: *they* worked on language, *I* love it. To read *al-Saq ʿala al-saq* is to read this division. It is to read the compulsive and insomniac relation to time to which language, in al-Shidyaq, points.

§

Al-Shidyaq left Mount Lebanon on December 15, 1826, "without bidding his family, or friends, farewell," and following the imprisonment of his brother, Asʿad al-Shidyaq, by the Maronite patriarch.[51] Asʿad had been the first Maronite convert to Protestant Christianity, and Faris's abrupt departure in 1826 mirrors the death and loss of his brother, and the cut he wishes to install between himself and the Maronite teachers with whom he studied the Arabic language, on the one hand, and the tradition of Arabic lexicography, on the other. And it is this relation to death and loss that compels al-Shidyaq to read (one among other commands he received from his brother, Asʿad), and to remain with the divided materiality of words, *alfaz*. Al-Shidyaq describes his intention in *Sirr al-layali* as "to arrive at the knowledge of the secrets of its [language's] statements or utterances one word at a time [lafzatan lafzatan]" (*SL*, 113). The content of this knowledge involves a reorganization in the way in which meaning is identified in lexicography. Rather than locate meaning in what has already been given in written language, one ought to derive meaning based upon similarities in word sound. One may therefore replace letters in a word with similar and yet distinct ones, or invert the order of letters in a word, *al-qalb wa al-ibdal*, to account for word meaning. Al-Shidyaq explains of the tradition he wishes to contest, "You see them say, for example: to sell something means to sell it, which is to say, to acquire it [baʿa al-shay' ya'ti bi maʿna baʿahu, wa bi ma'na ishtarahu]" (114). But, he continues, to comprehend language through synonymy is not to understand the reason that gives place to the meaning of words. "They didn't clarify for us the reason for this, nor the ground [asl] of the meaning of buying or its aim. And without knowing the reason or becoming aware of the purpose, one will not have the pleasure of knowing that a single word can give place to two opposed meanings and two different intentions" (114). It is not that synonyms don't help to explain meaning but that to derive meaning based upon synonymy is to offer a derivation without reason. It is to understand language without understanding it, in relation to a derivation without ground.

Al-Saq 'ala al-saq, to which I turn in detail below, is at once a book of and about language. In it al-Shidyaq writes of language in terms of synonymy, and he does so to redesignate an understanding of what synonymy is. The discussion of the meaning of words, and of the way in which one may explain word meanings, becomes, he writes, a condition of reading, and I wish here to relate lexicography and reading to time. "Then my condition for the reader is that a compilation of synonymous words be drawn up in this book of mine, despite their great number. He might agree to pass by, on a single road, a herd of fifty words of a single meaning, or of meanings that are near to each other. If he doesn't, I won't allow him to read it or benefit from it. This, despite that I don't think that synonymous words [al-alfaz al-mutaradifa] have a single meaning [ma'na], or they would have called them equivalent, whereas they are synonymous, in the sense that some of them might take the place of others" (*FS*, 10).[52] Al-Shidyaq wishes to reorganize synonymy as substitution rather than equivalence, to explicate a project for the grounding of meaning. To run up against this understanding of language, and to be overwhelmed by it, is what it means, in al-Shidyaq, to read. On the one hand, to read in al-Shidyaq is to encounter a relation to the time of language and its origin. It is to read the origin of language in historical terms, and it is to do so through a privileging of a single figure: the reader. But if *al-Saq 'ala al-saq* solicits the figure of the reader, and if it does so by relating reading as a practice to an understanding of the time of language, it equally refuses to allow language to draw away. Language, in al-Shidyaq, is pleonastic. A single word is already "a herd of fifty words of a single meaning, or of meanings that are near to each other [sirb khamsin lafza bi ma'na wahid aw bi ma'anin mutaqariba]"). Language remains an unsettled temporal event. The stake of reading this temporality is particularly acute because it turns on the reading of "man," the figure solicited in the title of al-Shidyaq's text ("One Leg over Another"). Yet in al-Shidyaq the body of "man" is already confounded, his skin, in a passage I turn to read later in this chapter, "torn to shreads" (358). The privileging of *Bildung* in the colonies, where "man" is to become conscious of himself as a living being through the experience of his gaining literacy (as in al-Bustani and, differently, Husayn), is promised and stalled. This aporia is staged in *al-Saq 'ala al-saq*, where language is read as historical even as it interrupts reading as a practice for the giving of temporal sense.

In al-Shidyaq synonymy is to be understood as substitution rather than equivalence, and to articulate this understanding of language al-Shidyaq must substitute himself for others. He must take the place of the lexicographers he deposited at the opening of *Sirr al-layali* and the teachers of language of whom he speaks in *al-Saq 'ala al-saq*. He explains in the latter text that "their interest was to teach some of the rules of grammar [qawa'id nahu] of the Arabic and Syriac languages, only in order to recognize them, and to no benefit" (*FS*, 15). Recognition without benefit is also how he describes what he calls the shortcoming, *khalal*, of the Arabic lexicographers, and most prominently among them al-Fayruzabadi. He writes in *Sirr al-layali* that in the former's *al-Qamus al-muhit*, "If you want to search for a word, for example, 'to be averse to something' [a'rad 'an al-shay'], you have to read everything given under the heading 'to show or demonstrate' ['arada], from beginning to end. You'll pass by 'to oppose,' 'to show,' and 'to object,' and then the names of writers and scholars and jurists and poets and animals and countries, and then all of the words derived from each, before you arrive at 'to be averse to something'" (*SL*, 172). In place of a reflection on the reason for the meaning of words based upon a notion of derivation through an understanding of the transformation of meaning with the addition of letters to root words, he offers a theory of imitation that is also a theory of institution. "The one who instituted language [al-wadi'], when he instituted *qad* and *daq* and *daf*, did not intend with them, in the first instance, that they be a verb or a noun but only the imitation of a sound that he imagined without regard to anything else" (177). If the linking of the origin of word meanings to the imitation of sound is not new in the Arabic language, what is new, even as it appeals to something very old, is that this rendering of the origin of language translates. It reorganizes a conception of language that repeats and displaces an older practice and series of categories (the oppositions of *lafz* [utterance] and *ma'na* [meaning] and *asl* [ground] and *far'* [derivative or branch], which I considered in chapter 1), to give place to a new understanding of time. The time of language is to be historical, the time of life ("al-Shidyaq realized that language was the child of life, for life was what brought language into being, and what nourishes it allows it to grow"), and this rendering is offered to leave the present, a time said to be decadent and in decline, behind.[53]

Al-Shidyaq emphasizes the word *meaning* (ma'na) in several places, some of which I have underlined in the passages I have cited here. And meaning, al-Shidyaq recalls, divides. "A single word," he writes in a passage in *Sirr al-layali* I cited above, "can give place to two opposed meanings and two different intentions" (*SL*, 114). If al-Shidyaq underlines that a single word may give place to two—two meanings, two intentions—this implies a reading of language in relation to doubling and multiplication. Language doubles and multiplies without end, to become an event of writing that is a compulsive practice of pleonastic iteration.[54] As I discussed in the introduction to this book the name "al-Fariyaq" points to the division and fusing together, *naht*, of the names Faris and al-Shidyaq. Here, *naht* appears as a form of addition where one plus one does not equal two but two squared. Al-Fariyaq splits into the narrator of *al-Saq 'ala al-saq* and al-Fariyaqiyya, al-Fariyaq's wife. Four (two squared) mirrors the number of books in *al-Saq 'ala al-saq* to yield sixteen (four squared), an event of mathematical expansion that does not lead back to "one" but that, in al-Shidyaq's words, "surprises." "To speak of two surprises more so than does speaking of one" (FS, 401). In al-Shidyaq "one" already splits, placing in question more than one inheritance, where a single being said to belong to time and the immanence of its relation to itself, "man," would occasion a grounding of being in history. In *al-Saq 'ala al-saq* one is already a "created being," and such a being must love. This imperative and its anteriority point to the understanding of language in al-Shidyaq, to give the thought that reading must remain with language and the interruptive understanding of time it gestures. Language refuses to withdraw, *lafz* (linguistic utterance), refuses to subordinate itself to *ma'na* (meaning) but pluralizes it. In *al-Saq 'ala al-saq* difference already divides to be more and less than itself. The stakes of this division, and its relation to the political order, were, al-Shidyaq knew, high. "For a single word from a single mouth may lead to either life or death" (434).

Al-Shidyaq explains in *al-Saq ʿala al-saq* that al-Fariyaq, whose story its narrator tells, was a good reader as a child. "Al-Fariyaq took an innate pleasure, from the time he was a child, in reading eloquent words, examining them closely, and picking out the strange expressions he found in books" (*FS*, 22). Reading and picking out strange expressions, *al-alfaz al-ghariba*, in relation to clear speech, *al-kalam al-fasih*, gives place to an understanding of language and its sound based upon which al-Shidyaq comes to understand language differently. "I've learned from experience that these rhetorical figures and flourishes, with which so many authors are so careless, preoccupy the reader with what is apparent, with the linguistic utterance [lafz] at the expense of reflection on what is most intrinsic: meaning [maʿna]" (12–13). Al-Shidyaq writes of his learning about language in relation to his experience as a reader ("I've learned from experience," he writes), but to write of himself as a learner, and to write of language in relation to sound, he must borrow old words. Already, the newness he solicits is confounded through the articulation of what the new takes itself to be leaving behind. The words *lafz* and *maʿna* are repeated, as an older inheritance is reorganized and domesticated, and as al-Shidyaq argues that the origin of language is derived from the imitation of word sounds. "Even someone who knows nothing about the Arabic language, if he were to hear, for example, the words *tantana*, *dandana*, *jaljala* or *rannama* [to ring, hum, rattle, sing], and if he had sound judgment, it would have to occur to him that what is involved is the imitation of sounds" (*SL*, 184). What takes place with language is, then, al-Shidyaq argues, a human event, and such an event is "gradual." "Nothing comes from language, or from other human arts and objects, complete and whole from the first moment but gradually ['ala al-tadrij]" (184). This gradualness articulates, in this passage, a belonging of language in time, in relation to an understanding of time as a temporal progression, and in particular, historicist terms.[55] But if al-Shidyaq solicits a historicist—and historical—and, in a certain sense, philological understanding of time and language, it is overwhelmed by his text. If in al-Shidyaq time is a form of belonging, it is one that takes place in relation to the imperative to love, *la budda*, which *Sirr al-layali* repeats, confounding the temporally coherent figure of the reader ("I've learned from experience"), in relation to language and time. And if al-Shidyaq is to be read, this reading must, then, yield to the interruptive dimensions of language his text compels us to consider, and which al-Shidyaq imposes as a condition for the reading of *al-Saq 'ala al-saq*.

Al-Shidyaq's text is new. But his work on language is all about substitution, and one doesn't substitute one for the other simply. If al-Shidyaq works to displace an older understanding of language—"he broke our chains and liberated our minds from the veneration of the ancient and eternal," Marun 'Abbud wrote—this is because his writing preserves and transforms an older set of oppositions.[56] On the one hand, it articulates a new series of divisions as it translates itself into a European, philological idiom. In *Sirr al-layali*, and through his writing on the time of language as historical, he privileges an understanding of the present as in decline, on the side of rhetoric, emptiness, and ugliness ("I found that it [the Arabic language] had been praised with rhetorical flourish, and adorned with superficial beauty, which caused it to appear ugly, solely for empty show" [*SL*, 112]). But al-Shidyaq is unable to replace what he tells us he must replace: an older, Arabic understanding and practice of language, which he repeats to produce a historical ground for the explication of the meaning of words, and which he repeats by articulating that ground through an understanding of *lafz* and *ma'na*. Al-Shidyaq does so, he demonstrates the impossibility of substitution—himself for others—as he produces a theory of language as a theory of substitution. Al-Shidyaq describes in the understanding of language he wishes to articulate what he is unable and still desires to do with that explication. And he does so even as he substitutes, one word for another, one word at a time, and he does not and cannot stop. Al-Shidyaq's text—in *al-Saq 'ala al-saq* and *Sirr al-layali*—exceeds the giving of grounds it wishes to have secured as it performs, if repeatedly and without end, a temporal excess. It performs and stalls the love it tells us is what the created being must do: to love a person, thing, or—and as al-Shidyaq closes this decisive sentence—a meaning, *ma'na min al-ma'ani*. This imperative may not be said to belong to its time, and it is not classifiable: neither secular nor religious, modern nor classical, colonial nor precolonial. It—and the text to which it gives place—confounds the language one is compelled to use to speak of it, to teach us that to speak of al-Shidyaq is to have it out with this confounding. It is to decline to yield to the demand for translatability, to which one already responds, prior to any decision, anterior to any act or event of reading.

When they [the Orientalists] translate a book, they piece together whatever they have understood and shape into the form [qalib] of their language.

AHMAD FARIS AL-SHIDYAQ, *Kashf al-mukhabba 'an funun Urubba*

Remember that we can't share with Christ his greatness if we don't also share his pain. So be joyful and happy whenever you are tested, and don't be sad, because your faith is strong.

BUTRUS AL-BUSTANI, *Qissat As'ad al-Shidyaq*

In *al-Saq 'ala al-saq* al-Shidyaq put language to the test. It is not only that al-Shidyaq tells us that al-Fariyaq was tested ("I mentioned at the end of Book Two that God tested al-Fariyaq with many books and illnesses and then saved him from all of them" [*FS*, 365]), but that his being put to the test gives place to language. The place of this test is a place of love, and al-Shidyaq's love for a brother who had died, As'ad al-Shidyaq. American missionaries had arrived in Palestine in 1819, and As'ad al-Shidyaq became a teacher of the missionary Jonas King and, later, Isaac Bird. As'ad registers, for his brother, a relation to memory, death, and the future. "Even though my brother, God have mercy on him, has died, his memory will not" (138), he writes in *al-Saq 'ala al-saq*, mournfully inscribing the thought that death is related—as al-Shidyaq elsewhere writes in *al-Saq 'ala al-saq*—to surprise, love, numbers, multiplication, and the future, and to what already will have been more than one. I will turn below to elaborate the imperative of love in Ahmad Faris al-Shidyaq in relation to the figure of the body, which is articulated through the voice of al-Fariyaqiyya in the twelfth chapter of the fourth book of *al-Saq 'ala al-saq*. But this love ("Is it not a disgrace that the men of this land [England], the land of science, technology, culture, and civilization, only marry a woman if she has a dowry. And worse than that, that the influential men here do not marry out of love ['an hubb] but out of a desire to increase their wealth?" [601]) is already routed through a relation to death and reading. Reading occupies a privileged place in As'ad al-Shidyaq's writing, and in the framing of that writing in Butrus al-Bustani's *Qissat As'ad al-Shidyaq* (Beirut, 1860). Before reading the body in *al-Saq 'ala al-saq*, then, I turn to al-Bustani's text about the life and death of Ahmad Faris al-Shidyaq's brother.

Al-Bustani reports in *Qissat As'ad al-Shidyaq* that following the missionary Jonas King's departure from Lebanon, As'ad wrote a response to King's letter of departure. The letter turns on reading and its relation to the Maronite Church. "But when, in his response, he came to Jonas King's objection to the Catholic Church's prohibiting its children from reading the Bible, and when he considered the force of this objection, he came to be quite influenced by it, and he decided to throw off the yoke of his obedience to the Church. The veil which covered his sight was then lifted, and he began to feel the force of the other objections and the demonstrations and proofs [al-barahin wa al-adilla], which the Biblemen had presented to him to refute some of the opinions of the Church and its teachings."[57] "So," al-Bustani continues, "he [As'ad al-Shidyaq] started to argue with whoever would sit with him, affirming the Protestant religion and relying upon the citation from the prophet Isaiah about the necessity of reading the holy books, as becomes clear from the story he wrote about himself in his own words" (16). The word *reading* appears twice in these sentences in which al-Bustani renders—and translates—what he calls in the title of the text, "the story of As'ad al-Shidyaq." The question of reading is underlined by al-Bustani in relation to the institution of the Maronite Church and the reading practices of the American missionaries. In response to both of these, al-Bustani offers the form of the story, *qissa*, in order to frame As'ad al-Shidyaq's life. In *Qissat As'ad al-Shiduq*, life is framed in terms of its relation to a narrative—from birth to death—and in terms of the subject of such a narrative. "Life," in al-Bustani's reading of As'ad al-Shidyaq, comes to be reorganized in relation to the totalizing figure of the work as *qissa* and the being that subtends it: "man."

But As'ad al-Shidyaq reads compulsively. He can't stop. Al-Bustani explains, "During this time As'ad would fervently search the holy books, to the extent that he had no time for anything else, and to the extent that he found no pleasure in anything except in reading the Bible and striving to understand its meanings" (18). It is as if As'ad had fallen in love with the Bible, pointing to an experience or event of reading al-Bustani was at pains to manage, even as he couldn't help but report on it. Returning to live at the mission house on December 12, "resolved to bear all of the resistance and all of the losses to which he would be exposed because of his contravening the order of the Patriarch" (19), As'ad al-Shidyaq is described by al-Bustani in the following terms: "At that time As'ad would say about himself that he was restless and anxious, that he didn't know what to do and that he couldn't find a place to rest his two feet. He would say that he thought that the Maronite Church had many errors, and that the missionaries had some as well, and that he was surprised at the calmness that he would find in them" (19). Al-Bustani points again to As'ad al-Shidyaq's comportment in relation to the Maronite Church authorities ("He would also say that however true the things that people said about the intention of the missionaries in their coming to this country were, I think that their teachings are in accord with the truth. And so I am resolved to hold tightly to them" [19]), and he can't put an end to it: As'ad al-Shidyaq holds tight, repeating himself over and over again. For Butrus al-Bustani, al-Shidyaq must—like language—be settled down, and the staging of "the story of As'ad al-Shidyaq" points to a desire to do so. To get language under control, the time of life must appear as readable, it must take the form of a story of a life that ends in death, yielding a reassuring, if harsh, closure of time.

Al-Bustani's indirect citation of al-Shidyaq ("He would also say") absorbs al-Shidyaq's language into the whole he wishes *Qissat As'ad al-Shidyaq* to have been. But As'ad al-Shidyaq interrupts himself. He cuts himself off, abbreviating the story of his "own" life. After submitting, again, to the patriarch, on March 30, al-Shidyaq composed a text in response to a request of the missionary Isaac Bird. This text is included by al-Bustani in his account of the story of As'ad al-Shidyaq, doubling the citation of al-Shidyaq I have gestured to above. As'ad wrote his story, he writes, so that after reading it each person may decide on his own regarding his affair. "Many have received word that I've gone mad and others that I'm a heretic, and so I wanted to write down my story, in an abbreviated form, so that then anyone who has an intellect may decide whether I'm mad or am following in the footsteps of the Heretics or of true Orthodox belief" (22). To tell his story he must abbreviate: the story, *qissa*, of his life must be shorter than itself; it must stall and interrupt itself to be what it is, and this is its "truth," a word underlined by As'ad al-Shidyaq in his description of a debate he had with the Armenian archbishop Ya'qub and the Maronite patriarch, where As'ad refuses to subordinate "the truth that is clarified in the book of God [al-haq alladhi yattadih min kitab Allah]" (37) to the words of these leaders of the church.

If As'ad al-Shidyaq speaks of the truth, his text remains in compulsive iteration: he must keep reading. The whole al-Bustani desired to secure, and to which al-Shidyaq also points ("so I wanted to write down my story"), is stalled in the abbreviated event As'ad al-Shidyaq's life is. If, in al-Bustani's reading, al-Shidyaq's desire is formed into the decision of an autonomous subject—al-Bustani writes of As'ad that "he decided to throw off the yoke of his obedience to the Church"—this autonomy points to an iterated event of stuttering repetition. Makdisi has suggested that al-Bustani's reading of al-Shidyaq occasions a "literary revolution" that is also an event of "secularization" ("His call for Arab cultural 'awakening' generalized and secularized the deeply personal struggle with faith that awakened an evangelically minded person from so-called spiritual death and the challenge to prevailing orthodoxies that it entailed").[58] But this "secularization" installs and proliferates a new, colonial, philological understanding of language in relation to the time of life and death, and, as Makdisi has made clear, in relation to the social and political order. This understanding remarks, I wish to argue, a generalized reorganization of language to which the discipline and practice of Arabic literature studies belatedly bears witness. And this event, I also wish to argue, is carried out against the backdrop of a single, if divided figure—"man"—a figure that cannot stop falling into pieces, stalling, stammering, and repeating itself in *al-Saq ʿala al-saq*.

Faris appears twice in *Qissat Asʿad al-Shidyaq*, first on the occasion of his mother's visit to him while he was being held by the Maronite patriarch. He is described as a close listener ("Her youngest son, Faris, had come with Asʿad's mother, and he spoke, for a while, freely and easily, and listened closely to all the arguments Asʿad presented to substantiate his opinions and determination"), and after having listened he is called by his brother and commanded to read.[59] "After his mother left he called his brother Faris and said to him: I want you to understand that I love you. I have one thing to ask of you, and it is that you take the Gospel and read it closely. He immediately said, Give me one, and he did. And then he left. And it was clear that this conversation impacted Faris and soothed his heart" (43). The second appearance follows an altercation with his brother, Mansur, who had struck him with a rifle butt. Al-Bustani reports that Faris, speaking in the first person to the missionary Isaac Bird, said, "I remained sitting and didn't move, with the book in my hands, until someone came and took it from me. Then the brother who I mentioned took out his rifle and pretended to shoot at me and kill me—and my mother came between us and stopped him from doing it. When the news spread to the rest of my brothers one of them came and entered with a stick in his hand and hit me with it without stopping to ask why. As he was hitting me he screamed: Leave your heresy and go to church like everyone else! Then Mansur stood before my brother Asʿad's chest, which was beside me, and took out all the Hebrew, Arabic, Syriac, and Italian books that you'd given him, and burned them" (44). Having commanded Faris to read, As'ad instructs him not to mourn. "So be joyful and happy whenever you are tested, and don't be sad, because your faith is strong" (45). If reading is solicited to domesticate death in time, it already points to a mournful relation to another who has died. The appropriation of language in the formation of a subject through its recognition of itself as a literate being is interrupted, even as it is immediately solicited, to impart a legacy in language in relation to a privileging and stalling of a coherency of form.

> It is clear that the first person who wrote about lexicography was only interested in gathering words, despite that one of the requirements of any act of gathering together is order and organization, which is to say, putting each thing in its place.
>
> AHMAD FARIS AL-SHIDYAQ, *al-Jasus 'ala al-qamus*

If language, in *al-Saq 'ala al-saq*, is a pleonasm, this use of words does not point to a "meaning" that stands behind language but interrupts it. Pleonasm does not secure the being of an entity that would be called upon to read or write language but places that entity and its understanding of itself as a coherent temporal being in question. I underline this dimension of language because, read in relation to al-Bustani, and the understanding of the political body privileged in his text, and read in relation to the new, Ottoman political and juridical order, language, in *al-Saq 'ala al-saq*, declines the terms of that order. Never having been its own, *al-Saq 'ala al-saq* compels one to stutter and stammer before the massive inventory of language it supplies, forcing its reader to repeat the interruptive quality of its prose. Mohammed Bakir Alwan, Stephen Sheehi, and Kamran Rastegar have underlined, differently, that this text is unclassifiable.[60] Yet if this is so, and if this unclassifiability points to the impossibility of domesticating al-Shidyaq's language into a literary critical institution, and into the terms for reading privileged in al-Bustani—and if also, differently, in Husayn—*al-Saq 'ala al-saq* solicits the thought of a unitary work, and the coherent figure of its reader, only to decompose each. It is in this decomposition that one may consider that if the test to which al-Shidyaq points repeats ("I have to keep on talking in this chapter, to test the patience of its reader"), pointing to an interruptive relation to death, and to the death of As'ad al-Shidyaq, in *al-Saq 'ala al-saq*, this test continues, unabated, until, at the close of this text one reads its epilogue, *khatima*, and then its tail or appendage, *dhanab*. The epilogue is not an ending, it does not seal the wholeness of the work but completes the text by appealing to a second part, closing it by cutting into it and cutting it into parts, *ajza'* ("the first part of the book *al-Saq 'ala al-saq fi ma huwwa al-Fariyaq* is complete, and a second one will follow after its author is stoned or crucified, by the grace and generosity of God" [*FS*, 702]), to point to the matter and form of language.

The epilogue underscores a relation to reading, *qira'a*, and understanding, *fahm* ("I made this book [ana 'amaltu al-kitab di], that is to say I composed it [allaftuh], I neither printed it nor bound it nor placed it in your hands. I know well that my Lord Shaykh Muhammad would laugh at it [yidhak minuh; also, "make fun of it"] were he to read it because he knows in his Spirit that he would be able to do better than it [annu y'dar ya'mal ahsan minnu], and because he thinks that it is something useless [shay' farigh], even if I've filled it with letters. But our Lord, our Father, and our Sir will not be able to read it or understand it [bal ma yi'darush yifhamuh], and so I ask them that before they light a fire to burn it, they ask about what is good and what is not good in it, and if what is good is disagreeable then leave it with me, and if not, burn it between its covers. And I ask that if they find in it lapses or mistakes, it would be unjust [fa ma yikunsh min al-'adl] to burn it because each of us has lapsed or made lots of mistakes, and God doesn't burn us in Hell because of it" [703]). The passage opens with the word *I* ("I made this book [ana 'amaltu al-kitab di]"), an opening that would be redundant in written Arabic but that in spoken Arabic—the passage I have translated here is written in spoken Egyptian Arabic—is not. The contestatory valance of this passage is doubled in this word, pressing the noun *I* and its grammatical staging over against the legacies touched upon in the words *nahu* and *adab*. Each of these categories—"grammar" and "literature"—is solicited to be understood differently, in relation to the time of life and death. Yet if "I" solicits a figure of comprehension and learning in relation to language, through the presentation of an equivalence between the words *reading* and *understanding* ("But our Lord, our Father, and our Sir will not be able to read it or understand it [bal ma yi'darush yifhamuh]"), this figure comes apart. Al-Shidyaq privileges a historical and temporal capacity of the reader, *al-qari'*, to understand language, but language, in al-Shidyaq, is not simply something that may be understood in time. And to read, in al-Shidyaq, is, then, to hold language, to remain with language during the time of its devastation ("and so I ask them that before they light a fire to burn it, they ask about what is good and what is not good in it, and if what is good is disagreeable then leave it with me and if not, burn it between its covers"). It is this, perhaps, that "understanding" in al-Shidyaq is, a way of remaining with the time of language, and of declining to leave that time behind in the act of comprehension reading is solicited to enact.

The first reader solicited in the epilogue is "my Lord Shaykh Muhammad," and al-Shidyaq returns to this figure as it progresses. "Oh my Lord Shaykh Muhammad, I know that the books of jurisprudence and grammar [kutub al-fiqh wa al-nahu] are more important than this one of mine, because when someone reads one of those books they scowl and knit their brow in order to understand its meaning, and you know that reverence and loftiness comes only with knitting one's brow. But the books of jurisprudence don't say that laughter is forbidden or hateful" (703). This passage situates itself in relation to two of the Arabic disciplines, *fiqh*, which is most often, and if problematically, translated as "jurisprudence," and *nahu*, "grammar." I privilege this reference here, allowing others to shade for a moment into the background (the reference to "Father Hanna," a metonym for the Maronite Church hierarchy and its teachers and functionaries, and who al-Shidyaq mocks, and "Monsieur, Mister, Herr, and Señor," a parade of Europeans who "do not have an obligation to print my book because I'm not writing for cattle or donkeys or lions or tigers but for all people, all created beings [bal huwwa 'ala al-nas, bani Adam]" [704]), to underline the relation of language to inheritance, which al-Shidyaq asks us to read. I have pointed to the reading of al-Shidyaq offered by al-Baghdadi, where *al-Saq 'ala al-saq* occasions an "anthropocentric" rather than a "theocentric" understanding of language. This transformation has been discussed by Geoffrey Roper in terms of a "demystification of language and literature, a revival of the classical heritage, and a new self-awareness."[61] And it has been read by Rastegar through what he calls "the emergence of a largely autonomous category of secular literature outside of religious or monarchical systems of legitimation."[62] This autonomy is occasioned in the formation of "a field no longer deriving legitimacy either from sacred or theological utility" "but from an entirely self-sufficient system of values and legitimation" (7), and in relation to "the social contestations that are present in this histories of the productions of all texts" (29), literary and others. Yet if the reading of an "autonomy from traditional forms of legitimation" "needs to account for the shift away from pre-modern sources of legitimation of cultural productions" (72, 31), this "shift," as Rastegar also underlines, never takes place once and for all. To be what it is, and if it is to be itself, it must be reenacted in and through acts of reading and writing. Language, in al-Shidyaq, is an aporetical, untimely event, that is unable to leave the past, and its linguistic and juridical disciplines, behind. The "autonomy" of literature, then, if there is one, and like the change pointed to in al-Baghdadi (a shift away from "theology") and Roper (where language in al-Shidyaq is a "demystification"), is undercut by the iterative, if aporetical, quality of language in al-Shidyaq.

Al-Shidyaq's gesturing to the disciplines of *fiqh* (jurisprudence) and *nahu* (grammar) is also, in the passage I am reading here, an event of citation. The sarcasm of al-Shidyaq's remark ("Oh my Lord Shaykh Muhammad") underlines the distance he wishes to place between himself and the disciplines he is to name in the following clause in this sentence ("Oh my Lord Shaykh Muhammad, I know that the books of jurisprudence and grammar are more important than this one of mine, because when someone reads one of those books they scowl and knit their brow in order to understand its meaning [Ya sayyidi al-shaykh Muhammad ana a'rif anna kutub al-fiqh wa al-nahu ajall min kitabi di, li anna al-wahid lamma yi'ra kitab min dol yu'attib wijhu wa yu'abbis hatta yidar yifham ma'nahu] [*FS*, 704]). This distance points to the one he wishes to install between himself and the older tradition of Arabic lexicography in *Sirr al-layali* ("If the ancients have worked on this noble language, I've loved it passionately" [*SL*, 111]), and it points to his language project as a project about authorship. The author, in al-Shidyaq, and the practice of composition, is offered as a way of restaging a relation to the past. Here, the past comes to appear as if it belonged to another time, a reading affirmed, as we have seen, through a principal line of interpretation of al-Shidyaq in literature studies ('Imad al-Sulh, the principal biographer of al-Shidyaq, to mention one other, writes in these terms, underlining that *al-Saq 'ala al-saq* represents a "difference in kind" in relation to language practices of the nineteenth century).[63] Yet this reorganization of terms, where writing comes to appear as a kind of "making" (writing that he "composed" *al-Saq 'ala al-saq*, al-Shidyaq underlines that he is the one who "made this book ['amaltu al-kitab di]"), a practice and a word that accumulate and decline to seal into the past the legacies al-Shidyaq gestures to in this "epilogue." Rastegar has underlined this passage in relation to writing and authorship ("This act—of writing—is what defines the book's creation, and his [al-Shidyaq's] authorial role in its production"), suggesting, compellingly, that *al-Saq 'ala al-saq* both promises "and fundamentally undermines the aim of creating a stable subjectivity" in language.[64] Both mirroring and interrupting the form of life—and the understanding of life and death—solicited in the Arabic, Ottoman nineteenth century (through the *Hatt-i Şerif-i Gülhane*, and in relation to the expansive and destructive force of capital in relation to language and being), *al-Saq 'ala al-saq* becomes a text that signals this form of life (and death) and remains inappropriable in relation to the terms it privileges.

If *al-Saq 'ala al-saq* gives place to itself by displacing a series of disciplines in Arabic, it is not able to leave this act of displacement behind. Language, in *al-Saq 'ala al-saq*, remains with, and it keeps repeating, the division (and divisions) it desires to have installed, once and for all, between itself and more than one other. The negotiation of a relation to an "older" tradition gives place to the time of *al-Saq 'ala al-saq*, confounding its belonging to a single period, genre, literary institution, or form. In *al-Saq 'ala al-Saq* "the peculiarities of language appear to be the essence of the work," and this "essence," in al-Shidyaq, is already interrupted, ruining the understanding of the work as a whole of interconnected parts.[65] The ruin of language and form in *al-Saq 'ala al-saq* bears a relation to laughter ("But the books of jurisprudence don't say that laughter is forbidden or hateful" [*FS*, 704]), and laughter, in al-Shidyaq, is mournful. It points to a desire to install a firm break between the present and the past. And it teaches us that reading, if also understanding, *fahm*, may not be separated from the materiality of letters. "I know well that my Lord Shaykh Muhammad would laugh at it were he to read it because he knows in his Spirit that he would be able to do better than it, and because he thinks that it is something useless, even if I've filled it with letters" (704). To read letters, then, is to read in relation to a materiality, and a relation to time, that may not be domesticated or transcended: letters, in al-Shidyaq, already come apart. Stopping by adding an epilogue and an appendage, it is as if *al-Saq 'ala al-saq*, "a text that nearly eludes prior—or subsequent—categorization," couldn't end but had abruptly to interrupt itself to bring itself to a close.[66]

The language of *al-Saq 'ala al-saq* is said to have been "without mannerism or obscurity"[67] and to have broken with the "burdens and fetters that had frozen [also, "hardened," "caused to clot"] Arabic literature for many decades," yet clarity of expression is ridiculed in *al-Saq 'ala al-saq*, and its narrator tells us that he—or al-Fariyaq, or al-Shidyaq—has been unable not to carry with him al-Fayruzabadi's dictionary on his travels as he composed the text.[68] "I've written it having no Arabic books to turn to or rely upon other than the dictionary [of al-Fayruzabadi]" (*FS*, 10–11). This inability is repeated in *al-Saq 'ala al-saq* in its relation to the *maqama*, an older Arabic genre written in rhymed prose, of which the two most prominent examples are those of al-Hamadhani (967–1007) and al-Hariri (1054–1122). "Rhymed prose [saj'] for an author is like a wooden leg for someone walking. So I must not lean on it, in any of its forms of expression, so its doctrine doesn't constrain me, or entangle me in a situation I can't get out of" (*FS*, 61). But, and as this passage also makes clear, al-Shidyaq is already caught up in language. It is something from which he will never have been simply free.[69] *Al-Saq 'ala al-saq* mimes the *maqama* by including four of them within itself, and by giving its narrator, "a wretched servant, the writer of his [al-Fariyaq's] story, thinking of composing a *maqama* that would delight the married and unmarried among you" (463), to tell al-Fariyaq's story. If *al-Saq 'ala al-saq* was an attempt to render the *maqama* in a "contemporary form" this is not, then, because it exemplifies "a possible modernity," "a modernity opposed to colonial modernity, which is built upon a historical and cultural break, and which adopts an Orientalist view of the self," but because it ruins the temporal terms of contemporeneity.[70] In the field of language, "colonial modernity" may not be said to have been "adopted" or not but is a name for an event of violence in language, which touches in advance upon acts of writing and poetic statement.

I underlined in the preceding section of this chapter that in al-Bustani a totalizing form of the body is privileged in relation to reading. If for As'ad al-Shidyaq belief is to be linked to the heart, and to the word of God, unmediated by human institutions, the simplicity of form this linkage solicits imparts the division of the letter, *al-harf*, from the spirit, *al-ruh*, in the letters of Paul ("But we have now become free from the law, for that which we held tightly to has died, so that we may serve the newness of the spirit, not the ancientness of the letter" [Romans 7:6, tr. Ahmad Faris al-Shidyaq]).[71] This understanding of form is reiterated and changed in al-Bustani, where a Pauline political theology is indexed in the privileging of a single body in relation to a new series of divisions (life from death, the human from the animal, childhood from adulthood, Europe from Africa, and others, and in which al-Shidyaq, in part, shares).[72] If in al-Bustani this privileging is, as it were, privileged, in al-Shidyaq it is catachrestically repeated. Distinctions—for example, the distinction between al-Fariyaq and al-Fariyaqiyya—are not affirmed, and neither are they opposed. They are entered into and accelerated, forced open, written, to give place to the textual event al-Shidyaq named "al-Saq ʿala al-saq." The linguistic excess that this text is—it is catachresis, pleonasm, parabasis, allegory (because to speak of himself al-Shidyaq must speak of another—like all created beings, he must love)—dislodges it from, even as it will never have simply have been other than, the juridical, social, and political forms privileged in the Arabic nineteenth century. In this book I read texts in Arabic (Mahmoud Darwish, Elias Khoury), Hebrew (Shimon Ballas), and French (Edmond Amran El-Maleh), each of which takes up the question of form as it is gifted to them in al-Shidyaq. Al-Shidyaq's displacement from Mount Lebanon led to his residence in Egypt, Malta, England, France (where *al-Saq ʿala al-saq* was published in 1855), Tunisia, where he converted to Islam and took the name Ahmad, and, finally, Istanbul. If this conversion points to a relocation of sorts, a setting up of place within a new economy of terms, *al-Saq ʿala al-saq* repeats al-Shidyaq's persisting displacement. This text may be said to be an event of displacement, because, from the start, it displaces itself from itself, to point to a declining of the coherent form of the work as linguistic or social totality.

Were you to say that children now go to schools, where they learn reading and writing, I would say that what they learn there does not do away with the delusions their mothers impart to them at home. For they memorize the word of God by heart without understanding its meaning. Even their teachers themselves do not understand it.

AHMAD FARIS AL-SHIDYAQ, *Kanz al-ragha'ib fi muntakhibat al-Jawa'ib*

An excess of laughter is the beginning of weeping.

AHMAD FARIS AL-SHIDYAQ, *al-Saq ʿala al-saq*

In *al-Saq ʿala al-saq* what called itself "al-lisan" or "al-lugha" is conscripted into the historical, anthropocentric understanding of language this text promises and stalls. It is not that this event comes later—it is not that at first there is language and that then a colonial violence befalls it, as if from an outside—but that language already takes place in the fallout of this violence. And it is a violence, I have underlined, that is not simply historical, but that repeats itself—already, and as if for this first time—in acts or events of language. The beginning, then, will already have been lost, and in the beginning, in al-Shidyaq, there is sadness. It is not only that when reading *al-Saq ʿala al-saq* one cries out of laughter—and one does—but that in the beginning one will already have laughed, and one will, then, already have cried. To read this beginning I turn to the twelfth chapter of the fourth book of *al-Saq ʿala al-saq*, titled "Fi khawatir falsafiyya" (On Philosophical Thoughts). There al-Fariyaqiyya, after losing her patience, offers a reading of England, of the village in the country where she and al-Fariyaq had been staying, and the city of London. "I thought, while we were on the island of Malta, that the English lived under the best conditions, and were the most at ease. But when we came to their country and lived among them, we saw that their peasants were the most miserable of God's creatures. Look at the people of this village who are all around us, look closely at them and you'll see that there's no difference between them and a band of flies. Those who work in the fields leave in the morning to toil and exhaustion and return home in the evening without seeing any of God's creatures—and without anyone seeing them. They go to sleep after dinner, and wake in the morning to what had been before, and so on, and so on" (*FS*, 597). The *fallah* is like a tool, and he works without rest. On Sundays he goes to church and remains there for two hours, as if he were a statue, yawning for one and sleeping for another, only to return home. These passages, and the ones I shall read in what follows, turn on the institution of world and its relation to justice. After remarking the class distinctions to which he points—if also the distinction between human beings and insects—and after underlining that "the need of the wealthy for the poor is, in fact, stronger than the need of the poor for the wealthy" (599), al-Fariyaq figures people, *al-nas*, as the parts of a body. "If people are slaves of God upon his earth, irrespective of the difference in their condition or station, they are like a single body [ka al-jism al-wahid], with the difference between its lofty and the vulgar parts [aʿda'; also "members," "organs"], so why is the relation between people not just, as it is between the parts of this body" (598). This passage solicits the thought of a single body—an anthropotheologism that will have come, suddenly, to take the place of an older understanding of language and world. "The world, during the time of your grandfather and father, peace be upon them, was not as it is now" (518). But if the world's being different gestures to a new understanding of time and language, the writing of this difference occasions a repetition. Language sets itself apart from something else, remarking an indebtedness to it, to point to an inability to cut off what is said to belong to the past.

This older understanding of world is pointed to in the legacies received by several of the Arabic words we have considered in al-Shidyaq: *adab*, *fiqh*, *nahu*. The words *lugha* (language) and *'ilm* (knowledge) are equally decisive. One may consider this understanding through the dispute over the being of the world and its knowability in al-Ghazali's *Tahafut al-falasifa* (The Incoherence of the Philosophers) and the response to it offered by Ibn Rushd in *Tahafut al-Tahafut* (The Incoherence of the Incoherence). If this dispute turned on the question of the createdness of the world in relation to an understanding of the attributes of God, an understanding of world that privileges its coherency and that of the being that resides in it—the human being as a figure of juridical and ethical obligation—is presupposed in each. This understanding is articulated in relation to *adab* perhaps most incisively in Miskawayh's *Tahdhib al-akhalaq* (The Refinement of Morals) and, differently, in Ibn Khaldun's *Muqaddima*, texts which were first published as printed editions in the later half of the nineteenth century. Yet, in *al-Saq 'ala al-saq*, the figure of a single body, *jism wahid*, already divides, and one of the names of this division is al-Fariyaqiyya. It is not that this text separates itself from the inheritance I point to here, or from an older reflection on and understanding of language in Arabic. In al-Shidyaq this inheritance is mournfully, interruptively retained—*al-Saq 'ala al-saq* cannot stop dividing itself from it—to give place to the body of the work in pieces. Form interrupts the colonial, philological grounding of world. The chapter titled "On Philosophical Thoughts" is staged as the presentation of the narrator of *al-Saq 'ala al-saq* reporting al-Fariyaqiyya's words as she relates them to al-Fariyaq. If, in al-Shidyaq, the sensible is to be privileged over the intelligible in relation to language and its origin ("It is clear that mental, ideational matters are derived from sensible ones" [*FS*, 411]), this derivation does not point to or come down to "one," an atemporal ground, because the dividing function of this derivation is, in al-Shidyaq, what a ground, *asl*, is. It is not that al-Fariyaqiyya is derived from the name al-Fariyaq but that this pair—al-Fariyaq/al-Farayqiyya—is an allegory of what language is and does. This pair mirrors others—the pair Ahmad Faris al-Shidyaq/As'ad al-Shidyaq, and the twinned time of the world "during the time of your grandfather and father" and "as it is now"—to iterate, in *al-Saq 'ala al-saq*, the interrupted time of language. Already, whatever will have grounded language and its reading divides. Origin or ground is in excess of itself. It is not that this excess belongs to history but that it speaks to us of the historicity of language, because it teaches us to read the relation of language to time and loss.

It is in relation to this understanding of loss that one may read what al-Shidyaq calls "surprise." "And for whoever has each day one hundred dinar, what is the difference [al-farq, one of the words encrypted in the names al-Fariyaq and al-Fariyaqiyya] between him and one who has fifty or twenty? For whoever is not content with this, a world filled with gold would not suffice. And even when a woman is rich this wealth must be followed by pain ['ina'; also "toil," "work"], because she must prepare dinners, banquets, and parties, and visit and be visited." And, al-Shidyaq continues, "Don't the wealthy receive the gift of illness and disease like the poor? Does death not surprise them, when they are absorbed in the abundance of their pleasures?" (*FS*, 602). Surprise multiplies these "Philosophical Thoughts," to give al-Shidyaq to compare England to Egypt. To do so he gestures to the figure of a merchant in Egypt at the close of the day sitting on a couch, one leg resting over the other, as if he were repeating the title of this book, *al-Saq 'ala al-saq*. "It is not a crime that the fellahin in our country are happier than all of these people. Even the merchants here are miserable, despite their wealth and riches. Each of them spends the entire day and a third of the night standing on his two feet. I once asked one of them, Why don't you sit down on a chair, when you've got so many of them? He said to me, Because of our supervisors, who visit us to buy from us. Were I to sit with them, I'd become one of them. As for Sunday, their bodies and thoughts remain numb." "So where are merchants like this among us," al-Fariyaqiyya continues to ask, "ours who bend one leg over the other for a few hours on a couch? And who then, in the afternoon, put their cloaks away behind them and go out, walking proudly? If civilization and science have caused this, ignorance is bliss" (603). To compare Egypt to Europe, and to solicit, through this comparison, an understanding of justice ("How could this happen in a country [England] that presents its justice as an example?" [602–3]), al-Shidyaq must encrypt the title of his text into his explication of comparative differences. To offer a sentence in language *al-Saq 'ala al-saq* must cite itself, at the border—the title—that is to divide its inside from its outside. Taking the title of this text into its interior—consuming it, as if it were an unmournable object—*al-Saq 'ala al-saq* ruins the border between the interior and the exterior, which his text also solicits. The political body al-Shidyaq promises—and which he locates on the side of justice—may be compared to the body of his text. Each may be said to be what it is only insofar as it already relates itself to another, only insofar as it falls into pieces, where form takes place in mutilation.[73]

"I've learned now, from the barbarity and primitive simplicity I've found in their country, how to live in ours, if I return safely to it" (*FS*, 604), but the "learning" al-Shidyaq underlines ("I've learned now [qad ta'allamtu al-an]") disrupts the understanding of learning—and of knowledge, *'ilm*, a word encrypted in the Arabic verb al-Shidyaq uses here—privileged in the Arabic disciplines. If learning, in al-Shidyaq, is to solicit justice, this is only insofar as a just social and political body—and a just understanding of world—will never have turned on an understanding of the world as totality, as a body the parts of which combine into a whole. If the body in al-Shidyaq is one, if it is a single body, this is because it already bears a relation to pain and toil, and illness and disease. And the diseases may not be counted. After offering a list of illnesses lasting several pages, he gestures to "those diseases whose name is not yet known" (357). This excess mirrors the excess of language in *al-Saq 'ala al-saq*, to point to a time of sorrow. "Is it not sufficient for human beings that their lives are short? That their sorrows are long and many? That their affair is difficult? Each has pain, anguish, and toil that suffices both for him and others. The student stays up all night explaining problems and clarifying issues and questions. One who practices a trade spends the whole day devoted to his work to the point of exasperation merely to make a living"—al-Shidyaq goes on to describe others, the minister, the king, and the merchant, the doctor, the judge, the naval captain, the teacher, the singer, the musician, "and the author [al-mu'allif] who, like me, is among those who are crazy (or, who remains wary of them, and is not one) who are accosted and whose books are burned and whose skin is torn to shreds" (357–58). The skin of the body of man—the surface that divides its inside from its outside—is torn from it. If in justice, as in love, a single body is solicited—"We are two bodies in a single spirit, or two spirits in a single body" (370), al-Shidyaq writes—this body already tears apart. It declines to assume the form of a coherent political—or social—body. It interrupts, even as it promises, the aesthetic, historical, and philological terms for the domestication of language in the Arabic nineteenth century—as in *Sirr al-layali*, and as in the passage from *Kanz al-raga'ib fi muntakhibat al-Jawa'ib* that I have placed at the opening of this section, which points to an understanding, *fahm*, that will have left memorization (also retention, preservation, and inscription, as we have learned through Mahmoud Darwish), *hifz*, behind.

Readings of al-Shidyaq have underlined that his writing "sets out from the burden of tradition in a completely subjective way," but language, in *al-Saq 'ala al-saq*, already forms an occasion for what al-Shidyaq calls "love."[74] There are three kinds of love in al-Shidyaq: balanced, where the lover loves the beloved as he loves himself; excessive, as if the lover loves the beloved more than he does himself—"and this is the kind of love of a father or mother for their child, and of some lovers" (*FS*, 371)—and what al-Shidyaq calls "well known [ma'luma]," "and this is when a person loves his beloved out of a preference or feeling of affection for him, and this is the most common" (372). This tripartite division is preceded by an appeal to human nature and the course of life in time and its consummation in death ("I say: love is among those things that are implanted in human nature from the day they are placed in the cradle until the day they are placed in a bier" [371]), but it gives place, immediately, to further distinctions of love. "For there are also three other conditions: those in relation to place, and they are being nearby, being distant, and what lies between them" (372). This condition or state prompts the word *difference* ("They influence people differently according to the difference in their nature") to give place to further distinctions. "And three others, which are temporal: they are childhood, youth, and mature age" (372). These—three times three—give place to others: in terms of poverty and wealth, and in terms of humility, strength, and equality, "and humility is most often the character of the lover, and strength that of the beloved" (372). This series of divisions closes with a reflection on the image of the beloved, and to read these divisions is to read their relation to this closure. "It is my opinion," al-Shidyaq writes, "that the lover must already have formed in his mind the characteristics and qualities of what is good and yearn for them, until he sees them in reality in a living being, just as he had imagined them" (373). But if this image must have been formed in the mind, its staging in relation to the divisions of love ruins the oppositions it generates: imaginary from real, sensible from intelligible. These divisions are ruined because one is already in love, and this anteriority gives place to *al-Saq 'ala al-saq*, to teach us that this text mirrors the mathematical expansion I have underlined. To read this expansion is to do so as if one were al-Shidyaq reading grammar—al-Fariyaq, the narrator of *al-Saq 'ala al-saq* explains, suffered from ophthalmia (*FS*, 329), and he would read grammar, *nahu*, until his eyes hurt. And it is to read by yielding to this expansion, allowing language to point to the many relations—and there are always others—which *al-Saq 'ala al-saq* compels us to consider. This compulsion is itself a form of love, a practice of reading in which one is schooled in the writing of Ahmad Faris al-Shdiyaq.

§

After traveling to Malta al-Shidyaq comes to interpret dreams—just as he comes to be an expert at curing bad breath (*FS*, 438). The subject whose dream he interprets, Sayyed Dhahul bin Ghaful, whose name means "the absent-minded, son of the forgetful" (also, "heedless," "inattentive"), has dreamed that he wishes to write a speech to read in public to the people. In the dream he takes a paper and pen, writes a single letter, and is then interrupted by a woman who calls him to her room. He goes, leaving the single letter written on the paper, and when he returns he sees that a second letter has been added to the first. He takes up the pen to write another letter, and he does, and he is then immediately interrupted to be called again, and when he returns he finds that "another letter had been added to the first three so that they formed a single word" (430). He begins to write, and after writing a single word he is called again only to find another word, and then a page, until a book has been completed. In what remains in the dream he climbs up to the top of a pulpit and reads from the book to the people "and those who had come to listen are surprised by its eloquence, the harmony of its expressions [insijam 'ibaratihi], and the precision of its meanings." The woman who had called him earlier in the dream now appears as his wife, and, after completing fifty books in the manner in which the first was written, they decide to travel "to some Eastern countries" so that he can read what he has written to people there. Yet after arriving in an unnamed country, where a massive gathering of people have come to hear him speak, he opens the first book he had composed, and all but the letters he himself had written had been erased. "So he tried to link them together so that he might infer from them a meaning, and he was not able to. So he came down from the pulpit and woke up" (431–32). The interpretation al-Fariyaq offers is that the writing he had taken himself to have produced was appropriate for his own country but not others. Al-Sayyed al-Dhahul bin Ghaful is upset by the interpretation, and al-Fariyaq explains to him that "our country" is the origin of dreams and the birthplace of their interpretation. One may read this passage in relation to the figure of man. If this figure is solicited, and if it points to the totality of a social body, this is only to give this totality, like the unreadable letters with which the dream ends, to fall into pieces. The coherency of the social and political order—and its interruption in the form of unreadable letters, and if also of the undomesticated fellah—is given to be at stake in the act or event one calls reading. In al-Shidyaq language is to its fulfillment in reading as the single body is to love. The task of reading, as one is taught in *al-Saq 'ala al-saq*, is to refuse the translation of the unreadability of these letters into the pacified simplicity of legible speech.

TESTING LITERATURE STUDIES

Even the least study of this poetry will convince you—if you are among those who compose modern research—that this poetry which is attributed to Imru' al-Qays and which is related to his story is Islamic—and not jahili—poetry.

TAHA HUSAYN, *Fi al-shi'r al jahili*

The institution of a literary object in Taha Husayn responds to the call of the juridical violence of the colonial state.[75] A practice of historical categorization gives place to this object, to mirror the violence of the law and the being it solicits and privileges in the field of language, "man." The first sentence of *Fi al-shi'r al-jahili* (Cairo, 1926) states that "this kind of research on the history of Arabic poetry is a new one, which no one among us has composed before" (*F*, 13), and the newness of the research Husayn takes himself to have carried out mirrors the sovereignty and autonomy of "man" it presupposes. The practice of reading in relation to the designation of a literary object is to be new ("I want to follow in literature [al-adab] the philosophical method that Descartes invented for research into the reality of things at the beginning of this modern era. Everyone knows that the essential rule of this method is that the researcher be freed from everything that he knew before, and that he receive the object of his research [mawdu' bahthihi] with his mind entirely clear of what has been said about it" [23]), and this newness, and Husayn's cosigning the era to which his project belongs as "modern," reiterates the historical procedure of the reading practice he privileges. What comes to appear newly as a past—the Arabic nineteenth century, and, through Husayn's reading of Ibn Khaldun, the thirteenth and fourteenth centuries—appears on the side of stillness and death. It is to be left behind to give place to the freedom of a subject and its clear mind ("with his mind entirely clear of what has been said about it [khali al-dhihn mimma qila fihi khuluwwan taman]"), one that is to have been installed through a new experience of reading.

To know the cause of a phenomena is already a step taken in the direction of controlling it.

RANAJIT GUHA, "The Prose of Counter-Insurgency"

And what's the loss in translating classical Arabic poetry into the modern Arabic language?

TAHA HUSAYN, *Hadith al-arbi'a'*

The law's solicitation of an understanding of the "human body" and the time of its life from birth "until death" points to a juridical violence, which privileges a historical understanding of time.[76] As Samera Esmeir has underlined, and in relation to the work of Khaled Fahmy and Talal Asad, "The coloniality of the law is found in the forceful elimination of past legal traditions, in the conquest not only of a territory and its inhabitants, but also of the past."[77] It is this dimension of the law that gives place to Husyan's writing on what he called "the history of Arabic poetry" (*F*, 13). The past is to be left behind and included, differently, as having passed. The newness of the object Husayn wishes to install mirrors his desire to historically locate the jahili ode: it is to have succeeded rather than preceded Islam. The category "history" had been privileged as a literary term through a series of introductions, university lecture courses (at the Egyptian University, which had been founded in 1908), and translations. Texts published during the last decade of the nineteenth century and the first decade of the twentieth—Sulayman al-Bustani's introduction to his *Ilyadhat Humiros* (1902), Ruhi al-Khalidi's *Tarikh 'ilm al-adab 'ind al-Afranj wa al- 'Arab, wa Victur Hugo* (1904), Jurji Zaydan's *al-Falsafa al-lughawiyya* (1886), *al-Lugha al-'arabiyya ka'in hayy* (1904), *Tarikh adab al-lugha al-'arabiyya* (1911), and others, including the lecture courses given by Carlo Nallino and Louis Massignon at the Egyptian University, both of which were attended by Husayn—compelled a reorganization of language in historicist terms.[78] Husayn's intervention absorbs these texts, if also earlier and other ones, by forcing them to belong to its past. His text decides on their time, just as it had decided, and installs itself by deciding on the time of the ode. The text of literature studies—and the invention of the literary monograph as the product of the labor of a "researcher" in a field that takes "literature" as its object—mirrors the violence of the law as it desires "to constitute its own grounds of citability and legitimation."[79] Such grounds are given in the disavowal of literature studies of its relation to the past, its presentation of itself as if it were starkly new—"Promoting itself against what it articulated as the violence of the khedival legal order and its inhumanness, colonial law detached itself from the checks of the past and established its authority in its own present" (16)—a time that will have repeated itself to be itself, yet again.

Fi al-shi'r al-jahili points to "the metainscription of colonial conflicts in texts, both literary and material," yet it is not that in the 1920s and 1930s "Egyptian liberal reformers were trapped in the language of the Other" but that language's being itself occasioned its repetition, as if for the first time, of an event of destruction that hierarchically redescribed the distinction between more than one inside and outside.[80] And it is not that in Husayn an understanding of language is transposed from European languages to Arabic, or from Syria to Egypt, a reading that would allow Husayn to appear as the "logical end" of the writings of those "Lebanese Christians" studied by Albert Hourani in the early chapters of *Arabic Thought in the Liberal Age*.[81] To read the relation between Husayn and Europe, on the one hand, and al-Bustani and al-Shidyaq, on the other, as one of provenance and derivation would recognize language in relation to a site of origination, muting the interruptive materiality of language. It is not only that writing practices of the Egyptian khedival state were proliferated in Syria during the period of the Egyptian occupation (1831–40), that al-Shidyaq read the well-known *rihla* (travelogue) of the nineteenth-century Egyptian writer and scholar Rifa' Rafi' al-Tahtawi,[82] and that in *Khutba fi adab al 'arab* al-Bustani praised the printing press established by the Egyptian viceroy Mehmed 'Ali, gesturing to it as a model for the re-forming of language of which he wrote, but that language, in Husayn, confounds its tethering to historical grounds.[83] *Fi al-shi'r al-jahili* writes itself as the linguistic performance and staging of its relation to what it compels to appear as a past, and it does so as it responds to the call of the law.[84] In this response—a response that is juridically and linguistically constituted—*Fi al-shi'r al-jahili* institutes a tradition of reading by relating itself temporally to that event of institution. It is not only that this instituting event divides, but that it is a division—the present from the past, but also the object of study from literary researcher, literature studies from autobiography, and literary understanding from mere repetition. And it is not, then, that in relation to Husayn one may capture an "originary" moment, because in his writing one is given to read the ways in which the paths of language confound their comprehension in relation to demarcated temporal ends, where language discombobulates the understanding of time it solicits in historiographical reflection.

> The Arabic language had remained until this recent time unchanging, in a single form, as if the door of juridical interpretation had been closed in its face.
>
> SULAYMAN AL-BUSTANI, *Ilyadhat Humirus*

> The sender is the one who sends his speech unbound by the rhyme of poetry or prose, by meter, or by anything else. His speech is released without constraint.
>
> RUHI AL-KHALIDI, *Tarikh 'ilm al-adab 'ind al-Afranj wa al-'Arab, wa Victur Hugo*

> Languages are sounds with which each group expresses its intentions.
>
> JURJI ZAYDAN, *al-Falsafa al-lughawiyya*

What is at stake in *Fi al-shi'r al-jahili*, and as Sayyed al-Bahrawi has taught us, is "the issue of method" ("Taha Husayn's issue in this book was not the issue of his attacking religion, but it was, essentially, the issue of method").[85] But if in Husayn "the method of humanist positivism" takes the place of "the metaphysical interpretation of things and the world" (42)—and it is toward a critique of the former, and its relation to what al-Bahrawi calls "intellectual dependency" (115), that his *al-Bahth 'an al-manhaj* aims—the separation of "religion" from "method" repeats the principal gesture given—and repeated—in Husayn's work.[86] Abdelrashid Mahmoudi has argued that Husayn's literary critical writing points to a movement from theology to literature.[87] "For him, the study of literature constituted a release from the oppressive dominance of religious subjects," but the division pointed to here—between language and "religious subjects"—is one that Husayn's writing actively works to install as it renames the differences.[88] Said to have left "metaphysics" (al-Bahrawi), "religion" (Mahmoudi), and, as we shall see below, "theology" (Faysal Darraj) behind, Husayn's text privileges a single category: history. Charles D. Smith has argued that what is at stake in *Fi al-shi'r al-jahili*, and other writings of Husayn's during this period, including *Qadat al-fikr* (1925), is "the establishment of the idea of the historicity of the Qur'an."[89] This idea, for Smith, is installed in relation to an understanding of text critical reading as a science. "Literature had to be desacralized and treated in the same manner as the natural sciences" (93), but if what is at stake is the historical reading of "sacred" texts ("literature had to be desacralized"), this is so only insofar as this reading occasions a reorganization of the way in which meaning is to be secured and policed in the giving of sense. What appears as a separation of "religion" (or "metaphysics" or "theology") from language is a restaging of language in colonial and philological terms.[90]

Faysal Darraj has read Husayn in *Fi al-shi'r al-jahili* as exemplifying what he calls "the rationalist method," which is to stand in contrast to the knowledge of "the traditional shaykh," and I turn here to consider Darraj's reading in detail.[91] In Darraj, the "rationalist method" appeals to a division of science from religion and to an understanding of science as a practice "founded and instituted only with the separation of science from religion" (37), while "tradition" points to to a mode of reflection where "the only role of science was to recall the sacred ground [al-asl al-muqaddas] from which it was derived" (46). In Husayn, "the liberation of knowledge from religious authority" (30) gives way to the institution of sciences, including a science of literature, which discovers and secures objects through testing procedures. As Darraj clarifies, "We are talking about the contradiction between theological consciousness and scientific theory, in the precise sense of the word, insofar as it is a theory that produces objective knowledge and binds science to technique, through research, verification, comparison, experimentation, and continual correction"

(48). In Darraj's reading the installation of an object of study points to a secularization of language, where a "theological consciousness" is displaced through the formation of a science of literature. "Taha Husayn did not explicate literature using theological categories, but in his studies of the history of literature he produced theoretical concepts that corresponded to the object they studied. That is to say that the designation of the object imposed the designation of the concepts that treated it" (50). Darraj designates Husyan's literary critical project as one that transcends a "theological" ground of reading through a historical, scientific practice of interpretation in literature studies. Darraj calls attention to *Fi al-shi'r al-jahili* as a text for which the question of legibility and its relation to institutions and to the state is at stake but brackets the question he provokes by subordinating language to time through a reading of the past as "theology," and by subordinating language—and time—to historical categories.

"The sacred text requires reading, syntactical analysis, explication, and interpretation," Darraj writes. "That is to say, it requires sacred modes of knowledge, such as jurisprudence [fiqh], the fundaments of religion [usul al-din], and the grammar of the Arabic language [nahu al-lugha al-'arabiyya]" (47). But Darraj's reading rescripts, as it also teaches us to read, the domestication of the past, and the new institution of the "past" as a historical category, carried out in Husayn, and if also in al-Bustani, and, differently, and as I will consider in some detail below, in Rifa' Rafi' al-Tahtawi (1801–73). Darraj's text cites the words *fiqh*, *din*, *nahu*, and *lugha*—as al-Bustani cited passages from Ibn Manzur's *Lisan al-'arab* in the entry under "adab" in his dictionary, *Muhit al-muhit*—to relocate them in relation to a colonial idiom. This relocation redesignates the past in particular kinds of ways. It is—or is to have been—left behind, even as it is retained, confounding the divisions Darraj wishes to have secured. Husayn, Darraj writes, "pulls out from beneath language its presupposed sacredness" (39), yet Husayn does so only insofar as he recognizes language in relation to a past that at once is—and is not—its own. And if, for Darraj, the falling away of "religion" and "theology" in secularization has taken place in Husayn, it has not done so in colonial Egypt. What appears to Darraj as an absence is explained by pointing to a contradiction in relation to capital: early-twentieth-century Egypt is a society in which precapitalist relations dominate, and Egypt has therefore not broken with "religion" and "theology," as had taken place, for Darraj, in Europe. There, during the "middle ages," the "college" "liberated the human being from the man of religion [din], and it liberated science from the bonds of theology [al-lahut]" (43). In "al-Shaykh al-taqlidi wa al-muthaqqaf al-hadith," modernity is European, it is Europe, and colonial Egypt appears as "malformed" or "bastard," *hajin* (58).

You see that taking up this method is not necessary only for those who study science and write about it, but it is also necessary for those who read.

TAHA HUSAYN, *Fi al-shi'r al-jahili*

The reflection on Arabic literature studies presupposes the institutionalization of the object it takes to be its own. In this book I do not present a history of Arabic literature studies, as should be clear, but I offer readings of selected texts to elaborate the terms of the institutionalization of a literary object in relation to the legacies of Orientalism and the juridical violence of the colonial state. What appears in scholarship as Husayn's participation in "the new culture" points to an event where the past is relocated to give place to a practice for reading said to be starkly new.[92] If in this event, and as Joseph Massad has written, the "Egyptian belletrist Taha Husayn had called upon the Arabs to accept modern civilization smiling and not frowning," what took place as he opened his mouth points to a mournful relation to loss, including his text's loss of itself.[93] And if in *Fi al-shi'r al-jahili* the texts of the immediate and distant past are interiorized and buried, this event points to a generalized, if stalled and unfinished, mournfulness in Husayn. It is not only that the jahili poetry bears mournful motifs, but that the firm temporal boundaries Husayn desires to install point to the mournful comportment of scholarly writing. This mournfulness translates a series of separations, and it responds in advance to an obligation. This obligation gives place to the single question privileged in the historical, philological project Husayn pursues. "We are obligated to ourselves and to science to ask: was not this jahili poetry which we have demonstrated does not represent the life of the jahili Arabs or their mentality, their religions, or their civilizations, that it does not represent their language, was this poetry not written down and ascribed to its authors after Islam?" (*F*, 53). This obligation turns on the self's obligation to itself, to point to a law of reading that the text of criticism gives. This law institutes separations—between the scholar and the object of study, literature and its context, religion and language, life and death, and more—and these separations stage the ruined adjudication among the gestures of proof, verification, falsification, demonstration, and certainty, as Husayn invents the privileged figure of the literary scholar as a researcher in the field of language. If he does so in relation to reading, and if this privileging solicits the figure of "man" as a site of autonomy and sovereignty in language, this figure is already stalled and bereaved, in iteration. The sovereign reader—a locus for the domestication of language in the colonies—is promised and ruined in Husayn.

Husayn's scientific and scholarly project involves the subordination of an object to a regime of testing protocols, and it therefore participates in what Avital Ronell has called "the test drive."[94] Testing affirms in a mode of rescindability, offering and withdrawing the ground upon which knowledge will have staked its claims. The test inaugurates the newness and originality of its practices and discoveries under the sign of repetition, and it is in relation to this dimension of the test that one may read Husayn's constant affirmation and retraction of what he wishes to prove. "The first thing with which I shall surprise you in this book is that I have doubted the value of the jahili poetry and have insisted in doing so—or, *this doubt has forced itself upon me* [my emphasis]. For I began to research, think, read and ponder, until all of this led me to something which, if it is not certain, is nearly so. That is that the vast majority of what we call jahili poetry is not jahili at all, but rather was forged after Islam. It is Islamic, and it represents the life of Muslims and their tendencies and desires more so than it represents jahili life. *And I almost don't doubt* [my emphasis] that what remains of authentic jahili poetry is very little, that it does not represent or mean anything, and that one need not rely upon it in order to infer the true literary image of this jahili period" (*F*, 19). Interrupting itself to be itself, halting and hesitating as it demonstrates its claims, this text suggests the compulsive dimension of scholarly writing. *Fi al-shi'r al-jahili* delimits the bounds of its object and that object's time only insofar as those bounds will have been ruined in advance, and it may then be said to be "a founding text that never quite manages to ground the very experimental culture for which it remains nonetheless responsible."[95] Disavowing hesitation and weakness ("I appreciate the serious implications of this theory, but I nevertheless do not hesitate to demonstrate and disseminate it. And I am not too weak to proclaim to you and other readers that what you read as if it were the poetry of Imru' al-Qays or Tarafa or Ibn

Kulthum or ʻAntara [Husayn offers here a list several of the canonical jahili poets] is not theirs at all. It is the forgery of transmitters, the false attribution of the Bedouin, the invention of grammarians, the dissimulation of storytellers, or the invention of commentators, moderns, or theologians" [*F*, 19]), Husayn's text resembles those of Asʻad and Ahmad Faris al-Shidyaq—each is compulsive, neither can stop reading—as it institutes a discipline of literature studies. The undermining of what it presupposes remarks this text in relation to an "ambivalent demarcation," where it gestures and effaces "the strategic nature of apparently constative academic discourse," in the stalled labor of philological, critical statement.[96] *Fi al-shiʻr al-jahili* bespeaks the registers of Husayn's depletion, to which the law of reading this text gives ("We are obligated to ourselves [min al-haq ʻalayna li anfusina] and science"), compels us to attend.

At the beginning of this book we defined *nahu* as the knowledge through which one knows correct Arabic speech, in reading and in writing, and we mentioned those rules that yield the precise regulation of the tongue using correctly inflected words.

RIFAʻ RAFIʻ AL-TAHTAWI, *Kitab al-tuhfa al-maktabiyya li taqrib al-lugha al-ʻarabiyya*

One must excel in clarity of expression [bayan] to the extent that it is possible.

RIFAʻ RAFIʻ AL-TAHTAWI, *Kitab manahij al-albab al-misriyya*

One of the many pasts Husayn disavowed was a more recent one, pointed to in the work and writing of Rifaʻ Rafiʻ al-Tahtawi (1801–73), a principal builder of educational and language institutions in nineteenth-century Egypt. Yet a new sense of the historicity of language is remarked in al-Tahtawi's *Kitab manahij al-albab al-misriyya fi mabahij al-adab al-ʻasriyya* (1867), to which I turn here.[97] Tahtawi had been a part of the first educational mission sent by the Egyptian viceroy Mehmed ʻAli to study in France, from 1826 to 1831, and the pages of his travelogue *Takhlis al-ibriz fi talkhis Bariz*, which was published at Mehmed ʻAli's Bulaq press in 1834, reorders language in relation to the time of the life and death of man. Al-Tahtawi defines language as follows: "Language as such is specific words that denote specific meanings, and its paths are two, reading and writing, which differ in the way that nations differ the one from the other."[98] But having divided what he calls language "as such [min haythu hiyya]" in two, language is divided again, into those that continue to be used and those that have died out, *lughat musta'mila*, *lughat mahjura*. While in Paris al-Tahtawi had studied with the Orientalist Silvestre de Sacy, just as he had read Rousseau, Condillac, Montesquieu, and the grammar of the Port Royal, and these divisions point to these readings.[99] An understanding of language in relation to "classical," "dead" languages—al-Tahtawi lists Coptic, Latin, and "the ancient Greek language called 'al-Ighriqiyya' [al-Yunaniyya al-qadima al-musamma bi al-Igriqiyya]" (273)—points to the appropriation of language into the time of the state. This appropriation is elaborated in *Manahij*, where the present is described as a return of past greatness. "Everyone who loves the beauty of civilization and who smells the fragrant scent of this time, will be delighted with happiness and his heart will be filled with joy when he sees, with an eye of love, that Egypt's ancient greatness, brilliant splendor, noble grandeur, and early fortune, have returned to her."[100] But the return of the past compels further labor, that of modernization or civilization, *tamaddun*, which al-Tahtawi explicates by dividing. "It is understood from what we have said that civilization has two sources" and the first is "*ma'nawi*, which is civilization in morals, behavior, and *adab* [comportment], that is to say, civilization in religion and law [al-tamaddun fi al-akhlaq wa al-'awa'id wa al-adab ya'ni al-tamaddun fi al-din wa al-shari'a]" (9). "The second division," al-Tahtawi writes, "is *taqaddum madi*, in relation to the general welfare, like agriculture, commerce, and crafts" (9). The understanding of *Manahij* as a book about general welfare, *al-manafi' al-umumiyya*, becomes one that reads this text as an event of language that reorganizes terms. It translates those terms—*din*, *shar'*, *nahu*—and the ways of being to which they point into this understanding. Citing these words, al-Tahtawi, and with the force of a single, if divided gesture, relocates them in relation to a new, colonial idiom.[101]

This idiom is elaborated in relation to what al-Tahtawi calls "al-bulitiqyya." "The grounds and laws through which a state is administered is called the art of state politics [fan al-siyasa al-mulkiyya], and it is also called the art of administration, or the science of the organization of the state, and the like. And reflection on this science, its circulation on people's tongues, their speaking of it and carousing about it in gatherings and parties, and their diving into it in journals [al-ghazitat]—all of that is called politics [bulitiqiyya], or siyasa [politics], and one can form it into an adjective, political [bulitiqi] or siyasi. So politics [al-bulitiqiyya] is everything related to the state [al-dawla] and its laws, relations, and what binds it together" (350). What al-Tahtawi transliterates as "bulitiqiyya" and translates as "politics" (siyasa) compels a reorganization of *adab*, and of language, in relation to this new understanding of the political. In al-Tahtawi *adab* is routed through an elaboration of a racialist idiom in relation to the Sudan, which is to be located on the side of animality ("As he described it, half of its inhabitants were like beasts and others like stones," Eve M. Troutt Powell has written), to separate Egypt from the Sudan and bring it closer to Europe.[102] This restaging of borders is historical, giving place to a new understanding of language and the ways it may become an object of reflection. It is not that al-Tahtawi "liberated" language by giving to it a "natural, simple form" but that in his text language is relocated into a new pedagogy of reading, in what al-Tahtawi called "politics."[103] "In civilized countries it has become customary to teach children the Qur'an (in Islamic ones) and books of religion (in others), before teaching them crafts, and that is fine in itself," al-Tahtawi writes. But "what would be wrong were there to be in each administrative district a teacher who would read to the children—after they have completed learning the Qur'an, and their religious obligations, and the principles of the Arabic language [ba'd tamam ta'lim al-Qur'an al-sharif wa al-'aqa'id wa mabadi' al-'arabiyya]—the principles of political and administrative affairs."[104] Politics is not added as a supplement to what will have appeared as "religious" content (the Qur'an, religious obligations, the Arabic language). Rather, language and the older institutional practices in relation to it, including the memorization of the Qur'an, are appropriated into the state, and into a certain conception of life and death. Appropriating "adab," "politics" is to occasion a new a mediating practice in relation to singular beings—what al-Tahtawi calls "rawabit"—to give place to a new understanding of time and language in relation to form.

To elaborate his discussion of "politics" al-Tahtawi recalls the story of Abu al-Aswad al-Du'ali (603–88) in relation to the invention of *nahu*, a word that has come to be translated as "grammar" but which relates to the giving of place to sense in the faculty of language.[105] The reading al-Tahtawi offers mirrors that of Ibn Khaldun in his *Muqaddima*, but if the latter's discussion turns on a reading of language in relation to an Arabic-Islamic logocentrism, in al-Tahtawi the staging of the origin of "grammar" locates that origin in relation to, and subordinates it within, his explication of *tamaddun*, civilization.[106] Ibn Khaldun discusses language in the following terms: "Know that language, as this term is commonly understood, is the speaker's expression of his intention. This expression is an act of the tongue [fi'l lisani], which derives from the intention to convey the meaning of speech, so language must become a faculty established in the organ that gives place to it—the tongue."[107] With the expansion of Islam, the Arabs of the Hijaz "came to mix with non-Arabs, and so their linguistic faculty changed, because of the incorrect usage of the non-Arabs who had learned Arabic" (634). And with the corruption of the linguistic faculty—and "listening is the father of the linguistic faculties"—"the Qur'an and the hadith would no longer be understood [fa yanghaliq al-Qur'an wa al-hadith 'ala al-mafhum]" (634). It is in relation to this threat, the threat of the nonunderstanding or miscomprehension of language, that Abu al-Aswad al-Du'ali offered the following instructions. "Abu al-Aswad said to him: whenever you see me open my mouth when uttering a letter, place a dot high up at its top; when I draw my mouth together, put a dot mid way down the letter; and when I narrow my mouth, put the dot beneath the letter."[108] The shaping of the mouth in the imparting of sense in language is what Ibn Khaldun calls, in the passage I cited above, "an act of the tongue." This act is not the act of an autonomous subject, it is not a sovereign act of man, but forms the occasion for an iterated practice in relation to what Ibn Khaldun calls the "malaka," faculty or habitus, of language.[109] If in *Manahij* and, differently, *Takhlis*, a labor of domestication is both carried out and interrupted, if only because al-Tahtawi must repeat the event of the colonization of language his text also enacts, this domestication gives place, in *Fi al-shi'r al-jahili*, to the instituting designation of the monadic form of a literary object.

THE TONGUES OF LANGUAGE

Knowledge of literature—this is a kind of knowledge that does not have an object, which one would study in order to affirm or deny its attributes.

IBN KHALUDN, *al-Muqaddima*

In the strict sense of the term, it [*Fi al-shi'r al-jahili*] added nothing to our understanding of this poetry.

ABDALLAH LAROUI, *L'idéologie arabe contemporaine*

Fi al-shi'r al-jahili was presented as a lecture course at the newly refounded Egyptian University in the fall of 1925.[110] Upon its publication in 1926 it was attacked on the ground that it defamed religion, and complaints brought before the public prosecutor led to the investigation of Husayn by the state. If Husayn interrupts the philological invention of the corpus of jahili poetry as the ground of "Arabic literature," *adab al-'arab, al-adab al-'arabiyya*, because he places the historical time of the ode in question, his gesture reorganizes and affirms this invention. *Fi al-shi'r al-jahili* retains the privilege of this poetry as it is articulated in Orientalism (from Sir William Jones, for whom Imru' al-Qays was "the *Ovid* of *Arabia*," to Wilhelm Awlhardt, Theodore Nöldeke, Hamilton Gibb, and others) to reorganize language as an object of literature studies.[111] A new understanding of *'ilm* as "science" (rather than knowledge), and of *adab* as "literature" (rather than a practice of language, an "act of the tongue"), is called upon, and in this redesignation the reflection on the time of the ode as a historical question—when is the time of the ode?—touches upon the disciplines of reading and the comprehension of language in Arabic. In chapter 1 I underlined the hermenutic function of poetry in the clarification of the meaning of words in the Qur'an. Al-Suyti explains that this is not to make poetry a ground for the Qur'an ("He [Abu Bakr ibn al-Anbari] said: the matter is not, as they claim, that we made poetry a ground for the Qur'an, but that we wished to clarify [tabyin] strange letters in the Qur'an through [or with] poetry") but points solely to a lexicographical use of poetry.[112] Poetry is to be subordinated to the Qur'an as a linguistic source to clarify, *tabyin*—al-Zarkashi, citing the same passage, uses the word *ithbat*, to settle, establish, determine, firmly demonstrate—the latter.[113] But if this corpus of poetry is subsequent to the Qur'an, then the hierarchy privileged in al-Suyuti and al-Zarkashi is placed in question. Reading, understood as the giving of sense in language, ceases to give place to sense.

The question is elaborated in Husayn as one of citation.

> For this research will lead us to the conclusion that from the linguistic and artistic point of view it is not possible that this poetry, which is attributed to Imru' al-Qays, al-A'sha, and other jahili poets, is theirs, or that it was spoken or disseminated before the appearance of the Qur'an! Yes! This research will lead us to a strange conclusion, which is that it is not necessary to cite this poetry in order to interpret the Qur'an and the hadith, but rather one must cite the Qur'an and the hadith in order to interpret this poetry. I wish to say that these poems do not render anything certain [la tuthbitu shay'an] [Husayn points here to the passage in al-Zarkashi I am discussing, by gesturing to the word *ithbat*, which the latter used to describe the relation of poetry to the Qur'an] and do not mean anything [wa la tadullu 'ala shay'in] and that they ought not be treated as a means [wasila] to authoritative knowledge of the Qur'an and the hadith in the manner in which they have been. (*F*, 21–22)

The inversion of the relation between the Qur'an and poetry disrupts the possibility of the production of linguistic meaning. It interrupts the possibility of language's making sense, and the jahili poetry, in Husayn, therefore does not indicate or point to anything. It does not mean and it does not signify: *la tadullu 'ala shay'in*. It is this disruption that subtended the attacks on *Fi al-shi'r al-jahili* and the call for the banning of the book and for Husayn's being removed from his position as professor of Arabic literature at the Egyptian University. The stakes of this disruption are related to language and to modes of life and the recognizability of world. The capacity of language to make sense is privileged in Islamic jurisprudence, *fiqh*, because in this discipline juridical decision requires a clear understanding of the Arabic language. This privilege is explained by al-Shafi'i (discussed in chapter 1) and is linked to the understanding of juridical content and religious obligation. Al-Shafi'i underlines the word *bayan* to point to "the sum of what God has made clear in his book [the Qur'an] to his creatures [jima' ma abana Allah li khalqihi fi kitabihi]," and the event of making juridical content clear in language relates to obligations imparted in the law.[114] *Bayan* points to meanings that are "a clear statement to those to whom they are addressed and in whose language the Qur'an was revealed," and ignorance of the Arabic language introduces difference, the possibility of the disruption of linguistic understanding: the meanings of *bayan* are "different for those who are ignorant of the Arabic language" (60). The explication of language in relation to the law in this passage uses a passive voice verb—*bayanun li man khutiba biha mimann nazala al-Qur'an bi lisanihi*—to gesture to a scene of address, the explication of which points to the rhetorical and juridical tradition in which it shares.

One may consider this tradition as it is discussed in the pages of Ibn Khaldun's *Muqaddima* I recalled in reading al-Tahtawi above. Ibn Khaldun explains the relation between the sciences of language and the law in the following terms. "Knowledge of them [the sciences of language] is necessary for those bound by the law [al-shar']. For the source of all legal judgments are the book [al-kitab, the Qur'an] and the *sunna*, and they are in the language of the Arabs, and those transmitters who were companions or followers of the Prophet were Arabs, and the explication of problematic passages is from their language."[115] He underlines the disciplines of "lexicography [lugha], *nahu*, *bayan*, and *adab*," and he explains that "the most important of the preceding is *nahu*, because with it the origin of what one intends by means of signs is clarified" (633). Here Ibn Khaldun follows the rhetorical tradition he has inherited. Al-Jahiz explains that "what is at stake in the matter and in the intention towards which the speaker and listener aim is understanding and giving one to understand; for with whatever thing you give one to understand or clarify meaning, that is *bayan*, in that place."[116] *Bayan* is further linked to the presentation or bringing forth into visibility of meaning, *izhar al-ma'na*, through signs, *dalalat*, one of which is the utterance, *lafz*. It "makes the hidden clear, the absent present, and the distant near" (56). Ibn Jinni (932–1002) summarizes the privileging of intention where he defines language as "sounds with which each group expresses their intentions."[117] *Nahu* is the means by way of which such intention is clarified. This clarity is linked to knowing the difference between two moments in a grammatical determination. "One knows the subject of the verb from the object [al-fa'il min al-maf'ul] and the subject from the predicate [al-mubtada' min al-khabar]."[118] Here, *nahu* works to secure the unsettling force of the linguistic utterance in relation to an inheritance that is, and at the same time, ontotheological (it grounds being in something—a Being—outside of time), logocentric (it privileges the voice over writing in clarity of expression), and juridical (it grounds decision in respect to the law). Insofar as *Fi al-shi'r al-jahili* interrupts the production of linguistic sense in Arabic—and one would wish to underline that Husayn tells us that the jahili poetry "does not meaning anything [la tadullu 'ala shay'in]"—it opens, in language, a relation to non-sense, to an aporetical nonbelonging of language in time, which his writing immediately domesticates into the language appropriation protocols of the state.

But language, in Arabic—and as Ibn Khaldun reminds us—is also a practice lodged in the tongue. If the juridical and rhetorical inheritance Husayn engages in *Fi al-shi'r al-jahili* calls for the closure of language in comprehensibility, and in relation to a hierarchy (e.g., speech over writing), and if it commands the installation and sanctioning of meaning in relation to the sentence, *al-jumla*, in Ibn Khaldun language is faculty or habitus, which is given place to through iteration in acts of the tongue. Prior to the knowledge that attains in the clarification of meaning—"One knows the subject of the verb from the object and the subject from the predicate [fa ya'rif al-fa'il min al-maf'ul wa al-mubtada' min al-khabar]"—one will have developed the faculty or habitus, *malaka*, that language is. "Faculties result from the repetition of acts. When an act first takes place, and then one repeats it, it becomes a condition. A condition is an attribute that is not firmly established, but as one increasingly repeats the act, it becomes a faculty [malaka], which is to say, a firmly established attribute."[119] Ibn Khaldun offers the example of a child learning language. "The speaker of Arabic—for as long as the faculty of the Arabic language existed among the Arabs—would hear the speech of the people of his generation, and their styles of address and ways of expressing their intentions. Like a boy who hears the use of words in their correct meanings, and learns them first, and then hears words formed into expressions, and learns them in the same way. He keeps hearing something new from different speakers, each moment, and his use of language repeats until it becomes a faculty, a well-established attribute, and he becomes like one of them" (643). Language, *al-lugha*, and like *adab*, is a practice or mode of comportment learned in relation to passivity: one hears and repeats. *Fi al-sh'ir al-jahili*, inheriting al-Tahtawi, and, differently, al-Bustani, appropriates this passivity, in the temporally discriminating labor of historical reading.

> Science does not require any rules that come to it from the outside because it gives its rules to itself.
>
> MUHAMMAD 'ABID AL-JABRI, *Nahnu wa al-turath*

In 1980 the Moroccan philosopher Muhammad 'Abid al-Jabri published in Beirut a book titled *al-Khitab al-'arabi al-mu'asir*. Al-Jabri's concern is to address "modern and contemporary Arab thought" and its "limits," and this thought is instituted, for al-Jabri, as the repetition of a category of juridical reflection, which it takes itself to have left behind.[120] This text was to serve as a "preface" (15) to the three—and now four—volume project *Naqd al-'aql al-'arabi*, and al-Jabri discusses the category of juridical reflection he places at the center of his project in the opening section of its first volume.[121] There, he offers a reading of juridical analogy in the work of the jurist al-Shafi'i, who is said to have "established a theoretical framework for juridical thought."[122] Al-Jabri explains that "in order for there to be analogy [qiyas] there must be a *khabar* (that is to say, a text) from the Qur'an or the *sunna* which is taken as a ground [asl] or proof, and there must be agreement, in meaning or in correspondence, between the derivative or branch [far'], that is to say, the new, with respect to which judgment is sought, and the ground."[123] Thought, for al-Jabri, has come to take place juridically. "What interests us here is not 'what is thought' but the way in which thought takes place."[124] Analogy works to make legal determination possible when there is not a clear text to secure it, and the persistence of analogy, in al-Jabri's reading, designates thought's time. Al-Jabri presents his argument as a critique of the *nahda*, where, he argues, this understanding of time persists through sediments, *rawasib* (36), of this older mode of thought, and where the colonizing action of Europe remains invisible ("It sets as a condition for the *nahda* the simultaneous absence of the West of yesterday and today" [36]).[125] If in the thought, *fikr*, which is the object of his work, one must turn either to an Arabic-Islamic past or Europe "to prop oneself up upon the remains of the past, recalling and repeating the dream of the *nahda* amid the nightmare of catastrophe," al-Jabri offers what he calls a "critique" of that thought in order that a certain past, and present, may be left behind.[126] What al-Jabri calls "the concepts of modern and contemporary Arab discourse," then, "were—and remain—essential elements of the intellectual cultural structure which predominated before, and which the *nahda* ought to have set out by shattering and erecting another in its place" (198, 40). If, in al-Jabri, the beginning ought to have begun with the installation of a clear line dividing the present from the past, what took place in the *nahda* was the formation of a mode of reflection that thought "not with a post-*inhitat* 'reason' but with a pre-*inhitat* one; not with the 'reason' of tomorrow but that of yesterday" (42).

Al-Jabri underlines a series of temporal distinctions ("the period of *inhitat*, the Arabic-Islamic 'middle ages'" [42]) that mirror those other divisions upon which his work relies, including the separation of the preface (*al-Khitab al-'arabi al-mu'asir*) from what he calls "our essential project" (15): *Naqd al-'aql al-'arabi*. This separation repeats one said to hold between writing and thought ("The writer desires to present a thought or a particular point of view on a particular subject, and this is a discourse") and thought and reason (al-Jabri's project addresses "Arabic thought and the reason which produces it"), just as it relies on the hierarchical subordination of each of the former to each of the latter.[127] "We have taken 'contemporary Arab discourse' as the object of our research" (15), and the designation of this object turns on a cultural interiority ("whether one speaks from within our heritage or from within European thought—or from some place between the two" [59]) and a temporal horizon. He cuts himself off from "modern Arabic thought" and its past—from Butrus al-Bustani ("one of the pioneers in the liberal trend in modern Arabic thought" [28]) to Taha Husayn. "We do not wish to renew here the issue which Taha Husayn provoked before—the issue of the authenticity or lack of authenticity of the jahili literature, and thus of the classical cultural inheritance which is attributed to the pre-Islamic Arabs. The calling of such things into question must take place within limits, and if it does not it loses its methodological justification."[128] Citing these two names in order to offer a critique, he repeats what remains their decisive temporal gesture: the present is a time of *inhitat*. "We have now become certain that the time of modern and contemporary Arab thought is a dead time—or one which may be treated as such."[129] If al-Jabri wishes the *nahda* to have left its past behind, and if he appeals to an event of stark newness—critique is to "begin from zero anew" (196)—he does so by remarking death, to confound the difference between life and death he also presupposes. Depositing a dead body into the prose of philosophy, al-Jabri tells us that his project is new and has left *inhitat* and the modes of reflection that occasion it behind, teaching us to think its relation to that thought—*fikr*—which it takes as its object.

The "sediments" al-Jabri discusses are elaborated in details in the second volume of his project, *Binyat al-'aql al-'arabi*. "Thought bears with it, whether one likes it or not, the traces of what has constituted it, and the marks of the civilizational reality in and through which it is formed."[130] The civilizational reality in and through which thought is formed in Arabic, for al-Jabri, is linked to the writings of al-Shafi'i and his discussion of juridical analogy, *qiyas fiqhi*. "The importance of al-Shafi'i's rules lies neither in their number, nor, even, in their clarity or obscurity" but "in the epistemological orientation which they founded, which has dominated Arab reason for a period of many centuries, and the deep traces of which remain evident until today" (105). The deep traces al-Jabri wishes to unearth are described in *Binyat al-'aql al-'arabi* and turn on the tripartate distinction of *bayan*, *'irfan* (knowledge, which al-Jabri glosses as an Eastern, gnostic, mystical tradition), and *burhan*, demonstration. In what al-Jabri calls "bayan" meaning is subordinated to language, and derivative [far'] to ground [asl], and this subordination is deepened in the tradition he calls "'irfan." For al-Jabri these legacies are unsettled, if still not halted, in *burhan*, and in the writings of Ibn Hazm (994–1064), Ibn Rushd (1126–98), al-Shatibi (d. 1388), and Ibn Khaldun. Ibn Rushd is a privileged figure in al-Jabri,[131] and his writing is to point to "a new philosophical discourse, liberated from theology and its problematics."[132] In the terms of those problematics "God is eternal, absolute, complete, and omnipotent, while the human being is finite and lacking in his actions and attributes" (313), and al-Jabri wishes to leave them behind through critique. But to carry out "a critique of the epistemological foundations upon which the rhetorical epistemological field, since the [second Islamic century], has been based" (551), al-Jabri restages the past, what he calls "the Andalusi cultural project" (530), by appropriating it into the colonial terms I have tried to elaborate. The new is to install "theoretical practice" as "scientific demonstration" (552), and the break this is to remark multiplies others: the present from the past, science from theology, the time of history from the time of repetition. Al-Jabri remarks a Kantian, philological legacy in the colonies, as he offers a critique of the conditions of the possibility of knowledge, and he repeats more than one colonial legacy to do so. If "as always takes place the method is victorious over the problems of its object only if it adapts itself to the nature of the latter" (442), al-Jabri starkly renders those problems, giving us to read the impossibility of the victory for which he calls.

On May 30, 1926, a complaint was presented to the respected Public Prosecutor by al-Shaykh Khalil Hasanayn, a student in the upper division of al-Azhar, in which he accused Taha Husayn, the professor at the Egyptian University, of writing a book titled *Fi al-shi`r al-jahili* which he published for the public, and in which there is a direct attack upon the Qur'an, which attributes fables and lies to this divine and generous book.

MUHAMMAD NUR, *Qarar al-niyaba*

The question for me is above all else a question of the law.

TAWFIQ AL-HAKIM, *Yawmiyyat na'ib fi al-aryaf*

The prosecutor's report (*Qarar al-niyaba*) is a philological text. It reads the reading of poetry in relation to religion (and religions), language (and Semitic languages), literature (and its relation to history and the Qur'an), and the state. I begin with the state. On October 19, 1926, Muhammad Nur began his investigation into Husayn's *Fi al-shi'r al-jahili.* The prosecutor's report was completed on March 30, 1927, and remained out of print until 1972, when it was published in Beirut by the Egyptian novelist and critic Khayri Shalabi. After detailing the complaint presented to the public prosecutor by al-Shaykh Khalil Hasanayn, the report specifies the accusation offered by the Shaykh of al-Azhar. "On 5 June 1926 the Shaykh of al-Azhar sent the Public Prosecutor a letter in which he described a decision taken by the scholars of al-Azhar regarding the book titled *Fi al-shi'r al-jahili* which Taha Husayn, who teaches at the Egyptian University, wrote, in which Husayn openly accused the Qur'an of lying, in which he attacked the Prophet, peace be upon him and his noble descendants, by which he incited the fervor of the religious, and by which he brought what would upset the general public order and call the people to chaos, and demanded that effective, useful legal measures be taken against this attack upon the official religion of the state, and that he be brought to trial."[133] The attacks focused on Husayn's discussion of the qur'anic presentation of Ibrahim and Isma'il in relation to the building of the Ka'ba and his depiction of the relations between Islam, Christianity, and Judaism. The discussion turns on language. Husayn writes that the transmitters agree that prior to Islam the Arabs were divided into two groups: those from Yemen, the Qahtaniyya, who "are Arabs ever since God created them, with the gift of the Arabic language," and those from Hijaz, the 'Adnaniyya, who "learned the language of the Arabs, and so their first language was erased from their minds, and this second, borrowed language was firmly secured in them" (*F*, 37). Husyan wishes to dislodge this understanding, to argue that the poetry attributed to the poets whose lineage was linked to Yemen, including that of the poet Imru' al-Qays ("he is from the tribe of Kinda, that is to say, Qahtan" [44]), did not precede Islam and that they did not speak the Arabic language.

To address this linguistic situation is to speak of Isma'il and Ibrahim, because the transmitters "agree that the lineage of the 'Adnaniyya, who learned Arabic, reaches back to Isma'il the son of Ibrahim" (*F*, 37). The events to which Husayn points remark Hagar's having been expelled to Mecca with Isma'il (Ibn Khaldun writes that "[Ibrahim] took her to Mecca and put her and her son at the site of Zamzam, by a large tree there, and left") and to Isma'il's learning Arabic from Jurhum there.[134] "Isma'il lived with Jurhum in Mecca and married from among them, he learned their language and spoke it, and he became the father of those who came after him of the generations of the Arabs" (45). To secure the time of the ode in relation to language Husayn drops the Semites—and literature. "So we are able to say that the connection between the classical Arabic language spoken by the 'Adnaniyya and the language spoken by the Qahtaniyya in Yemen is like the relation between the Arabic language and *any other known Semitic language* [my emphasis] and that the story of those who spoke Arabic originally and those who took it on later, and Isma'il's learning Arabic from Jurham—all of this is mythical, is of no importance, and there is nothing to learn from it" (*F*, 41). This story, *qissa*, is decisive because it bears upon the building of the Ka'ba. Ibn Khaldun explains, "Then Ibrahim came a third time, God having commanded him to build the house [al-bayt, the Ka'ba], and he commanded Isma'il to help him, so they built it [rafa'uha, raised it up] upon its foundation, and when it was finished people were permitted to make pilgrimage to it."[135] This event is gestured in the Qur'an ("And when Ibrahim, with Isma'il, raised up the foundations of the house: Our Lord, receive this from us; you are the all-hearing, the all-knowing" [Qur'an 2:127]), and in *Fi al-shi'r al-jahili* it appears as "myth." Husayn tells us that it is untrue and that it does not belong to history. It is, for Husayn, literature, and so is the Qur'an. "The Torah speaks to us of Ibrahim and Isma'il, as does the Qur'an. But the occurrence of these two names in the Torah and the Qur'an does not suffice to confirm their historical existence [la yakfi li ithbat wujudahuma al-tarikhiyy]. Not to mention the story which speaks to us of the migration of Isma'il the son of Ibrahim to Mecca and the settling of the originally non-Arabic-speaking Arabs there. We are forced to see in this story [qissa] a certain deception in the affirmation of the connection between the Jews and Arabs, on the one hand, and Islam and Judaism, on the other" (*F*, 38).

The division of literature from history points to the institution of religion—and Semitic religions—as the unity of a divided family. Husayn explains of the affirmation of the connection between Jews and Arabs, and Judaism and Islam, "The oldest period in which this idea could have arisen is that one in which Jews began to settle in the northern Arab countries and build colonies there. We know that violent wars took place between them and the Arabs who were living there, and that they ended with something of peace and quiet, with a treaty and an agreement. So it is not far fetched that this agreement was the origin of this story that made the Jews and the Arabs cousins, especially since each of them had seen that between the two there was something of a resemblance worth mentioning—for each of them were Semites" (*F*, 38–39). The philological family resemblance is a resemblance of religion: divisions of war and the difficulty of temporally and historically placing the jahili odes are brought back to the stable, clear peace of Semitic religion(s). "As for the religious connection it is stable and clear [amma al-silla al-diniyya fa thabita wadiha], because between the Qur'an, the Torah, and the Gospels there is a common subject, image, and intent. Each calls for unity and relies upon a single basis, that one which the Semitic religions share" (39). The reorganization of Islam, Christianity, and Judaism, as religion(s) (*din* [pl. *adyan*]) redesignates the word *din* in philological terms, and in doing so it institutes a discipline—Arabic literature studies—through the privileging of a legible object in language. If the reading of the time of the jahili ode as historical placed in question the organization of language in legibility and sense, the economy of terms remarked in these passages—history, religion, literature, race—reorganizes and domesticates language on a new series of terms. And these terms are—and perhaps one may be forgiven for repeating this yet again, through yet another text—historical. Names, he writes, are to be recognized historically: "But the occurrence of these two names in the Torah and the Qur'an does not suffice to confirm their historical existence."

The new privileging of a legible object in language is appropriated and repeated in the prosecutor's report. In it Nur cites a misquotation in *Fi al-shi'r al-jahili*. He underlines that Husayn misquotes the words he attributed to Abu ʿAmru bin al-ʿAla' to separate Qahtan from ʿAdnan. "What Abu ʿabd Allah ibn Sallam al-Jumhi, the author of *Tabaqat al-shuʿara'*, says about Abu ʿAmru bin al-ʿAla' is, 'The language of Hamir and the most remote parts of Yemen is not our language, nor is their Arabic ours,'" and Nur explains that here Husayn substitutes "nor is their language ours" for "nor is their Arabic ours."[136] He comments as follows: "But what we wish to point out is the error that the author has become accustomed to committing in his research, where he begins with a hypothesis he has imagined and then ends by organizing rules based upon it as if they were stable truths, as he did in the matter of the differences between the language of Hamir and that of ʿAdnan, then in the matter of Ibrahim and Ismaʿil and their immigration to Mecca and building of the Kaʿba: he began his research displaying his doubt and ended with certainty" (74). Nur both responds to the criticisms of *Fi al-shiʿr al-jahili* and cosigns the project Husayn wished to advance in it. According to the prosecutor's report the book is a work of scholarship that treated a clearly delimited object, *adab*, and this is what must guide, Nur underlines, the reading of Husayn's work. And reading requires a securely delimited context and an understanding of intention so that language may be comprehended in time.

> The expressions in which the claimants say that there is an attack upon the Islamic religion appear in the book in the context of speech about topics each of which is linked to the aim for the sake of which the book was written. In order to make a determination regarding this complaint, it is not permissible to tear these expressions [intizaʿ tilka al-ʿibarat] from their place and consider them separately. Rather what is required to arrive to a sound determination is to consider them from where they are, in their place in the book, and to discuss them in the context in which they appear. In that way one may grasp the intention [niyya] of the author with respect to them, and soundly determine his responsibility. (59)

What remains crucial for Nur is that "the aim of the author was not to defame or attack religion, but rather, the expressions that touched upon religion, and which he quoted in certain parts of his book, were quoted for the sake of scientific research, with the assumption that his research required them" (98–99). The analysis Nur presents participates in the reading of *Fi al-shiʿr al-jahili* that has become canonical: it is a text that exemplifies the application of a method in the study of a literary object. Linking reading to intention, authorship, and context, the prosecutor's report inscribes a historical, contextual notion of language in literature studies. In order to make what Nur calls a "sound determination" with respect to Husayn's case what is required is that words not be torn from their context ("it is not permissible to tear these expressions from their place [la yajuz intiza' tilka al-'ibarat min mawdi'iha]"), and the prosecutor's report, then, reenacts the instituting event Husayn's text performs. If literature studies labors, in Husayn, to "repeatedly demarcate the boundary in relation to which language and religion could be constituted," this labor also stalls and interrupts itself, in Husayn and elsewhere.[137] And the printed text of *Fi al-shi'r al-jahili*, and like language, had therefore to be domesticated and incorporated into the interior of the state. Ahmad Lutfi al-Sayyed, Husayn's mentor and the rector of the university, purchased at Husayn's request all of the extant copies and had them placed in the university storerooms "sealed with red wax."[138] If *Fi al-shi'r al-jahili* produced a crisis in reading, the prosecutor's report marks the intervention of the state in the appropriation of linguistic disruption and non-sense—a gesture that mirrors the management of populations and what, in the words of the shaykh of al-Azhar, "would upset the general public order and call the people to chaos."

CITATION II

True literature deserving of the name is eternal, whatever matters or temporal events have befallen its authors or their environment. This is the secret which explains why the literary and artistic heritage is cherished by cultured humanity: it portrays beauty to them. And beauty is eternal, untouched by death.

TAHA HUSAYN, *Khisam wa naqd*

"Anything one says about Taha Husayn ought to begin with his famous book *al-Ayyam*," including, and if not solely, the reading of *Fi al-shi'r al-jahili*.[139] The separation of the one from the other—of *al-Ayyam* from *Fi al-shi'r al-jahili*—mirrors the many divisions Husayn was compelled to install in his writing, and as the writing of an Arabic literary object. The installation of literature studies in Husayn, then, works to separate life from death, literary criticism from autobiography, and language from loss. Yet if in Husayn's autobiographical *al-Ayyam* (Cairo, 1926–27 [1929]), "the center of this book" is the story of a "tireless struggle for knowledge," it is a book that relates knowledge to time and death.[140] Telling the story of a blind child who comes to study at al-Azhar in Cairo, and, later, the Egyptian University and the Sorbonne, it calls for a movement from simplicity ("The country people, their old men, youth, young men and women, have a particular mentality in which is naïve simplicity, mysticism and ignorance") and repetition ("It [the four years I had spent at the Azhar] was an unchanging monotonous life, nothing new from the time of the beginning of the academic year until its end") to reason, science, modernity, and Europe.[141] If it is a text of *Bildung* in the colonies, where the experience of reading is to give place to the emergence of an autonomous subject in language, this experience and its coherency is confounded through the iteration of a relation to death and loss, where autobiography occurs as the writing of the loss of another who has died, and of a language said to be no more.[142] The understanding of time privileged in *Fi al-shi'r al-jahili* is preserved from Husayn's 1918 dissertation on Ibn Khaldun, written in French at the Sorbonne under the direction of Emile Durkheim, to the rewriting and republication of *Fi al-shi'r al-jahili* as *Fi al-adab al-jahili* (Cairo, 1927), in *Mustaqbal al-thaqafa fi Misr* (Cairo, 1938) ("Our intellectual life, irrespective of the way in which it appears, is purely European," Husayn writes there), and if also elsewhere.[143]

The dissertation was to explicate the "social philosophy" of Ibn Khaldun, but if the historian's intention had been "to explain human history in the widest sense of the term, and in this his social thought far surpassed that of Aristotle and Plato" (*IK*, 56), he failed to install sociology as a science. Husayn focuses on Ibn Khaldun's *Muqaddima*, the first volume of *Kitab al-'ibar*, and like the village from which Husayn came it shared in a simplicity it was not able to leave behind. "We are surprised when we compare his writing about history [the later volumes of *Kitab al-'ibar*] with the introduction to this book [the *Muqaddima*]. For in the book of history Ibn Khaldun seems to us to be the simple Arab transmitter who reports everything without stopping to examine or scrutinize the matter, whereas when you read the *Muqaddima* you think that there is going to be a real revolution in historical research" (35). Ibn Khaldun's simplicity turns on his not checking sources. History, in this text of Husayn's, is understood as a discipline founded on philological, source-based, text criticism ("the aim of history as we understand it today is to determine the events of the past based upon sources" [48]), and this is something that, for Husayn, appears absent in Ibn Khaldun. Ibn Khaldun is on the side of disorder and lack of clarity ("the *Muqaddima*, as we have remarked, is not an example of clear, ordered research" [84]), and this is because, for Husayn, it was not possible for sociology to become a science with a distinct object at the time in which Ibn Khaldun lived, because fourteenth-century North Africa was not—and for Husayn, not yet—Europe. It was not a society, and one could not study it—or, one could not study it scientifically. Husayn explains that "with the exception of the first Islamic century,"

> Islamic society does not present to us a social force. For the caliphs, kings, and rulers always (apparently without doubt) governed and administered the Islamic world as they saw fit. If we have in reality today come to see in society something truly autonomous, that has taken place only following the great advancement that a strong democratic movement brought to European societies in the modern period. And this movement has never existed in the East and it does not exist there in our time. (61)

Husayn's reading works to appropriate and manage Ibn Khaldun. Husayn keeps criticizing him, remarking that the *Muqaddima* contains errors ("despite the fact that he also commits many errors" [*IK*, 61]) and repetition (*tikrar*) (67), only to explain that Ibn Khaldun invented something new. "Ibn Khaldun was the first philosopher to take society as the object of an autonomous science" (58), but Husayn subordinates this autonomy to history. He explains of what he calls "sociological research," "there is no justification for its existence other than the clarification and verification [tahqiq; also, "confirmation"] of historical events. It is a supplementary science. The study of society does not lead to results of any value in themselves, which convince the mind that is interested in them" (59).

Yet this reflection on time is also undermined in *Fi al-shi'r al-jahili*, even as it is repeated in later Arabic critical, theoretical writing, some of which I have considered here (in Adunis, Darraj, and al-Jabri). I underscore that this understanding of time is undermined to point to the institutional dimension of literary formations: literary institutions must keep instituting themselves, their time is a time of repetition, a time that confounds the historical understanding of language, which those institutions also privilege. The traces of this are marked in the opening pages of the 1927 edition of *Fi al-shi'r al-jahili*, which Husayn titled *Fi al-adab al-jahili* (On Jahili Literature). The substitution of the word *shi'r* with the word *adab* absorbs the former (poetry) into the newly instituted understanding and practice of the latter (literature). As literature, *adab*, and if also *shi'r*, is to be on the side of life, breath, and movement rather than death and stillness. And death is to be left behind through the institution of the Egyptian University, which in *al-Ayyam* is a site of liberation from confusion and repetition, from words without sense. "It took him from the confined, confused atmosphere of al-Azhar and of Hawsh 'Atta and Darb al-Jamamiz, to another that was vast and unlimited, which allowed him to fill his lungs with fresh air on his way to and from the university, and to fill his mind with open knowledge not bound by the timidity of the Azhar professors in their lecturing, nor ruined by all of the back and forth citation and arguments about this word and that."[144] In "life," "breath," and the mind's openness to knowledge ("to fill his mind with open knowledge"), what had appeared as the incompetence of his teacher at the village school, his repeated attempts to memorize the Qur'an, and the contradictions of learned men in the countryside (74/52), is to be buried, lodged in the past.

In *Fi al-adab al-jahili* Husayn writes:

> If our schools remain as they are, and literature in them remains bound by these chains and shackles, monopolized by this group that is able neither to renew nor to enliven, but that is compelled by its nature to quiet and stillness—and I almost said the word death—Arabic literature will not be able to take from life the share that it is able, and the Arabic language will not be able to take its share in strength, or to become a living, scientific language in the true sense of the term.[145]

Science, if also freedom, belongs to the time of life. It is a time that works to appropriate the ease of youth ("But what comes more easily than the laughter of youth?") and the simplicity of the countryside.[146] The installation of literature studies "without confinement or constraint," where "we must be bound by nothing, and submit to nothing, other than the methods of scientific research," remarks a mournful, if scholarly, gesture in the desire to install firm boundaries, including the boundary between life and death, and, in *Fi al-shi'r al-jahili*, what came before and after Islam.[147] The installation of such boundaries points to an unfinished relation to mourning, in the loss of a brother and the death of a sister, each of which is narrated in *al-Ayyam*. The work of the scholar repeats these losses in acts of compulsive iteration. "What a terrible hour it was, that third hour of Thursday the twenty-first of August 1902,"[148] Husayn wrote, and his marking the date of his brother's death points to that of his sister, "who was four years old and the youngest of the children in the family" (98/70). If Husayn insists on the separation of life from literary criticism, the *bios* of autobiography and that *dhat* of *al-sira al-dhatiyya* from *naqd*, and the present from "the period of intellectual and political stagnation" that preceded it, his text also calls upon us to read these relations, telling us that the iteration of loss gives place to and stalls the institution of a literary object.[149] If, as 'Abd al-Muhsin Taha Badr has written, "we cannot consider the book *al-Ayyam* merely an autobiography,"[150] this is because to be itself language speaks to us in the voice of another, as the labor of literature studies points to a desire to bury something or someone, and "to do away with" what Husayn also called "myths and illusions."[151] Here, autobiography remarks a confounding of the time of life it is said to confirm, to take place as what I read in chapter 3, in relation to the novelistic writing of Elias Khoury, as allothanatography, a writing of the self as the writing of a relation to others and to death.

§

The installation of a colonial order in language, in Husayn, stalls and interrupts itself. "And you see that I'm not being excessive when I demand, beginning right now, of those who are not able to free themselves of the old and to do away with the shackles of emotion and desire when they read science or write about it, that they not read these chapters. For they will only benefit from reading them after they have become truly free" (*F*, 26). To read freely is already to have the left the shackles of the past behind, but it is also to read in relation to that past and one's desire to have compelled it to appear as having passed. If Butrus al-Bustani reads language in relation to a sociality of form where form is thought as a locus for the domestication of language and politics—where the members of the social and political body are to form "a single substance"—and if this domestication is mirrored, in al-Bustani, in a mournful historicism, in Husayn a free subject of language is promised through the institution of reading.[152] This institution, in al-Shidyaq, and in *al-Saq 'ala al-saq*, is at once presupposed and given to be read as an event of temporal excess. *Al-Saq 'ala al-saq* inherits the reading practice of As'ad al-Shidyaq, who couldn't stop reading, like al-Fariyaq, as it gives us to read a displacement and an interruption of social and political form, where reading occurs as an event of permanent interruption. I have argued in this chapter that philology is a colonial, Orientalist discipline, which privileges an originary sense of language, and I have argued that it is also something else. Philology points to another, more originary relation to language, where language already pauses, where it displaces itself from itself, and where its time is a time of interruption—an understanding of language one is taught to read in *al-Saq ʿala al-saq*. In this understanding of language—and philology ("Philology: in the pause of language")—language may not be said to have been owned, or to have been the language of a self.[153] "The idea of philology, like the idea of language, forbids us from regarding them as something had" (25), Hamacher also wites. That language may not be said to have been owned means that it does not belong to the institutions that emerge to domesticate it. Language is inappropriable into a "language of propositions" ("Propositional language is the medium and object of ontology, as well as of all the epistemic disciplines under its direction" [26]). Yet philology also comes to forget itself in order to morph into "logology," where it occurs as "the study of language, erudition, and finally as the scientific method of dealing with linguistic, in particular literary, documents" (26). The institution of literature studies as I have sought to discuss it, through Husayn's *Fi al-shiʿr al-jahili*, is a proliferation and interruption of reading as a logological practice. To read such a practice—to read the formation of literary institutions, and to consider that formation in its relation to poetic statement—would be to read philologically, it would be to learn that reading is to take place slowly, "for philology is that venerable art which demands of its followers one thing above all: to step aside, to take time, to become still, to become slow."[154]

Excursus: *Names*

In a wooden box, inlaid with pearl, covered in marble, he held fast to a package of letters, those which his grandfather had sent and which took months to arrive. Letters written in Hebrew characters but expressing themselves in Judeo-Arabic. Letters which came from a distance, from far away, filled with affection, with vigilant, restless, tenderness. Letters cast like a bottle at sea; but no one would be able to be certain that they would arrive safely to port.

EDMOND AMRAN EL MALEH, *Mille ans, un jour*

The safe arrival of letters sent—of missives offered and of language given—is a matter upon which judgment must remain suspended. Language in Edmond Amran El Maleh's *Mille ans, un jour* (Paris, 1986) partakes in a certain errance. It withdraws from that space said to have remained peacefully within the bounds secured by context and reference. If what *Mille ans, un jour* relates is the story of Nessim, who "according to tradition, bore the name of his grandfather" (*MA*, 14), this name bears a relation to mourning and loss. Its repetition mirrors that of the letters written in Hebrew characters to which Nessim repeatedly returns. If what has been lost is irretrievably remote, if what has been lost is no longer, this remoteness reiterates the distance that opens between Nessim and his name. "From where has this name surged forth? From the Bible, from biblical times! It appears, rolling across one's lips, calm, soothing. It comes, like an announcement, bearing all kinds of things. To a stormy and tormented environment, it offers welcome, a serene refuge" (9–10). The welcome El Maleh's text offers, the surprise that occasions the surging forth of the name, speaks to us of something other than what takes place, where "the past and the future fuse in the same incandescence" (10). It disrupts the time of speech to gesture to a relation to more than one other, and more than one language, and which inscribes itself upon language prior to any comportment or intention. And names, that of Nessim and of others, speak to us of loss, dividing El Maleh's language across one thousand years that join and cut on a single day.

One waits for the book of this Lebanon war, this war about which one does not know if one may name it in this way, if there is a way of naming it at all.

EDMOND AMRAN EL MALEH, *Jean Genet: Le captif amoureux*

The days that gather and divide in *Mille ans, un jour* form a clot. "The fluidity of past days, days which resemble each other, until the moment at which a clot of blood forms" (*MA*, 16). El Maleh names this wound using an Arabic word, and his text then bears a relation to the Arabic texts I study in this book, and to the older legacies incribed in those texts. "A tear, line of fracture, *inshiqaq*. Nessim repeated the word in Arabic because Moha Aït Wattas was there before him" (18). But if Moha Aït Wattas stood before Nessim, he did so like the word *inshiqaq* he repeated, and like the return of a ghost from a past one will never have left behind. "He thought of him at that instant, of their recent conversation in Marakesh while waiting for a common friend. He returned to him pushed by a torrential force of voices, of faces. Moha was there, before him, each of them in place on the veranda before a tray of glasses of tea, a plate of *féquas*—homemade biscuits scented with anise" (18). The return of Moha, like Nessim's return to the letters of his grandfather, points to a return of and to the Arabic language. "Moha, the old rebel who had left prison, punished for eight years for his oppositional opinions. Moha spoke. Nessim listened to his running words. The story knotted at its origins. It came, hurling itself. It grew from others to form the rising waters of an overflowing *'oud*. Moha spoke slowly, like a long walk, speech entirely interior, without accident, without rupture, without affect—the resonance, the vibration of the string of a *guenbri*, a song at the birth of memory" (18–19). This song points to the rupture of a friendship ("His neighbor, his friend, it was of him that Moha spoke. They were both from Talha, a Berber village in the Anti-Atlas mountains. He evoked the communal life, kneaded into the land. That red wall encircled by white lime on the windows of communal residences. He spoke of the detail of the religious festivals, of giving and exchange, the same love songs, the same dances, the explosion of the voice of the celebration—deep and beautiful" [19]) and to El Maleh's break with the Moroccan Communist Party in 1959, in which he had been an active militant, to write and teach.[1] "Moha spoke soberly now, a kind of suspension that bordered on fatality. He spoke of his meeting with Isaac. He spoke of him with extraordinary precision: It was a Wednesday. He, Moha, had just arrived at Casablanca. It was 1953, and he had come to join the resistance groups, the *fida'iyyin.* It was a decisive moment in the anticolonial struggle" (*MA*, 19). Depositing a date, 1953, into this text of literary prose, language asks us to attend to its losses. The writing of a break, *inshiqaq*, is also a writing of language's declining a final break with more than one past, and with more than one language, even as Isaac had come, unlike Moha, only in order to close off relations and to leave. When Moha asks Isaac if this is so Isaac falls silent, and so, too, does Moha; Moha's words, his recalling to Nessim that he had seen Isaac, close. This doubled falling silent—Moha's muteness repeats that of Isaac, mirroring and interrupting it—points to the line of fracture, "la ligne de fracture" (19), that generates the divided origin of *Mille ans, un jour.* It points to a relation to loss, and to the Arabic language, inscribed in names. I turn to read the relation of language to names in El Maleh here.

§

El Maleh asks us to attend to names, and I read *Mille ans, un jour* in relation to two: that of a friend, Ahmed Cherkaoui, a painter who died at the age of thirty-seven, and Hamad, the name of Palestinian child killed at Sabra and Shatila in 1982. One is asked to read names in this text because it underlines that Nessim bears the name of his grandfather, and this repetition of names is intensified in Nessim's returning to his grandfather's letters. "The envelopes, a little creased, yellowed more often than not, sometimes a stamp or a postmark, were, for him, the only opening to the pages of a moving epic. Nessim, dreamy, meditative, during these June days, like the other moments of his life, took in his hand one of the letters—dated Cairo, 1880!" (*MA*, 11). The measure of the distance marked by this letter is impossible to take, and to gain specificity with respect to it one must compare. "But one must, in order to be sure of it, compare the Jewish and Christian calendars" (11). This passage marks an imperative, and it asks us to trace the iteration of bereaved utterance in *Mille ans, un jour.* It asks us to attend to its dates, to address its wounds, the cuts and fractures, *inshiqaqat*, that mark its language. In *Mille ans, un jour*, language, in the words of Muhammad Barrada, is "plural language," and writing is already "digression," yielding to another.[2] This yielding, I have begun to argue, is mirrored in Nessim's returning to and rereading his grandfather's letters. The letter Nessim's hand touched and that he had taken out of the wooden box was "one of those he loved to read and reread with emotion, without doubt because it was charged with so many evocations, and because on those days in particular they awoke, suddenly, profound resonances" (*MA*, 11). The return trip of these letters is anything but certain, and they must pass a series of places—Alexandria, Cairo, Tangiers—El Maleh names. Like in the poetry of Mahmoud Darwish, the naming of place shares in a mournful register, to gesture to the inscription of loss on the body of the letter and the letter of language. But the naming of place is also expansive, in excess of the form of the colonial state, to give language to be read differently.

> To reach its destination this letter cleared many obstacles. It took on the burden of its long wait, which became a festival of joy and happiness the day it finally arrived. From Alexandria to Tangiers, entrusted to the care of a ship's captain who wanted to be charged with it and placed it upon its arrival with a merchant from Tangier who did business with a house in Cairo. But once there it had to be entrusted to the postal service, which was organized at that time by the German consulate. The letters were given to couriers, *reqqas*, who ran from village to village, would meet halfway after having covered more than forty kilometers on a journey to exchange letters, take a night to rest, and set out again at dawn. (11–12)

The expansive geography the letter's itinerary remarks does not point to a moment prior to European colonialism—("But once there it had to be entrusted to the postal service, which was organized at the time by the German consulate")—nor does it suggest that colonial violence may simply be transcended or left behind. The exigencies the letter faced, as it passed over sea and from hand to hand, do not come to the letter, or to language, from an outside to impinge upon it as if they were an empirical accident. The letter's having been sent marks it from the beginning in relation to repetition and repeatability: the repetition of names, and the giving of my name as the name of another who has died. "Nessim, according to tradition, bore the name of his grandfather. The force of a name, of an untamable river, gushing from unknown sources, clearing victoriously the torments of its journeys, its sovereign light assuring the dark tumult of tossed waters" (14). But if the name participates in a sovereignty ("its sovereign light"), it also, immediately, splits. "Nessim—was it him or his grandfather who entered like a child who comes to be born on that legendary dawn, the high capital of a millennial memory. Safad, Tiberius, Jerusalem—the letters crowded upon the wooden box whose scent was alive, still green, looking after an intimate presence" (14–15). And the letters that had been inscribed upon the wooden box come to life. "The letters come to life, opening to the sky, to faces, bearing within their folds the beauty of women, the friendship of speech, the burning flame of faith, amusement, astonished exposure, the maturity of wisdom, the flavor of fruit, the softness of a garment gathered, waiting, surrounded by a dream, by a body, Bethsheba, Judith, Sarah" (15). If the letters point to life, what is given is neither a vitalism nor a genetic understanding of time. It is as if the box to which Nessim returns, at which he lingers, feeling the thickness of the aging paper of the letters it holds, marks the retention of more than one relation to loss.

> The letters follow the mad flight of birds, the enchantment of fountains in the gardens of Paradise, filled with the immense rumor of people tossed into infinite space, in the fire of a search thirsty for the absolute, trembling beneath the anger of the Eternal! The letters opened, the high mountains parted, Nessim trembled, lowered his head in submission, dazzled. He advanced, with a step heavy with the weight of the world. He advanced as if he held the entire earth in his hand. (15)

The letters he touches are thick. He describes the paper ("With his pointed fingers, Nessim felt the dull and pat thickness of the paper of the letters and the envelopes" [15]), and he returns, and remarks his return, to the letters. "He took, that morning, the wooden box inlaid in pearl. The live scent of greens overtook him, enveloped his entire body. He trembled, dazzled. What was he looking for in those letters which he knew by heart and to which he constantly returned?" (16). The return to the letters gestures to a physical relation to the paper on which they had been written: he touched the paper with his hand and felt its thickness, pointing also to a relation to language, and to a materiality and a temporality of language, where "the name calls upon the name" (19).

> To be named—even if the name-giver is godlike and saintly—perhaps always brings with it a presentiment of mourning.
>
> WALTER BENJAMIN, *Ursprung des deutschen Trauerspiels*

Reading Walter Benjamin, here and elsewhere, is among those rare things which immediately, imperatively stops you, forcing you to abandon well-known paths.

EDMOND AMRAN EL MALEH, *Lettres à moi-même*

This leaves, in a hollow, a certain wound.

EDMOND AMRAN EL MALEH, *Entretiens*

Taking the wooden box in his hand routes Nessim, like the letters he had read and reread and whose trajectory he traced, to a burial site and to a site of ruin, to Paris, Essaouira, Beirut, and, finally, to Sabra and Shatila, and to June 1982. This gesture points to the first lines of *Mille ans, un jour* and "The Lebanon war! June days, summer days beneath a Parisian sky, hot, torn by a stormy violence. The Lebanon war! Did it really take place!" (*MA*, 9). The unsettling of place, *lieu*, in the text's opening lines points to the immeasurable comparison for which El Maleh's writing calls. Words appear without context or attribution, to erupt onto the page leaving one with nothing but the words of another, already sent and underway. It is as if the beginning opens, already, in response, marking a loss. This loss points to a friend, Ahmed Cherkaoui, who died suddenly in 1967. Cherkaoui's work has been collected in two volumes—*La peinture de Ahmed Cherkaoui* (Casablanca, 1976) and *Ahmed Cherkaoui: La passion du sign* (Paris, 1996)—and each contains an essay, "Les pierres blanches," contributed by El Maleh.[3] The opening page of the essay situates the work in relation to life and biography.

> One cannot summarize a life and say that a particular event was decisive in the awakening of a vocation, in the formation and development of a body of work. Biography would be of slight importance did it not provide more than one point whereby a body of work may be situated and studied. Thus if chance, his father's ruin, led Ahmed Cherkaoui to learn a trade, calligraphy, if desire agreed with necessity, this is not an indifferent biographical detail. It is added to others to make the story of a life. What was only a fortuitous circumstance changes, it is charged with meaning, to become a decisive factor in the unfolding of a body of work.[4]

Writing about Cherkaoui, for El Maleh, recalls the biographical and the word *life*. Pointing to the time of life and death in the elaboration of the work, and asking us not to be indifferent to it, El Maleh teaches us to listen to the place of Cherkaoui's work in his own. Calling attention to life and death, and to loss and language, El Maleh asks us to listen to the bereaved quality of his own prose. Reading Cherkaoui in "Les pierres blanches" El Maleh points to the dimensions of inheritance given in the practice of Arabic calligraphy ("It is firstly a sacred kind of writing, and we must not forget for a single moment its place of origin, the Qur'an" [35]), and in calligraphic form. "We are therefore in the presence of a dynamic structure, not a static one, a matrix generating a whole combination of forms" (39), El Maleh writes. In the calligraphic practice El Maleh is reading "any element may be developed in any direction whatsoever," "there is neither beginning nor end," and, further, "no motif has its end or logical limit in itself" (39). The reading El Maleh pursues asks whether painting may be said to be a "universal tongue" ("to paint would then be to handle a universal tongue" [47]), and El Maleh elaborates in terms of life, mourning, colonialism, and language. "The power exerted by colonial domination is not confined to force of arms, as is too summarily and superficially assumed" (33), El Maleh writes early in the essay, and to read this exertion El Maleh compares painting to language, drawing an analogy between the two. "In comparison with a Maghrebi writer using French, the painter would seem to enjoy a privileged position of almost complete freedom. The writer is tied to the French language, which defines a culture with specific habits of feeling and thought" (45). Yet the events of "life" which touch upon language, and painting, relate, El Maleh writes, to Cherkaoui's mother ("we may not treat with indifference the love Ahmed Cherkaoui had for his mother, who died when he was still a child" [50]) and his father, who El Maleh describes as a figure of authority through whom "the voice of the Qur'an resounded" ("It was through him that the voice of the Qur'an resounded and he transmitted a family mystical tradition linked to an ancestor, Muhammad Cherki, whose Sufi experience is well known and has been preserved" [51]). El Maleh's reading then points to a doubling of obligation (the death of the mother, the father) which further multiplies (in relation to the Qur'an and "a family mystical tradition") complicating the "almost complete freedom" of which he writes. The analogy between painting and language is further linked to Cherkaoui's training at the École des Métiers d'Art in Paris, where he had earned a diploma in 1959, and to labor, effort, practice, and meditation. "These were years of slow, laborious effort to master his craft as a painter, but also and above all constant meditation on painting, against a background of the Moroccan reality which was the very stuff of his life" (43–45).

Calling attention to the matter of painting and its practice, it is as if in writing of Cherkaoui El Maleh is writing of himself, and it is as if in *Mille ans, un jour* what is given to be read is a devastated relation to the loss of a friend. The confounding of the time of the "author" is mirrored in the interrupted time of narration. "That day, the morning on which he took the wooden box in this hands, Nessim felt in a strange state, a sense of absence where everything, for him, collapsed, without sense, with the fatality of something completed, a disquiet at once passive and lucid. Where was he, on those days, that June day, since a single one counted for all? In Paris, or in that distant Essaouira—distant because it was enveloped in a time without measure, distant and nevertheless so close?" (*MA*, 21). Writing of distance, El Maleh routes Nessim to the old Jewish cemetery, the burial of Nessim's grandfather, Beirut, and the Aramaic word *kaddish*. "*Kaddish, kaddish!* Nessim surprised himself, saying this word, but he couldn't say the prayer in its entirety. *Kaddish*, the prayer for the dead, for dead children. He couldn't say the prayer—he had never thought of doing it. He didn't know Hebrew, just a few formulas learned by heart for his bar mitzvah. Rudiments quickly forgotten" (23). The name of the prayer for the dead repeats as he looks into the eyes of a child. "Disconcerted, set in his place, without reaction, Nessim took in his hand the newspaper that he had come to buy. There, in all of the breadth of the first page, there, the look of the burned child, there, on the counter, among the magazines, illustrated in loud colors, the faces of all of the greats of the world, pornographic scenes crying with the grotesque, in Arabic, in French, stupidity and vulgarity, of things, of people," "He was alone before the burned child, at a scene of ruins, an anguished cry without echo, the dust had covered and eaten away at the bodies, the last signs of life. He looked at the burned child who, now, also looked at him" (24). The child burned by an Israeli phosphorous bomb in Beirut, 1982, returns him to "kaddish." "*Kaddish, kaddish*, the prayer for the dead child. Absurd! For him, who does not know how to pray, a few quick forgotten words. For him, who had never set foot in a synagogue! If, even so, perhaps three or four times when he was a youth, the Yom Kippur, in order to greet his father at the moment at which one would hear the shofar, the emotional moment which marked the end of the fast" (25). The words repeat, marking the name of more than one other who has died.

> *Kaddish, kaddish!* The murmuring, the rustling of lips, all of the bodies bowing in prayer, all of the bodies praying. *Kaddish!* Resonances,

> spacing, solemn silence before his eyes, his hesitant steps, the vision of a charred land, Beirut, he was there, that man, he roamed, walked upright among the ruins, the familiar layout of streets, the tenderness that once appeared in the windows, a light shiver, the down of a bird still warm after its death, life had still not abandoned these places, he recognized children's toys, one would say, something that survived a star that had exploded; he advanced, mastered his steps, the story knotted at that enclave, a rock, the waves split and it was drowned beneath them. *Kaddish, kaddish!* The resounding noise, a muffled burst, the chant, the prayer for the dead child, the shofar in stifled, sharp cascades climbed in immense echoes, a quickened breath announcing the end of time, thousands of heads covered in prayer shawls of white silk with blue stripes, still impregnated with the odor of mothballs, among those who pray only one time during the year. An immense crowd praying with fervor and contrition. The mourning of light. (26–27)

And loss—here and elsewhere—is gestured in iteration.

> He repeated the word 'kaddish' like a slow and solemn meditation, because he suffered a desire for silence, for respect, fervor in that love that didn't stop growing within him for that child. A Hebrew word for the Arab child, the pain knotted in itself. (30)

§

The giving of names is mournful, because it points to the death of the one named, and to the afterlife of the name following death. "Nessim, a name, condensation dense with energy. A true name through which time, light and speech come, the irruption of a singular pain" (*MA*, 140). This pain points to the name of the Palestinian child, Hamad, into whose eyes Nessim had looked. "Truth crying out, flesh and blood: a body has gushed from the canvas of the painter and all of space denies time and its procession of deceitful appearances. Hamad! The body of the burned child perforates space, denies time" (140). This cry, encrypting a relation to Cherkaoui and his death ("a body gushed from the canvas of the painter"), does not recoil into a self but gives us to read the disarticulation of the self in another, a "sustained dispossession of this I," an "interruption at the heart of the ipseity that I am."[5] The cry of Majid echoes that of Hamad ("The beautiful summer which in this cursed month of June had dared to stain the sun with innocent blood, flesh torn by a sure science. Disfigured bodies which drowned the light in mourning, ransacked the garden, opened the veins of hatred. Burned with napalm, phosphorus:

the child, Hamad! A long, tearing cry of pain echoing of that of Majid!" [*MA*, 137]), even as it ciphers "those things one does not say, upon which one's heart closes like a sacred coffin" (172). The coffin is already "truth crying out" (140), and it points, like Hamad, to "this cry lost in the silence of the desert" (100)—and to "Beirut—a reality of flesh and blood!" (140).

In an untitled painting dated 1967, and which appears as a frontispiece to this book, the canvas is cut by a downward-running line. The line divides, just off the center of the canvas, to give two further downward-running lines, asymmetrically diverging from the first. Each of these two lines curves, asymmetrically, one to the right and the other to the left, drawing one's eye to the top of the canvas and the curved line which opens out from the "original" line. The painting may be read as a series of four sections, carved out through these lines, yet each is interrupted, open to an outside, and cut into by further strokes of the paintbrush. The canvas draws the eye to what may be a self-portrait in profile overlaid through the four sections. The openings created through the fractured lines of the canvas reiterate that self-portrait, and mouths open, crying out. If this painting is a form of self-portraiture, then, it is one where the "self" is already overlaid with others. It is one where the mouth that opens gives, as its own voice, the voice of more than one other. And this self-portrait, if that is what it is, splits, it is riven by cutting lines, pointing to the word *inshiqaq* to which I have drawn attention in El Maleh. This splitting or cutting draws the eye toward the openings in the canvas—there is no section of it that is closed off—giving place to a movement that presses upward, toward the sky. Each brush stroke is displaced, suggesting a multiplication that moves outward, where the time of the image, if also language, "prevents it from ever being simply itself," to recall, as Eduardo Cadava has written, "the deaths and losses for which we remain, still today, responsible."[6] Here, the "subject" of the painting withdraws, giving it to be read in relation to the relations it asks us to read, where the consideration of painting, and of its relation to written language, cannot occasion "the act of a comprehension that begins by taking hold of something, by laying one's hands on something."[7] In the reading he offers of Cherkaoui, El Maleh wrote of the relation between calligraphy and the Qur'an ("the art of calligraphy participates in an act of divine creation").[8] If in an older Arabic-Islamic inheritance, which I considered in chapter 1 in relation to Adunis, the Qur'an is *asl*—root or ground—in Cherkaoui this root is already plural. "The root takes leave of itself, to vibrate in the wind," Abdelkabir Khatibi has written of Cherkaoui in an essay that came to be incorporated into *Maghreb pluriel* (Paris, 1983).[9] If El Maleh cites Cherkaoui to give place to his writing, and if this writing may then be said to be called "a structureless poetic composition," this is to render this writing as the writing of another, as the citation of the painting of Ahmed Cherkaoui.[10] Writing, in El Maleh, is "diffuse, without form," yet it gives "a poetics of lucidity," which teaches a relation to death and writing.[11] Writing, in El Maleh, borrows calligraphic practice to remark "the weight of a past that is not yet over," as it places itself in debt, interrupting the form of the work to which language is also constrained.[12]

When on his journeys during June he read the letters of his grandfather, these letters which came from elsewhere, an intimate correspondence had already taken shape within him. He felt as if he were on the point of a new departure, and he had already written to himself, to himself and to another at the same time. And, in that open space, incitement to move, toward the density of a look, which was destroyed and reborn in the ashes at each moment

EDMOND AMRAN EL MALEH, *Mille ans, un jour*

The story told in *Mille ans, un jour* is already, itself, more than one. It is the story of Nessim, Moha Aït Wattas, Hamid, Ruben, Ari, and Majid, if also of Nessim's grandfather. Ari wrote to Nessim, "*Alef*, a pure breath, the point of indifference of all speech. *Yod*, 'the brilliant source,' *ot*, *otiyot*, letters of the alphabet, writing and discourse. 'The Torah was originally written with black fire upon white fire,' Nahmanides said. Writing and discourse in language's permanent act of creation which is present in all things" (*MA*, 140). This letter both replaces and repeats, it takes the place of without taking the place of Nessim's grandfather's letters. "*Alef*, but the letter was not written in Hebrew characters, in Hebrew. It was Ari who wrote to Nessim at great length and in French. An envelope without address, crumpled, which Nessim had slipped into his pocket, which he felt in order to assure himself that he had not lost it" (140). The letter from Ari, "a distant cousin of Ruben" (141), points to the context of Jewish life in North Africa following the colonization of Palestine. "He explored the folds of the envelopes with his fingers. Eager, impatient, he wanted to know what was happening in the heads of people there, in Tel Aviv, in Jerusalem, in Israel—this name hardly uttered here, encircled in black writing" (140–41). The relation to Ari, to whom I shall turn, is routed through his cousin Ruben. Reading and rereading the letter from Ari, whose name was not Ari ("Guy, that was his name! That obsession of families at the time of the Protectorate to give Christian names to their children!" [141]), Nessim thinks of Ruben. "Nessim grew sad. With tears in his eyes he thought of Ruben, of his laugh, of his friendship, of his generous affection. Does this child, this boy, know what has happened? Ruben gave in to the general movement. He also decided to leave. He sold his furniture, his belongings, confident that he would begin a new life. He was there with the parents of friends, with official support, since he had until that time contributed to the managing and editing of the Zionist journal, and had maintained a quasi-correspondence with the great names—Ben Gurion, Golda Meir, and many others" (141). Remarking a correspondence with names, this text underscores a relation between language, mourning, and the political reorganization of states. The unsettled errance of language is drawn into its domestication in the state form, in Ruben's expectation that he would be well received in the "promised land."

> Without being militant—the least in the world—he thought that the doors of the promised land were going to open grandly before him and that he would be welcomed as a friend, a person of importance. Then that cruel disillusion, the drama. Nessim thought of him with an inexpressible sadness. The arrival in Tel Aviv, the anonymity, the silence of all of those upon whom he believed he could count, the contemptuous bureaucracy. He was an Arab before everything—Jew or not—old and unusable. Ruben, without resources, living in shelters among the beggars, all of this debris of the Oriental communities. All of those who no longer had the strength to work, to go and build with their hands the new colonial cities. Ruben, worn out, humiliated, took the path of return and went back to his country in order to die there in the greatest sadness. (141–42)

The death of Ruben shuttles us back to Ari and to the letter he had written to Nessim in the French language about the Hebrew letters *alef* and *yod*, where names fold across names. "What could he have known—Ari, who left so young, who returned here as a tourist from time to time. When he would also confusedly feel that he was not a stranger in this city. When he would find himself recognized, surrounded by friendly sympathy—people who spoke to him, evoking memories, rebinding the interrupted thread, these people nevertheless were not Jews. So what his parents said wasn't a tall tale, the dim shadow of nostalgia" (142). Ari's letter turns to the war in Lebanon, and to the leaving behind of ashes. "You know, one stays up to shelter our soldiers from their mothers' tears. Yes. But finally we are a State, a Nation. We are leaving prayer, the ashes of ashamed shadow, books closed upon by pain and hope. We have effaced the infamy of the ghetto. From the hell of the holocaust we are here, in the sky of resurrection. We are making the desert bloom. We are bringing the flower of justice, of straightforward speech, of the purity of heart, to the world. Peace in Galilee! Black light upon white light" (142–43). The installation of the Iraeli state manages the past by disburdening itself from it in disavowal, a past it compels to appear as prayer, the ghetto, closed books, and pain, to manage the future in justice, freedom, and the purity of colonization ("the flowers of justice, of straightforward speech, of the purity of heart"), in a secular, if theological, settler colonialism. "But who is able, who dared to see clearly on that night of blindness, Ari said. That general who bears his name, there on the roof of a building, directs the bombardment. He had left his farm, his orange trees. Tranquilly he does his work. He makes war. Admirable modernity. Technical perfection" (143). In all of the bright light, the difficulty of reading and language, of tradition and death, is obscured in the clarity of technical precision. "The shock. One knew it that morning. That night one sensed that something was not normal in the nearby camps. But what was most terrible was that it passed as if nothing had taken place. That morning someone told us about it. Someone had seen it. No one wanted to believe. It was the Phalangists who did it—not us. We argued among ourselves. Then all of the fingers pointed at the calm man" (144). Gesturing to the massacre of Palestinian civilians at Sabra and Shatila in 1982, responsibility is disavowed ("blood everywhere, men masked in black hoods cutting the throats of children, entranced, a drunk orgy amid cries of anguish" [144]). And Ari is installed as a witness, asking us to read *Mille ans, un jour* as a text in bereavement, to point to the mournful dimensions of the colonial topography of language and loss it traces.

CHAPTER THREE

Repetition

And what if prose were to steal something from poetry?

MAHMOUD DARWISH, *al-Rasa'il*

To begin—as Mahmoud Darwish has taught us—is to begin "here." In *al-Dhakira al-mafquda* (Lost Memory) (Beirut, 1982), a collection of literary critical and theoretical essays, Elias Khoury names this beginning a starting point, *nuqtat intilaq*. Its time is the time of the present and it gestures to a practice of historical reading. "Between the history of criticism and the critique of history lies a single issue from which every historical reading sets out: the present."[1] Yet to set out from the present, and to read historically, is to set out from a moment of interruption, when "suddenly, nothing remained of Beirut except demolished walls upon which the posters of martyrs have been pasted," and where "everything disappeared" (27–28). The present is a time of loss and devastation, in the legacies of the First World War, the Lebanese civil war (1975–90), the 1982 massacre of Palestinian civilians at Sabra and Shatila, and beyond, to point to what Khoury calls "Arab modernity." "Arab modernity is a child of the colonial relation" (32), and this modernity privileges the state and its institutions, including the institution of reading in literature studies, in an ideology of aesthetic recuperation, where memory is muted in what appears as a "present without a past" (29). "With the transformation of war into daily life, into a slow burning fire which runs and grows at the interior of the Arab continent, culture and modern ideology thought that everything had returned or was on the path to returning to what had been, and that what was important was to build a unified state, and that the old, beautiful, Lebanon was going to return to be what it was, and that what had happened must be erased from memory, after memory had been recuperated" (28). Lebanon points to a general condition ("For Lebanon transformed from an Arab laboratory into an Arab condition" [28]), and the present "is repressed, crushed, and destroyed, and the state becomes the absolute repressive apparatus which bears an absolute future" (26). To think another future is the stake of Khoury's writing. If it is a writing that begins here and now, in a "historical reading," it is one that compels us to consider the essentially unfinished, excessive dimension of language, as the present, from "Mehmed 'Ali to Gamal Abd al-Naser" (28) and beyond, remains nightmarish and bloodied. In Khoury, and in his critical and novelistic writing, one begins where "we stand without memory" (29), where the bright light of renaissance and Enlightenment—of *nahda* and *tanwir*—is touched upon in advance by the bodies of the dead: "In the dark where there is nothing—pen and white paper, obscure thoughts, and blood" (29).

The "historical reading" (17) Khoury offers bears a relation to writing and to what it means to begin. "But we can only begin critique with criticism" (29). The overlay between criticism and critique, each of which is rendered with the word *naqd*, gives place to the beginning of which Khoury wishes to write. To begin is to engage in an act of critique, which begins in the practice of literary criticism. Thought, *fikr*, is not taken to be untouched by the dense, aporetical dimensions of language. Criticism, if also critique, is "writing upon writing, and language upon language" (11), and when one begins one therefore already bears a relation to others, to death and time. And one therefore begins by repeating. "Despite the linkage of the critical process to a diverse number of human sciences, it is only able to set out from the text itself" (11), and criticism—or critique—therefore resembles what we have come to call "literature." To think the present is to read it as if it were a text, "to discover, in the middle of this total darkness, points [niqatan] which may lend themselves to a dialogue around what we are writing or what we desire to write, around the new text that is no longer able to be a text, around the reality we desire to read like a text and the text that we really and urgently need" (29). Rather than a mode of reflection that will have privileged a distinction of thought from language, subordinating the latter to the former, critique, in Khoury, declines to leave language behind. This declining is given in Khoury's novelistic and critical, theoretical writing, where language is touched upon in advance by unmournable losses. Such losses interrupt the recuperative form of the circle to which language in Khoury returns. From the circle deposited and repeated in Khoury's first novel and in its title, *'An 'alaqat al-da'ira* (Beirut, 1975), geometrical forms proliferate in his writing, to teach us to read language through an anterior, interruptive relation to loss and death. To read this anteriority, and consider its relation to language, I turn in this chapter to Khoury's *Bab al-Shams* (Gate of the Sun) (Beirut, 1998), where, as Khalil Ayyoub explains to Yunus al-Asadi, who had suffered a stroke and fallen into a coma, and whom Khalil seeks to nurse back to life with words, "The beginning of the story says that you were like a dead man, and there was no hope of reviving you" (*B*, 32/30).[2] In the beginning there will have been death, if also a confounding of a harsh opposition between life and death ("The beginning of the story says that you were like a dead man [yaqul awwal al-hikaya inaaka shibh mayyit]"), and this confounding points to the place of words, devastated and in mutilation, in Khoury. In this chapter I consider this mutilation to read its relation to a persisting legacy of the word *adab* in the time of its loss.

SENTENCES

I memorized literature [al-adab] because it was my refuge.

ELIAS KHOURY, *Bab al-shams*

To read *Bab al-shams* is to read its title, and to do so involves addressing the dimensions of repetition in which it shares. One may not read this text from an outside, a place that will be said to have remained untouched by the rapport that opens among Yunus and Khalil, and the stories the latter tells and retells: Khalil's repeating the stories that Yunus, Umm Hasan, Nahila, and others had told him. The repetition of another's words points to a relation to loss, just as the title *Bab al-shams* repeats the title of an earlier text, *Abwab al-madina* (City Gates) (Beirut, 1981). This repetition registers a movement from the plural to the singular, and it asks us to read the mournful dimension of writing. "He was a man and he was a stranger," *Abwab al-madina* opens.[3] The man is a stranger to himself, and this loss mirrors his not being named ("The principal character in the novel *Abwab al-madina* is the strange man who, like the city, does not have a name," Sonja Mejchar has written), even as this sentence calls for the name it also declines to offer.[4] Language has been a privileged site of reflection in the reading of Khoury's work, and in this chapter I reiterate this privilege. As Mejchar further explains of *Abwab al-madina*, "It is not the events [it narrates] but the practice of narration that occupies a privileged place in the novel" (86), and in its reading.[5] Language, in Khoury, is what Sami Suwaydan has called an "event," and the time of this event stalls the hermeneutic comprehension of writing in relation to the legible, coherent form of a social or political body.[6] "Writing in *Abwab al madina* is not able to gather together the pieces of the social-psychological body, because it is formed and built of words which may not be gathered, and which, like memory in this novel, are unreadable."[7] If in Khoury language occasions what Muhammad Barrada has called "the shards and fragments of speech, conversation, and memory [that] grow according to their spiraling movement,"[8] a writing of "non-identity,"[9] to read these shards and fragments is not to comprehend them in relation to "an internal logic that binds them," but it is to give them to decline the figure of totality to which the shard and fragment also point.[10] This declining solicits, in *Bab al-shams*, what Khoury has called "critique." It is a labor of reading where critique—*naqd*—already takes place in the fallout of the Arabic nineteenth century and the destruction it imparts, and with "the stubborn negativity of the past" to which the writing of Elias Khoury recalls us.[11]

The first chapter of *Abwab al-madina* is titled *mubtada'*. This word bears a relation to "beginning" (*bid'*, *bidaya*, *ibtida'*), and it is also a category in *nahu* (grammar). Ibn Jinni explains, "As for the sentence it is any meaningful speech that is independent in itself, and it is of two types: a sentence that is composed of *mubtada'* and *khabar*, and a sentence that is composed of a verb and a subject or agent."[12] Meaningful speech is language that signifies. In the words of Ibn Hisham al-Ansari (d. 1397), it is speech that indicates a meaning, *al-dal 'ala ma'na*.[13] Meaning is articulated according to an order of foundation: the *mubtada'* is a noun, *ism*, "which you have made the first of something that comes second, wherein the second informs you about the first and rests or is founded upon it."[14] If reading privileges the institution of meaning in the force of an unwritten copula—Ibn Jinni and Ibn Hisham explain that the words in a sentence composed of *mubtada'* and *khabar* do not have a written marker that indicates the imparting of syntactic force, they are *mujarrad 'an al-'awamil al-lafziyya*—the sentence that opens Khoury's text is already cut into and interrupted, pointing to the colonial, linguistic violence I considered in chapters 1 and 2.[15] Whatever precedes this violence is already given in relation to it, where the past will already have been lost. "He doesn't remember how his story began, because he doesn't know. He saw himself in the middle of the story and didn't ask how it began, because he was busy with its ending. And when the ending came he found that he didn't know the ending either, and that the others didn't know the ending, because the ending can't be known, because the ending is an ending."[16] The disappearance of the beginning points to the sea, *al-bahr*, if also to lines of poetry, *buhur al-shi'r*. "In the beginning they said the sea" (75/66), Khoury also writes, gesturing to a bereaved relation between novelistic writing and poetic statement. The disappearance of prose, where prose takes place as if it were poetry, mirrors the repeated shattering of "I," solicited as the subject of the literary work. "The sea was night and I was alone. Then I felt that everything was shattering. The sea was glass and I was thrown in the middle of shattering black glass. And the glass changed into tiny pieces and the tiny pieces pierced through my body and the salt. The salt was in my eyes, the taste started to seep through the eye into the chest. I was shattering into tiny pieces [atakassar ila qit' saghira]" (76/66–67). In this shattering, where the subject of language may not be separated from the verb that is called upon to write of it—*atakassar*, I shatter, I am shattering, or, "I" am the event of my shattering into pieces—reading in literature studies, where events of language are conscripted to be "transformed into historical and aesthetic objects," is confounded.[17]

To read this transformation as it is textually performed is one intention of this book, and the word *bab*, cited in the title of *Bab al-shams*, points to this transformation through its relation to the tradition and practice of *adab*. If *adab* has been understood in literature studies in generic terms, as one kind of writing among others, it points, as I underlined in chapter 2, to what Ibn Khaldun called "malaka," a way of being with language.[18] And if in *Bab al-shams* the word *adab* is routed through a relation to its devastation and loss in colonialism, this loss is repeated in Khoury's citation of the word *bab*, which gestures to the partitions into which a text may be divided, just as *Bab al-shams* is divided in two, "The Galilee Hospital" and "The Death of Nahila." In the fallout of the loss of tradition, *Bab al-shams* is an event of writing already cut into in relation to a colonial "logic of separation and division," and the textual, institutional practice to which it gives place in the Arabic language.[19] If, as Khoury has written in relation to a reading of Darwish offered in *Dirasat fi naqd al-shi'r* (Beirut, 1979), "the past does not exist except as a part of a present that has been pulverized and stands in ruin [la wujud li al-madi ila ka juz' min hadir suhiqa wa dummira]," then language is already touched upon by the Galilee Hospital, the death of Nahila, and the stories Khalil Ayyoub tells and retells.[20] Writing, in Khoury, is not offered "in the name of recovering a lost essence or an undamaged self"[21] but takes place as an inability to leave the losses behind, to compel what Khoury has called a "patience without condition."[22] The partitioning of *Bab al-shams* in two cuts into the figure of the book—*al-kitab*—pointing to the occurrence of tradition in the fallout and persistence of colonial legacies. Yet this division gives place to a newness in language—it gives place to novelistic writing, if one that never ceases to remark its relations to others—in the wake of the First World War, the French occupation, the institution of sectarianism in the 1943 National Pact, and, in the years leading up to the civil war, the expansion of capitalist relations. The word *bab* also cites itself, repeating in *Bab al-shams* the legacy remarked in its name. And this name will already have pointed to the word *adab*, which solicits and recalls a tradition that is "irretrievably past," in the time of language's devastation, and in the stalled, melancholic repetition of its loss.[23]

Khoury has underlined that in "Arab modernity," and in what called itself *nahda* and *tanwir*, the present is understood in relation to "a beginning whose history is external to it," where the past will already have been lost, and language, in Khoury's novelistic and critical writing, repeats and displaces this beginning.[24] At the opening of *Orientalism* Edward W. Said wrote of the city of Beirut ("On a visit to Beirut during the terrible civil war of 1975–1976 a French journalist wrote regretfully of the gutted downtown area that 'it had once seemed to belong to the Orient of Chateaubriand and Nerval'").[25] The time of the present appears, in this journalistic prose, as one that has already ended. "Now it was disappearing; in a sense it had happened, its time was over" (1). The tradition of which Said writes reaches back to Aeschylus ("To Asia are given the feelings of emptiness, loss, and disaster that seem thereafter to reward Oriental challenges to the West" [56]) and "Latin Christianity" (61), and is routed through the legacies of European philology. This legacy, as I have tried to show in chapter 2, is proliferated within the Arabic language, redrawing the terms for the giving of sense. If Orientalism privileges and imposes a harsh division of life from death (Said writes of Ernest Renan that "his Oriental languages, the Semitic languages, are inorganic, arrested, totally ossified, incapable of self-regeneration" [145]), Khoury approaches these legacies in relation to the damage they impart to language. Declining to write as if colonial violence, including the losses imparted through the *nahda* and its historical, philological practice, will simply have been mournable, Khoury's writing points to the historicity of language. If Said, in Orientalism, teaches a persistence with and critique of these legacies, I have sought in this book to aggravate the attention to loss Said underlines ("To Asia are given the feelings of emptiness, loss, and disaster"). Orientalism, an event of compulsive, philological discrimination, is a machine for the proliferation of what Stathis Gourgouris has called "a cadaverous approach to culture," an approach imparted with asymmetrical, unequal consequence.[26] One measure of this consequence is taken in Khoury, where repetition, said to be on the side of death and ossification, is written, anew, through an older Arabic inheritance. Beginning in relation to the legacies imparted in colonialism—and language, as Said underlined in *Beginnings* (1975), "precludes a fixed beginning, even an arbitrary one to which one can refer retrospectively"—Khoury offers writing as a practice of repetition.[27]

FORM IN MUTILATION

> Languages may be an easily learned method of communicating ideas, but by 'language' shouldn't we really mean something else?
>
> JEAN GENET, *Prisoner of Love*

> The life he had written down came to him like dismembered, incomplete stories.
>
> ELIAS KHOURY, *Yalu*

In poetic statement, Khoury has written, "writing abandons its author," and so, too, in novelistic prose.[28] If, in *Bab al-shams*, "narration itself is the central form of action,"[29] this form does not point to a "nostalgia" but an unfinished relation to loss and death.[30] One is given to read the unfinished dimension of this relation, and therefore of relations in general, in the proliferation of figures—points, circles, triangles—I have begun to underline, and to which I turn. This proliferation points to an event of language where prose comes to appear as if it were poetry, where prose takes place as what de Man called an "enumerative stutter,"[31] an event of language that at once promises and confounds "the reconciliation of knowledge with phenomenal, aesthetic experience" (258), a reconciliation that is privileged in the reading of Khoury. In this privileging language is said to be "harmonious,"[32] and writing appears as "a fragment that we are then entitled to reconstruct, to identify, and implicitly to complete,"[33] as literature studies occasions a desire to carry out "the possible convergence of aesthetics and of history" or of its end in a totalizing form of temporal coherency.[34] In the pages that follow in this chapter, and to elaborate the discussion of *adab* in relation to colonialism I have offered thus far, I consider the relation of poetry to prose, and of writing to repetition—and citation—in Khoury. I do so because it is as if, in *Bab al-shams*, Elias Khoury, to sign his text, with "the signature of a single subject no longer folded back upon itself in mirror-like self understanding," had to do so in the name of another, and of more than one other, of the Palestinian novelist Emile Habiby (1922–96), of the novelist, literary critic, and militant Ghassan Kanafani (1936–72), and of Mahmoud Darwish.[35] It is as if the beginning had to repeat, and it is as if prose, and if it is solely itself, had to take place as poetry. And "poetic language," as de Man also wrote, "can do nothing but originate anew over and over again."[36]

The multiplication of geometrical figures I have underlined—points, circles, triangles—mirror the man in *Abwab al-madina* who drew far away. "And the man was far away. In the square, far away. He bent down over himself as if he were a circle and moaned faintly."[37] This man involves a relation to an emaciated and collapsing body and the breakdown of words ("his words" were "breaking down with him" [7/3–4]), and language becomes an event where one begins by repeating. Unlike the "Once upon a time" of the tradition of oral storytelling, upon which Khoury draws, what is given is an interrupted time, the erring, already reiterated gift of language. "So, you want the beginning. In the beginning they didn't say, Once upon a time [kan ya ma kan], they said something else" (*B*, 31/29). The displacement of "Once upon a time" means that the time of the beginning is the time of that displacement. It is the time of the dissonant fragility of an "or," which haltingly repeats the fragility of the beginning of the story, "For in the beginning it was—or it wasn't [fa fi al-awwal kan aw ma kan]" [31/29–30]). If what the story gives is this fragility, and if this fragility involves a relation to the interruption of surprise ("Do you know why they said that? When I first read this expression in a book about ancient Arabic literature it took me by surprise" [31/30]), this surprise gives place to an event of reading that confounds the notion of experience it is said to confirm. If what is at stake in *Bab al-shams* is the telling of the story of 1948, the story of the loss and destruction of Palestine, this telling occasions a passage through a circle that repeats. In this repetition the beginning draws away, like a point that turns into angles, angles into circles, and circles into a distant and withdrawing point. “Like a man he walked to his death, but I spotted him, but I tried to approach him, but I tried to say to him, I saw him in the distance, and like this distance he was, like a point turning into angles, and like an angle turning into circles, and like a circle withdrawing into a distant point.”[38]

This withdrawal points to the form of the stories told in *Bab al-shams*. Khalil repeats to Yunus the stories Yunus and others had told him of their lives and of the events of 1948. “My grandmother said she found herself in the middle of a group of about thirty women, old men, and children from the village of al-Safsaf wandering in the hills looking for the Lebanese border. ‘With my daughters and my son, we walked with them. I don’t know how we ended up in that terrified group. We were afraid too, but not like them. When they spoke they whispered. When we got to Beit Jann, they refused to go into the place. Their leader said they’d rob us and ordered us to continue marching. I told him not to be afraid, but he told me to shut up, and we left. When we got to Lebanon, we’d lost our voices because the old man had made us whisper so much’” (*B*, 213/218). Two versions of a story are told, and this doubling is mirrored in the loss of voice of which Khalil’s grandmother speaks. A child cries out, and his mother tries to quiet him. Khalil’s grandmother gives the child a piece of bread, and while the boy is crying an old man approaches and eats the pita. “‘Kill him,’ he hissed” (215/220), and the mother takes the child into her arms. “He went toward the child, whose screams grew louder and louder. The woman took a wool blanket, wrapped her son in it and picked him up. She put his head on her shoulder and kept pulling him down onto it as she walked, stifling the child’s cries with their blanket. The old man walked behind them; my grandmother said he walked behind the woman and kept pushing the child’s head down onto its mother’s shoulder. In Tarshiha the mother put her son down on the ground. She pulled back the blanket and started weeping” (215/220). The story—told through Khoury’s staging of the flight from Palestine in 1948, and telling the story of the death of a child—is told differently in Umm Fawzi’s recounting. Khalil tells Yunus, “His mother killed him—do you hear, Father—his mother killed him because she was afraid of the old man, who was afraid of the Jews. The mother didn’t carry her child on her breast, and she didn't support his head on her shoulder the way that my grandmother had told me. She wrapped him in the blanket and sat on him until he died. That's the way our relative, Umm Fawzi, told it. Umm Fawzi said they walked for five days without a sound so the Jews wouldn't hear them, and when the boy cried his mother killed him because the old man threatened to kill them both" (216/221). A historical recording of this event—through a narrative practice exterior to its telling—is precluded. In a way which parallels the understanding of history in Darwish's lyric, a historical telling that would account, finally, for death and loss, is displaced, as the category history is patiently redescribed through novelistic practice. The historical is given to be read as what refuses the domestication of loss, and this refusal is written, in *Bab al-shams*, through a practice of narration. Failing to be simply itself, language—as a matter of form—repeats the devastation it is called upon to describe, to become an originary stutter, a doubling in linguistic utterance: it was or it was not.

The stories of *Bab al-shams* are "painful, oppressive, pressing on the reader with the heavy burden of suffering they bear," and their form repeats that pain.[39] In this pain the bodies of the dead keep returning, as does the body of Umm Hasan, which opens the novel. "Umm Hasan is dead. I saw everyone racing through the alleys of the camp and heard the sounds of weeping. Everyone was spilling out of their houses, bent over to catch their tears, and running" (*B*, 9/5). Bending down, the inhabitants of the Shatila refugee camp mime the work of Umm Hasan and prefigure her repeated return in the novel. "Nabila, Mahmoud al-Qasemi's wife, our mother, was dead. We called her mother because everyone born in the Shatila camp fell from their mother's guts into her hands. I too had fallen into her hands, and I too ran the day she died" (9/5). The death of Umm Hasan mirrors the deaths of others, to point to "the mass grave of the victims of the 1982 Shatila massacre, where children now play soccer and trash is scattered all over the place"(37/35–36), the War of the Camps ("Our world wasn't destroyed during the great massacre, when our faces were covered with corpses; it was destroyed by what we call the War of the Camps, between 1985 and 1988, when we were besieged from every side" [454/465]), and the suicide of Aziz Ayyoub and the deaths of Khalil's father, Yunus's son Ibrahim, and his wife, Nahila.[40] The death of Umm Hasan points, I have begun to suggest, to the practice of storytelling in *Bab al-shams*. And her death compels attention to this practice in relation to loss and death, and in relation to the responsibility of reading to which we are recalled through Khoury's prose. "The narrator cuts off his speech [yabtur al-rawi al-kalam; also, "amputates" his speech] and interrupts the story to open a space for another to begin, or to continue a story that had begun and been interrupted," 'Aliya Mamduh Salih has written, and the cutting and amputation gestured in this reading ask us to consider the melancholic relation to loss generalized, in *Bab al-shams*, in novelistic form.[41] In this text's "poetics of melancholia," to borrow the words of Ranjana Khanna, novelistic form takes place as a mutilated event of language, to mirror the body of Yunus, which grows smaller and smaller as it withdraws, a circle withdrawing into a circle, over the seven months that is the time of the telling of Khalil's stories.[42] The iterated, painful retention of loss is repeated in the stories *Bab al-shams* tells—stories of unburied corpses and failed surrenders, the devastating pain of suicide, and the progressive dilapidation of the Galilee hospital. And the ciphering of this unfinished relation to loss as a practice of form—a practice which, I have argued, gives us to understand the category "history" in Khoury, and through Darwish, differently—helps, if however partially, to explain why "even Amin, the young man in charge of the emergency room, disappeared" (*B*, 120/123).

Since the significance of these words could not be assimilated, they were instead incorporated, at once mutilated and preserved.

LAURENCE RICKELS, *Aberrations of Mourning*

"We're back at the beginning" (*B*, 298/303), and *Bab al-shams*, like Umm Hasan, involves a relation to telling the truth. "No one would question Umm Hasan because she always told the truth" (10/6). To tell the truth is to tell the stories of the unburied bodies of which Yunus had told Khalil. "You couldn't dig a grave. You dug with your hands because you'd left your rifle in a cave three hours away from Deir al-Asad. You dug, but you couldn't make a grave that would hold the four of them. You dug a little grave for the child but then had second thoughts: Was it right to separate it from its mother? In the end you didn't bury any of them. You broke off olive branches, covered the bodies and decided to come back later with a pickaxe to dig them a grave. You covered them with olive branches and continued on your way to Lebanon. And all the many times you went back to Deir al-Asad, you never found a trace of them" (22/18). The dead who remain unburied haunt *Bab al-shams*, and one such death is that of Yunus, who grows smaller as the novel proceeds. "And this Yunus, Abu Salem, look at him. He's shrinking and becoming a child again. Look at his face and eyes. His face is the size of a child's palm, which means he wants his mother. Why are you keeping him here?" (374/383). The shrinking of Yunus points to and promises his end ("I know you're waiting for the end, but I assure you, as I have in the past, that the end can only be a man disappearing into the cave of Bab al-Shams" [244/250]), which is interrupted in a still birth. If Khoury's writing solicits a "freedom," then, it is one that will not have been free to mourn the dead.[43] *Bab al-shams* repeats this unmournability in relation to loss, gestured to in Yunus's inability to cry. "Weep a little, father. Just one sob and everything will be over. One sob and you'll live. But you don't want to, or you no longer want to, or you've lost your will. And I'm with you and not with you" (235/241). The impossibility of mourning points to a relation to language and names. If in *Bab al-shams*, "naming has an ontological power," this power interrupts itself, it is a sort of nonpower or an inability, and it teaches us to recall, in relation to language and names, a more originary repetition.[44] This repetition asks us to read a relation to loss, which is repeated—yet again, and we shall turn to others—in the disappearance of the Galilee hospital. "During these months everything has changed, as you know. Dr. Amjad comes only rarely, I've become head nurse and acting director of the hospital, the nurses have disappeared one after another, the hospital's been converted into a warehouse for medicine, but Zeinab's still here, immovable. She limps a little, toward her left foot, her shoulders droop, she has a short neck and small eyes. She moves like a ghost and takes care of everything" (487/498). And this disappearance mirrors—it repeats—those of Yunus, Shams, and the story's beginning.

> The theory has changed. The true novel is the one which comes from an interior rhythm, for I imitate neither the *maqama* nor Joyce.
>
> NAJIB MAHFUZ, *Najib Mahfuz yatadhakkar*

> But where does the circle begin, and where does it end?
>
> ELIAS KHOURY, *'An 'alaqat al-da'ira*

The relation of language to literature studies, and the "culture of forgetfulness" institutionalized in the philological practice of literary historiography, is placed in question in Khoury's novelistic writing.[45] Yet Khoury's first major publication was a book of literary criticism, and to read the relation of literary history to language in Khoury is to read the relation of language to history in his critical and literary critical writing, some of which I have cited thus far in this chapter (*Zaman al-ihtilal* [1985], *al-Dhakira al-mafquda* [1981], and *Dirasat fi naqd al-shi'r* [1979]). Criticism, in Khoury, is, perhaps first, an act of reading and citation, what he called in *al-Dhakira al-mafquda* "writing upon writing, and language upon language," and the relation that holds or fails to hold between literary criticism and literature points, then, to the rapport between writing, citation, and death. Citation forms an occasion for the mournful interruption of speech, to gesture the death of Ibrahim, Yunus's first son, whom his wife, Nahila, was unable to mourn. "The woman wept because she needed to weep. Nahila needed a false death in order to cry because a real death doesn't make us cry, it demolishes us. Have you forgotten how the death of her son Ibrahim annihilated her? Have you forgotten how she was incapable of weeping and sank into moaning?" (*B*, 134/137). It is a relation to loss that remains unfinished—"Our story has no end" (440/451)—and to which one repeatedly returns. It is for this reason that the telling of stories, in Khoury, is mournful. And it is for this reason that this telling must begin in death, citation, and literary criticism. The relations among these are pointed to in Khoury's *Tajribat al-bahth 'an ufuq* (Beirut, 1974), in the reflection he offers there on the novel and its history in the Arabic language. "The novel is not a part of our literary heritage. If some who study the theatre attribute its first seeds to *al-Bukhala'* [The Misers] of al-Jahiz or to the ancient civilizations that originated here before the arrival of Islam, we don't find, in Islam or what preceded it, a novelistic development," Khoury writes, to underline that were one to consider the relation between the novel and popular stories and the *maqamat*, "we insist that each may be included within an art that is specific to itself, and that it is possible to find links that relate them to the theatre more so than to the novel."[46] The novel, in the Arabic language, Khoury further writes, occasions a "literary break" in relation to European colonialism and "the challenge of European thought and conquering, European armies" (12). The return to loss in novelistic writing—and in *Bab al-shams*—is repeated in the explication of the relation of European colonialism to the institution of the genre and practice of the novel in Arabic. To tell the story of each is to tell the story of a death—of a "literary break" and of the stories of loss (and, as we shall see, love) told by Khalil and Yunus. And yet this break, and like the finality of death, its harsh designation as exterior to the time of life, is already interrupted, as Khoury makes clear, in relation to events of repetition in the fallout of loss.[47]

The novel, in the Arabic language, is said to have been a new form, one that will have originated in Muhammad Husayn Haykal's *Zaynab* (1914 [or 1913?]),[48] or, earlier, in al-Shidyaq's *al-Saq ʻala al-saq* (1855),[49] Salim al-Bustani's *al-Huyam fi jinan al-Sham* (1870),[50] ʻAli Mubarak's *ʻAlam al-din* (1882),[51] and Muhammad al-Muwaylihi's *Hadith ʻIsa ibn Hisham* (1907).[52] But the originarity of what is said to have come first, and to have occasioned "a radical break in the form and thematic content of Arabic prose fiction," already, in Khoury, points to a relation to loss.[53] If this gestures to an understanding of language in relation to its having been tethered to, and its taking place in the wake of, a point of origin, this event of hermeneutic designation is already confounded in Khoury, if also, differently, and in terms of the readings I offered in Chapter 2, in Ahmad Faris al-Shidyaq.[54] And if Khoury's writing occasions a break from earlier, modernist, Arabic prose, if his work comes, "after Mahfouz," if also in the fallout of Husayn's *al-Ayyam* (1926–27 [1929]), Tawfiq al-Hakim's *Yawmiyyat na'ib fi al-aryaf* (1933), Ibrahim ʻabd al-Qader al-Mazini's *Ibrahim al-katib* (1931), and Yahya Haqqi's *Qindil Umm Hashim* (1943), his language does not break, finally, from these texts but gives a bereaved, unfinished relation to them.[55] In Mahfouz's late work, Khoury wrote, "it is as if we stand before the end of a period that does not wish to end," to teach us, and not solely, that language already appeals to another, in relation to a loss that does not simply cease to take place.[56] The "literary break" of which Khoury writes, then, does not effect a break, but it repeats a desire to have broken with a past, which Khoury's writing also teaches us to read. A break has taken place—something or someone has been lost, an event of devastation has occurred—and Khoury's writing of a "literary break" teaches us to attend to this loss and its iteration, as it declines the privileging of a historical, philological understanding and practice of form.[57] It is not that the novel, as a distinct literary genre in the Arabic language, may be said to have begun at one point among others in time, or that this beginning may be said to have been exemplified in one text among others, but that the question which asks into such a point of origination shares in a desire to domesticate loss through a practice of historiographical reading.[58] If, in Arabic literary modernity, the past appears as if it has already been lost, where "what took place, on the literary level, was that the classical model lost, in a single moment, all of its exemplarity and all of its magic,"[59] reading in literature studies compels attention to the losses Khoury's explication repeats, and it teaches us to read, including, and if not solely, the loss of the simple interiority of "Arabic literary modernity."

In Khoury, the beginning already cites the words of another, and this citation points to the practice of *adab* in Arabic letters. This citationality repeats the text and practice of *Alf layla wa layla* (The Thousand and One Nights), a text that bears a relation to *adab* and to *zarf*, etiquette or manners.[60] In this text, "there is neither an original text nor an original author,"[61] and as Abdelfattah Kilito has written of its stories, "Their narration is an act which repeats an indefinite number of similar, previous acts, without its being possible, or conceivable, to go back to an initial source that would lie at the point of their emergence."[62] The practice of *adab* gestures, in *Bab al-shams*, to the Qur'an, to circles, to the name of God, and to language. I turn here to the name of God, Allah, which wraps and protects. It offers itself, as if it were literature, as a refuge ("I memorized literature because it was my refuge [hafiztu al-adab li'annahu kana malja'i]," Khoury has written). Khalil, Khoury writes, brought the name of God and placed it over Yunus's bed in the Galilee hospital. "But then, after having put you to bed and cleaned everything up, I went home to get my things and remembered the picture [al-lawha]. Something told me that it belonged here. Allah in Kufic letters wraps you in its aura and protects you" (*B*, 127/130). Unlike the posters of martyrs, and unlike the lives of finite beings, the inscription of the name of God, for Khalil, is eternal. "I brought you the picture, saying to myself that the name of Allah in Kufic lettering would remain however circumstances and conditions changed. The photographs and posters were ephemeral, but the name of the Almighty will not move from its place, and it will remain suspended before our eyes for eternity" (128/131). *Bab al-shams* stages this name in relation to its loss. To bring this name to Yunus is to do so following a sudden, interruptive injunction ("Something told me that it belonged here [qultu inna makanuha huna, I said to myself: its place is here]"), an interruption that repeats the sudden eruption of violence that colonialism (in *Dirasat fi naqd al-shi'r*) and the Lebanese civil war (in *al-Dhakira al-mafquda*) are. The name of God is cited—it is repeated—and this repetition points to the inscription of loss, and of a destruction imparted to language, in novelistic writing. The loss of the giving of sense, through the tradition that bears the name *adab*, is iterated in Khoury, not to point to a lost origin, or a tradition that is no more, but to inscribe tradition in relation to its belated repetition. The name of God is cited in the text of literature, as writing's relation to language and death. Literature, in Khoury, is one name for this relation.

Khalil: "Everything is relative. Even the Arabic calligraphy that I've hung on the wall above you is relative, since it isn't a work of art [lawha] in the precise meaning of the term, though it is beautiful. I brought it from my house because Shams refused to take it. A beautiful work with the name of the Almighty written in Kufic script. I like that script. I see its angular forms as if they are redrawing the boundaries of the world, and I see it curving and rounding everything off. It's true it's not a curved script, but everything's round in the end" (126/129). If, for Khalil, "everything's round in the end," then language, as the angular writing of Kufic script—as the writing of the Qur'anic text—interrupts the temporal, hermeneutic comprehension, which language also solicits. If the end solicited in language is pointed to in Khalil, and in what Khalil calls "a work of art [lawha; also, "a painting" or "a picture"]," the end, in Khoury, is interrupted without end. Hermeneutic closure, if also aesthetic totality, is confounded by a displacement and a distance, *bu'd*, which refuses to draw away. The confounding of the resolution of temporal incoherency is staged in literature—it is staged in *Bab al-shams*—and this confounding repeats as the form of the work. To place in question the grounding of language through a political, theological understanding of form—an understanding of form solicited in post–civil war Beirut, and, if differently, in Butrus al-Bustani's *Nafir Suriyya* (1860–61), which we read in chapter 2—becomes in *Bab al-shams* a principal intention. Khoury approaches this intention through a practice of writing that is also, immediately, a practice of repetition. The old words are retained, as they are patiently read in relation to a literary practice of language and of writing. Language, like literature, will never have let go of loss ("For the principal matter of literature," Khoury writes, "is language [fa madat al-adab al-ra'isiyya hiyya al-lugha]"), and *Bab al-shams*, then, schools its readers in the relations among loss, mourning, and aesthetic form.[63] Literature, in Khoury, may be said to iterate a relation between form and death, teaching us to read language differently, and anew.

This iteration declines a sociality "founded through the efficacy of language," where a domestication of loss in aesthetic form would mirror, in politics, what Marc Nichanian has called a "manipulation of mourning within the reconstitution of the city reconciled with itself."[64] Khoury has written, in relation to a discussion of Said's *Orientalism* (1978) and *The Question of Palestine* (1979), that "the history of the region witnessed, during the nineteenth century, and through European, and particularly French, intervention, the establishment of what resembled independent rule for the Maronite minority in Lebanon, following the crushing civil war (1860), which had led to the intervention of the French army, and whose clashes extended into the heart of the city of Damascus."[65] Remarking a violence, and placing a date between parenthesis—cutting into his text and pointing to the place of dates, and of particular losses, in relation to writing—Khoury offers a critique of the project of the institution of "confessional states [iqamat duwaylat 'ala asas ta'ifi]" (52) and their racialist and colonial practice. If, in the Arabic language, and in the writing of Butrus al-Bustani, a relation to the past is restaged in colonial philological terms, where, in those terms, the "native" is instituted as the one who witnesses her or his culture ("He is its witness because he has lost it," Nichanian writes), and where, through "the operation of philology," "he is the archived trace of his own temporality, of his own immemorial past," in Khoury, a refusal to separate this archivization of the past from writing becomes a locus of novelistic writing, and of the pratice of language and critique.[66] If al-Bustani—and, differently, al-Shidyaq, al-Tahtawi, and Husayn—perform "autoethnography," where "the subject of culture" is transformed into "a carrier of tradition" (14), and if not solely, Khoury teaches us to read the devastating iteration of this loss, "a past event that cannot become past," in relation to novelistic form.[67]

The calligraphic inscription of the divine name is rounded off by Khalil ("It's true it's not a curved script, but everything's round in the end"), but the angular corners of Kufic script interrupt the hermeneutic comprehension of language and the specular figure of consciousness solicited in the circle. If Taha Husayn's *Falsafat Ibn Khaldun al-ijtima'iyya*, *Fi al-shi'r al-jahili*, and *al-Ayyam* privilege the figure of a reading subject that would come to know and understand itself and others as a historical subject through an experience of reading, this subject is solicited and confounded in *Bab al-shams*, where "everything has already begun to dissipate and to withdraw," including the beginning.[68] And if literature studies labors, in the legacies of the European Enlightenment, to install distinctions as a domesticating event of integration—"the vastness of light is like the capacity of the mind to make endless distinctions, or the power of calculus to integrate by ways of infinitesimal differentiation," de Man has written—language both calls for and ruins that integrating and differentiating capacity.[69] In language "there are always at least two texts, regardless of whether they are actually written out or not" (260), and this excess is remarked in the divided call of *Bab al-shams*. The "specular structure" (252) of reading, where language would appear as "the monumental stability of a completed entity" (254) in relation to a desire for "mastery over form," is solicited in the repetitive structure and narrative practice of *Bab al-shams*.[70] Acts of repetition become metonymic, the part points to a whole, even as this whole can do nothing but fall into pieces, as in Ahmad Faris al-Shidyaq's *al-Saq 'ala al-saq*. The framing of the name of God in Kufic script solicits an aesthetic understanding of language and of history, as it places that understanding in question. If this framing points to a desire to domesticate language in relation to the state, it disrupts that domestication, to solicit a reading practice that declines, even as it will never simply have separated itself from, a coherency of form.

To read this domestication is to do so in relation to a desire to domesticate loss, including the loss and destruction of Palestine in 1948, and the events of colonizing violence that preceded and succeeded the events of that year. This domestication is, I have suggested, promised and stalled in Khoury, where writing is not recuperable into what Cynthia Chase has called the "stories of the victory of voice over meaningless repetition or over mute textile and mutilated figure."[71] This irrecuperability confounds the reading of loss in relation to what David Lloyd has discussed as "therapeutic modernity" and "the mournful logic of historicized events," which that modernity compels.[72] "That historical conception is not merely an ethical ideal but also an end that regulates historical method and evaluation, from the selection and legitimation of archives and sources to the organizing modes of narrative. It bears, moreover, an idea of the human subject that is the product of that narrative and the ideal of the discipline itself—the disinterested subject of modern civil society" (220). The event of language in Khoury declines this understanding of history and the subject, where "the social forms of the colonized become 'survivals,' of a precapitalist, precolonial past, survivals that effectively have no future" (217), and it does so as a matter of form. Writing, in Khoury, becomes a writing of relations, where there will never have been a text that does not relate itself to others, a text that, in its mute interiority, will solely have been itself. "The various ways in which a text entangles itself with other texts, articulates itself in terms of other narratives, or produces articulations with other texts or contexts," become, in Khoury, a site to which one is compelled to return in reading.[73] Language calls for, and recalls us to, a responsibility in reading that is also a responsibility to the relations inscribed in language. In such a thinking of relations, language, for example, the name, declines to come down to one. A name is already names—in the plural. And the name of God will have been indistinguishable from that of Yunus, just as Yunus's name, and its origin, will never have been solely its own.

> You said your father had first wanted to call you Asad. So you would have been Asad al-Asadi and everybody would have been terrified of you. He did name you Asad but changed his mind after a couple of days because he was scared of his cousin Asad al-Asadi, a village notable who'd indicated displeasure at his name being given to the poorest of the poor in the family. So he named you Yunus. He chose Yunus to protect you from death in the belly of the whale. But your mother didn't like the name so she said 'Izz al-Din and your father agreed, or this was what she thought, because when she started calling you 'Izz al Din your father kept calling you Yunus. Then he decided to put an end to the litany [thumma qarrara al-shaykh wad' had li al-mas'ala] and he said that the name Abd al-Wahid was better. He started calling you Abd al-Wahid, and you and everyone else became confused. (*B*, 118/120)

§

The beginning involves a relation to Ayyoub—to 'Aziz Ayyoub, to Uncle 'Aziz Ayyoub, to Sheikh 'Aziz Ayyoub, and to White Ayyoub. "One day a woman came to the lotus tree to fulfill a vow, and she saw him. She threw down her candles and ran to al-Jdeideh and everyone came. Ayyoub was dead beneath the holy tree, his neck tied to a rope, the rope on the ground, as though the man had fallen from a branch of the tree" (*B*, 341/349). The story of Ayyoub is the story of a saint who died and who had lived his life alone. Villagers would visit Ayyoub and the lotus tree to be healed from illness, and Ayyoub came to resemble what Khoury has called literature: he became a site of refuge, and his name encrypts a relation to loss and devastation, as it points to a futurity. "Umm Hasan told me about my grandfather's uncle, 'Aziz Ayyoub. She said he'd become a saint and that people made oaths in his name and that he cured illnesses. She said that during her visit to her brother in al-Jdeideh, she'd remembered her promise to my grandmother to visit al-Ghabsiyyeh and light a candle under the lotus tree" (339/347). 'Aziz Ayyoub is a saint and he is ghostlike. The oval shape of his face repeats the points, circles, and triangles that give place to Khoury's text. "It was as if he were from another world, it was as if he were a ghost, his eyes sunken into his oval face and his shoulders that drooped as if his body was no longer capable of holding them up" (340/348). Sunken and bending over, like the inhabitants of Shatila who bent over picking up their tears at the opening of *Bab al-shams*, he bears a ghostly dimension. He may not simply be buried. "Ayyoub, or 'Aziz Ayyoub, lived his life a solitary phantom in a village inhabited by ghosts. He lived alone close to the tree and the mosque, sleeping in the mosque with cows and eating plants that grew on the land and the remains of provisions that had been left behind in the abandoned houses. They'd see him walking through the fields or sitting under the lotus tree or praying in the mosque or giving the call to prayer. His clothes were a brilliant white, as though all the muck that surrounded him left no mark" (341/348–49). Ayyoub continues to live, somewhere between life and death, beyond death and burial. If Ayyoub may have committed suicide ("Umm Hasan said she thought 'Aziz Ayyoub had committed suicide" [342/350]), it is an act that may have been thwarted by the generosity of the lotus tree. "'Listen Khalil,' said Umm Hasan. 'It could be that he hung himself, or it could be that the man tied the rope around his neck and climbed onto a branch of the tree to put and end to his misery and loneliness, but the tree took pity on him and broke so as not to allow him to commit the defilement of suicide'" (343/351–52). Or—*kan aw ma kan*—he may have been strangled. "The tree, which is ruled by a saint, proclaimed him a saint, so now it has two: the first one, whose name we don't know, and Ayyoub, of our village, whose name was 'Aziz. The sheikh of al-Jdeideh has a different opinion. He believes the Israelis strangled him, then tied a rope around his neck to make people think he committed suicide" (343–44/352). If one must tell stories—"I had to gather your parenthetical sentences and mumblings and transform them into a story I could tell you" (34/32)—this telling points to the necessity of repetition without end, where writing occurs "as a form recording its own impossibility,"[74] and where one is left to read the unreadable story of 'Aziz Ayyoub, without consolation, and in loss. "He's now a saint to whom people make vows, and we're on our own" (*B*, 344/352).

ALLOTHANATOGRAPHY

Holding fast to origins is not a natural quality of our people or our language. It is one that was imposed upon us by others, from the outside, and from outside our language.

EMILE HABIBY, *Khurafiyyat Saraya bint al-Ghul*

"I'll tell you everything, from the beginning" (*B*, 298/303), and in the beginning one will have cited the words of another. Language begins in citation, as Khalil repeats the words of Yunus and Umm Hasan. Like Khalil, *Bab al-shams* becomes a citation machine: it cites al-Mutanabbi, Ghassan Kanafani—whose novel *Rijal fi al-shams* (Men in the Sun [Beirut, 1966]) Nahila, Khalil's wife, had copied out by hand ("You'd bring me books and go away. And I'd read. I read all the novels and the poetry, and I learned the stories by heart. Do you know what I used to do? I used to copy the books by hand. I wrote out Ghassan Kanafani's *Rijal fi al-shams* longhand innumerable times" [395/405])—Ahmed Shawqi, Imru' al-Qays (who is on the side of beauty, and "there's nothing more beautiful than the poetry of Imru' al-Qays" [68/68]), the Qur'an, Mahmoud Darwish, Jabra Ibrahim Jabra, "the novels of Jurji Zaydan on the history of the Arabs, and the books of Taha Husayn" (356/364), and Jean Genet and his *Un captif amoureux* and "Quatre heures à Chatila" ("Here, after having given up writing for so many years, he returned to it, because, with the terror he felt inside of him moving among the piled-up corpses, he found that he had to bear witness").[75] These names, like that of Khalil's father, point to the beginning, and to a death that has already taken place, a death that was missed and that will have been lost. "At the beginning I see my father. I see him and I don't see him, for Yasin Ayyoub died before I could set eyes on him" (*B*, 298/303). In Khoury narration is a practice of interruption ("The narrator cuts off his speech and interrupts the story to open a space for another to begin, or to continue a story that had begun and been interrupted," Yumna al-'Id has compellingly written of Khoury's *Rihlat Ghandi al-saghir* [Beirut, 1989]), and this practice points to a relation to death and repetition.[76] In this practice writing becomes allothanatography, where to write of one's self is to write of a death and of more than one other who has died and is said to be no longer.[77]

The story of Palestine cannot be told smoothly.

EDWARD W. SAID, *After the Last Sky*

The old paths do not necessarily disappear altogether. They may well remain dimly visible along with remnants of the languages that articulated them.

DAVID SCOTT, *Conscripts of Modernity*

We constantly betray the dead.

ELIAS KHOURY, *Mamlakat al-ghuraba'*

In an essay titled "al-Akhta' . . . al-addad (Errors . . . Opposites)" (Beirut, 1996), Khoury explains that "Emile Habiby never stopped talking about Ghassan Kanafani's error in his novel *'A'id ila Haifa*. It's strange that he didn't speak about the structure of the novel—because like all of Kanafani's novels it is closer to a sketch of a novel than a novel—and that he spoke about the character Duv or Khaldun, the Palestinian child who was left behind in Haifa and who transformed into an Israeli soldier."[78] The discussion of Habiby and Kanafani leads Khoury to attend to a question of names. "In the intensity of his reaction against the novel Habiby forgot—or pretended to forget—that the hero of his novel *al-Mutasha'il* bore the same name as that of the Palestinian father of the two boys: Khaldun, whose name had changed and become Duv, and Khaled, whose name will change when he joins the Palestinian *fida'iyyin*, as was the custom in those days" (152). The question is reformulated as a question of citation: one takes on the name of another and speaks with his or her voice. "Emile Habiby spoke about a borrowed name and forgot the real one. He spoke about Khaldun and forgot Sa'id S., who was to transform in his novel into Sa'id the Pessoptimist" (152). And it is reformulated again as one that bears upon a return to the beginning. "What if we were to ask the two Sa'ids to tell us what they've never spoken of? To speak of their inability to speak? And to return to the beginning, to the moment of the question of the meaning of the *nakba* and its stories?" (153). The beginning that repeats in *Bab al-shams* is also this beginning, and it entails a relation to others who have died within us ("Others die, and things die inside of us. Those we love die, and limbs from our bodies die, too" [*B*, 505/517]), and to the voices of others coming out of my throat. "I'm tired of talking, too. I stop speaking, and then the words come. They come like sweat oozing from my pores, and rather than hearing my voice, I hear yours coming out of my throat" (20/16).

Such voices include those of the poet, Mahmoud Darwish, and that of the Palestinian novelist Emile Habiby and his *al-Waqa'i' al-ghariba fi ikhtifa' Sa'id abi al-nahs al-mutasha'il* (The Strange Events Concerning the Disappearance of Sa'id Abi al-Nahs the Pessoptimist) (Haifa, 1972–74). This text tells the story of a disappearance, *ikhtifa'*, and this disappearance mirrors that of Khalil's mother, the Galilee hospital, Yunus, and Shams, and it gestures to the death of Nahila, Yunus's wife. "As for me," Sa'id explains of himself in *al-Mutasha'il*, "I've disappeared."[79] But if Sa'id has disappeared Habiby does not wish to recall him to the plenitude of his having been there. What is offered is patience. "Patience. Patience. Don't ask: Who is this Sa'id abu al-Nahs al-Mutasha'il? He drew no attention to himself throughout his life, so why should we pay attention to him now?" (13/3). The imperative, "Don't ask 'Who?,'" gestures to a patience in reading, as did Khoury in the passage cited above in *Zaman al-ihtilal* (Beirut, 1985). The reader of *al-Mutasha'il* is asked not to understand this text by asking about its author but to remain with the disruptive, dislocating dimensions of language. One ought therefore not rush to explain. "Take it easy, Take it easy. Don't rush my explanation, sir. Everything will come in its time."[80] But if time anticipates a future wholeness where "everything will come," where everything is as sweet as honey, *kull shay' fi waqtihi ya'sal*, this future repeats. Habiby's text holds time in reserve, declining to manage it according to the protocols of hermeneutic interpretation or the aesthetic imperatives of the colonial state. For the beginning repeats. "Let's begin from the beginning" (16/6). The beginning solicits the question of its origin, but to ask for the beginning the text proliferates and multiplies beginnings. "When was the beginning? The beginning was when I was born again thanks to a donkey" (16/6). The desire to know the beginning requires that it multiply, and it must, again and again. And there are at least five beginnings in this sentence, which I underline here as I repeat and reread it. "When [1] was the beginning [2]? The beginning [3] was when I was born [4] again [5] thanks to a donkey."

The beginning withdraws, and this withdrawal points to the bereavement of language I am exploring throughout this book. If

Khoury's writing of the beginning cites Habiby, Habiby, in turn, cites *al-Saq 'ala al-saq*, a text which, in Khoury's words, "came close to inventing a new literary approach based upon autobiography, and based upon a language that mixes the style of the *maqama* with the prose of everyday life."[81] Sa'id's name, in Habiby's text, and like that of al-Fariyaq, cuts into itself to combine two, it is *naht*, just as this name, like the birth of al-Fariyaq, points to a misfortune ("The birth of al-Fariyaq took place at the time of the greatest misfortune [nahs]," al-Shidyaq writes" [*FS*, 13]). The beginning, in the passage in *al-Mutasha'il* I am reading here, is citational, and it points, as Khoury also wrote of Habiby, to a future. *Al-Mutasha'il*, Khoury writes, "bears its particular future and its new language."[82] It is a future one is given to read in the confounding of the beginning, in the event of repetition that citation is. Already language is entangled with the language of another, just as the telling of stories points to the "entanglement of one story with another."[83] It is as if the question that asks about the beginning is already ambushed, just as Sa'id and his father were ambushed in 1948. "During the events they ambushed us and opened fire. They hit my father, may he rest in peace. As for me, a stray donkey came between me and them, and they brought it down. It died in my place. My life that I've lived in Israel since that time is a gift of that poor beast. How, then, are we to evaluate my life?"[84]

This beginning is repeated throughout *al-Mutasha'il*, as it is in *Bab al-shams*, and it bears a relation to devastation, to Abjar ibn Abjar, the first Pessoptomist ("That's the way our family is, and it's why we bear the name Pessoptimist. For this word is a fusing together of two—optimist and pessimist—which have blended into the character of each member of our family ever since our first divorced mother, the Cypriot"), and to the giving of the name "Pessoptimist."[85] "It is said that the first to so name us was Tamerlane, following the second massacre of Baghdad" (22/12). The firsts that repeat here ("ever since our first divorced mother," "the first to so name us") reiterate the devastation of 1948 ("After the first misfortunes in 1948 the members of our great family became scattered, living in all of the Arab countries not yet occupied" [19/8–9]), to point to the beginnings we have already traced. They link the beginning to the iteration of loss gestured in the dismemberment and unfinished burial of Sa'id's older brother. And they mirror the return of Yu'ad, whose name repeats those returns. Yu'ad first appears when Sa'id arrives in Acre after having left the headquarters of the military governor, to which he was taken as he sought refuge with Adon Safsarsheck. She returns as a memory, and she begins, then, by returning ("Akka welcomed us as we entered the city, cloaked in the darkness of an Abbasid night. I remembered my girlfriend Yu'ad, who never smiled at anyone but me on the train, making my heart beat rapidly" [28/17]), only to appear later with her sister from Haifa, and for the first time, in the chapter "Is Sa'id the Hooded Informer?" "Yu'ad's sister now told me that Yu'ad had arrived on foot that day from Nazareth by way of the villages of Shafa Amr and Ibtin, alone over the mountains. She had come to tell her sister in Haifa that they had arrested their father in Nazareth and that I, Sa'id, was the cause, since I had informed on him" (72/55). Sa'id convinces them that he had not done so, and they decide that Yu'ad should stay overnight in his house. Yu'ad's sister leaves, pointing to more than one loss, to those who disappeared ("she was waiting for the return of her husband, who had gone out one morning saying: wait for me, I'll return" [75/58]), and those mutilated or killed by land mines (74/57).

Sa'id's house is raided, pointing to the instituting, persisting violence of the state of Israel, which Sa'id reports and does not recognize. But the novel is a novel in iteration, declining to repeat the pretension to sovereignty, which the authorities to whom Sa'id gestures, and who are raiding his house, claim. And Yu'ad is then shoved into a car "full of others like herself" (79/62) and deported. But the chapter closes with the word *return*, an active participle that is able to function as both a noun and a verb, *'a'ida*, and which repeats the title of Kanafani's *'A'id ila Haifa*, of which Khoury wrote in "Errors . . . Opposites." This iteration within iteration punctuates the events Sa'id narrates, if also the sovereignty of the state, to decline the closure of time in aesthetic form. Sa'id's nonrecognition of the colonizing dimensions of the violence he nevertheless describes repeats the unrecognizability—the nonsovereign dimensions—of that violence. In Habiby, the colonial state already stalls, it already interrupts itself, in nonsovereignty. "As the car moved away I heard her, calling out at the top of her voice: Sa'id, Sa'id. Don't worry. I'll return!"[86]

Sa'id elaborates as follows:

> They had seized her along with other 'infiltrators' to Haifa, people from Nazareth, Jaffa, Maalul, Shafa Amir, Iblin and Tamrah, each worker who had slipped into the city to feed his family, and tossed them on the Jinin plain amidst the land mines of the British, the Arabs, and the Jews.

> Some of them hid in the ruins or amongst the trees and did not cross over into Jordan. They waited until it was dark and slept by day, so they could retrace their steps. They returned and were expelled. Again. So they would return and be expelled, yet again. Right up to the present day.
>
> Some of them kept on walking until Jordanian soldiers met them with curses, and they are still swearing at them today.
>
> Yu'ad was among those who did not return. (80/63)

If Yu'ad does not return, the second Yu'ad, "Yu'ad al-thani," the daughter of the first Yu'ad, does. Following the disappearance of Sa'id's wife, Baqiyya, and their son, Wala', Sa'id meets the second Yu'ad's brother, whose name is also Sa'id, in jail. "I learned from the prisoners that he was a Palestinian *fida'i* who had crossed over from Lebanon and had been taken prisoner when wounded. They also told me that his name was Sa'id. 'Just like me,' I commented" (173/133). The second Yu'ad had come to search for her brother, and her explanation of who she is deposits into Habiby's novelistic prose yet another body. "She said I had been mistaken about her, that I had confused her with the Yu'ad I had been waiting for, a woman who was in fact her mother! And she was now dead" (195/150). The repetition of names—Sa'id and Yu'ad—and the repetitions within names—Yu'ad is also a passive voice verb: "to be repeated"—points to the losses and a beginning that has been lost, which *al-Mutasha'il* stages. The soldiers come to take the second Yu'ad, as they had the first, marking a compulsive iteration in state sovereignty, and the following conversation ensues.

> She sat me down at her side:
>
> Do you love me, uncle?
>
> With all the anguish of my life.
>
> Would you like to marry me?
>
> Until death do us part.
>
> Should I marry an old man, coming to the end of his life?
>
> But I'll return to the beginning.
>
> Impossible!
>
> Then how can your brother believe that things will return to where they began?
>
> He got the idea from his elders. Of his beginning an old man remembers only the prime of youth and so he thinks fondly of it. Do you really know how the beginning was, uncle? The beginning was not merely sweet memories of pines over Mount Carmel, or orange groves, or the songs of Jaffa's sailors. And did they really sing anyway?

> Do you really want to return to the beginning, to mourn your brother torn to pieces by the crane as he carved his living from the rocks. You want to do it all again, from the beginning?
>
> But your brother, Sa'id, said they had learned from the mistakes of their predecessors, and would not commit them again.
>
> If they had, they wouldn't have spoken at all of returning to the beginning. (199–200/154)

If Sa'id, whose collaboration with the Israeli state marks his complicity with its institution, wishes to return to the beginning ("But I'll return to the beginning"), *al-Mutasha'il* stages the impossibility of such a return in the fractured, interrupted iteration of the "first."

> From above, from my house, I heard a woman screaming and the noise of kicks and punches and tumult. I saw a violent battle raging between Yu'ad and the soldiers. I saw her resist, shouting and kicking. And I saw her bite the shoulder of one of the soldiers who cried out in pain and retreated. Then I saw them all charge together and force her into the deportation van. As it pulled away I heard her shout: Sa'id don't worry! I'll return!
>
> Then I opened my eyes, sighed deeply, and said: So here we are, back at the beginning. (200/155)

That the origin occasions this repetition is one lesson imparted by Yu'ad, and it solicits a futurity. "Yu'ad had returned, but it was not Yu'ad. She was a bouquet of roses for a wedding of the future and at the same time a wreath of fresh flowers on the grave of the past" (203/157). The closure of death pointed to in this passage ("a wreath of fresh flowers on the grave of the past") is interrupted in an early scene in this text, in relation to a debt that increases in the measure in which it draws away. Writing of a Sa'id speaking of a Palestinian woman and child in 1948, Habiby offers, "The more the woman and her son drew away from us, the governor standing on the ground, and me sitting in the jeep, the taller they grew until they merged with their shadows in the setting sun, having grown longer than the plain of 'Akka. The governor stood, waiting for them to disappear, and I waited, sitting, hunched over, until the governor asked himself, astonished: When will they disappear?" (26/15). Later, those who had been cordoned off with Sa'id inside the Jazzar mosque in 'Akka tried to determine who the woman he had seen in the field was. "I am from al-Manshiyya. There's not a stone left standing there except the tombs. Did you meet anyone from al-Manshiyya? No. We are from Amqa. They plowed all its houses under and spilled its oil onto the ground. Did you meet anyone from Amqa? No. We over here are from al-Birwe. They expelled us and obliterated it. Did you meet anyone from al-Birwe? I did see one woman from there hiding with her child among the sesame stalks" (32–33/21). If the others who had gathered in the mosque stop guessing who the woman and child were, they do not stop naming the names of villages that had been destroyed, to the point that Sa'id is unable to recall them. "But soon voices erupted again, persisting in drawing out their relationships to their villages, all of which I understood to have been razed by the army" (33/21). In this excess of names, "damage itself becomes the locus of survival, the pained trajectory of what lives on" in the interruption of historical and hermeneutic closure.[87] And this interruption is repeated—Habiby's text is catachrestic—when, in the reiteration of the names of the villages, a corpse is remarked. The mother who had covered the mouth of her daughter to quiet her as Sa'id entered the mosque smothered her. "An infant began to cry but was soon hushed."[88]

KANAFANI, JABRA, HABIBY

The word *Khaldun* remained a single point [nuqta wahida], nothing else, which swam, lost, amid that unending overflow of voices and names.

GHASSAN KANAFANI, *'A'id ila Haifa*

The disasters we've endured can no longer be addressed with words. All of the words have been pulverized.

JABRA IBRAHIM JABRA, *al-Bahth 'an Walid Mas'ud*

"Don't be afraid. We can return to the beginning" (*B*, 302/307). If Ghassan Kanafani "went to his death to announce that the story of the writer was more important than the writing of the story," Habiby's *al-Mutasha'il* involves a novelist who sought to imitate literature.[89] "Why did he imitate the story rather than write it? Why did he try to be the hero that he invented rather than write one?" (156). But Jabra Ibrahim Jabra's *al-Bahth 'an Walid Mas'ud* (The Search for Walid Mas'ud) (Beirut, 1978) occasions the transformation of the story into culture. "And Jabra Ibrahim Jabra came to the novel from everywhere else and transformed it into a scene for all of the arts: he made the story into culture."[90] This transformation involves a passage through literature. Khoury writes in *Bab al-shams* that "Sana', the wife of the *kunafa* seller, came. She came and stood at the open door of your room and knocked. I was sitting here reading Jabra Ibrahim Jabra's novel *al-Bahth 'an Walid Mas'ud*. I was drowning in Walid

Mas'ud, this Palestinian who disappeared leaving behind an obscure tape in his car radio. To unlock the mystery of this tape Jabra had to write a long, beautiful novel. I love Jabra because he writes in an aristocratic way. His sentences are well chosen and beautiful. It's true that he was poor as a child, but he wrote like a writer. He wrote literary, well-formed sentences [jumalan adabiyya baligha], ones that you have to read the way you read literature and not the way I'm talking to you now" (*B*, 99/101). If *al-Bahth 'an Walid Mas'ud* consists in well-formed literary sentences, *Bab al-shams* is already contaminated by the disruption of colloquial speech. Without consoling recourse to genetic or temporal sequence, all Khalil can do is to try to gather the shards of words. "I'll try to gather the shards that I heard from you and from others. When I make an error, correct me. And I won't begin from the beginning, because I'm not like you. I'm not able to say, 'In the beginning'" (*B*, 221/226). Khalil, unlike Dr. Jawad Husni in *al-Bahth 'an Walid Mas'ud*, is not able to return to the beginning, or to a tranquil interior or anterior moment, said to have remained untouched by time. "At the center of the turmoil, a settled voice. In the thick of contradictions, a hidden, perceptible, harmony. Between the poles of attraction and repulsion, a deep silent point [nuqta sakina 'amiqa]: the eye of the storm, an ecstasy that words are incapable of touching, in a world of babbling and masked fear."[91] *Bab al-shams* repeats this point, to give it to divide and disappear. If "words are everything," they gesture, immediately, to a devastation of world, and of language, in the fallout of persisting losses.[92]

Given over to the haunting words of others ("I light a cigarette, gaze at its glowing end in the dark, and my eyelids start to droop. I put out the cigarette, close my eyes, and let the phantoms take over" [*B*, 52/51]), the austere and privileged figure of the author withdraws. And what one does, listening to another, is nothing, *la shay'*. "I sit next to you in silence. I listen to the rasp of your breathing and I feel the tremor of tears, but I don't weep. I say, 'That's it, I won't enter your room again. What am I doing here? Nothing'" (20/16–17). It is perhaps for this reason that Khalil never met Jabra Ibrahim Jabra. And it is perhaps why Jabra never wrote a novel about Jamal, "whose chest was torn open by an Israeli bullet near the Beirut airport during the siege" (424/435), and whose story he could have made into an epic. "I don't know why I told her about Jamal. I think his story deserves to be made into a book. If only I'd told it to a great writer like Jabra Ibrahim Jabra, he could have made it into an epic. But Jabra's dead now, and I never met him. And all I had in front of me was this French woman half of whose face was hidden behind the bottle of white wine, and I wanted to explain things to her" (424/435). In the fallout of more than one death—that of Jabra Ibrahim Jabra and others—what is left is for words to repeat, as Dr. Jawad Husni repeats, in Jabra's novel, Walid Mas'ud's reflection upon the relations between memory and writing. "Perhaps it is my right, now, to take recourse in this expression of Walid Mas'ud that he so often repeated in his last months."[93] Taking on the voice of another, and speaking to us as if it were another, language implies a relation to something other than itself. Already in relation—and in relation to relations—one is left, without certitude, to read. And one is left with the responsibilities of reading. As Khalil says to Yunus, "Where are the landmarks, my friend? How will I know the road, and who will guide me?" (*B*, 16/11). What is gestured is an idiom schooled in the stories of *Alf layla wa layla*, giving us to read the historicity of language in the devastation and loss of words. "Three novelists who wrote a great deal but who in the end became the heroes of the story they didn't write—and which became the memory of their literature."[94]

I memorize poetry but I don't want to be a poet.

ELIAS KHOURY, *Ka'annaha na'ima*

"So, you want the beginning" (*B*, 31/29). The beginning points to the death of Nahila, to Yunus's seven sons, three daughters, and fifteen grandchildren, and to Ghassan Kanafani. "Ghassan Kanafani came, you told him your story, he took notes, and then he didn't do anything. He didn't write your story. Why didn't he write it? Did you really tell him your story? You never used to tell anyone your story because everyone knew it, so why tell him?" (43/41). The story that must be told is the one that has not been told. It is the one that was not told to Kanafani when he came to meet Yunus and when Yunus told him his story. "Writers are strange. They don't know that people don't tell real stories because they're already known. Kanafani was different though. You told me you liked him and tried to tell him everything. But he didn't write anything. Do you know why?" (43/41). But the pen of Kanafani did write, to transform story into symbol and literature into the author's story. "It was the late 1950s when he came to see you, and your story hadn't yet become a story.

Hundreds of people were crossing from Lebanon to the Galilee. Some of them came back and some of them were killed by the bullets of the border guards. That, maybe, is why Kanafani didn't follow up on the story, because he was looking for symbolic stories, and yours was just the story of a man in love. Where's the symbol in this love, which has no justification? How did you expect he would believe the story of your love for your wife? Is a man's love for his wife really worth writing about?" (43/41). The relation between Khoury and Kanafani is mournful ("But you became a legend without realizing it. And I want to assure you that if Kanafani hadn't been killed by the Israelis in 1972—when they blew up his car in Beirut and ripped his body to shreds—he'd be sitting with you now in this room, trying to piece together the shards of your story" [43/42]), and it teaches us to read citation in *Bab al-shams*, where language occurs as "the unsovereign speech to which the writer is both constrained and compelled."[95] Kanafani, in Khoury, points to a question (Khoury wrote of *Rijal fi al-shams* in 1974, two years after Kanafani's assassination, "His engagement with oppressive, monotonous life began to produce its questions. And the principal question called for an answer"), and to reply to this question and the legacy it imparts compels attention to Habiby, Kanafani, and Jabra, and to Darwish's *Limadha tarakta al-hisan wahidan?*[96] "Mahmoud Darwish recorded that he was an Arab to remain there as an Arab. And then, after his long journey in the Arab world, the first question came: Why did you leave the horse alone? Why did you leave the horse? The question begins here: perhaps we must ask how and not why? Perhaps the how will allow us to understand the why?"[97]

One among other firsts and beginnings in Khoury stands Mahmoud Darwish's *Limadha tarakta al-hisana wahidan?* (discussed in chapter 1) ("And then, after his long journey in the Arab world, the first question came: Why did you leave the horse alone?"). If, for Khoury, in Darwish, language points to a "fracturing of the self and its inability to become a unity," this fracturing is repeated—and cited—in *Bab al-shams*.[98] Such language relates to names (Khoury writes of language in Darwish that it becomes "a new name for the Palestinian name, which has not ceased, since the *nakba*, to search for its names" [135]), to gesture, in Khoury, to an encryption of names in novelistic language. Such an encryption points to the bereavement of writing, and if this bereavement remains secret, it gestures, in Khoury, to Darwish, if also others, "because secrets, like love, are only spoken poetically."[99]

Love, in Darwish, implies a relation between two—"There is no love without two," Darwish explained in a 1999 interview—and two, in Darwish, is anterior to one.[100] The implication of love with writing, the poetic, and relationality is ciphered in Khoury in relation to Darwish. "With Darwish," Khoury writes, in an essay that appeared in the year following the poet's death, "my ink became colored with the scent of the Galilee," and writing shares its indebtedness to others.[101] If this indebtedness is untranslatable ("for language reveals what is particular to it only in those of its expressions which are untranslatable"), it is given to us to be read.[102] Darwish, in Khoury, is "simply a poet,"[103] and his name points to a discombobulation of the time of prose, its scattering, dispersion, and dissemination as *nathr*, several of the other meanings of the Arabic word that renders "prose," to give place to "the futures of language" (35) and its time. "The text, from the beginning, is excess," Said also wrote in *Beginnings*, in a passage that teaches us to read the beginning in Khoury, and which compels attention to Said's name—a name that is both uttered and withheld in the essay I have underlined in the latter half of this chapter, and which was published in Beirut in 1996, just two years before *Bab al-shams*.[104] "Perhaps my hypothesis has been that the novels *The Pessoptimist*, *Return to Haifa*, *Arabesques* ["Once again I stand at the gate that is ajar," Anton Shammas wrote there], and the book *After the Last Sky* [by Edward W. Said] form a single novel whose hero is a man named Sa'id," Khoury writes, and this hero disappears in *Bab al-shams* to morph into the figure of Khalil.[105] This disappearance points to the bereavement of language, where one is given to "remain mindful of the alterity of the departed addressee," to gesture to "a disorienting loss of hermeneutic foundations"—a loss that Khoury declines to appropriate into the reading institutions of stately intention.[106]

FIRST(S)

> Every triangle, whatever its form and whatever the size of its angles, is able to enter a circle. And circles necessarily burst apart. This is how I discovered our story. I wasn't able to start with events. Events are ambiguous and distorted—they can't form a beginning. We began as a triangle.
>
> ELIAS KHOURY, *al-Jabal al-saghir*

"Lets go back to the beginning" (*B*, 208/213), to recall that *Bab al-shams* is a love story. The title of the novel names the place in the

Galilee where Yunus and Nahila would meet. "This is Acre. Here's Tyre. The plain runs to here. These are the villages of the Acre district. Here's Ain al-Zaitoun, and Deir al-Asad, and al-Birwe, and here's al-Ghabsiyyeh, and al-Kabri, and here's Tarshiha, and here's Bab al-Shams. We, kids, are from Ain al-Zaytoun. Ain al-Zaytoun is a little place, and the mountain surrounds it and protects it. Ain al-Zaytoun is the most beautiful village, but they destroyed it in 1948. They bulldozed it after blowing up the houses, so we left it for Deir al-Asad. But me, I set up a village in a place no one knows. A village in the rocks where the sun enters and sleeps" (24/20). This love story is also the story of this place and its institution, a site of a refuge that mirrors the literature, *adab*, Khalil tells us he memorized. And yet to speak of Bab al-Shams is also to tell the story of Shams, who Khalil buried the way people bury their stories ("I have to bury her as people bury their dead and their stories" [473/484]). Shams was married at fifteen to Fawwaz Mohammed Nassar and taken from ʿAmman to Lebanon to live in the Tel al-Zaʿatar refugee camp. Fawwaz's withdrawal from the camp with the Tel al-Zaʿatar militia leads to her running into Ahmad Kayyali, "who gave me a Kalashnikov and said 'Come with us'" (481/492). Shams's return to Fawwaz anticipates her coming to live in Beirut with him. "'For six years in Beirut I can only remember myself as naked, crucified, with bullets exploding around me, and then the man would come to me, erect boring into my body with a savage shout that emerged from between his thighs" (500/512). After their departure from Beirut in 1982 Fawwaz morphs into a stammering adolescent ("It seems the demon left him, and he became a different man, stammering in front of his father, addressing his mother respectfully and coming to me calmly" [501/512]), and his violence returns after his father's death. In the fallout of her repeated rape, Shams consumes images of Fawwaz, to eject them from her mouth. She is inconsolable, and the interruptive dimension of mourning ruins the desire to sever the ties to the dead. "Everything in Shams wept as she mutilated Fawwaz Mohammed Nassar and spat out the little shreds of paper she was chewing. And then suddenly she'd wipe away her tears as if it were nothing. As if the woman who had wept were another woman. And she'd start gobbling the dish of pasta for which she'd made a special sauce of cream and basil leaves" (476–77/487–88). Stalled in melancholia, as if she were "another woman," Shams repeats the bereaved condition of the stories Khalil tells.

The shredding of Fawwaz anticipates the murder of Shams, who had been accused of killing Sameh Abu Diab. Khalil describes his relationship with Shams as follows: "She'd tell me she saw me every day and heard my voice calling to her every morning. She'd ask me to repeat her name over and over again, and she'd never get tired of hearing it. I'd say it once, twice, three times, ten, then I'd stop, and I'd see her face crumple like a child's, so I'd start again, and we'd start making love again" (46/44). The repetition of Shams's name in this passage urges us to consider Khalil's account of Shams's death, and the mutilation of her body. "There's no need to describe the shreds of woman stuck to the metal of the burned out car" (47/45–46). This mutilation communicates with the pulverized words of which Jabra Ibrahim Jabra wrote, with the iteration of misfortune in Habiby, and with the death of something inside of Khalil. "No, my beloved child, I wasn't afraid of her or of revenge. I was afraid of myself. Something suddenly died inside me. When someone we love dies, something dies in us. Such is life—a long chain of death" (505/517). The chain of death involves the cutting links of relation, where the incessant, stalled interruption of the telling of stories "can be repeated indefinitely,"[107] not to give place to communication ("Death is not, then, an obstacle to communication" [50]), but to confound communicative privilege in language, to which Khoury has called our attention, pointing to others within us. "Others die, and things die inside each of us. Those we love die, and limbs from our bodies die, too." (*B*, 505/517). The shards of Shams's body and the limbs Khoury points to in this passage gesture to further amputation, and something's having been cut off. It is a relation to destruction that may not be transcended but that forms a condition for words. It is Shams who has taught Khalil to be attentive to the relations between death and love ("Before Shams I didn't know this. When she died I became aware of my amputated limbs and the parts of me that had already been buried. I became conscious of my father and my grandmother. Even my mother, who I had forgotten. I saw her as if she were a part of me that had been ripped out of my body by force" [505/517]). The torn limbs of the body mirror the tearing apart of Shams's, and the story of *Bab al-shams* "mirrors its form," pointing to a loss that compels Khalil to interrupt himself, as if mourning were necessary and interdicted, in loss.[108] "She told me she loved me and then she left to kill Sameh. I didn't do anything wrong. I loved her the way one loves, but she left and was killed. She killed him and then was killed, and that's enough. I don't want to say anything else about her" (*B*, 39/37).

The interdiction of mourning is given to be read in Elias Khoury's signing his name. "But tell me, what is the story of that spirit woman and that man who drowned in the circles of the red sun? That happened at the beginning, but even so, it comes just at the end of the story" (485/496). Nahila was married to Yunus in 1943 at the age of twelve and came to resemble her son who had died, and who explained to Yunus that he had misunderstood what he thought he had seen. "Nahila explained it to you, it was a simple misunderstanding. You thought she was a spirit, and she thought you were a prophet. You ran away, she knelt down, and Nahila laughed and laughed" (485/496). It is the story of Yunus's mistaking a Yemenite Jewish woman for a spirit, and of her mistaking Yunus for the prophet Elias. "'She was wearing a long black dress,' Yunus said, 'and she had covered her hair with a black headscarf. She saw me and came toward me. I shrank back against the tree. I was wearing my long, olive-green coat and carrying my rifle like a stick. The woman was approaching me. She was far away and the sun was in my eyes so I couldn't see her clearly. I saw a phantom emerging from among the red rays of sun, with black slipping through them like a thread, and walking'" (485/496). The approaching woman stops in a way that mirrors Khalil's jumping from story to story, teaching us to consider, as in *Alf layla wa layla*, "the twisting back of narrative on itself," where the time of narration is the time of language's relations.[109] And where language asks us to read—again and again—more than one relation to loss. "'I leaned against the tree and saw her coming toward me. Then, when she was two hundred meters away, she stopped in her tracks as though she were rooted to the ground, knelt down, rubbed her brow with dust, and raised her face toward me. She put her hands together and said something in an Arabic that I wasn't familiar with. Then she rose, stumbling over her long dress. I took advantage of the moment to hide inside of the trunk of the tree, slipping inside it with my heart beating like a drum. I stayed inside the trunk until night had covered everything. There was something strange in her eyes. I thought she was a spirit even though I don't believe in spirits. But I was afraid, very afraid'" (*B*, 485–86/496–97). The story *Bab al-shams* tells is repeatedly interrupted by its telling, gesturing to this text's indebtedness to time and death. This interruption points to the historicity of literature—a historicity that is historical only in the sense in which we have been taught, newly, to read that term here.

What remains, then, of *adab*?

ABDELFATTAH KILITO, *Les séances*

It is a perhaps well-studied dimension of Frantz Fanon's *The Wretched of the Earth* that it underlines that colonialism was—and is—an activity of division and separation. "By its very structure, colonialism is separatist and regionalist," Fanon wrote.[110] What Fanon called "decolonization" points to the placing in question of such a structure. "In decolonization, there is therefore the need of a complete calling in question of the colonial situation" (40/37). This situation is one that is linked—as Said underscored, in the pages of *Orientalism* I cited earlier in this chapter and in the introduction to this book, and, as I shall argue in chapter 4, as the writings of Jacques Derrida on language and repetition also teach us—to a colonial, philological understanding of time, death, and language. "The settler makes history; his life is an epoch, an Odyssey. He is the absolute beginning: 'This land was created by us'; he is the unceasing cause: 'If we leave, all is lost, and the country will go back to the Middle Ages'" (52–53/51). In the "calling in question of the colonial situation" Fanon underlines the "colonial bourgeoisie," which "has done nothing more than take over unchanged the legacy of the economy, the thought, and the institutions left by the colonialists" (169/176), to point to a "concrete praxis" in relation to what he calls "a new politics which in no way resembles the old" (140/147), undertaken "to suspend the static period begun by colonialism, and to make history" (69/69). Khoury's writing intervenes at this point, to underline that language, in colonialism, is already devastated. Language, in Khoury, ruins the division of the "new" from the "old"—a division that is both historical and philological—to give one to read a political praxis that is also a practice of repetition, in a refusal of a final break with a past time ("to suspend the static period begun by colonialism [à interrompre le temps mort introduit par le colonialisme]"), and if also with a relation to loss and death. To disavow the historicity of colonial violence, and not solely in relation to language—a disavowal one is taught to read in the pages in Fanon I have cited here—would be to read as if "in relation to such a disaster" one "thinks that tradition has continued," as if in relation to colonial violence there is a temporal continuity.[111] One already writes, Jalal Toufic has further underlined, "in the aftermath of disaster" where "what survives was also destroyed" (72), and where nothing will have been left untouched. And "tradition" or the "past," whatever will be said to have come before, will never have been "something so substantial to have produced debris," but already and only takes place, then, in devastation.[112]

The story of the spirit woman and her words point to this anteriority, and they are explained to us by Nahila. "Yunus said that when he told Nahila how he'd stood close to his tree, wrapped in the red rays of the sun, and how the spirit woman had appeared to him at a distance and how she was going to carry his mind off like in the stories, Nahila laughed for a long time. 'There's no spirit woman or anything like that! The Yemenis are everywhere. That was a Yemeni Jewish woman'" (486/497). The story of Yunus's misrecognition of the Yemeni Jewish woman involves a relation to bodies and history ("the body of a single human being contains the entirety of human history" [158/161]), and this relation mirrors the one between death and beginning. "Nahila told Yunus about the sobs they'd heard coming from the kibbutz the Yemenis had built on top of al-Birwe and about the mysterious rumors of children dying and disappearing. She said the Yemeni women would go out into the fields and weep like Arab women and that she'd started to fear for her children. 'If the children of the Jews are disappearing, what will happen to ours?'" (486/497). Death, in Khoury, opens a relation to the future ("what will happen?"), and it refers us to the gift of language. No longer simply with, yet neither starkly without, the legacies of philology, language gestures to a relation to names, and the story that opens with Yunus looking into the circles of the sun ends with a single one. "'That spirit was no spirit,' said Nahila. 'She was a poor woman like us who must have lost one of her children. So when she saw you, she probably thought you were a vision of the prophet Elias'" (486/497). This name recalls the giving of language ("Nahila laughed at you and called you Elias, saying that with your beard you'd started to look like a Jewish prophet" [486/497]) as it disappears, like Yunus, Nahila, and Shams. And language withdraws, it divides, like *adab* and the tradition to which this word points, to give place to a new, if still also however old, practice of form. "I promised you I'd start with the end, and the end will come when you've left this coffin of a bed. You'll get up, tall and broad shouldered, walking stick in your hand, and return to your country. You'll go first to Bab al-Shams. You won't go to Nahila's grave, as everyone expects. You'll go to Bab al-Shams and enter your village—cave and disappear" (34/32).

CHAPTER FOUR

Literature

What will you do, then
When words are finished?
A bird searches for sky.
That's what "sky" is
going leaving with "wings."
Take me, for example.
A word or two is left to me.
And what, finally,
when words are finished?

SAMI SHALOM CHETRIT, *Petikha*

If "words are finished," if they may no longer be given, language also tells us that words, if only one or two, have been left me. I turn in this chapter to consider the citation and recitation of words as events of literature. "'I won't yield to Aunt Zakiya.' She recalled her sister's voice as she repeated her daughter's words with a satisfied smile. Her only reaction had been to nod and lower her eyes to her hands folded in her lap. She had already told her sister many times that she would not burden Muhyi by sharing the single room with them, but Naima needed to hear her say it over and over again. Her remorse was repugnant to her, and at that moment she felt hurt by the demand to evince compassion and consolation, when she was the one who deserved them. Could she have imagined that this was the way things would turn out, and that she would have to end her days at her niece's? Going back to the family—people say—like a man who departs for foreign lands and returns to die at home" (*I*, 9/69).[1] Opening at the end and in relation to death ("Could she have imagined that this was the way things would turn out"), the first words of Shimon Ballas's *Iya* (Tel Aviv, 1992) yield to the citation of names. Its first words are an event of citation, where Iya recalls her sister's voice repeating her daughter's words, and this citation points to another, the act of recitation and diminutive reorganization, which Iya's name is. "Iya" is the nickname given to Zakiyya by the children she raised in the home of the Jewish neighbor's daughter in which she had come to live. "Iya. That was what the children called her. Like all toddlers, they had had difficulty pronouncing her name, and in time it had become an endearment. She had watched over their cradles, and they had grown and matured in her care. She had no children of her own, nor had she her own home, but she had never eaten the bread of charity. Ostensibly, her status was a servant's. While her own family treated her like a stepchild, to her many acquaintances she had become a part of her adoptive family since the day she had left her sister's house and gone to live with the Jewish neighbor's daughter" (10/70). If *Iya* is displaced in and through language, and in and through citation, it also, immediately, teaches us to read its language in relation to Arabic, and in the fallout of the devastation in language, in the Arabic nineteenth century, which I read in the preceding chapters of this book.

The story *Iya* tells is a story of language, of languages, and of literature. In *Iya* the bereaved dimensions of its idiom are reiterated, just as the name "Iya" is repeated by Sophie, Sarah's daughter. "Three who grew up in her arms, but she would never rejoice at their weddings, throw sweets over their heads, see their offspring. Iya, Sophie pronounced from her cradle, smiling sweetly, and Sarah laughed: 'Do you hear, she calls you Iya'" (11/71). The word *Iya* is an Arabic one, lodged untranslated within the Hebrew text, marking a relation to loss and language I read in this chapter, a relation to fathers and sons (Saul and Ephriam), sisters (Iya and Naima) and those like sisters (Iya and Sarah) ("You are a sister to me" [29/84]), generation and lineage, and recitation and the Qur'an. If *Iya* is to tell the story of the departure of the Iraqi Jewish community from Baghdad in 1951, it returns to this beginning by way of the Hebrew language, which Ballas will have learned only "after" this event. And it returns to the beginning of a new exile, which will have taken place in the place to which one is conscripted to returned.[2] The beginning to which one is conscripted, with the institution of the state and the negation of exile (Hebrew, *shlilat ha galut*), remains, in *Iya*, displaced onto its fragile exposition.[3] And if this beginning refers to a place, it is one that, both earlier and later, in the words of Yitzhak Laor, "is not stable, is not solid, does not stand in its place, and is not empty," because "in this 'place' there is always already language and power."[4] In Ballas language is neither a site of gathering nor a site of return, and to read *Iya* is to read its relation to the language it will never simply have left behind: Arabic. Hannan Hever writes that "Israeli literature is understood, as a matter of course, as a direct continuation of Hebrew literature,"[5] and he underlines that this understanding conceals a certain violence. "The accepted historical account presents a smooth and direct continuity between the two, and conceals what was bound to the passage to national independence: the struggle over the Israeli territory" (8). *Iya* stalls this account to invite Ballas to be read in relation to the destruction imparted to language, and the reorganization of the giving of sense, in the Arabic nineteenth century. To read *Iya* in this way is not to secure its belonging to "Arabic literature" but to point to language's nonbelonging to a single literary tradition, history, institution, or language. It is to read where *Iya* declines to be itself, where it takes place as an event of translation.

THREADS OF LANGUAGE

> A State of the Jews, only Jews, even the fellah a Jew, whoever heard of such a thing in the past?
>
> SHIMON BALLAS, *Iya*

The repetition of Iya's name points to a mournful relation to language. I have underlined that the name "Iya" is an event of citation, and this text's calling itself "Iya" redoubles this mournfulness, asking us to read *Iya* in relation to language and loss. "Iya. Two joyous syllables in Sophie's mouth, which had just started to sprout teeth. Come to Iya, come. First daughter, a darling girl who found warmth and comfort in her bosom just as Hamida had done before her. There would be no one to call her Iya anymore, and Sarah would no longer have a sister to support her and be her confidante" (*I*, 29/84). This loss gestures Iya's departure from her sister's home and the violence to which she is subjected by the man to whom she was married. But if following his conscription into the Ottoman army she begins a new life to leave her old one in the past ("That morning she went forth to a new life, the five years of her marriage wrapped in shrouds of oblivion, like a heavy, repulsive bundle she cast behind her" [12/71–72]), this newness does not leave the past behind. Ammiel Alcalay has underlined that in Ballas "memory" confounds "the legitimacy of forms,"[6] just as the distinction between the new and the old drawn in these passages is overwhelmed by detail ("She [Iya] remembered how Farumi loved to hear the story of that day. She stretched her legs out on the cold cement floor and leaned back against the wall. Small beads of sweat appeared on her brow and on the sides of her straight, angular nose. She rested the cup in its glass saucer on the floor and lifted her gaze to the mulberry tree visible from the high window, the afternoon breeze rustling its dense leaves" [*I*, 12/72]). The temporal movement of the narrative is stalled in repetition, as more than one story is told. The language of *Iya* is a language of "discontinuity" ("Ballas fashions a type of identity based on the heterogeneous, the contradictory, the discontinuous, the irredeemable," Hever has also written), which discombobulates the order of language—and languages—compelled in the state form.[7] This discombobulation in and of language repeats the loss of world and sense narrated in *Iya*. They, Sarah's family, are to leave for Palestine, while Iya is to be left behind, in Iraq, to move in with her sister. If *Iya* stages a repetition in language, it also stages this loss of world, compelling one to consider the relation between the institution of states and the appropriation and management of language with the imparting of sense. I have sought to elaborate this question in detail, and in relation to the institution of a literary object, and of a subject of language, through a reading of citation (chapter 1), philology (chapter 2), names (Excursus), and repetition (chapter 3), to argue here that what is at stake is a reflection on the category—and the event of writing—that literature is. If this event—and this European, Latinate, and Christian word—belongs to the institution of world in the fallout of the European Enlightenment (even as this event is also older and other than that), it gives place, between and within languages, and in the fallout of 1948, to a displacement of temporal categories, to become an event of form. For literature—and if also, differently, *adab* (Arabic), *sifrut* (Hebrew), *littérature* (French), and *Literatur* (German)—declines to be itself or what it is, interrupting the categories—historical, hermeneutic, and philological—that labor to domesticate loss and death in time.

The end Ballas stages at the opening of *Iya* points to others, and to the end of Iya's marriage. "A young girl, a violent man, and five years of suffering and miscarriages. And when she returned to her mother after her husband's departure for the war, her body was small and tough, the skin covered with bruises" (*I*, 30/84). This loss communicates with other losses, pointing to a reiterated relation to loss, and to a loss that will have been more than one. The disappearance of Iya's husband, her brother Mahmoud, and her father, who had died ("Her father was no longer alive [Hebrew, aviha lo haya od bayn ha chayim]"), repeats the disappearance of the story *Iya* is to tell. This disappearance points to the loss and destruction of tradition and the past, and a relation to death that is inscribed in language. What attention to language in Ballas compels is not a reading of his text as inside or outside of a single literary or linguistic tradition—for example, Hebrew or Jewish literatures, or Israeli literature, but also, differently, Arabic literature—but as an event of language that gives us to read his text as one that will never have simply belonged inside of any single one of these.[8] If I have argued that Ballas's text—and like those of Mahmoud Darwish, Elias Khoury, and Edmond Amran El Maleh—remarks a relation to the event of destruction and restaging in language I have studied in chapter 2, this has not been in order to bring any of these texts into the inside of "Arabic literature," nor has it been to argue that any one among them belongs to a "cosmopolitan" practice or way of being, if there is one, but it has been to suggest that each of the texts I have considered disrupts its relation to language and time and that to read this disruption is to read a relation to language—and to languages—and to loss.[9] The relation to death given in the passages in *Iya* I am reading is imparted with, and as, the being of this text and its story, to confound the categories that give place to understandings of language and time. In the passage we are considering this confounding is inscribed in relation to the First World War and the conscription of Iraqis by the Ottoman army ("She had no other brothers, and her mother had remained alone, going to live in the big house her sister lived in, where they found her a dark room near the gate. She stayed there with her mother and waited for the end of the war. The British entry to Baghdad, which followed the return of the surviving Turkish conscripts, brought terror with it, and she frequented the alleys to hear what she longed to know" [*I*, 30/84]), and to the reorganization of the political order in what was to emerge as the British Mandate in Iraq—and Palestine—in the aftermath of that war, in relation to the impacts of this event on language and the way it came to appear as an object of study. If Iya's husband never returns ("no one knew what might have happened to him"), he, and the solicitation of death—and language—in relation to the state form to which he points, haunts Ballas's writing, declining, finally, to draw away.

Sadness has many facets. In my view the worst is related to supposedly fleeting, unimportant acts.

SHIMON BALLAS, *Ve hu akher*

Be patient until God judges between us. He is the best of judges.

QUR'AN, Surat al-A'raf

Ballas describes Iya's relation to the Jewish family with whom she lived, where she was to become "Iya." There, "she also learned to adapt her tongue [Hebrew, lashona] to the Jewish dialect [Arabic, an tu'awwid lisanaha 'ala al-tahadduth bi lahjat al-yahud], to use the turns of phrase peculiar to them and to weave Hebrew words into her speech as they did [Hebrew, lishabetz et diburah ba milim 'ivriot kamohem] until it was impossible to discern her difference [Hebrew, zrutah]" (*I*, 32/86).[10] The impossibility of discerning Iya's difference with the adaptation of her tongue compels us to read language in *Iya*. It tells us that *Iya* remarks a relation to language, and to the loss of a tongue, *lashon*, which touches upon the language of Ballas's novelistic writing. In an interview published in the journal *al-Karmel*, Ballas explains that, after having taken up residence in Israel, and after having given up the Arabic language to write in Hebrew, and to publish his first novel, the Arabic language returns. "I had prohibited myself from reading Arabic or listening to the Arabic radio station, for the entire period during which I wrote my novel *Ha ma'abara* [The Transit Camp], which was a period of two years. I wanted to forget the language to be able to make myself anew, and to build a new world around me."[11] Ballas's desire to forget the Arabic language gives place to what he has called its "revenge." "After transcending the crisis of my first writings in Hebrew, I regained a certain relation to the Arabic language, by way of the story *Du'a' al-karawan* by Taha Husayn, and it was entirely by coincidence. I remember that I read the book for the whole night, after returning from work at the printer unable to fall asleep. I felt that my world was collapsing all around me. It was a strange experience for me. Arabic words, expressions, vocabulary, and sayings overcame me, they overwhelmed my entire being anew" (222). Pointing to a loss of world ("I felt that my world was collapsing all around me"), and given place to through an event of chance or coincidence (in the Arabic of the interview I am reading here, *sudfa*), one is compelled to attend to language—and the Arabic language—in Ballas. The practice of Iya's tongue mimes the event of language Ballas describes in the passages from the interview I have translated here. If, in the adaptation of Iya's tongue, difference withdraws, confounding the categories called upon to compel language to appear as recognizable (Iya is "more Jewish than Muslim and a Muslim among Jews" [*I*, 39/91]), in *Iya* the Arabic language is retained, it is included while never simply interiorized, like a foreign body installed within the interior of the Hebrew language, confounding that interiority as it promises and interrupts it.[12] To decide on the place of *Iya*—as interior or exterior to one or another time or language—is a decision that one will have to have refrained from taking, because *Iya* interrupts the terms for the comprehension of language in time. And language, then, as literature, as an event of citation, recitation, and iteration, "prevents literature from assuming form as a stable object of study."[13] Ibrahim Taha has underlined that the story of Iya points to "a total loss and destruction,"[14] but literature repeats the losses—it repeats, as *Iya*, and as if for the first time, its loss—if also the loss of the word *adab* in the Arabic nineteenth century. Language will never simply have left the losses behind, to ruin the finality of loss, which Taha also teaches us to consider. To read this loss in *Iya*—to read the loss of the finality of loss—I turn here to Husayn's *Du'a' al-karawan* (Cairo, 1934), a text about loss, citation, and language.

GHOSTS, CITATION, IDIOM

But I soon begin once more to lose myself in my sadness and distraction.

TAHA HUSAYN, *Du'a' al-karawan*

Iya points—in more than one way, and again and again—to a relation to the Arabic language—to the spoken Arabic language, to the Qur'an (with which *Iya* closes, in a scene to which I turn below), and to Taha Husayn.[15] Ballas's citation of Husayn's *Du'a' al-karawan* (The Call of the Curlew) points to a devastated relation to the loss of a language, and to the reordering of language—and languages—in relation to the state form. *Du'a' al-karawan* is a novelistic text that inscribes itself in a genetic, masculinist, and Orientalist economy. "I took Amina, who was maturing and growing like a young, green tree in the garden, fresh and tender, radiant and beautiful, away from them."[16] Telling the story of a family that is destroyed and remade through the fateful decision of Amina, the family's youngest daughter, the narrative of *Bildung* in the colonies—the narrative privileged in *al-Ayyam* and remarked in the reading practice exemplified in *Fi al-shi'r al-jahili* and *Falsafat Ibn Khaldun al-ijtima'iyya*—is repeated, to suture loss in a figure of wholeness. Following the death of her sister Hanadi, Amina renames herself Su'ad to mourn the losses, even as the losses remain inconsolable, remarked in the event of naming that is to have left loss and death behind. Su'ad comes to live with the young man who had been Hanadi's lover, pointing to a desire to mourn the losses in the circular simplicity of love, "a single thing that takes on different forms and shapes without changing in its essence," but this desire points to a repetition, which confounds the essential nature of the essence it solicits.[17] The pattern repeats throughout the novel, giving that pattern to be read. Haunted by images of her sister, Amina returns "to my calm, peaceful and sad life, without the burden of sadness or joy" (154/124), but the calm and peace solicited here, and in the union of Su'ad and her lover, a union sealed with the name of God ("The burden would be too heavy for you to bear alone, and it would be too heavy for me to do so. So we shall bear our misfortune together until God carries out what has already been determined" [160/130]), is interrupted in the stalled, distracted melancholy of language.

The "strange friendship" (154/125) Husayn describes elaborates the "logic" of *Du'a' al-karawan*. It guards an itinerary that moves from west to east and from the placid, quiet simplicity of the country ("the quiet village I had grown up in" [54/42]) to the urbanity of civilization and the city, and from stupidity ("What would I do in that village and what would my life be like there? Coarse and vulgar, I would spend it in ignorance and stupidity" [54/42–43]) to *nahda* and *tanwir*, if also understanding, *fahm*, and judgment, *hukm*. Yet the movement from the village to the city is also a movement toward literature, civilization, and death. After leaving her village Amina takes up a job at the house of the Ma'mur as the companion of one of his daughters, Khadija. Her arrival at the home entails a relation to pain ("At first my service seemed odd and painful to me, but soon I began to like it and find pleasure and interest in it" [18/10]), and this pain is relayed elsewhere in the novel. The voice of Hanadi, in the figure of the curlew, returns to wake Amina from her sleep to a "pained wakefulness" (22/14), and this pain is reiterated in the demarcating of Amina's relation to Khadija. Amina was to be near to, but not share in, Khadija's learning. "I was to accompany her in her play, but not play with her; to accompany her to the *kuttab*, but not learn with her; to be present with her when her private tutor came before sunset, but not to follow her lessons" (18/10). But this division falls away and Amina comes to share with Khadija her activities, repeating the theologism that closes the novel, and giving it to stutter in its finitude: "Constraints ceased, we became companions and friends" (18/11). This gives Husayn to describe Amina's relation to language, with the oppositions he cannot stop repeating: Khadija speaks the "sweet, pleasant, and refined language" of Cairo; Amina, "a vulgar, rough, and boorish one, that of the peasant of the *Bani al-warkan*" (19/11).

The difference between Amina and Khadija closes just as that between Amina and her mother and sister does not, and this difference is expanded to include Europe. Following the death of Hanadi, Amina returns to Khadija's home. She learns that Khadija had begun to study French, and to describe this new language situation Husayn complicates Amina's earlier discussion of language to reference the language of the countryside, of Cairo, and of books. "She tells me that she had begun to learn a new language which she calls French. I do not understand anything. Another language! How can it be? I know there is the provincial language which I used to speak, the language of Cairo which Khadija speaks, and a third language which we read in books; though we are not unable to understand it, we find some difficulty in it. Another language! How can it be? How can people set about learning it?" (88/70). The illegibility of French, and the inability to determine the beginnings and endings of its letters ("I try to look at the letters but I don't know their beginnings or ends; I recognize neither their heads nor tails. Khadija laughs gently, feeling proud because she knows something I don't. When she deciphers what's in them she achieves something I can't. She translates some of what she reads and I understand what she says in Arabic. I am completely amazed" [88/70]), gives place to understanding, *fahm*, through translation. Reading French gives the gift of *nahda* and *tanwir* in Arabic. It gives place to the Arabic language as its translation of itself into French, and into the discursive terms of legibility in the legacies of Orientalism and the European Enlightenment. Reading is reorganized as an event of temporal domesticity, mirroring the founding, mournful gesture of literature studies. With Amina's learning French, "the curtain falls slowly between me and that terrible and recent past until gradually it is erased" (89/70).

§

But Amina leaves the home of Khadija, who learns she is to be engaged to the young man with whom Hanadi had fallen in love, to live with the family that had earlier employed her mother, Zahra. Her new home is with another family, and if Zannuba, who found her new living situation for her, explains that life there will be "simple" (118/94), the move aggravates her movement away from the city as it propels her toward it. The house is out of step with what it ought to have been in its becoming modern. It is a site of failed, poorly educated modernity, surrounded by the modern but not of it. "We arrived at one of those provincial houses which seem wealthy and whose inhabitants lived a comfortable life. But despite that they only took from the luxury of civilization what was easy and comfortable, maintaining what they were accustomed to in this country life, which tolerates no precision, refinement, or mastery of the satisfaction that comes with taste, and that hates order and flees from it. For them, order and arrangement are a burden and an effort without use—they have no need for them" (120/95). Using energy and resources in vain—the daughters are educated at home, the sons in Cairo—and expenditure without yield mirrors the arrangement of the home and the mixing of animals into its interior. "There was virtually no difference between the people and the animals of the house: the chickens wandered freely everywhere, settling here and there, dragging with them their squalor and mess" (121/96). The interrupted economy of the home gestures to a relation to death and the economy of decline that institutes the reflection on modernity in Arabic. It is here translated into the division of the rural from the urban, and the human from the animal, the former pointing, in Amina's new home, to where "reason comes to be as if it were dead" (121/96).

Amina arrives at the home of her new employer having not taken any books with her. The time of her reading with Khadija is lamented. What has been lost is the time of reading and books. "Where are those times I spent reading, either with Khadija or alone? Where are the Arabic and French books with which I used to spend a good part of the day and some hours of the night?" (122/97). To read, Amina borrows books from her new home. The narrative elaboration of this borrowing ("What harm would there be in taking stealthily a book, looking at it for some time or for just a short while and then putting it back in its place without ever spoiling it? [123/98]) is interrupted by the news that Khadija was not, after all, to be married to the young man with whom Hanadi had fallen in love. The breaking up of the engagement and the splitting of opinions about it ("People disagreed about it" [124/99]) mirror the interruptive economy of the narrative and the relations it installs. The reading lesson given in these pages is intensified when the father discovers that the book with which his children have been spending time ("I had noticed this miserable-looking book, badly printed on poor-quality paper. The young people were really obsessed by this book, they would read it endlessly, rush and vie with one another to get it, and argue about who should have it" [131–32/104]) is *Alf layla wa layla*. "The book is now in my hands; it is ugly, miserable-looking, its paper is of poor quality and the print is bad, but it is called *Alf layla wa layla*. I read, I read more, I forget myself, I lose all sense of time and space. Suddenly, what do I hear? What do I see? The door is carelessly opened, the master of the house enters" (132/105). The entry of the master of the house disrupts the reading scene staged in the text, pointing to the excessive economy Husayn's text remarks but cannot control. This excess points to a time of catastrophe, *bala'* (131/104), which is also the time of literature. "They not only waste their time and effort and their father's energy and money, but they ruin his house with their own hands as if they did not know that this book could not enter a house without bringing it to ruin" (133/106). If Husayn's novel participates in an economy of substitution—it comes to take the place of *Alf layla wa layla* and the ruin it invites—it also stalls that economy and the categories it privileges. The desire to domesticate language is ruined by a past that keeps arriving, and a relation to death that cannot be securely managed, and that gives place to the time of writing.

Amina and Hanadi's uncle, Zahra's brother Nasir, had arrived to bring them back to the village they had left. "The two camels were carrying us toward security and calm, toward honor and protection, and toward where we would spend our lives the way other young village girls like us had become accustomed, quietly and tenderly, until they would grow into the prime and bloom of youth, and the young men from their village or the surrounding ones would come to ask for their hand in marriage" (59–60/47). The uncle commands them to stop while they are journeying at night. "Here we are getting down bewildered and stumbling around. Our mother wants to know why he stopped the camels, and why we are getting down when there is no place to go. Here I am about to say something, but I have scarcely opened my mouth and understood what my mother said before the air is torn by an ominous, horrifying scream, and a body falls on the sand with a dull thud" (64/51). Responsibility for the murder of Hanadi is displaced ("You know, by God, that Hanadi, like many inhabitants of the town, was the victim of this epidemic which she caught a few weeks ago! [66/53]). The novel—like literary history—must cover the tracks of the murder, even as it asks us to read them. If the task of reading in literary history is the comprehension of language in time, *Du'a' al-karawan*, with and against Husayn, offers a treatise on ghosts. Already, the call of the curlew—Hanadi—interrupts Husayn's organicist privilege. Ballas's citation of the title of this Husaynian text recalls us to the time of death and loss in relation to literature, and it asks us to read the Arabic language, in *Iya*, as an event that interrupts a presumed interiority of the Hebrew language, where language will, finally, from before the beginning, have been lost, and where language occurs as a practice of the tongue—*lisan* (Arabic), *lashon* (Hebrew)—that exceeds itself and the time said to be its own.

THE TIME OF LITERATURE

Who can foresee time's upheavals?

SHIMON BALLAS, *Iya*

The losses pointed to in *Du'a' al-karawan* ask us to read *Iya* in relation to loss and to the Arabic language. It is a loss—the loss of language, and of a language—that is gestured to in the narration, and the impossibility, in *Iya*, of simply narrating, the departure of Baghdad's Jewish community in relation to the loss and destruction of Palestine in 1948. "They never imagined it would be like this. Baghdad without Jews? How would Baghdad look without Jews, they say to me" (*I*, 26/81). So, too, Sarah's family is to leave, and the great hall of the synagogue had been transformed into an emigration center. "The crowd formed into groups in the great hall. Since its transformation into an emigration center, the benches had been pushed to the walls and the crystal chandeliers burned day and night" (39/91). It is here that Iya finds herself catching sight of Juliet, who had been a teacher of Sophie years before as a child. "She listened to the exchanges, leaning against the fence with her face to the courtyard, where she saw the teacher, Juliet, with her little brother. She had lost a little weight, but was still full-figured, and her dress fit too tightly about her hips. It had been a while since she had run into her, but she had heard that her two brothers had fled to Iran while she stayed behind with her mother and little brother. A wonderful girl, and how she had suffered in that first year! Sophie had loved her and would recount angrily how the little girls tormented her and how one day she had cried in class. And she loved Sophie, too" (35/88). But the love to which Iya points in this passage, of teacher and student, falls away and disappears—as does Juliet—repeating the immanent departure of the Jews of Baghdad. Iya's line of sight is interrupted twice as her head jerks, first responding to Salha the matchmaker and then to the voice of Abraham the carpenter. "How are you, Zakiya? And how are the children?" (39/91). The call of her name, Zakiya, as if Iya had already been lost, interrupts itself—*aval*—to repeat itself—maybe, perhaps, *ulay*—to repeat the disappearance of Juliet ("But where has Juliet disappeared [Hebrew, aval la an ne'alma Juliet]? Just now she was standing here with her brother. Maybe she's gone into the building" [36/89]) and of the Iraqi Jewish Arabic Iya had learned to speak impeccably ("her impeccable Jewish dialect" [38/90]).

> The push to enter, which he renewed when the gate was opened, gave her an opportunity to leave her place and distance herself from the woman wearing the flowered scarf. She stood now at the edge of the crowd, and a hostile, accusatory voice echoed in her head: *Wa-allah*, she's not a Jew, she's pretending! The woman had been standing behind her in line at the butcher's and she had not reacted. She swallowed the insult in silence [Hebrew, bal'a et 'alvona ve shatka; Arabic, bal'at al-ihana wa samatat]. For some reason, she had been at a loss for words and did not retort scornfully [Arabic, li sababin ma tawahanat anadhak wa lam tarf' sawtaha]. Pretending? Did she pretend? The wickedness of some people. (38/90–91)[18]

Iya's loss for words points—again—to the losses at stake in the reading of *Iya*. Not simply able to speak of loss, or to narrate the loss of Iraq, and of Baghdad, language produces a catachrestic performance of the losses. It is not—as in the other texts I have considered in this book—that what is at stake is a nostalgia for a lost place or a relation to language that is no more but that the losses one is given to read have not simply ended, they may not be said to simply belong to a past, to ruin—and give place to—the event of narration that *Iya* is. This excess is pointed to in Iya's accidental use of the Jewish, Baghdadi dialect in conversation with Naima. I cite here a passage in *Iya*, a portion of which I have cited above, where the loss of language gives place to words that take place in translation. "And when, in conversation with Naima, she was caught using words and phrases in a Jewish accent [Hebrew, ve ka asher hayta nitpeset ba amirat milim ve mishpatim ba matba yehudi], she would laugh contentedly. 'You are more Jewish than Muslim,' Muhyi would chide her jokingly. Yes, more Jewish than Muslim and a Muslim among Jews" (39/91). Iya's use of "words and phrases in a Jewish accent" is accidental—she would catch herself or be caught using them—and this use points to the coincidence or chance, *sudfa*, in relation to which Ballas deposited the name Taha Husayn, and the novel *Dua' al-karawan*, in the passage from the interview I translated above. The interruption of language—and of the time of language—by chance, points to the untimely event that literature is, and this untimeliness is repeated, in the passage in *Iya* we are considering here, in Iya's laughter ("she would laugh contentedly"). The interruption of laughter, in this passage and elsewhere in *Iya*, declines the temporal and linguistic protocols privileged in the disciplines of literature studies—a privilege I read over against the institution of literature in Arabic (in chapters 1 through 3 of this book) and the institution of literature—and practices of reading—in the fallout of the European Enlightenment and Jena Romanticism (in the introduction to this book and chapter 1, and, in the pages that follow in this chapter, in Walter Benjamin's "The Task of the Translator" ("Die Aufgabe des Übersetzers") and the reading of it pursued by Jacques Derrida). Through this interruption *Iya*, like the story it tells, withdraws, confounding the possibility of discerning an "original" language from one taken on only later. And Juliet disappears, while Iya searches for her in the Iraqi synagogue that had been transformed into an emigration center for Jews, pointing to a relation to language and institutions, teaching and reading, memory and recitation. "She wanted to take her into her arms and kiss her farewell. But she had disappeared. It was as if she had flown into the air [Hebrew, ka ilu farkha ba avir; Arabic, ka'annaha talashat fi al-hawa']" (*I*, 41/93).[19]

§

The time of literature is the time of its form. To read this time in relation to language—and languages—in *Iya*, I return to the legacies of Jena Romanticism and Kant's third *Critique* I considered in earlier chapters of this book, to offer a reading of Jacques Derrida's "Des tours de Babel" (Paris, 1985). In this essay Derrida traces the relations among language, translation, the name of his mother ("Safah, the name of the 'lip' and of my mother"),[20] and the name of God ("And the war that he declares has first raged within his name: divided, bifid, ambivalent, polysemic: *God deconstructing*" [207/196]). The occasion for "Des tours de Babel" is Walter Benjamin's "The Task of the Translator," and Derrida reads Benjamin there alongside Genesis 11:1–9, to argue that if the word *Babel* must be translated, it remains untranslatable, "it improperly means the improper, to wit: Bavel, confusion" (207/196). This double injunction points to the division of the name of God, and it is approached in Derrida in order to illumine the understanding of language, translation, indebtedness, and originarity in Benjamin. In "The Task of the Translator," Derrida argues, Benjamin promises an origin that would stand anterior to translation, an original language, even as this promise is interrupted. To suggest this Derrida underscores that in Benjamin translation is a task, *Aufgabe*. That translation is a task, Derrida argues, points to an indebtedness to mark "the authority of what he [Benjamin] still calls 'the original,' not insofar as it produces its receiver or its translators, but insofar as it requires, mandates, demands, or commands them in establishing the law" (216/205). Yet insofar as it lays down the law the original is already indebted (Benjamin writes, "Translation is a mode. To comprehend it as a mode one must go back to the original [gilt es zurückgehen auf das Original], for that contains the law governing the translation: its translatability"), and it may not therefore be said simply to be or to have been an origin.[21] God, like the origin, is indebted—"He is also indebted"—and this indebtedness interrupts the philological and hermeneutic privileging of legibility and sense.[22] In Benjamin relations of kinship between languages are thought "in a sense that is no longer tributary of nineteenth-century historical linguistics, without being totally foreign to it" (212/201), and this sense is read, in Derrida, to recall—as I have tried to offer for consideration through the readings pursued in this book, both between and within languages—language's already being more than one. "Not the origin of language but of languages—before language, languages *plural*" (219/209).

If language is already more than one—"languages plural," as this passage has been compellingly rendered in the English translation—then it is already bereaved, it has already lost itself. This bereavement implies a reflection on form—one which I have pursued throughout, and which I turn to below in relation to the category literature. This category—literature—has become the title of this, final, chapter, to underline that literature—and what is always this act or event of literature—is also a performance of form and its interruption. This interruption is given to be read—in Benjamin and Derrida—in relation to the origin of language and historical linguistics, perhaps the principal philological discipline (Derrida writes of Benjamin's essay, "Perhaps what is here being proposed to us is that we think the very possibility of a historical linguistics" (212/201). In "The Task of the Translator" Benjamin writes of events of translation in German letters ("Luther, Voss, and Schlegel, are incomparably more important as translators than as creative writers"),[23] to underline what he calls a "kinship of languages" (53/72) that will not simply have been historical. The legacies of Jena Romanticism, through Benjamin's reading of "the task of the translator," rescore the European reflection on the origin of language. Translation, in Benjamin, no longer occasions "the imparting of sense" (59/78), and it no longer shares in the historical and philological designation and institution—the invention and proliferation—of language "families," to become what he calls "pure language" (54/74). At the origin of language there will already have been returns and repetitions. Derrida underlines that repetition remarks a haunting dimension of Benjamin's writing on translation and that this repetition confounds the division of life from death ("Neither life nor death, but the haunting of the one by the other").[24] Derrida's "Des tours de Babel" cites the words of another, repeating the indebtedness and the originary pleading Derrida has given us to read ("it begins by lacking—and by pleading for translation"), and which remarks what is most essential about translation: translatability. Underlining the privileging and the interruption of originarity in Benjamin ("There would thus be an original and inaugural way of indebting oneself, it would be the place and date of what is called an original, a work" [231/221]), "Des tours de Babel" teaches us to read the division, and the pleading for another, that already takes place in the "original," and which Benjamin has recalled for us through his writing on the task—*Aufgabe*—of the translator.

> The confusion of languages happened miraculously, creating many different tongues all at once.
>
> GIAMBATTISTA VICO, *The New Science*

> It is as if the very word "tongue" were a catachresis.
>
> DANIEL HELLER-ROAZEN, *Echolalias*

In the introduction to this book I read a passage in Derrida's *The Post Card*, where he writes, "It's always the same thing that comes back, the same wound, it speaks in my place as soon as I open the lips, my own, however" (*P*, 134/122). "Des tours de Babel" is also a writing of words, of "the same thing that comes back," of lips and tongues, and I turn to this text here to read it in relation to the consideration of loss I offer in this book. "Let us not forget that Babel names a struggle for the sur-vival [survie] of the name, the tongue, or the lips,"[25] and this "sur-vival" points to a body and a death, to memory and interiorization, mourning and melancholia, incorporation and introjection, and the "metonomy of the other in ourselves" (20/9). The Hebrew word *safa* may be rendered as "language" or "lip," and it appears in the first verse of the chapter of Genesis Derrida reads in "Des tours de Babel" ("Ve haya kol ha aretz safa ekhat udevarim akhadim [Everyone on earth had the same language and the same words]" [Genesis 11:1]).[26] In the beginning there will have been one language and one lip, *safa ekhat*, but "one," in this passage, is already more than one. A single language, if there is one, already harbors a relation to scattering, a word that appears in three different verbal forms in these passages. "Come, let us build a city, and a tower with its top in the sky, to make a name for ourselves, or else we shall be scattered all over the world [pen nafutz al pnay kol ha aretz]" (11:4). It is then that God goes down to confound language, *nurda venevla sham safatam*, and scatter, *ve yafetz*, the speakers of language and the builders of the tower of Babel "over the face of the whole earth" (11.8). The final verse links language's having been confounded with the scattering of language and its speakers. Derrida's repetition of the word *lip*, and his enjoining us not to forget it, to hold words and names in memory ("Let us not forget that Babel names a struggle for the sur-vival of the name, the tongue, or the lips [une lutte pour la survie de num, de la langue ou des lèvres]), points to the moistened opening of the eye, the mournfulness of reading ("setting your eyes on it in turn like moistened lips [des lèvres humides], you cry and it becomes our bed, the bed—like an opened letter" [*P*, 40/34]), and, in Derrida's text, to a brother, "Paul-Moïse, whom I replaced,"[27] and whose name interrupts a unicity and simplicity of time, an atemporal understanding of form in relation to language.[28]

In a text that was published following his death, and which suggests a reading of the repetition of lips and words, for example, the words *Paul-Moïse*, in his text, Derrida points to the relation between "I" and another. The "question of 'I,' of 'I am' or 'I think,' would have to be displaced," Derrida writes, "toward the prerequisite question of the other," "the other me that I am (following) or that is following me."[29] This question points to an understanding of form in relation to being ("before the question of (the) being as such, of *esse* and *sum*, of *ego sum*, there is the question of following" [94/65]), where a reflection on being presupposes a relation to death and time. The "as such" to which Derrida points in this passage ("before the question of (the) being as such"), gestures to the philosophical tradition Derrida places in question, a tradition that, Derrida also underlines, understands form in a particular way. The "as such" is a hierarchizing gesture, where the universal is distinguished from the particular, the ideal from the factual, and the transcendental from the empirical. The "as such" Derrida recalls in *The Animal That Therefore I Am*, what he elsewhere discusses as "the *as*, the *comme*, the *as such* of the essentiality, of the essential property or propriety" (*G*, 20/13), and which privileges "the monotony of a principle of identity, which, thanks to the copula and sense of being, would here take over alterity itself, nothing less than that, in order to say: the other is the other, that is always so, the alterity of the other is the alterity of the other," this "as such" relates perhaps most essentially to form, where form, *edios* or *morphe*, would remain on the side of the atemporal, and matter, *hyle*, on the side of the temporal.[30] "All the concepts by means of which *eidos* or *morphe* have been translated or determined refer to the theme of presence in general. Form is presence itself [la forme est la présence même]," Derrida also writes.[31] "Formality is whatever aspect of the thing in general presents itself, lets itself be seen, gives itself to be thought," and this thought "is a thought of Being as form" (188/158), where form would remain untouched by death and the divided, interruptive force of time. To think form differently, then, would be to do so not by inverting the privilege Derrida has underlined but by thinking that privilege as producing and being produced through the institution of a border that "no longer forms a single indivisible line but more than one internally divided line," a border—between the temporal and the eternal, between time and being—that repeats itself, giving place to and proliferating a tradition, if one which fails to cease being—and if it is or has been—simply itself.[32]

This border—one I underlined in the first paragraph of the introduction to this book—is solicited to secure a unicity of form. I have read form in this book through the reading Derrida has pursued in the texts I have cited here—and through the discussion of form and breath in Benjamin (in the book on the German mourning play) and in the late lyric poetry of Mahmoud Darwish—and form is addressed, in a fourth sentence in *Margins of Philosophy* I wish to cite here, in the following terms. "Metaphysics—the white mythology which reassembles and reflects the culture of the West: the white man takes his own mythology, Indo-European mythology, his own *logos*, that is, the *mythos* of his idiom, for the universal *form* [my emphasis] of that which he must still wish to call Reason."[33] And so, too—and if through a violent relocation of the terms for the giving of sense in language—are the terms Derrida has underlined here privileged in the Arabic nineteenth century (as in the readings I offer, differently, of al-Bustani, al-Tahtawi, al-Shidyaq, and Husayn, in chapter 2). "For philosophy, the world divides into matter and form," and form, understood as "self-identity," gives the reading of loss—and mutilation—as accidents that happen to an already self-constituted being.[34] "Immediacy," Derrida writes, "is derived."[35] "The speculary dispossession which at the same time institutes and deconstitutes me is also a law of language. It operates as a power of death in the heart of living speech" (204/141), and this power interrupts the fullness and plenitude of speech—of language understood as a form of temporal coherency—in relation to an interruptive relation to death. There will have been no language "without difference as temporalization, without the nonpresence of the other inscribed within the sense of the present, without the relationship with death as the concrete structure of the living present" (103/71). To underline this temporalization, Derrida also writes in *Of Grammatology*, has been to place in question the values of the present, the proximate, and the proper, if also others, and, Derrida underlines, "To make enigmatic what one thinks one understands by the words 'proximity,' 'immediacy,' 'presence' (the proximate, the own, and the pre- of presence), is my final intention in this book" (103/70). Speaking to us of what is final ("my final intention in this book [la dernière intention du présent essai]"), Derrida asks us to read a relation to time and loss. And one is given, then, to hear the name "Paul-Moïse" in the placing in question of the privileging of the *pr*esent and speech, *parole*, in the reading of *pas*,[36] the fold ("since everything begins in the fold [pli] of citation"),[37] re*pe*tition ("law is always a law of repetition" (153/123), and s*pe*cters ("There are several times of the specter" [*SM*, 162/99])"—to stop here. "We all," Derrida also writes, "have so many first names" (*P*, 82/74). An attention to sound teaches one to read "traces of Algeria"[38] in Derrida—traces of more than one name, and of a single name that is already more than one—to become a protocol for reading, and for reading loss.

We always ask to be forgiven when we write or recite.

JACQUES DERRIDA, *Parages*

Literature—if also *Iya*—interrupts its time. It is indebted, already, to more than one other. "A text," Derrida also writes, "has several epochs and reading must resign itself to that fact."[39] To compel language to belong to a single period among others—where new and different "information" would everywhere be called upon to refine or redesignate literary understanding—would point to the differentiating and discriminating practice of reading privileged in the legacies of Europe ("The logocentric longing par excellence is to distinguish one from the other" [237/167]).[40] *Iya* confounds this longing, if also its institutional form in the state and in stately reading institutions. Iya, perhaps more than anything, is a name, and it recalls us to an interruptive understanding of death and time. I have read this understanding in relation to what I have called "iterations of loss," to point to what Derrida—in relation to the pages in *Of Grammatology* I have cited above, where "difference as temporalization" and "the relationship with death as the concrete structure of the living present" are elaborated—called "iterability." Yet iterability—a capacity for citation and repetition—does not come later to language but is constitutive of writing in general. "And what would a mark be that one could not cite? And whose origin could not be lost along the way?"[41] If "iterability" points to citationality and repeatability—events I have tried to read in detail in chapters 1 and 3—this is not because iterability is iteration—it is not repetition—but its possibility, a generalized relation to death that "belongs however to the structure of all writing" (372/313) and language. "A writing that was not structurally legible—iterable—beyond the death of the addressee would not be writing" (375/315). This book has read "iterations of loss" to point to this relation—the relation of death to writing—to underline a contamination of the formal and the empirical, the atemporal and the temporal, and to read this contamination in relation to languages and literary institutions. And I have done so to underline that, in relation to iteration—and what Derrida called "iterability"—aesthetic form becomes an interruptive event, where language "carries with it a force of breaking with its context" (377/317), a "disruption of presence," which Derrida names "writing" (390/327). In this disruption lines of lineage and descent, of paternity and inheritance—lines that are presumed in the institution of states and in the philological idiom

I considered in the introduction to this book (in relation to Kant's "Analytic of the Sublime"—and one may underline that, in Rousseau, "aesthetics passes through a semiology and even through an ethnology") and in the reading of mourning in Hegel (in chapter 1)—become confounded.[42] And Derrida's "Des tours des Babel" becomes, in a certain sense, a postphilological reading of relations—of the relations between and within languages, and of the relation of language to loss. And the name "Iya," then, draws us out toward others, and toward the mournfulness of writing. Such mournfulness points to what Benjamin called the "afterlife" of translation ("Just as the manifestations of life are intimately connected with the phenomenon of life without being of importance to it, a translation issues from the original—not so much from its life as from its afterlife [Zwar nicht aus seinem Leben so sehr denn aus seinem 'Überleben']).[43] Already taking place after itself—already coming later to itself, already having received the gift of an "afterlife," and never simply becoming something that *is*—*Iya* interrupts the terms called upon to read language. The time of literature—the time of *Iya*—a time already "divided from itself—because it is inhabited by another," is an interruption.[44] And *Iya* comes to resemble Juliet, who will already have been lost, and who disappeared as Iya searched for her. "It was as if she had flown into the air" (*I*, 41/93).

ARS MEMORIA

> I never distanced myself from the world in which I was born and in which I grew up. I moved from one place to another in the Arabic-speaking region.
>
> SHIMON BALLAS, *Be guf rishon*

It is not, I have wished to argue, that loss is readable but that reading forms the occasion for a relation to loss and death that interrupts the economy of hermeneutic and historical interpretation I have considered in this book. The mournfulness of language, the unfinished relation to loss language remarks, is given in *Iya* in the figure of Farumi—Ephriam—one of the children of Sarah who is to leave Iraq with the rest of the family for Palestine. Farumi is a nickname, and I turn to it because its shortening repeats the giving of the name "Iya," and because this repetition mirrors others, in relation to language, the Arabic language, and the Qur'an. I linger with the giving of names and nicknames, and with the labor and the iterated movement of the tongue, because Ballas asks us to. And I do so because the departure of Sarah's family points to a reorganization of language in the monolingualism—and in what may perhaps be called the monotemporalism—installed in colonialism and in the state form, in the fallout of the nineteenth century, where a temporal "distinction between the originary and the derivative" in relation to language and an understanding of "historicity" will have been affirmed.[45] "The Jews are going, the Jews are going. It was a grand time for the tinsmiths and the suitcase dealers. Liquidation sale. The seasons of sales to the Jews were over. Earthenware platters for Passover, palm fronds and pomegranates for Sukkot, noisemakers and masks for Purim. There would be no more Jews and their holidays would no longer be felt in the market" (*I*, 47/97). This departure is also a replacement ("Muslims and Christians were replacing Jews, and by summer's end the street would change its face, like many of the other streets in the new quarter beyond the eastern gate" [29/83–84]), which reiterates the reorganization of and violence imparted to populations at more than one site and in relation to more than one language. Yet this violence is also a domestication of the time of life and death—including what Michael Naas has called "an excess of life over itself"—in relation to the giving of sense in language.[46] What Benjamin called "afterlife," then, points to an "irreducible sur-vival or surviving," which interrupts an opposition "between living and dying" (*SM*, 235–36/147), to teach, in *Iya*, a different reflection on time and language, where "the promise of a return to the homeland of language is never fulfilled."[47] The relation of language to loss, and of *Iya* to Arabic, remains unfinished, it becomes relations, ruining the "contemporaneity of the present to itself" (*SM*, 72/39), and the simple interiority of what is said to be "a" language.

Like Ballas, Farumi is a writer, and the decision to leave Iraq is a decision to burn his writing and leave his books behind. "I'm sorting. I'll only send what I need" (*I*, 20/77). Reuven Snir has read Farumi in "autobiographical" terms and in relation to Ballas's "voice," yet one would wish to underline that this "self" already takes place through *Iya*'s—and Iya's—bereaved relation to language, to which the burning of Farumi's writings points.[48] It is not that this text is nostalgic—it is not—or that it mourns the losses—it does not—but that it mirrors a relation to loss and death. The departure of the Iraqi Jewish community does not solicit an origin ("Such panic. As if their house had collapsed on them. The law for the cancellation of citizenship was to be in effect for a year, and only a few had registered when the bombs fell. Had the Jews themselves thrown them as people said? Who knows. A tangle of threads whose beginnings were lost. In another few days, all these people would no longer be here" [*I*, 36/89]). Rather, it points to a doubling and repetition—a historicity, as Darwish and Benjamin have taught us to read it—at the origin, as it declines to subtract out pain and loss from language and from writing. In Ballas there is already "a surviving inherited at the origin" (*SM*, 259/163), to point to "a mourning in fact and by right interminable, without possible normality, without reliable limit" (160/97), and that will never, simply, have been mourned. The interminability of mourning points to the interrupted time of language in Ballas. Language, in Ballas, is already routed through this loss—through the loss of mourning—and *Iya* repeats the loss of the meaning of words Iya experiences. "All the words had lost their meaning [Hebrew, kol ha milim ivdu mashma'uten; Arabic, kul al-kalimat qad faqadat ma'naha], with the gaping suitcases before her, and Sarah's quick hands folding and stowing things within them, back and forth" (*I*, 47/97).[49] Interrupting itself—declining the resolution of loss it also promises—*Iya* mirrors Sophie's laughing at Saul's plan to open a new business once the family will have left Iraq. "Sophie's short laugh sounded like a hiccup [Hebrew, tzkhok katzar she nishma' ka shihuk]" (25/81). This hiccup-laugh recalls the interruptive event of form that literature is. And language, then, "can only communicate itself, and not some signified content."[50] Language is neither a "property" nor a "substance," and, for this reason, it may be generalized in relation to being, where "everything speaks."[51] In this excess of language, one is given to read language differently, otherwise than through its domestication in the historiography of the state form.

> Those that cry lies to Our signs and wax proud against them—the gates of heaven shall not be opened to them, nor shall they enter Paradise until the camel passes through the eye of the needle.
>
> QUR'AN, Surat al-A'raf

> In this way al-Shafi'i confirmed the privileging of the text, and determined for a long time—and we are still living its effects until now—the privileging of the authority of the text over that of reason and human experience.
>
> NASR HAMID ABU ZAYD, *al-Nass wa al-sulta wa al-haqiqa*

In *Iya* the decision to leave Iraq repeats Ballas's decision to write in Hebrew. This decision touches on and is touched by threads, "a tangle of threads [Hebrew, pik'at khutim] whose beginnings were lost" (*I*, 36/89), and by mourning and melancholia, and language and generation. Memory is discussed in relation to loss and birth, and the beginning, in the passage I am going to cite here, will have been twice lost. The date of Hamida's birth has been lost and remains irrecoverable, as has the loss of the ability to securely locate that beginning in time. "For a long while she reproved herself, but the memories would not leave her. They came on together like a long continuous chain, or attacked her in a stampede, so that she could not fix them in time and place. The head is too small to hold them, and things get foggy and are forgotten. Here, she tries to seize the end of the thread and remember how Hamida was born—was it before her husband was taken to the war or afterwards, and the thread slips away from her [Hebrew, ve ha khut nishmat mimena; Arabic, wa al-khayt yanfalit minha] and she cannot decide" (44/95).[52] The time of this loss is the time of decision and its threads, and these threads point, throughout *Iya*, and as the name "Iya," to the time of language and loss.

The losses remarked in this passage and elsewhere ("The days of splendor were over and gone, when the hall would be filled with people in holiday dress come to pray, while the cantor stood at the ark trilling his sweet and melodious voice [42/93]) are already touched upon by language. Loss is already inscribed in language, just as the Qur'an is deposited in *Iya* on its closing page, as if it were a body, as if it pointed to a loss one will never have been able to mourn. "So she [Iya] sat in the shadowy kitchen, emptied of thoughts, stupefied as if in a faint. After some minutes she heard Ephriam's steps on the stairs. Immediately after, she saw his shadow in the doorway. 'Why are you sitting in the dark?' He turned on the light and entered. 'Alone like that in the dark!' She blinked from the light and did not answer. 'I brought you something,' he said, standing beside her. He handed her a book, bound in green and adorned with gold letters. 'The Qur'an I give to you'" (50/99).[53] The Qur'an is a gift, and with Farumi's giving of the Qur'an to Iya, *Iya* repeats the text and the language of the Qur'an. "And we gave Moses the Book [wa atayna Musa al-kitab] and made it a guidance to the children of Israel" (Qur'an 17:2). "The Book" points to the Qur'an ("The clear Book, we have made it into an Arabic Qur'an so that you may understand. It is in the mother of the Book, with us, elevated, wise" [Qur'an 43:2–4]). The repetition in *Iya* of the Qur'an's gesturing itself as a gift teaches us to read a mournful relation to language, and it institutes literature, in *Iya*, as that repetition. Al-Zamakhshari (1075–1144) explains in his *al-Kasshaf ʿan haqaʾiq ghawamid al-tanzil* that the Qurʾan gestures to itself as the mother of the book, *umm al-kitab*, because it is the ground from which other books "are copied and transcribed," and this ground, in Ballas, already will have been in repetition.[54] Literature—if also the Qurʾan and its words—is older and other than itself, at once more and less than what it is, otherwise than its persisting institution as a temporally legible object.

The question of time in the Qurʾan has been addressed by Nasr Hamid Abu Zayd in a text titled *Mafhum al-nass: dirasa fi ʿulum al-Qurʾan* (The Concept of the Text: A Study of the Sciences of the Qurʾan) (Cairo, 1990), and I wish to elaborate the stakes of reading language in Ballas through a consideration of this text. *Mafhum al-nass* draws upon al-Zarkashi's *al-Burhan fi ʿulum al-Qurʾan*, al-Suyuti's *al-Itqan fi ʿulum al-Qurʾan*, which uses the former as its source, and Ibn Khaldun's *Muqaddima* to read "the temporality of the revelation [wahi]."[55] To read this temporality Abu Zayd situates it in relation to two figures: God and man. "If the nouns 'the book' or 'the Qurʾan' are among those that are tantamount to proper names, the noun 'revelation' in its gesturing to the Qurʾan is not. Its meaning expands to include all Islamic and non-Islamic religious texts, for it is a concept that includes all of the texts that signify the discourse of God to man" (31). To read this relation Abu Zayd indexes Ibn Manzur in *Lisan al-ʿarab*, where "the origin of *wahi* [relation] in language in its entirety is communication in secret" (31), and Abu Zayd translates this understanding to explain that *wahi* is a process of communication. "If the central meaning of *wahi* is 'communication,' one condition of this communication is that it be hidden, in secret. One may say otherwise that *wahi* is the connective relation between two points and that it is this which comprises communication—a message [risala]—in hiding, in secret. And if 'communication' is only realized in the process of communication through a particular code, the concept of this code must be presupposed in the concept of *wahi*, and this code, which is used in the process of connection and communication [iʿlam], must be shared between the sender and the receiver, between the two poles in the process of communication/revelation" (31–32). Having understood language in the Qurʾan as an event of communication between two, Abu Zayd then delimits the discussion of *wahi* he offers to prophetic revelation, in order to consider the question of temporality in relation to the Qurʾan.

If what is at stake is to read the time of revelation, this time is thought, in Abu Zayd, in relation to language. To think *wahi* is to think the relation between language and time. "How did connection or communication at the horizontal level, between God and the angel Jibril, take place, and what code was used?" (42). Abu Zayd cites al-Zarkashi to reply as follows: "God gave Jibril to understand his speech while he was in the heavens, in a high place, and he taught him to read it, and then Jibril took it to earth as he descended from the place" (42). He continues, "The expression 'he taught him to read it' ['allamahu qira'atahu'—he taught him to recite it] leaves a wide space of conjecture, but the problematic is posed by the scholars of the Qur'an in another way when they wonder, what is it that Jibril has brought down in the Qur'an? Is it its *lafz* [material utterance] and *ma'na* [meaning]—the text in its content and its form—or is it the content and the meaning, over all of which the Prophet places the clothing of the Arabic language?" (42). Abu Zayd details two sets of responses to this question. The second entails the thought that what was revealed was a set of meanings, *ma'ani*, in isolation from language (44). Abu Zayd cites al-Zarkashi, who writes that "Jibril revealed to the Prophet, prayers and peace be upon him, particular meanings and he, prayers and peace be upon him, came to know them and expressed them in the Arabic language" (44). The first response conceives that revelation was at once *lafz* and *ma'na*, and to describe this reponse Abu Zayd cites a passage in al-Zarkashi, who, in turn, cites al-Ghazali. "*Lafz* and *ma'na*. Jibril memorized the Qur'an from the preserved tablet and revealed it. Some mention that each of the letters of the Qur'an inscribed upon the preserved tablet is the size of *jabal qaf*, and that beneath each are meanings the number of which is circumscribed only by God the powerful and exalted. This is the meaning of al-Ghazali's statement: these letters are a covering over of its meanings" (42).

In both instances what al-Zarkashi points to, for Abu Zayd, is an understanding of the Qur'an as outside of time, and this atemporality points to its "sacredness" (43). "Sacredness," in Abu Zayd, is a mode of understanding language through the grounding of the time of the linguistic utterance in an eternal meaning. If there is a depth and multiplicity in what the Qur'an signifies, "meaning and signification must be reconciled, on the one hand, with eternal speech—which is unified in divine knowledge—and on the other with this great mass of the eternal letters of the Qur'an" (43), and this understanding binds language, for Abu Zayd, to a theological ground. This binding is linked to a reading of language that, he also writes, became hegemonic in the past and continues to be so in the present. "The hegemony of this concept of the meaning of the text and its domination in culture led in the end to the transformation of the action or effectivity of the text from the sphere of linguistic signification, where the text is a message, to the sphere of semiotic determination, where the text is an icon" (44). This event points to the Quran's distinguishing itself from other texts, at the time of the institution of Islam, and perhaps most importantly poetry. "The matter was more serious than determining something permissible or impermissible, it was the attempt of the text [the Qur'an] to impose its hegemony and authority on cultural reality" (140). With the emergence of disciplines for reading, poetry comes to be appropriated into the discourse that instituted itself in the study of the Qur'an, by becoming a "frame of reference" (141) for it. And the qur'anic text is then, in the terms through which Abu Zayd reads language, reified, it is transformed "from a linguistic text that signifies into a mere sacred thing, into a collected text that derives its sacredness from its mere existence as something that represents its eternal ground" (67), and this understanding marks, in Abu Zayd, the discursive terms of Arabic-Islamic "theology."[56]

The gesture that remains decisive, in Abu Zayd, is a historicizing one: the Qur'an is an event that took place in time, and the task of reading—a task exemplified in "a critical position with respect to the inheritance"—is to read the text, *al-nass*, insofar as it is a linguistic, historical event, insofar as it is a linguistic event which took place at a particular place and time.[57] To do so is to bring the study of the Qur'an into contemporary literature studies, *manahij al-dars al-adabi al-mu'asir* (19), through the privileging of a hermeneutic, historical understanding of language. The Qur'an belongs to time, and to read this time is to leave behind the "medieval" and Ottoman periods of decline (language's becoming reified precedes and follows the Crusades to persist during the rule of "military elements of the Seljuks, the Turks, and the Justanids, then the domination of the Ottoman state over the Islamic world, until the First World War").[58] Noncritical reading, in Abu Zayd, "isolates the 'text' from the context of its objective, historical conditions, so that it is distanced from its originary nature as a linguistic 'text,' and is transformed into something that is sacred insofar as it is a thing."[59] To define language in relation to the "two essential poles of communication" (40)—the "sender" and the "receiver"—Abu Zayd cites the first revealed verses of the Qur'an: *iqra' bi ismi rabbika alladhi khalaka*. To read them he underlines that the imperative *iqra'* is to be read as "to repeat" and not "to read" (66). But in the reading Abu Zayd pursues this opening imperative is a first: it is *al-mawqif al-i'tisali al-awwal*, the first communicative position or place.[60] The thought *Iya* imparts, what it stages and performs, is that if the Qur'an is itself ("The Qur'an, as Taha Husayn said, is neither poetry nor prose. It is the Qur'an"), it is only as if the copula ("It is the Qur'an") pointed to a relation to being.[61] The doubling of negation ("neither poetry nor prose") does not yield identity or the secure giving of sense through a transcendental—or historical—ground, because it gestures to the relentless repetition of difference in absolute singularity. To read *Iya*, and to read with *Iya*, is to yield to the iteration of language, where language is "words without final destination" (*P*, 200/185), in the giving of the Qur'an from Farumi to Iya.

INTERRUPTION III

The beginning is always difficult—every beginning is difficult.

SHIMON BALLAS, *Iya*

The dimensions of repetition *Iya* invites us to read are already remarked with its first words. The citation to come, which appears on its closing page, with Farumi's giving the Qur'an to Iya ("He handed her a book, bounded in green and adorned with gold letters. 'The Qur'an I give to you'" [*I*, 50/99]), repeats at the "end" to recall the text's opening iteration. Describing the action as he performs it, in response to Iya's blindness ("Rooted to the spot, she stared at him mutely, and his features blurred gradually before his eyes" [50/99]), Farumi's act mirrors the event of citation, which the gift of the Qur'an, in *Iya*, is. *Iya* stages itself as the repetition of its beginning, where the name "Iya" is at once cited and recited. If in doing so *Iya* recalls a gift of language given in the opening imperative of the Qur'an—*iqra'*, recite—it teaches us that to read is to decline to leave this opening behind. *Iya* points to and undermines the reorganization of this declining as the giving of sense in legibility, in the institution of states and disciplines of reading prior to and following the First and Second World Wars, as do the other texts I have read in this book, and if differently: al-Shidyaq's *al-Saq 'ala al-saq*, El Maleh's *Mille ans, un jour*, Khoury's *Bab al-shams*, and the late poetry of Mahmoud Darwish. To read is to refuse the setting up of literature as an object of discriminating pedagogy in the university, and it is, at the same time, to allow language to teach us, in a pedagogy of interruption without end. And to read, then, is to decline to domesticate that interruption, "A disjointed or disadjusted time without which there would be neither history, nor event, nor promise of justice" (*SM*, 270/170). Such a promise points to an understanding of relation, where relation gives place to a nonserial, atheological practice of relations, a practice that the texts I have considered give us to read. What appears as having passed will never simply have been left behind in the giving of sense, to give language to point elsewhere and toward another, to become what it already is: something else. The texts I have considered give—like Iya, who couldn't decide ("And the thread slips away from her and she cannot decide" [*I*, 44/95])—a politics or ethics, a relation to a responsibility, in the declining of the "uninterrogated clarity"[62] to which language is solicited, something the word of the poet, if also the Qur'an, will have taught us, as one responds in advance to the call of more than one other, "until the white thread of dawn shows clear to you from its black thread [hatta yatabayyan lakum al-khayt al-abyad min al-khayt al-aswad min al-fajr]" (2:187).

NOTES

INTRODUCTION

1. Martin Heidegger, *Was Heißt Denken?*, 40/*What Is Called Thinking?*, 100.

2. Karl Marx and Friedrich Engels, *Manifest der Kommunistischen Partei*, 22–23/*The Communist Manifesto*, 38–39.

3. On the iteration of loss remarked in the refusal to mourn, and in relation to the apparatus of the state and its death—and life—imparting practices, consider the illuminating readings pursued by Avital Ronell in *The Telephone Book: Technology—Schizophrenia—Electric Speech*, *Stupidity*, and *The Test Drive*. And see also the incisive discussion of reading and mourning in Anselm Haverkamp, *Leaves of Mourning*. "The question is less how much mourning is done in reading than how much reading is needed in mourning. Mourning becomes the term for what reading might be all about: a coming to terms with what is on the page, just as what is (left) on the page was a coming to terms with what was not on the page before" (104–5). "Consequently," Haverkamp further writes, "the impossibility of mourning becomes the exemplary instance of the unreadability of writing" (105).

4. "After the War [the Second World War] it turned out that the Jewish question, which was considered the only insoluble one, was indeed solved—namely, by means of a colonized and then conquered territory—but this solved neither the problem of the minorities nor the stateless. On the contrary, like virtually all other events of our century, the solution of the Jewish question merely produced a new category of refugees, the Arabs, thereby increasing the number of the stateless and rightless by another 700,000 to 800,000 people. And what happened in Palestine within the smallest territory and in terms of hundreds of thousands was then repeated in India on a large scale involving many millions of people" (Hannah Arendt, *The Origins of Totalitarianism*, 290). Historical writing on the colonization of Palestine in 1948—and before and after—is vast. Walid Khalidi's *All That Remains: The Palestinian Villages Occupied and Depopulated by Israel in 1948* is an invaluable documentary resource. The history of the notion of population transfer in Zionist thought and its persisting legacies on the ground are discussed in a growing body of scholarship. I have learned from the work of

Nur Masalha, *Expulsion of the Palestinians: The Concept of "Transfer" in Zionist Political Thought, 1882–1948*; Salim Tamari, ed. *Jerusalem 1948: The Arab Neighborhoods and Their Fate in the War*; Ilan Pape, *The Ethnic Cleansing of Palestine*; Rosemary Sayigh, *The Palestinians: From Peasants to Revolutionaries*; Rochelle Davis, *Palestinian Village Histories: Geographies of the Displaced*; Gershon Shafir, *Land, Labor, and the Origins of the Israeli-Palestinian Conflict*; Zachary Lockman, *Comrades and Enemies: Arab and Jewish Workers in Palestine, 1906–1948*; and the essays contained in Ibrahim Abu-Lughod, ed., *The Transformation of Palestine*. And see also, differently, and in a broad temporal frame, Rashid Khalidi, *The Iron Cage: The Story of the Palestinian Struggle for Statehood*.

5. I remain deeply indebted, both in this sentence and throughout this book, to the work on the legacies of the question of Palestine pursued in Edward W. Said, *The Question of Palestine* and *Orientalism*; Ammiel Alcalay, *After Jews and Arabs: Remaking Levantine Culture*; Ella Shohat, *Taboo Memories, Diasporic Voices*; Amnon Raz-Krakotzkin, *Exil et souveraineté: Judaïsme, sionisme et pensée binationale*; Aamir R. Mufti, *Enlightenment in the Colony: The Jewish Question and the Crisis of Postcolonial Culture*; Gil Anidjar, *The Jew, the Arab: A History of the Enemy*; Joseph Massad, *The Persistence of the Palestinian Question*; Gabriel Piterberg, *The Returns of Zionism: Myths, Politics, and Scholarship in Israel*; Gil Hochberg, *In Spite of Partition: Jews, Arabs, and the Limits of Separatist Imagination*; Samera Esmeir, "Memories of Conquest: Witnessing Death in Tanturah"; Sherene Seikaly, "Return to the Present"; and Abraham Serfaty, *Ecrits de prison sur la Palestine*. Alongside the work of Anidjar, where the European, Christian legacies imparted through the division of the Jew from the Arab are discussed in detail, one may also underline the compelling reading offered by Ariella Azoulay, where the division of, and within, Jews from Arabs is related, through a reading of Walter Benjamin's "Critique of Violence," to the constitutive violence occasioned in the institution of the state of Israel in 1948. "Rather than drawing a line between Jews and Arabs, I try to understand its institutionalization as a central principle of the Jewish state. I do so by reconfiguring the disaster imposed on the Palestinians as a *catastrophe* (from a civil perspective) and by presenting it not as the outcome of a war that preceded the creation of the Israeli regime but as a component and product of the new regime's becoming legitimate, that is, of the law itself" (Ariella Azoulay, "Declaring the State of Israel: Declaring a State of War," 276). And see also Azoulay's *From Palestine to Israel*, and, differently, *The Civil Contract of Photography*.

6. Adunis, *al-Kitab: ams, al-makan, al-an*, 1:291.

7. "Comparability" is not intended here to privilege equivalence, understanding, comprehension, or identity but is offered to contribute to the reading of incomparability, untranslatability, incommensurability, and unreadability pursued, in different ways, in the discipline of comparative literature. The reading I offer follows the discussion of "translatability" in Walter Benjamin's "Die Aufgabe des Übersetzers" (The Task of the Translator) and the reading of it pursued by Jacques Derrida in "Des tours de

Babel," where the original—if also, and as Derrida underlines, the word of God—is already indebted, pleading for comparison ("The original is the first debtor, the first petitioner; it begins by lacking—and by pleading for translation" [Jacques Derrida, *Psyché: Inventions de l'autre, Tome 1*, 218/*Psyche: Inventions of the Other*, vol. 1, 207]). My intention is not to argue that texts, or languages, are simply comparable or translatable. Neither do I wish to suggest that they are incomparable or untranslatable, a reading that would presume a linguistic plenitude or a sheer absence of sense. In this book I underline, differently, that events of language take place as comparability, as a pleading for comparison in relation to a catachrestic dimension of language. Here, language points to other configurations of being and relation, a "survival" of the "original" ("The original requires translation even if there is no translator fit to respond to this injunction, which is at the same time demand and desire in the very structure of the original. This structure is the relation of life to sur-vival" [216/205]) in and through languages and relations invented through acts of comparison, languages and relations that will never simply have been their own. Alongside work on literary comparison I read and cite below, I learn here from the reading of Benjamin offered by Samuel Weber in *Benjamin's—abilities*, where, in "translatability" "the original can only be itself by becoming something different" (61), and where comparison forms the occasion for the staging of "a convergence that does not result in simple identity" (230) but a parting and coming apart in "comparability."

8. See Sigmund Freud, "Trauer und Melancholie" (Mourning and Melancholy).

9. Paul de Man, *The Rhetoric of Romanticism*, ix. The discussion I offer in this book of the domestication of loss, language, and death through a privileging of the aesthetic as an articulation of relations that is at once legible and total remains indebted to the reflection offered by de Man on "the ideology of the aesthetic" (Paul de Man, "Aesthetic Formalization: Kleist's *Über das Marionettentheater*," 264). Reading with de Man's late essays on Kant ("Aesthetic Formalization," "Phenomenality and Materiality in Kant," "Kant's Materialism," and "Kant and Schiller"), I ask how de Man's text teaches us to attend to reading institutions—in European and non-European languages. And I ask how this attention teaches a critique of the proliferating desire to appropriate non-European languages and literatures, through a "stabilization of form and of reading" (Paul de Man, "Hypogram and Inscription," 43), into the disciplines of the humanities in the Euro-American university. The formulations I offer here and in what follows remain indebted to the discussion of the aesthetic offered in Marc Redfield, *Phantom Formations: Aesthetic Ideology and the Bildungsroman* and "De Man, Schiller, and the Politics of Reception," and the consideration of reading in relation to "the disruption of the specular structure of figuration" in Cynthia Chase, *Decomposing Figures: Rhetorical Readings in the Romantic Tradition*, 21–22. I learn to read the privileging of the aesthetic as a totalization of form in relation to European colonialism and the pacified form of the

work through the discussion pursued in David Lloyd, *Anomalous States: Irish Writing and the Post-Colonial Moment*, 26 passim.

10. The work of Maria Torok and Nicholas Abraham, and through their discussion of introjection and incoporation, remains a singular site through which such a declining is given. "While the introjection of desires puts an end to objectal dependency, incorporation of the object creates or reinforces imaginal ties and hence dependency. Installed in place of the lost object, the incorporated object continues to recall the fact that something else was lost: the desires quelled by repression. Like a commemorative monument, the incorporated object betokens the place, the date, the circumstances in which desires were banished from introjection: they stand like tombs in the life of the ego" (Maria Torok, "The Illness of Mourning and the Fantasy of the Exquisite Corpse," 114). And see also Nicholas Abraham and Maria Torok, *The Wolfman's Magic Word: A Cryptonomy* and "Mourning *or* Melancholia: Introjection *versus* Incorporation"; and the reading of Torok and Abraham pursued in Jacques Derrida, "Fors."

11. Jacques Derrida, *Mémoires pour Paul de Man*, 102/*Memoires for Paul de Man*, 98. The French passage I cite here from *The Post Card* is, "C'est toujours la même chose qui revient, la même plaie, elle parle à ma place dès que j'ouvre les lèvres, les miennes pourtant."

12. Avital Ronell, *Stupidity*, 252: "In the less *Bildungs*-driven texts under consideration, these preludes to *The Prelude* [of Wordsworth], the notch of mutilation points to something that is inassimilable, stunted, incapable of being marked or mourned."

13. Judith Butler, *The Psychic Life of Power*, 76.

14. Rei Terada, *Looking Away: Phenomenality and Dissatisfaction, Kant to Adorno*.

15. Paul de Man, "Aesthetic Formalization," 288, 267.

16. Walter Benjamin, *Ursprung des deutschen Trauerspiels*, in *Gesammelte Schriften*, vol. 1, pt. 1, 208/*The Origin of German Tragic Drama*, 28. All emphases in all passages cited in this book appear in the original unless otherwise indicated between brackets.

17. For a reading of language practices in relation to the maintenance of a social and political order, consider the discussion of insurgency in Ranajit Guha, *Elementary Aspects of Peasant Insurgency in Colonial India* ("Indeed it would be quite in order to say that insurgency was a massive and systematic violation of those words, gestures, and symbols which had the relations of power in colonial society as their significata" [39]). A reading of insurgency as an event of political and semiotic interruption is also underlined in *Elementary Aspects*, 56, 245. And see as well Guha's discussion of form in relation to peasant insurgency and various modes of containment in historiography, and in relation to the institution and preservation of a "body politic" (223) in colonial India. Aesthetic form as a political and social event, and if also as an interpretive one, may further be read in relation to Guha's underlining, in the institution of the Permanent Settlement in Bengal, an articulation of a historical distinction between the medieval and the modern, and the religious and the secular, with "a general division of society between

an enlightened minority in whom all authority was vested and a mass of people laboring for the few who acted as their guardians" (Ranajit Guha, *A Rule of Property for Bengal*, 113). And consider also, differently, the discussion of the "strategic use of inegality and violence" in relation to "the formal structure of property" and "the legally constituted domain of civil society" in Partha Chatterjee, *The Politics of the Governed: Reflections on Popular Politics in Most of the World*, 76, 74 passim. In the Arabic context, the readings pursued in Kenneth M. Cuno, *The Pasha's Peasants: Land, Society, and Economy in Lower Egypt, 1740–1858*; Nathan J. Brown, *Peasant Politics in Modern Egypt: The Struggle against the State*; and Sayyed al-'Ashmawi, *al-Fellahun wa al-sulta*, remain urgent diagnostic and historical studies. And see also the discussion of the domestication of the peasant, "a delightful, static and safely contained image of the domesticated collective," in relation to the totalizing form of the novel in Samah Selim, *The Novel and the Rural Imaginary in Egypt*, 114. "In its efforts to create its own social destiny, this artificial, autonomous self contains and resolves the ontological contradictions embedded in the novel and emerges as a kind of 'mirror' of the social body as a whole" (14), an understanding that also points, as Selim compellingly underlines, to "the question of language as a discursive formation" (54). This question is elaborated through the reading pursued by Omnia El Shakry of the fields of ethnography, peasant and population studies, and medicine in colonial Egypt, where the legacies of reading in "Oriental philology" are related to "the transition from a textually based Orientalism concerned with collection and commentary to an experimental and clinical science of native difference" (Omnia El Shakry, *The Great Social Laboratory*, 31), a transition El Shakry teaches us to read in relation to a desire to "contain radical social change in the countryside" through the domestication of "the figure of the undisciplined rural subject" (116, 202). And compare, differently, and in relation to "radicalism" in Beirut, Cairo, and Alexandria, the readings pursued by Ilham Khuri-Makdisi in *The Eastern Mediterranean and the Making of Global Radicalism, 1860–1914*.

18. I borrow the term *epistemic violence* from Gayatri Charavorty Spivak, *A Critique of Postcolonial Reason: Toward A History of the Vanishing Present*, 266, and offer a consideration and expansion of it in relation to language and to the forms of destruction imparted to language at a particular, multilingual, colonial site.

19. Timothy Mitchell, *Colonising Egypt*, 132, 158.

20. And consider that, for Mitchell, prior to "colonial or modern politics," "Muslim scholars" shared in an Aristotalean tradition that was ruptured twice: first in Europe ("Descartes announced the West's rejection of the scholastic tradition" [178]) and again "in the case of the Middle East" (177), in the nineteenth century.

21. "It was in the *Discourse* [of Descartes] that European philosophy broke with the method of scholarship it had shared with the Islamic world" (Timothy Mitchell, *Colonising Egypt*, 178).

22. I learn here from the discussion of the "work of death" pursued in Michel de Certeau, *The Writing of History* ("Between the seventeenth and

eighteenth century, what allows the seen body to be converted into the known body, or what turns the spatial organization of the body into a semantic organization of a vocabulary—and vice versa—is the transformation of the body into extension, into open interiority like a book, or like a silent corpse placed under our eyes. An analogous change takes place when tradition, a lived body, is revealed to erudite curiosity through a corpus of texts" [3]). And consider as well the compelling discussion of death and the "medieval" in relation to the practice of historicism pursued by Dipesh Chakrabarty in *Provincializing Europe: Postcolonial Thought and Historical Difference* and *Habitations of Modernity: Essays in the Wake of Subaltern Studies*. I learn in particular from the passage that reads "modernity" as a persisting site for the articulation of temporal and historical divisions. "It is, of course, entirely possible that the word *modernity* has outlived its utility as a rigorous concept and is mostly of rhetorical value in today's debates. Yet it is a word that we cannot do without in the everyday context of discussions of democracy and development. It comes into use in the same way as words like *medieval* or *feudal* circulate in ordinary speech as expressions of moral value" (Dipesh Chakrabarty, *Habitations of Modernity*, xx). And see as well the discussion of the "premodern" and "archaic" in Partha Chatterjee, *Lineages of Political Society: Studies in Postcolonial Democracy*, 134, and what he discusses as a "strategy of historicization" (2). A stunning consideration of the "medieval" and "feudal" as temporal categories, and to which I remain indebted, is offered in Kathleen Davis, *Periodization and Sovereignty: How Ideas of Feudalism and Secularization Govern the Politics of Time*. A critique of the reading of the Arabic-Islamic past as "theology" is pursued by Abdallah Laroui in *The Crisis of the Arab Intellectual: Traditionalism or Historicism?*, 65 n. 26, 44–80. And compare the discussion of "Islamic metaphysics" and "theology" offered in Fethi Benslama, *Psychoanalysis and the Challenge of Islam*, 37 passim. I offer a reading of the categories of the "religious" and the "medieval" in the work of Adunis, Muhammad 'Abid al-Jabri, Taha Husayn, Faysal Darraj, and others, below, in chapters 1 and 2.

23. Natalie Melas, *All The Difference in the World: Postcoloniality and the Ends of Comparison*, 37. Citations from Paul (in this instance and elsewhere in this book) are taken from *The New Oxford Annotated Bible*, ed. Herbert G. May and Bruce M. Metzger. The practices of reading I gesture to here may be considered in terms of the desire to secure legibility through acts of targeting identification in the wake of 9/11 discussed in Marc Redfield, *The Rhetoric of Terror: Reflections on 9/11 and the War on Terror*. Such acts point to legacies that are at once quite old, gesturing to "an onto-theological tradition that has arguably never been stronger or more capable of laying waste to the world" (46), even as they mark the proliferation of new divisions. A consideration of such divisions is offered in the discussion of targeting in relation to the disciplines of literature studies and the institution of a "linguistic cosmopolitanism and the peaceful coexistence of national and cultural traditions" in Rey Chow, *The Age of the World Target: Self-Referentiality in War, Theory, and Comparative Work*, 72; and Samuel Weber, *Targets of Opportunity: On the Militarization of Thinking*. Targeting, as

Weber explains, occasions an act of identifying designation that is equally an act of both objectification and differentiation. "What is involved here is the difference between something simply being 'seen' and something being 'sighted'—that is discovered, localized, identified in order to be hit or struck" (8).The reading I am pursuing in this paragraph learns as well from the argument offered by Weber in terms of the legacies of Christianity in relation to the practice of reading in literature studies, where literature is "construed as an artifact that both consumes and fulfills itself in the reception or readings it receives" (Samuel Weber, *Benjamin's—abilities*, 22). And see as well, on reading as an event of temporal domestication in relation to Christianity, Erich Auerbach, "Figura"; Jill Robbins, *Prodigal Son/Elder Brother: Interpretation and Alterity in Augustine, Petrarch, Kafka, Levinas*; and Kathleen Biddick, *The Typological Imaginary: Circumcision, Technology, History*.

24. Ibrahim Abu-Lughod, *The Arab Rediscovery of Europe*, 77. A transformation in "Arabic style" is discussed, following the reading of language pursued by Albert Hourani, Jamal Mohammed Ahmed, and others, in Irene Gendzier's study of the Egyptian playwright and journalist Ya'qub Sanu' (1839–1912). Pointing to a series of literary societies that had been formed in the Levant during the nineteenth century, and which formed an occasion for the work of Butrus al-Bustani (1819–83), who I discuss in chapter 2, Gendzier writes that "literary societies, such as those mentioned, contributed to the modernization of Arabic style" (Irene Gendzier, *The Practical Visions of Ya'qub Sanu'*, 42). Gendzier links this "modernization" to a withdrawal of "religion" ("they had redefined or given less priority to religion" [30]), which points to "fundamental change." "In itself, this implies a fundamental change in the place of religion in society, which in this case is equivalent to a change in the very nature of the society involved" (30). In this change, Gendzier reads Sanu' as privileging an understanding of *Bildung*, culture or formation, in relation to language and the British occupation of Egypt in 1882 ("While Sanu' did not formally establish institutions of learning, his work as a journalist was devoted to the education of both Egyptians and Europeans; and he was sensitive to the fact that education alone would ultimately prepare Egyptians for independence" [97]). Readings of language in the Arabic nineteenth century since this scholarship—which was published in the 1960s—have approached language differently, in relation to more than one juridical, colonial event of violence (in Timothy Mitchell's *Colonizing Egypt*), in relation to capital and a new privileging of form and harmony (in Beth Baron's *The Women's Awakening in Egypt*, which I discuss below in the following note), in relation to "social relations of authority" and class (in Juan Cole's *Colonialism and Revolution in the Middle East*, 112, 115), and in the compelling reading of language in terms of the domestication of the fellahin and the urban poor in relation to "the national struggle" offered by Zachary Lockman in "Imagining the Working Class," 181 passim. Another line of questioning has been offered in relation to pre-nineteenth-century dislocations and dislodgings of language in Arabic, and in relation to the force of capital, in Peter Gran's *Islamic Roots of Capitalism*, Nelly Hanna's *In Praise of Books*, and, perhaps most recently, Dana Sajdi's *The Barber*

of Damascus, where what Sajdi calls events of "disturbance in the literary order" (20) are read in relation to "the long eighteenth century" (97, 114) and, differently, and if earlier still, "the twelfth and thirteenth" (122). And compare the discussion of "education" and "individual reading," in Konrad Hirschler, *The Written Word in Medieval Arabic Lands: A Social and Cultural History of Reading Practices* (106, 124, 141 passim). In terms of the discussion I offer here, I underline only that a reflection on language in relation to what Gran called "the creation of a modern, secular culture" (Peter Gran, *Islamic Roots of Capitalism*, 154)—Gran writes that, "Clearly, the commercial revival of the eighteenth century triggered a renewal of vitality in the religious life of Egypt, which in turn gave birth to a nascent secular culture" (74)—compels attention to the ways in which the categories privileged in *Islamic Roots*—the modern and secular, life and death ("a renewal of vitality in the religious life of Egypt")—teach us to consider the event of language I study in relation to the historical and aesthetic categories that have been called upon to read it. And see as well, earlier—in 1957—and in relation to the temporal rupture this scholarship has opened, Albert Hourani, "The Changing Face of the Fertile Crescent in the XVIIIth Century," where, anticipating the language privileged throughout his work, Hourani points to a "revival of culture" (104, 113) in the eighteenth century. Through a discussion of the relation of the Maronite Church to Rome—and to Europe and its learning ("the Oriental Colleges in Rome")—Hourani further explains that "the level of intellectual life rose" ("The Maronites too had been Catholic since the time of the Crusades, and the Concordat of 1736 strengthened their relations with Rome. It was through this renewed contact with the Papacy, and in particular through the Oriental Colleges in Rome, that the level of intellectual life rose, first among the clergy and then among the laity" [105]).

25. Elizabeth Kassab, *Contemporary Arab Thought: Cultural Critique in Comparative Perspective*, 32. And consider also the discussion of language pursued by Beth Baron in relation to an "evolution in literacy" in late-nineteenth and early-twentieth-century Egypt (Beth Baron, *The Women's Awakening in Egypt*, 83). Baron argues that the "modernization" of the Arabic language ("In the pages of the women's press, writers explored a variety of forms, developed new styles, and helped modernize the written language" [54]) took place in relation to an "evolution" and a displacement of what she calls "religion" in relation to "the new ideology of domesticity" (165) and "innovations that broke with the patterns of the past" (124). "Language, which had traditionally been the preserve of religious scholars, underwent an evolution" (55). This "evolution" is further discussed in relation to "a new aesthetic" ("At the same time, writers developed a new aesthetic in prose that avoided the use of the more arcane vocabularies of the past, encouraged new forms stripped of rhyming schemes and other rigid structures, and emphasized directness and fluidity. Obscure words were cut back, and formalized writing gave way to a clearer style" [55]). One learns from Baron's elaboration, because it relates language to the "capitalist economy" (151), domestic harmony ("A harmonious home depended upon a healthy marriage, and therefore women writers pushed for reforms in marriage and divorce" [166]), and a privileging of enlightenment

("the sense that women were emerging out of darkness into light and learning" [180]). Yet if it is not, as Baron rightly argues, that in what called itself *nahda* (renaissance, awakening) "writers in the early women's press" were "merely echoing a colonial discourse" (167), one may ask whether, prior to what she calls a "strategic decision" taken by these writers, such a decision bears a relation to a colonial violence and a destruction in language. Already, the subject of language takes place in relation to this violence—a violence, Baron also suggests, imparted to each of what she also calls "the general" and "the women's nahda." "The general nahda and the nahda al-nisa'iyya diverged only at the choice of contents, with women often but not always preferring domestic and social topics" (56). And compare the discussion of colloquial poetry offered by Joel Beinin, where, to locate this poetry on the side of politics ("a mode of expression which, despite the antiquity of its form, was consciously chosen by nationalist intellectuals as a political intervention at a particular historical moment"), Beinin reads "standard Arabic" in relation to "religious associations" ("Because it did not bear the burden of the religious associations of standard Arabic, colloquial zajal was open to foreign influence and could more easily integrate language and experiences derived from the foreign presence in Egypt, even as the poets and their audiences mocked the foreigners and struggled against them" [Joel Beinin, "Writing Class: Workers and Modern Egyptian Colloquial Poetry," 195]). Underlining an opposition between this poetry and "elite aesthetic and linguistic conventions" (207), language, in Beinin's reading, privileges "active subjects" (203), where "workers" are called upon to "transform themselves from the subject and the audience of the poem into the authors of their own destiny" (204). Yet the privileging of the notion of the "author" as an autonomous subject, if a collective one—an "elite" notion?—may, in a way that collapses the firm distinction between spoken and written Arabic Beinin privileges, be read differently, in relation to an attention to form.

26. I borrow the word *conscription* here from the illuminating discussion offered by David Scott in *Conscripts of Modernity: The Tragedy of Colonial Enlghtenment.*

27. Judith Butler, *Giving an Account of Oneself*, 52.

28. Aamir R. Mufti, *Enlightenment in the Colony*, 20.

29. I learn here as well from the illuminating work of Ronald A. T. Judy, who elaborates the violence occasioned in the reading of a single non-European, Arabic corpus as exemplary, and therefore as appropriable into the discursive legacies of Enlightenment and the understanding of being in the European disciplines of reading ("The way in which writing relates to the discursivity of thought cannot be demonstrated by way of example" [Ronald A. T. Judy, *(Dis)Forming the American Canon: African-Arabic Slave Narratives and the Vernacular*, 99]).

30. See Jacques Derrida, "Signature Événement Contexte," in *Marges de la philosophie*, 365–93/"Signature Event Context," in *Margins of Philosophy*, 307–30.

31. The discussion of philology I offer in this book situates it in relation to the reflection on the origin of language in Europe, with the reorganization of non-European languages according to a domesticating grid of ontotheological

legibility. I follow here a protocol explicated by Jacques Derrida in the following terms. "The history of the alphabet is accepted only after recognizing the multiplicity of the *systems* of script and *after assigning a history to them* [my emphasis], whether or not one is in the position to determine it scientifically" (*De la grammatologie*, 112/*Of Grammatology*, 76). I also learn from the work on philology pursued in Edward W. Said, *Orientalism*; Tomoko Masuzawa, *The Invention of World Religions, Or, How European Universalism Was Preserved in the Language of Pluralism*; Amnon Raz-Krakotzkin, *The Censor, the Editor, and the Text: The Catholic Church and the Shaping of the Jewish Canon in the Sixteenth Century*; Jonathan Sheehan, *The Enlightenment Bible: Translation, Scholarship, Culture*; Gil Anidjar, *Semites: Race, Religion, Literature*; Daniel Heller-Roazen, *Echolalias: On the Forgetting of Language*; Stathis Gourgouris, *Dream Nation: Enlightenment, Colonization, and the Institution of Modern Greece*; John T. Hamilton, *Soliciting Darkness: Pindar, Obscurity, and the Classical Tradition*; and Michel Foucault, *The Order of Things* ("It is apparent, then, that historicity was introduced into the domain of languages in the same way as into that of living beings" [292]). A discussion of the privileging of the category "history" in the fallout of the Enlightenment is offered in Reinhart Koselleck, *Futures Past: On the Semantics of Historical Time*. The work of Hans Aarsleff in *From Locke to Saussure: Essays on the Study of Language and Intellectual History* and Maurice Olender in *The Languages of Paradise: Race, Religion, and Philology in the Nineteenth Century* has helped to situate the question I ask in terms of the persistence of older legacies. Bernard Cohn's *Colonialism and Its Forms of Knowledge* is an important intervention in terms of reading this persistence as it bears upon language practices in the colonies.

32. I learn here from the reading of Kant pursued in Sankar Muthu, *Enlightenment against Empire*, but wish to underline that, with and against empire, the idiom generalized in Kant shares in the colonization of more than one language, and in the destruction of certain forms of life and ways of being and the sanctioning of others. In what follows I am attentive to the argument, offered by Frederick Cooper, that colonialisms, European and others, are each more than one but wish to underline that in fallout of the sixteenth century, and with what Hans Blumenberg has called "the genesis of the Copernican world," the terms of life, being, and language have come to be fundamentally, if compulsively and interruptively, altered. If, in the terms Cooper underlines, "'the' Enlightenment implied no one view of race or difference. It provided no clear bases either for legitimizing the subordination of non-European societies on the basis of universalistic criteria or for claiming that cultural difference precluded criticizing different political practices, in Europe or elsewhere" (Frederick Cooper, *Colonialism in Question*, 21), what I wish to offer for consideration is not a reflection on legitimation or a desire to subordinate but one that would attempt to think the ways in which language, being, and life, prior to such acts, are already touched upon by the violence of colonialism and the juridical force of the colonial state.

33. And compare Horkheimer and Adorno, where in Enlightenment "Whatever might be different is made the same [Was anders wäre, wird

gleichgemacht]" (Max Horkheimer and Theodor Adorno, *Dialektik der Aufklärung*, 18/*Dialectic of Enlightenment*, 8). Horkheimer and Adorno's further discussion of "the subsuming of difference under sameness" (190/148) may be considered in relation to the reading of "dominant power" offered in Talal Asad, *Genealogies of Religion: Discipline and Reasons of Power in Christianity and Islam* ("To secure its unity—to make its own history—dominant power has worked best through differentiating and classifying practices" [17]). I remain indebted to a certain thread in Asad's work, and yet one would wish to underline that the institution of difference—and differences—is not proliferated and imposed through and in relation to "traditions" each of which is "not" the other ("The virtuous Muslim is thus seen *not* [my emphasis] as an autonomous individual who assents to a set of universalizable maxims but as an individual inhabiting the moral space shared by all who are together bound to God (the umma)" [219]) and each of which is said to stand in contrast to others ("This stands in sharp contrast to the Enlightenment view of criticism as a *right*, whose exercise is therefore optional" [215]) but already takes place in relation to an asymmetrical imparting of violence—juridical and other. This violence does not come later to "tradition" or the "past" but forms a condition of the possibility for tradition's being what it is at all. "Tradition"—if also "culture" and "religion"—is not anterior to the law (e.g., the institution of European forms and practices of the law in the colonies) but constituted through its operation. Asad has underlined that translation bears upon forms of life ("All successful translation is premised on the fact that it is addressed within a specific language, and therefore also to a specific set of practices, a specific form of life" [189]), but such forms of life—including, and not solely, those privileged in Kant—are already given, differently, through and in relation to practices of colonial and colonizing violence—a violence which may not be belatedly subtracted out. And see also, around a persisting series of questions, Talal Asad, "Conscripts of Western Civilization," *Formations of the Secular: Christianity, Islam, Modernity*, and *On Suicide Bombing*.

34. Jacques Derrida, *La vérité en peinture*, 153/*The Truth in Painting*, 134. And see the discussion of the third *Critique* in Gil Anidjar, *The Jew, the Arab*, 120–25, and of race in relation to religion in *Semites*. And consider as well, in relation to readings of Kant, Marc Redfield, *Phantom Formations*, 20–27, and Gayatri Chakravorty Spivak, *A Critique of Postcolonial Reason*, 10–37, to which I turn below. On race in relation to the state form, see David Theo Goldberg, *The Racial State*, and in relation to colonial legacies, Ann Laura Stoler, *Race and the Education of Desire*.

35. Jacques Derrida, *La vérité en peinture*, 128/*The Truth in Painting*, 112.

36. Marc Redfield, *Phantom Formations*, 53–54. And compare the reading offered in Jean-François Lyotard, *Lessons on the Analytic of the Sublime*. "Sublimity does not predicate the thing but the *Geistesstimmung*, the disposition of thinking that experiences or reflects on itself when it represents the thing to itself" (81).

37. Jacques Derrida, *La vérité en peinture*, 127/*The Truth in Painting*, 111.

38. Marc Redfield, *Phantom Formations*, 6.

39. A stunning discussion of the confounding of the privileging of autonomy in Kant is presented in Elizabeth Rottenberg, *Inheriting the Future: Legacies of Kant, Freud, and Flaubert*, 36 passim. And see also, in relation to the third *Critique*, Rodolphe Gasché, *The Idea of Form: Rethinking Kant's Aesthetics* ("From the very start, then, it would seem that, however important its function may be, the power of judgment is marked by a certain self-effacement, a subservience and a lack of independence" [13]). I learn as well from the reading offered by Peter Fenves, who writes that "the feeling of sublimity is *only* a feeling, not a secure basis for knowledge, not even knowledge of the self" (Peter Fenves, "Taking Stock of the Kantian Sublime," 66).

40. Immanuel Kant, *Kritik der Urteilskraft*, 110/*Critique of Judgment*, 103.

41. See Gayatri Charavorty Spivak, *A Critique of Postcolonial Reason*, 1–37. The passage in Kant I follow Spivak to read here appears in *Kritik der Urteilskraft*, 134/*Critique of Judgment*, 124.

42. Gayatri Chakravorty Spivak, *A Critique of Postcolonial Reason*, 13.

43. Immanuel Kant, *Kritik der Urteilskraft*, 134/*Critique of Judgment*, 124. And compare, in terms of the reading of this passage pursued by Spivak, the discussion offered by Marc Nichanian of "the invention of the native" (Marc Nichanian, "On the Archive III: The Secret; or, Borges at Yale," 12) in relation to European philology, Orientalism, historicism, and ethnology, and the distinction Nichanian draws between the native and the savage (13–14), and Marc Nichanian, *Mourning Philology: Art and Religion at the Margins of the Ottoman Empire*, 73–77. The "native"—what Nichanian also calls "the central invention of philological Orientalism" (173)—is formed, in Nichanian's reading, in relation to an "auto-orientalism" and an "auto-ethnography" (153), the "adoption" and "internalization" (76) of Orientalist, philological categories by, and as the invention of, "the native himself" (76). In terms of the reading I pursue of the distribution and proliferation of European philological and aesthetic categories in the Arabic nineteenth century, and which I study in chapter 2, I also remain indebted to the reading of "the negro" in Kant offered by Ronald A. T. Judy ("Kant's problem is how to think about the Negro, not as a phenomenal appearance, or undetermined object of an empirical intuition, but as an intellectual concept, a derivative of the concept of '*Man*'" (Ronald A. T. Judy, *(Dis)forming the American Canon*, 115).

44. The reading I offer of Kant—and of the legacies of Jena and of German romance philology—learns and diverges from the discussion offered by Pheng Cheah in *Spectral Nationality: Passages of Freedom from Kant to Postcolonial Literatures of Liberation*. In Cheah, a Kantian legacy is transposed from Europe to the postcolony, "from Kant to postcolonial literatures of liberation," where the latter is recognized through its derivative relation to the former ("The living people's vulnerability is precisely the aporia of *techne* and *physis* afflicting Kant's *inaugural* [my emphasis] explanation of organic life as the technic of nature" [229]). Yet Cheah's provocation compels the argument I offer here: that rather than an event of transposition that presupposes an understanding of being ("the living people's vulnerability

is"), the Kantian moment and the displacements it remarks—its "displacement outside the North Atlantic" (12) and "the displacement of a cosmological worldview by an anthropologistic and mechanistic modern worldview" (241)—compel attention to the polemological dimensions of writing in the language practices of Europe I read. And compare as well, differently, that Adorno, for his part, reads the third *Critique* in relation to Kant's "affirmation" of his "unquestioning complicity with domination" ("However, by situating the sublime in overpowering grandeur and setting up the antithesis of power and powerlessness, Kant directly affirmed his unquestioning complicity [seine fraglose Komplizität] with domination" [Theodor Adorno, *Ästhetische Theorie*, 296/*Aesthetic Theory*, 199]).

45. Immanuel Kant, *Anthropologie in pragmatischer Hinsicht*, 93/*Anthropology from a Pragmatic Point of View*, 86. I am indebted here to the work of Friedrich Kittler, *Discourse Networks 1800/1900*.

46. Immanuel Kant, *Kritik der Urteilskraft*, 147/*Critique of Judgment*, 135. Anidjar has pursued a reading of this passage in Kant, which I continue to cite below, in terms of its articulation of a "conflictual unity" (Gil Anidjar, *The Jew, The Arab*, 120), and which I consider here following a slightly different vector to underline its elaboration (and disarticulation) as a philological question—as the very question and practice of philology.

47. Immanuel Kant, *Die Religion innerhalb der Grenzen der bloßen Vernunft*, 172/*Religion within the Bounds of Mere Reason*, 156.

48. Immanuel Kant, *Kritik der Urteilskraft*, 134–35/*Critique of Judgment*, 125.

49. Immanuel Kant, *Kritik der reinen Vernunft/Critique of Pure Reason*, A 680, B 708. All references refer to the pagination offered in the edition of Jens Timmerman, and to the first and second editions, labeled A and B. And consider the discussion of "metaphysics" in Kant offered by Peter Fenves ("Now, all that remains to be seen is what it means to suspend this basic problem of metaphysics" [Peter Fenves, *A Peculiar Fate: Metaphysics and World History in Kant*, 112]), where the ground "man" is said to occasion ("The subjectivity of the human subject is therefore the final ground of every claim to know the world" [93]) is confounded through Kant's explication of its mournful relation to metaphysics. "The break with classical metaphysics thus presents itself in the figure of the cloud: a murky region that allows for no elucidation, much less final enlightenment" (55).

50. Cathy Caruth, *Empirical Truths and Critical Fictions*, 79.

51. Immanuel Kant, *Kritik der reinen Vernunft/Critique of Pure Reason* B xxxi–xxxii.

52. Cathy Caruth, *Empirical Truths and Critical Fictions*, 75.

53. I underline the term *political-theological* to point to a Pauline inheritance in relation to the figure of a coherent, whole social body ("For just as the body is one and has many members, and all the members of the body, though many, are one body, so it is with Christ. For by one Spirit we were all baptized into one body—Jews or Greeks, slaves or free—and all were made to drink of one spirit" [1 Corinthians 12:12–13]). In reading the privileging and interruption of the figure of "man" in Kant's third *Critique* as a

political-theological moment, I learn, differently, and alongside the work of Derrida, Ronell, Biddick, Robbins, and Anidjar cited thus far and in what follows, from Jacob Taubes, *The Political Theology of Paul*; Ernst H. Kantorowicz, *The King's Two Bodies: A Study in Medieval Political Theology*; Amos Funkenstein, *Theology and the Scientific Imagination*; Hans Blumenberg, *The Legitimacy of the Modern Age*; Giorgio Agamben, *The Time That Remains*; Hent de Vries, *Philosophy and the Turn to Religion* and *Religion and Violence*; and Carl Schmitt, *Political Theology* ("All significant concepts of the modern theory of the state are secularized theological concepts" [*Politische Theologie: Vier Kapitel zur Lehre von der Souveränität*, 43/*Political Theology: Four Chapters on the Concept of Sovereignty*, 36]). I have tried to offer a reading of Schmitt in *Political Theology* in relation to the nonsovereign sentences he has written about sovereignty and the sovereign decision in Jeffrey Sacks, "Untranslatability, or Mourning Translation."

54. Eduardo Cadava, *Words of Light: Theses on the Photography of History*, 37.

55. Edward W. Said, *Orientalism*, 155. And consider the compelling reading of Orientalism offered by Ali Behdad, where Orientalism, rather than a "general phenomenon of monolithic domination" (Ali Behdad, *Belated Travelers: Orientalism in the Age of Colonial Dissolution*, 136), is a complex rhetorical—if also military, political, cultural, and lexical—event, which works "through a kind of proliferation of difference" (91), imparting, as Said has also taught us, "the impossibility of occupying a position outside the orientalist formation" (111).

56. And compare Suzanne L. Marchand, *German Orientalism in the Age of Empire: Religion, Race and Scholarship*.

57. Edward W. Said, *The World, the Text and the Critic*, 259, 260. And consider: "But if these interconnected elements represent a secularizing tendency, this is not say that the old religious patters of human history and destiny and 'the existential paradigms' were simply removed. Far from it: they were reconstituted, redeployed, redistributed in the secular frameworks just enumerated" (Edward W. Said, *Orientalism*, 120–21). Alongside the work of Derrida, Olender, Masuzawa, Raz-Krakotzkin, Hamilton, Sheehan, Foucault, and Heller-Roazen, cited in note 31 above, the reading I offer of these passages in *Orientalism* learns from Gil Anidjar, *Semites*, 39–63; Aamir R. Mufti, "Orientalism and the Institution of World Literatures" and "Global Comparativism"; Stathis Gourgouris, *Dream Nation*, 91–105, 122–54; and Marc Nichanian, *Mourning Philology*, 66–77, 153–54.

58. Edward W. Said, *Culture and Imperialism*, 58.

59. One may also consider the passage in which Said underlines that "whenever 'philology' is spoken of around the end of the eighteenth century and the beginning of the nineteenth, we are to understand the *new* philology whose major successes include comparative grammar, the reclassification of languages into families, and the final rejection of the divine origins of language. It is no exaggeration to say that that these accomplishments were a more or less direct consequence of the view that held language to be *an entirely human phenomenon* [my emphasis]" (Edward W. Said, *Orientalism*,

135). I am not able here to read this sentence with the care it deserves, other than to underline that in it philology is described as an anthropocentric event that takes place in relation to secularization, and through the proliferation of a divided and dividing series of terms. A compelling discussion of the question of the origin of language, which points to its displacement of an older, Christian, understanding, is offered in Maurice Olender, *The Languages of Paradise*. A brilliant reading of philology in relation to Christian Hebraism and in terms of its relation to secularization, Orientalism, colonialism, and the redefinition of relations between Christians and Jews in Europe is pursued in Amnon Raz-Krakotzkin, *The Censor, the Editor, and the Text*, 181 passim. A reading of philological categories as giving place to a new, if also old, series of names—"world religions"—is pursued in Tomoko Masuzawa, *The Invention of World Religions*. A compelling discussion is further pursued in David Scott, *Refashioning Futures*, where "secularization" is read in relation to "forms of social life" (66) and the constitution of "religion" as an epistemic category. "At another level, secularization describes not only the formal institutional separation of church and state but an epistemic shift in which a field of discourse and practice comes to be constituted as 'religion' as such" (67). This shift is read in relation to "the need to understand the ways in which Europe, in its world-conquering project of empire, altered the conditions of the lives of non-European peoples in ways that obliged them too to reconstitute themselves as members of one exclusive 'religious' community *against* others" (56), an obliging I consider in what follows in relation to language, and languages, in the legacies of philology in the colonies.

60. Edward W. Said, *Orientalism*, 25.

61. See Edward W. Said, "On Mahmoud Darwish." And see also the essays collected in Edward W. Said, *On Late Style*. I wish to underline, again, that Said's text compels a reading I am not able to pursue here, other than to remark that a reading of Said would need to attend to the ways in which his text asks one to read, both his own words and the words of others, in a way that "provides no redemptive message or reconciliation at all" (160).

62. I learn here from the discussion offered by Wlad Godzich in *The Culture of Literacy*, where "the constructed and institutionally determined character of the object of literary study" (279) is read in relation to the European, philosophical privileging of a subject of language ("for modernity everything must be brought within the orbit of the subject" [280]) and "those literatures that cannot be readily comprehended within the hegemonic view of literature that has been dominant in our discipline" (291). And compare the reading pursued by Gayatri Chakravorty Spivak, who underscores that "part of our 'unlearning' project is to articulate our participation in that formation [what Spivak has called "the masculine-imperialist ideological formation"]—by *measuring* silences, if necessary—into the *object* of investigation" (*A Critique of Postcolonial Reason*, 284). One may read this insight in relation, on the one hand, to what Spivak also calls "the historical production of the colonial subject" (Gayatri Chakravorty Spivak, *An Aesthetic Education in the Era of Globalization*, 92) and "the transformation and displacement of writing into something readable" (58). And consider as well,

differently, the illuminating reading offered by Aamir R. Mufti of "the *Eurocentrism* of the knowledge structures we inhabit" (Aamir R. Mufti, "Global Comparativism," 472) in relation to "the *already translated nature* of the objects" (483) one approaches in the humanities. In what follows I argue that each of these—"the constructed and institutionally determined character of the object of literary study," "the transformation and displacement of writing into something readable," and the "mediation" ("Global Comparativism," 482) of Orientalism in relation to "the *already translated nature*" of objects—may be considered, together, in relation to Euro-American reading institutions and in relation to understandings of literature and the reorganization of language in the Arabic nineteenth century and its legacies—in literature, poetic statement, and theoretical and critical writing—in the twentieth and twenty-first centuries.

63. Here I remain indebted and hope to contribute to the work pursued in Stathis Gourgouris, *Dream Nation*; Aamir R. Mufti, *Enlightenment in the Colony*; Marc Nichanian, *Mourning Philology*; Kamran Rastegar, *Literary Modernity Between the Middle East and Europe*; Shaden M. Tageldin, *Disarming Words: Empire and the Seductions of Translation in Egypt*; and Nergis Ertürk, *Grammatology and Literary Modernity in Turkey.*

64. I point here to the illuminating discussion of this term offered by Nadia Abu El-Haj in *Facts on the Ground: Archaeological Practice and Territorial Self-Fashioning in Israeli Society.*

65. Consider also Adorno's discussion of lyric poetry in "Rede über Lyrik und Gesellschaft," 52/"On Lyric Poetry and Society," 39–40. "This demand, however, the demand that the lyric word be virginal, is itself social in nature. It implies a protest against a social situation that every individual experiences as hostile, alien, cold, oppressive, and this situation is imprinted in reverse on the poetic work: the more heavily the situation weighs on it, the more firmly the work resists it by refusing to submit to anything heteronymous and constituting itself solely in accordance with its own laws. The work's distance from mere existence becomes the measure of what is false and bad in the latter. In its protest against it the poem speaks of the dream of a world in which things would be different [Im Protest dagegen spricht das Gedicht den Traum einer Welt aus, in der es anders wäre]."

66. Werner Hamacher, "95 Theses on Philology," 42. And consider also the discussion offered by Paul de Man in "The Return to Philology," where philology is discussed in terms of "an examination of the structure of language prior to the meaning it produces" (24) and over against the "theological" dimensions of reading pursued in literature studies "as a humanistic and historical discipline" (21) ("Moreover, it ["the teaching if literature" as "an autonomous academic field"] has the task of determining the meaning of texts and this hermeneutic function establishes its kinship with theology" (22). And compare the reading of philology in Edward W. Said's *The World, the Text, and the Critic* and *Orientalism* (cited above), where philology is discussed in relation to what Hamacher has called its being forced to conform to "the norms of an epistemic discipline"—"The relegation of philology to an ancillary discipline of dogmatic theology, jurisprudence, historiography; its

shrinking into a disciplinary technique in pedagogical institutions; its contraction to literature studies; and above all the attempt to force it under the norms of an epistemic discipline: however destructive these institutions of repression were and remain for the experience and clarification of linguistic existence, they have not yet been able to destroy the philological impulse" ("95 Theses on Philology," 41)—in relation to Said's recuperation of philology as a practice of reading where "we encounter our own silence and mortality" and where language "depends on history but is not reducible to it" (Edward W. Said, "The Return to Philology," 83, 64). I discuss philology in relation to the institution of literature studies in Arabic in chapter 2, and wish to underline here the compelling discussion of philology offered by John T. Hamilton, where, following a reading of Said, de Man, Hamacher, and Nietzsche, philology points to a "resistance to reducing everything to phenomenal objects of understanding" (John T. Hamilton, *Security: Politics, Humanity, and the Philology of Care*, 24).

67. Alongside the work cited thus far, consider as well the discussion of the privileging of monolingualism as a practice of reading and "an acknowledged and unacknowledged ground of conflict" in relation to "the "intersection of research methodology with the reproduction not of methods so much as institutional positions for researchers" underlined in Brian Lennon, *In Babel's Shadow: Multilingual Literatures, Monolingual States*, 141.

68. Emily Apter, *The Translation Zone: A New Comparative Literature*, 249. And consider also the discussion of untranslatability Apter pursues in relation to language—and languages—and what she calls "anachronistic" temporal, literary historiographical categories ("These discrepant temporal measures may be defined as Untranslatables of periodicity" [Emily Apter, *Against World Literature: On the Politics of Untranslatability*, 61]). And consider as well Apter's discussion of "revolutionary untiming" (226) in terms of the interruption of the work as an "object owned by a single author" (293) in relation to translation. Pointing to the ways in which the names of others ("anonymous signatories"), and other languages, touch upon acts of writing, Apter underlines, further, that "mediated by unseen editorial hands, the text bears the imprimatur of anonymous signatories whose alterity redounds against the unregistered identities of the work's all-inclusive readership" (293).

69. Avital Ronell, *The Test Drive*, 19.

70. Gayatri Chakravorty Spivak, *Death of a Discipline*, 72.

71. I learn here from the reading pursued in Jacques Derrida's *Politiques de l'amitié/Politics of Friendship*, where Derrida asks whether politics may be given to be thought in relation to "the friendship we have striven to think beyond the homo-fraternal and phallogocentric schema" (340/306). I wish to underline as well—in relation to the political-theological figure of the body one receives in the fallout of Paul, and the privileging of which is generalized in language in the Arabic, Ottoman nineteenth century—what Derrida calls a "graft" at the "origin" of such a body. "We are here in the vicinity of a generative graft in the body of our culture. 'Our' 'culture' is such an old body, but such a young one too. It is a child's body, the body of so-called European

culture, between all these testaments, between Greek philosophy and the so-called Religions of the Book. A patriarch, born yesterday, who knows but forgets, too young and too old to remember that his own body was grafted at birth. There is no body proper without this graft [Il n'y a pas de corps proper sans cette greffe]. It 'begins' with this prosthesis or this supplement of origin" (212–13/185).

1. CITATION

1. Avital Ronell, *Crack Wars: Literature, Addiction, Mania*, 60.

2. The fourteenth-century lexicon *Lisan al-'arab* explains that the lexicographer Ibn Sidah (1007–66) glosses the Arabic word *hifz* as "the opposite of forgetfulness [naqid al-nisyan]" (Ibn Manzur, *Lisan al-'arab*, 7:498).

3. Subhi Hadidi, "Mahmoud Darwish fi 'khutbat al-hindi al-ahmar,'" 52.

4. Darwish offers an illuminating discussion of the word *mihna* in "Hiwar ma' Mahmoud Darwish," 67.

5. Ibn Manzur, *Lisan al-'arab*, 4:606.

6. In reading this passage in *Fi hadrat al-ghiyab*, and in reading Darwish in relation to form and the legacies given in the word *qasida*, I learn from Muhsin J. al-Musawi, *Arabic Poetry: Trajectories of Modernity and Tradition.* Al-Musawi opens his discussion in relation to the understanding of poetry remarked in Ibn Rashiq (d. 1064), who cites a passage attributed to Ibn 'Abbas (d. 687), "Poetry is the register of the Arabs" (cited in Muhsin J. al-Musawi, *Arabic Poetry*, xiii; and see Ibn Rashiq, *al-'Umda fi mahasin al-shi'r wa adabihi wa naqdihi*, 30). This passage points to an important interpretive legacy in relation to the Arabic language and the Qur'an: Arabic poetry is to serve as a lexical point of reference in relation to the comprehension of language. In recalling the citation of the name Ibn 'Abbas in Ibn Rashiq, al-Musawi points to these older and related legacies and asks us to read the sentences that surround the passage he has cited. Those sentences may be rendered in English as follows: "Ibn 'Abbas used to say: When you recite something from the book of God and don't recognize it, search for it in the lines of poetry of the Arabs; for poetry is the register of the Arabs. When asked about something in the Qur'an, he would sing a verse of poetry" (Ibn Rashiq, *al-'Umda*, 30). In this passage—a passage cited in a slightly altered form in some of the central texts regarding the disciplines of reading in relation to the Qur'an—the singing of poetry is called upon to give place to the giving of sense in language. An institution that desires to install sense and recognition in the field of language is pointed to through the relation of poetry to the Qur'an. In what follows I argue that in Darwish, and in poetic form, a negotiation of this legacy is routed through a citational poetic practice.

7. 'Abdu Wazin, "Qira'a fi a'mal Mahmoud Darwish al-jadida," 25.

8. The ellipses here, and in all of the passages in Darwish cited in this chapter, appear in the original.

9. And compare François Xavier, *Mahmoud Darwich et la nouvelle Andalousie*, 39.

10. Najat Rahman, *Literary Disinheritance*, 13, 56.

11. Throughout I cite and modify the translation of the Qur'an offered in A. J. Arberry, *The Koran Interpreted*. For an illuminating discussion of sound in the Qur'an, in relation to "the tension between syntactical rhythm and phonological cohesion" and "the intertwining of semantic and acoustic fields," and from which I learn here and in what follows, see Michael Sells, "Sound, Spirit, and Gender in Surat al-Qadr," 241, 254 passim.

12. Muhsin J. al-Musawi, *Arabic Poetry: Trajectories of Modernity and Tradition*, 259.

13. Mahmoud Darwish, *Yawmiyyat al-huzn al-'adi*, 5. The words I cite here appear in a short preface that Darwish appended to the 1978 and 1984 editions of *Yawmiyyat al-huzn al-'adi*.

14. Shakir al-Nabulsi, *Majnun al-turab*, 601.

15. Judith Butler, *Excitable Speech: A Politics of the Performative*, 34.

16. Ghassan Zaqtan, "Madha katabta ayyuha al-sha'ir fi al-harb?', 259. And compare the discussion of death in relation to the measurement of sound in verse offered in Khaled Furani, *Silencing the Sea: Secular Rhythms in Palestinian Poetry*, 183.

17. A foundational reading of this section of the ode appears in Jaroslav Stetkevych, *The Zephyrs of Najd*.

18. Sinan Antoon, "Returning to the Wind: On Darwish's La Ta'tadhir 'Amma Fa'alta," 220.

19. I'tidal Uthman, "al-Nass: nahwa qira'a naqdiyya ibda'iyya li ard Mahmoud Darwish," 121.

20. Here and in what follows I cite the 2007 edition of *Yawmiyyat al-huzn al-'adi*.

21. Ammiel Alcalay, *a little history*, 113.

22. Mahmoud Darwish, "Hiwar ma' Mahmoud Darwish," 151.

23. Mary N. Layoun, "Between Here and There," 142.

24. Mahmoud Darwish, "Mahmoud Darwish ... La ahad yasil," 37.

25. I follow and slightly modify here the translation offered in A. J. Arberry, *The Koran Interpreted* (Qur'an 5:31).

26. I'tidal Uthman, "al-Nass: nahwa qira'a naqdiyya ibda'iyya li ard Mahmoud Darwish," 122.

27. Najat Rahman, *Literary Disinheritance*, 60.

28. Mohammed A. Bamyeh, *The Social Origins of Islam*, 83.

29. David Lloyd, "The Indigent Sublime: Specters of Irish Hunger," 153.

30. al-Zawzani, *Sharh al-mu'allaqat al-sab'*, 17. I slightly modify the translation of A. J. Arberry, *The Seven Odes*, 61. And consider that this opening, in the classical commentaries, is not resolved into a single reading: the commentators do not decide whether in speaking in the dual the poet was addressing himself and another or two companions (see al-Zawzani, *Sharh al-mu'allaqat al-sab'*, 17; and al-Tibrizi, *Sharh al-qasa'id al-'ashar*, 11–12).

31. Selim Barakat, *Taysh al-yaqut*, 60.

32. Drawing on the work of Ghassan Kanafani, Barbara Harlow has offered a discussion of the literature of resistance, *adab al-muqawama*, that opens that term to the English language (Barbara Harlow, *Resistance*

Literature). 'Abdu Wazin, in "Qira'a fi a'mal Mahmoud Darwish al-jadida," writes, "It is impossible now to call Mahmoud Darwish 'the poet of Palestine,' the poet of the cause, or of the land, or whatever other metaphors or qualities have been attributed to him" (13–14). This is because, for Wazin, in Darwish's late poetry the political is subordinated to what he calls "the aesthetic." "The poet who has excepted himself from the enthusiasm of his beginnings, was able to make the historical moment into a quintessentially poetic one. In a similar manner, he was able to subordinate the political condition to the aesthetic one" (14). In this passage Wazin alludes to earlier readings of Darwish elaborated in the literary critical work of Ghassan Kanafani—*Adab al-muqawama fi Filastin al-muhtalla, 1948–1966,* and *al-Adab al-filastini al-muqawim taht al-ithtilal, 1948–1968*—and Raja' al-Naqqash, *Mahmoud Darwish: sha'ir al-ard al-muhtalla*. And yet it is not that in the late poetry politics is left behind, but that form becomes accentuated there as a matter of poetic writing, recalling us to a reading of the aesthetic in relation to the political in Darwish. See Kadhim Jihad, "Mahmoud Darwish fi majmu'atihi al-shi'iriyya al-ula wa qasa'idihi al-akhira"; and the discussion of form and politics in *Limadha tarakta al-hisana wahidan?* in Sinan Antoon, "Mahmoud Darwish's Allegorical Critique of Oslo."

33. 'Abdu Wazin, "Qira'a fi a'mal Mahmoud Darwish al-jadida," 34.

34. Salma Khadra Jayyusi, *Trends and Movements in Modern Arabic Poetry*, 2:560. Jayyusi's *Trends and Movements* is the most comprehensive reference in the English language, and perhaps in any language, on Arabic poetic modernity. Consider also the discussion of Badr Shakir al-Sayyab (1926–64) and Nazik al-Mala'ika (1923–2007) in relation to "what seemed a new and revolutionary technique" in Shmuel Moreh, *Modern Arabic Poetry*, 198. And compare the readings pursued in Ihsan 'Abbas, *Itijahat al-shi'r al-'arabi al-hadith*, 15–66; Muhammad Bannis, *al-Shi'r al-'arabi al-hadith: binyatuhu wa ibdalatuha*, especially vols. 3 and 4; and, differently, Muhsin J. al-Musawi, *Arabic Poetry.* A consideration of Darwish in relation to the transformations discussed in detail in Jayyusi, Moreh, 'Abbas, and Bannis—where the writings of the Mahjar poets, the Apollo group in Egypt, and the free verse movement in Iraq are underlined in relation to a question of poetic form—is offered in Shakir al-Nabulsi's extensive study, *Majnun al-turab: dirasa fi shi'r wa fikr Mahmoud Darwish*. Darwish's relation to these moments are considered in al-Nabulsi through the understanding of modernity gestured to in the passages in *Majnun al-turab* that I have cited and discussed above, note 14 (chapter 1). And compare the discussion offered by Terri DeYoung, where "free verse," *al-shi'r al-hurr*, is read as a rupture with tradition. "Certainly, it radically changed the form of Arabic poetry and constituted a direct and uncompromising challenge to the rules that had formed the traditional poetic canon" (Terri DeYoung, *Placing the Poet: Badr Shakir al-Sayyab and Postcolonial Iraq*, 192). Modernist Arabic poetics is discussed by M. M. Badawi in relation to what he calls "attitudes" ("It should be clear by now that what we have been dealing with in this chapter are not purely matters of the external form of verse, but questions intimately related

to attitudes taken with varying degrees of consciousness towards traditional Arab society and culture" [M. M. Badawi, *A Critical Introduction to Modern Arabic Poetry*, 228]) and by Hussein N. Kadhim through the metaphor of vision and a privileging of the notions of "ability," "transcendence" and "repudiation." In a reading of Badr Shakir al-Sayyab in relation to T. S. Eliott, Kadhim writes, "Moreover, by adhering to the general scheme of the ancient Mesopotamian myth of death and resurrection (the Tammuz Myth), the Arab poet is *able* to *transcend The Waste Land's vision* and ultimately to *repudiate* that vision" (Hussein N. Kadhim, *The Poetics of Anti-Colonialism in the Arabic Qasidah*, 141; my emphases). And compare the discussion offered by Khaled Furani, where poetic language in Arabic modernity privileges a relation to "the secular," which has "obliterated old modes of poetic involvement with politics and introduced new ones in their stead" (Khaled Furani, *Silencing the Sea*, 232). "He [Adunis]," Furani writes, "supplants the sovereignty of meter with self-sovereignty that becomes a synonym of his secular self" (243). And compare Rebecca Dyer, "Poetry and the Politics of Mourning: Mahmoud Darwish's Genre-Transforming Tribute to Edward W. Said," 1451.

35. Mahmoud Darwish, *Hirat al-'a'id*, 123.

36. Mahmoud Darwish, "Hiwar ma' Mahmoud Darwish," 88.

37. Mahmoud Darwish, "Hiwar ma' Mahmoud Darwish," 85.

38. On the practice of naming, and translation, in relation to Zionism and the colonization of Palestine, see Nadia Abu El-Haj, *Facts on the Ground*; Susan Slyomovics, *The Object of Memory: Arab and Jew Narrate the Palestinian Village*; Ted Swedenburg, *Memories of Revolt: The 1936-1939 Rebellion and the Palestinian National Past*, 38–75 passim; and the remarkable collection of essays, *Nakba: Palestine, 1948, and the Claims of Memory*, ed. Ahmad H. Sa'di and Lila Abu-Lughod.

39. Mahmoud Darwish, "Hiwar ma' Mahmoud Darwish," 74.

40. Jacques Derrida, *Schibboleth: Pour Paul Celan*, 36/"Shibboleth: For Paul Celan," 18.

41. And see also Mahmoud Darwich, *La Palestine comme métaphore*, 59; and Elias Khoury, "Su'al al-nakba: al-Sira' bayna al-hadir wa al-ta'wil," 48.

42. Kamal Abu Dib, *Jamaliyyat al-tajawur*, 81.

43. Najat Rahman, *Literary Disinheritance*, 93.

44. Jaroslav Stetkevych, *The Zephyrs of Najd*, 111.

45. al-Zawzani, *Sharh al-mu'allaqat al-sab'*, 16/Arberry, *The Seven Odes*, 61.

46. See the explanation provided by al-Zawzani in *Sharh al-mu'allaqat al-sab'*, 18. And consider as well al-Tibrizi, *Sharh al-qasa'id al-'ashar*, 13.

47. Theodor Adorno, *Negative Dialektik*, 158/*Negative Dialectics*, 155.

48. See Abraham Serfaty, *Ecrits de prison sur la Palestine*, 81, and the reading of Zionism pursued in Amnon Raz-Krakotzkin, *Exil et souveraineté: Judaïsme, sionisme et pensée binationale*, and the elaborations offered in "Galut be toch ribonut: le bikoret 'Shlilat ha galut' ba tarbut ha israelit" (pts. I and II), "A National Colonial Theology: Religion, Orientalism, and the

Construction of the Secular in Zionist Discourse," and "The Zionist Return to the West and the Mizrahi Jewish Perspective." On Jewish history and its relation to Christian polemics in the European "middle ages," in terms of which the reading of Zionism is situated in Raz-Krakotzkin's work, see Amos Funkenstein, *Perceptions of Jewish History*; and Israel Jacob Yuval, *Two Nations in Your Womb*. An illuminating discussion of the proliferation of the terms of these polemics in the colonization of the Americas is presented in Jonathan Boyarin, *The Unconverted Self: Jews, Indians, and the Identity of Christian Europe*. On historicism and Orientalism in European Jewish writing and thought beginning in the eighteenth century, see David N. Myers, *Re-Inventing the Jewish Past: European Jewish Intellectuals and the Zionist Return to History*; Susannah Heschel, *Abraham Geiger and the Jewish Jesus* and "Revolt of the Colonized: Abraham Geiger's Wissenschaft des Judentums as a Challenge to Christian Hegemony in the Academy"; and Jonathan Hess, *Germans, Jews, and the Claims of Modernity*. On the colonial and masculinist dimensions of Zionism, I have learned from the readings pursued in Daniel Boyarin, *Unheroic Conduct: The Rise of Heterosexuality and the Invention of the Jewish Man*; Zachary Lockman, *Comrades and Enemies*; and Joseph Massad, *The Persistence of the Palestinian Question*, 168 passim. The reflection pursued by Yosef Hayim Yerushalmi in *Zakhor: Jewish History and Jewish Memory* and *Freud's Moses: Judaism Terminable and Interminable* remains instructive in relation to Yerushalmi's privileging of historicist terms, which has been read in Amnon Raz-Krakotzkin, "Jewish Memory between Exile and History." An illuminating discussion of Judaism and Christianity as "religions" in late antiquity, and which complicates the terms of reference I gesture to here, is pursued in Daniel Boyarin, *Border Lines: The Partition of Judaeo-Christianity*. My reading learns as well from the work of Edward W. Said, Ammiel Alcalay, Ella Shohat, Aamir R. Mufti, Gabriel Piterberg, Gil Hochberg, Samera Esmeir, Sherene Seikaly, and Gil Anidjar, cited above.

49. Ella Shohat, "Taboo Memories, Diasporic Visions: Columbus, Palestine, Arab-Jews," in *Taboo Memories, Diasporic Voices*, 216. I learn from the intervention offered in this essay—which was published in an Arabic translation in *al-Karmel*, the literary and cultural journal edited by Darwish ("Kulumbus, Filastin, wa al-Yahud al-'arab: nahwa muqaraba 'ala'iqiyya li huwiyat al-majmu'")—and from Shohat's earlier and later writing, in *Israeli Cinema: East/West and the Politics of Representation*, "Sephardim in Israel: Zionism from the Standpoint of Its Jewish Victims," "The Invention of the Mizrahim," and the essays collected in *Taboo Memories, Diasporic Voices*.

50. Amnon Raz-Krakotzkin, *Exil et souveraineté: Judaïsme, sionisme et pensée binationale*, 38.

51. See the discussion Darwish offers of this volume in "Hiwar ma' Mahmoud Darwish," 147.

52. Fawwaz Traboulsi, *Guernica/Beirut*, 270. On poetic and cultural production in Beirut and during the Israeli siege of that city in the summer of 1982, see the remarkable work offered in Hilmi Salim, *al-Thaqafa taht al-hisar*.

53. Mahmoud Darwish, *Dhakira li al-nisyan*, 150.

54. Aamir R. Mufti, *Enlightenment in the Colony*, 224, 242.

55. ʻAbbas Baydun, "al-Mukhtalif al-haqiqi," 249.

56. Jacques Derrida, *Schibboleth: Pour Paul Celan*, 65/"Schibboleth: For Paul Celan," 35.

57. Qasim Haddad, "Fi shurfat Mahmoud Darwish," 121.

58. Ibn Manzur, *Lisan al-ʻarab*, 3:433.

59. I offer a discussion of al-Jahiz and his *al-Bayan wa al-tibyin*, in relation to a reading of Taha Husayn, in chapter 2. I remark here only that Arabic poetics presupposes linguistic categories. In a paper that addresses the formation of Arabic poetics in relation to four moments (Arabic philology, Qur'anic exegesis, the emergence of a modernist, *muhdath*, poetry in Abbasid Baghdad, and the translation of Greek philosophical categories into Arabic), Wolfhart Heinrichs underlines that the categories of "the first systematic treatise" on Arabic poetics, *Qawaʻid al-shiʻr* of Thaʻlab (d. 904), are thought and explicated in "grammatical" terms (Wolfhart Heinrichs, "Literary Theory: The Problem of Its Efficiency," 39). In a discussion of *Thaʻlab* in terms of what later came to be recognized in Qudama ibn Jaʻfar's *Naqd al-shiʻr* as poetic themes or aims, *aghrad*—e.g., *madih* (praise), *hija'* (invective), *marathi* (elegy), *wasf* (description), and *nasib* (opening)—Heinrichs explains, "Thaʻlab had no general name for what he enumerates; he simply introduces his list by saying that the *qawa'id* or *usul* [each of which are "grammatical" and "juridical," if also "theological" terms], the bases of poetry, which being a grammarian to the core, he identifies with the four basic types of sentences, 'branch out' (*tatafarraʻ*) into *madh*, *hija'*, and the others" (40). He further underlines in a discussion of the word *gharad* that it points to a more originary understanding of what it means to do something with language. "From the original—concrete—meaning 'target' (but perhaps also from the infinitive *gharad* of the verb *gharida ila* 'to yearn for,' this is difficult to decide) the term *gharad* acquired the more general meaning 'aim, intention' and, according to the indigenous lexicographers, becomes a synonym for *qasd*" (40–41). He then explains, "In other words, Qudama's use of the word shows that for him *gharad* has an even more general meaning, it is simply the 'aim' of the poet in writing a line of poetry" (41). The generalization of these categories in relation to language is further explained in a consideration of Ibn Rashiq and of Ibn Tabataba's *ʻIyar al-shiʻr*, where judgment in poetics is related to rhetoric. "The criterion of his judgment is, thus, to be found in the concept of *ijaz* or *ikhtisar* (terseness, conciseness) which is one of the basic ideas of literary theory, being the constituent quality of literary expression in general" (48). Gesturing to a moment that points to al-Jahiz and earlier—"Terseness is eloquence [wa al-ijaz huwwa al-balagha]" [al-Jahiz, *al-Bayan wa al-tibyin*, 79]—Heinrichs's reading underlines a legacy of the Arabic word *qasida*, where *qasida* generalizes a practice of language that relates language to the loss of the immanence of the giving of sense occasioned in the death of the Prophet. The argument I offer here is that the disciplines Heinrichs names—*nahu*, which has come to be translated as "grammar" or "syntax," and *adab*, which has come to be translated as "literature" (and Heinrichs links *ijaz* and *ikhtisar* to what he calls "the constituent

quality of literary expression in general")—index a relation to language that is remarked in Darwish, if through its destruction and loss in colonialism. If Heinrichs recognizes Arabic criticism in relation to what he calls its "lack of historical insight" (Wolfhart Heinrichs, "Literary Theory: The Problem of Its Efficiency," 55), and if "the concept of historical development in poetry was alien to the Arabs" (60), one would wish to read the understanding of language Heinrichs explains not through a privileging of what he takes the Arabic language not to be but as an eventfulness of language, or as an understanding of language as a practice of the tongue in the giving of sense. If, for Heinrichs, Arabic criticism, if also Arabic poetry, is not "historical" ("For our Western mind which is used to the concept of development in literary history, a phenomenon like Abu Tammam's poetry with its excessive rhetorization is almost predictable" ["Authority in Arabic Poetry," 267]), to read the relation of the Arabic language to the European understanding of literary history to which he appeals would compel attention to the translation of that understanding into Arabic, an event to which I turn in chapter 2. The discussion I offer here also learns from the reading of the word *history* offered in Wolfhart Heinrichs, "An Evaluation of 'Sariqa," 358, and from the discussion of language in his "On the Genesis of the haqiqa-majaz Dichotomy," 112 passim. See as well the discussion of Arabic criticism, *naqd*, in Suzanne Pinckney Stetkevych, *Abu Tammam and the Poetics of the 'Abbasid Age*; G. J. H. Van Gelder, *Beyond the Line*; and Amjad Traboulsi, *La critique poétique des arabes*. And compare the reading of Tha'lab and Qudama ibn Ja'far in Ihsan 'Abbas, *Tarikh al-naqd al-adabi 'ind al-'arab*, 70–77, 177–202; the reading of criticism, *naqd*, and eloquence, *balagha*, in Jawdat Fakhr al-Din, *Shakl al-qasida al-'arabiyya*, 29–64; and the discussion of the opposition of *lafz* and *ma'na* in Margaret Larken, *The Theology of Meaning*, 10, 33, 46–47. I also learn from the illuminating discussion of *adab* in relation to its social practice in the Arabic institution of *mujalasa* in Samer M. Ali, *Arabic Literary Salons in the Islamic Middle Ages*.

60. Ibn Manzur, *Lisan al-'arab*, 3:435.

61. And consider: "The best speech is that which, when it is of only a few words, suffices more so than what is of many [wa ahsan al-kalam ma kana qaliluhu yughnika 'an kathiruhu]" (al-Jahiz, *al-Bayan wa al-tibyin*, 61). The imparting of sense in language is further linked, in al-Jahiz, to intention, *niyya*, in relation to its location in the heart. The giving of sense in language is imparted through the tongue, pointing to a privileging of speech over writing, even as ideational content, thought, is privileged over sound. Al-Jahiz therefore also reports that "'Amir ibn 'Abd al-Qays said: When a word departs from the heart it falls upon the heart, but when it departs from the tongue, it doesn't reach the ears" (61).

62. I learn here from the discussion of Ibn Zaydun, Ibn Khafaja, Ibn al-Farid, and Ibn Hazm offered in Jaroslav Stetkevych, *The Zephyrs of Najd*, 74–102, 113–14, 130–32, 180–201.

63. The Arabic appears in the tenth-century translation of Abu Bishr Matta ibn Yunus (d. 940), which has been published in *Kitab Aristutalis fi al-shi'r*, 65. I follow the translation of Seth Benardete and Michael Davis.

64. Salah Fadl, *Asalib al-shi'iriyya al-mu'asira*, 169.

65. Ibn Manzur, *Lisan al-'Arab*, 7:246.

66. Hannah Arendt, *The Origins of Totalitarianism*, 292.

67. Timothy Mitchell, *Colonising Egypt*, 167. And consider also Timothy Mitchell, "The Limits of the State."

68. For a discussion of *ritha' al-mudun* in al-Andalus, see Alexander E. Elinson, *Looking Back at al-Andalus*, 15–49.

69. Ibn Khafaja, *Diwan Ibn Khafaja*, 354.

70. Jaroslav Stetkevych, *The Zephyrs of Najd*, 79.

71. Amjad Nasir, "Mahmoud Darwish wa qasidat al-nathr," 114.

72. Elias Khoury, "Rita wa shi'iriyyat al-muthanna," 141.

73. Sherene Seikaly, "Return to the Present," 238.

74. Elias Khoury, "Rita wa shi'iriyyat al-muthanna," 128, 126, 127.

75. Elias Khoury, "Rita wa shi'iriyyat al-muthanna," 128.

76. Judith Butler, *Excitable Speech*, 102.

77. Philippe Lacoue-Labarthe and Jean-Luc Nancy, *L'absolu littéraire*, 373/*The Literary Absolute*, 103.

78. The German may be consulted in Friedrich Schlegel, *Lessings Geist aus seinen Schriften*, 425–26.

79. Philippe Lacoue-Labarthe and Jean-Luc Nancy, *L'absolu littéraire*, 21/*The Literary Absolute*, 11.

80. Friedrich Schelling, "Das älteste Systemprogramm des Deutschen Idealismus, 70/"The Earliest System-Program of German Idealism," 511. A discussion of the "authorship" of this text appears in Lacoue-Labarthe and Nancy, *L'absolu littéraire*, 39–40/*The Literary Absolute*, 27.

81. Philippe Lacoue-Labarthe and Jean-Luc Nancy, *L'absolu littéraire*, 51/*The Literary Absolute*, 36.

82. Paul de Man, "The Rhetoric of Temporality," 222.

83. Paul de Man, "The Concept of Irony," 178. The reading I pursue of Schlegel learns from Avital Ronell's discussion in *Stupidity*, 95–161; and the pages devoted to de Man and Schlegel in Werner Hamacher, *Premises*, 181–260.

84. Friedrich Schlegel, "Über die Unverständlichkeit," in *Kritische Friedrich Schlegel Ausgabe*, 2:368/"On Incomprehensibility," in *Friedrich Schlegel's Lucinde and the Fragments*, 265.

85. Kevin Newmark, *Irony on Occasion*, 191. And consider as well the discussion offered in Marc Redfield, *Phantom Formations*; Cynthia Chase, *Decomposing Figures*; David Lloyd, *Anomalous States*; and the essays by de Man cited in the introduction, note 9.

86. "The certainty with which a 'comparative grammar' is spoken of ought not be misleadingly passed over; this name is here used *for the first time* and the matter of which it speaks is first originated" (Heinrich Nüsse, *Die Sprachtheorie Friedrich Schlegels*, 42).

87. Cited in Klaus Behrens, *Friedrich Schlegel's Geschichtsphilosophie*, 175. The passage appears in "Rede über die Mythologie," in *Kritische Friedrich Schlegel Ausgabe*, 2:320.

88. Cited in Klaus Behrens, *Friedrich Schlegel's Geschichtsphilosophie*, 176.

89. Friedrich Schlegel, *Über die Sprache und Weisheit der Indier*, in *Kritische Friedrich Schlegel Ausgabe*, 8:109/*On the Language and Wisdom of the Indians*, 426.

90. "The old Indian *Sanskrit*—the cultured [from *Bildung*] or perfect language, and *Gronthon*, the language of writing and books—has the greatest affinity with Latin and Greek, as it does with the German and Persian languages. The resemblance does not lie only in the great number of roots it has in common with them, but it extends to their inner structure and grammar. The correspondence is then not accidental, something that may be explained as a mixing of languages; rather it is essential, pointing to common descent. It is further shown by comparison that the Indian language is the most ancient, the others of later origin, derived from it" (115/429).

91. Friedrich Schlegel, *Zur Philologie I*, in *Kritische Friedrich Schlegel Ausgabe*, 16:46.

92. Friedrich Schlegel, *Zur Philologie II*, in *Kritische Friedrich Schlegel Ausgabe*, 16:80. Wolf's *Prolegomena* has been published in an English translation as *Prolegomena to Homer.* On Winckelmann and the *Altertumswissenschaft*, I have learned from the readings pursued in Stathis Gourgouris, *Dream Nation*; and John T. Hamilton, *Soliciting Darkness.*

93. Friedrich Schlegel, *Zur Philologie I*, 44.

94. Friedrich Schlegel, *Zur Philologie II*, 70.

95. Werner Hamacher, *Premises*, 254.

96. Friedrich Schlegel, *Zur Philologie I*, 49.

97. Walter Benjamin, *Der Begriff der Kunstkritik in der deutschen Romantik*, in *Gesammelte Schriften*, vol. 1, pt. 1, 72.

98. Here and in the following citation I follow the translation given by de Man in "The Concept of Irony," 182. It appears in *Der Begriff der Kunstkritik in der deutschen Romantik*, 84.

99. On the word *Darstellung*, see Carol Jacobs, *In the Language of Walter Benjamin*, 2, 18.

100. Samuel Weber, *Benjamin's—abilities*, 154.

101. Avital Ronell, *Stupidity*, 105.

102. Raymond Schwab, *The Oriental Renaissance*, 168.

103. Avital Ronell, *Stupidity*, 144.

104. Ibn Khaldun, *al-Muqaddima*, in *Kitab al-'ibar*, 1:468.

105. Adunis, *al-Thabit wa al-mutahawwil*, 2:137.

106. In pursuing the reading of Adunis reading al-Shafi'i I offer here, I have learned from the introduction appended to the English translation of his *al-Risala* (*Al-Shafi'i's Risala: Treatise on the Foundations of Islamic Jurisprudence*, tr. and introd. Majid Khadduri). I have also learned from Wael Hallaq, *A History of Islamic Legal Theories* and *The Origins and Evolution of Islamic Law*; Bernard Weiss, *The Spirit of Islamic Law*; and Joseph E. Lowry, *Early Islamic Legal Theory.*

107. Adunis, *al-Thabit wa al-mutahawwil*, 2:8.

108. Ibn Khaldun, *al-Muqaddima*, in *Kitab al-'ibar*, 1:469.

109. al-Suyuti, *al-Itqan fi 'ulum al-Qur'an*, 301.

110. See Muhsin J. al-Musawi, "Arabic Rhetoric," and the passages in *Arabic Poetry*, cited above in note 6 (chapter 1).

111. al-Suyuti, *al-Itqan fi 'ulum al-Qur'an*, 301. See also al-Zarkashi, *al-Burhan fi 'ulum al-Qur'an*, 1:294.

112. Ibn Khaldun, *al-Muqaddima*, in *Kitab al-'ibar*, 1:468.

113. And consider also the discussion of the opposition of *lafz* and *ma'na* in Wolfhart Heinrichs, *Arabische Dichtung und Greichische Poetik*, where this opposition "governs" "literary theory" and points to a more general understanding of language. "Naturally, the opposition *ma'na-lafz* applies not only to poetry, but to all linguistic utterances in general [nicht nur für die Dichtung, sondern für alle sprachliche Äußerung überhaupt]" (69).

114. Hichem Djaït, *La grande discorde*, 130.

115. Adunis, *al-Thabit wa al-mutahawwil*, 2:152.

116. Hichem Djaït, *La grande discorde*, 131. And see the discussion of the word *fitna* in relation to mourning in Leor Halevi, *Muhammad's Grave: Death Rites and the Making of Islamic Society*, 133 passim, and the reading of this term pursued in Michael Chamberlain, *Knowledge and Social Practice in Medieval Damascus*, as "less a temporary breakdown of legitimate political or social order than the inescapable environment, and even the very substance, of elite social life" (47), through a discussion of "the production of knowledge ['ilm]" (85) and its transmission. Differently, a historical, text critical reading of the Qur'an, and the bibliography to which such a reading would need to take recourse, is presented in Fred Donner, *Narratives of Islamic Origins*. And see the discussion of the formation of the qur'anic text in W. Montgomery Watt and Richard Bell, *Introduction to the Qur'an*, 40–56; and A. Jones, "The History of the Text of the Qur'an after the Death of Muhammad."

117. I have learned here, alongside Djaït, from the reading of the word *jahili* offered in Toshihiko Izutsu, *Ethico-Religious Concepts in the Qur'an*, 3–116.

118. Ibn Manzur, *Lisan al-'arab*, 9:223.

119. Ibn Khaldun, *Kitab al-'ibar*, 2:557.

120. And see also al-Suyuti, *al-Itqan fi 'ulum al-Qur'an*, 154.

121. Hichem Djaït, *La grande discorde*, 133.

122. Adunis, *al-Thabit wa al-mutahawwil*, 1:58.

123. Ibn Manzur, *Lisan al-'arab*, 13:202.

124. Adunis, *al-Thabit wa al-mutahawwil*, 2:73.

125. *Diwan al-hamasa* is remarked in Adunis, *Diwan al-shi'r al-'arabi*, 1:9. And consider also the discussion of *Diwan al-hamasa* offered in Suzanne Pinckney Stetkevych, *Abu Tammam and the Poetics of the 'Abbasid Age*, 239–356.

126. Adunis, *Fatiha li nihayat al-qarn*, 45.

127. Hegel, *Phänomenologie des Geistes*, 46/*Hegel's Phenomenology of Spirit*, 38.

128. The reading I offer here of "consumption" remains indebted to Werner Hamacher, *Pleroma—Reading in Hegel*, and to the illuminating reading pursued by Timothy Bahti in relation to what he has called "the tensions

between the interiorized, the digested, and the leftover, or between history as spirit's exteriorization and the concept as its reappropriation" (Timothy Bahti, *Allegories of History: Literary Historiography after Hegel*, 104).

129. And consider the reading of Hegel in Judith Butler, *Subjects of Desire: Hegelian Reflections in Twentieth-Century France* ("The subject of Hegel's *Phenomenology* emerges not only as a mode of intentional enthrallment and the reflexive pursuit of identity, but as a desire that requires Others for its satisfaction and for its own constitution as an intersubjective being. In the effort to gain reflection of itself through the recognition of and by the Other, this subject discovers its dependency not only as one of many attributes, but as its very self" [58]).

130. Hegel, *Phänomenologie des Geistes*, 14/*Hegel's Phenomenology of Spirit*, 10.

131. On Hegel as a thinker of identity, see Theodor Adorno, *Negative Dialektik*, 44/*Negative Dialectics*, 33–34, where Hegel is a figure with whom Adorno wishes to have broken. Yet consider also that, in Adorno, "the principal of absolute identity is self-contradictory. It perpetuates non-identity in suppressed and damaged form" (312/318).

132. Hegel, *Enzyklopädie der philosophischen Wissenschaften im Grundrisse, Erster Teil: Die Wissenschaft der Logik*, 20/*The Encyclopaedia of Logic, Part One of the Encyclopaedia of the Philosophical Sciences*, 1.

133. Hegel, *Enzyklopädie der philosophischen Wissenschaften im Grundrisse, Erster Teil*, 56/*The Encyclopaedia of Logic, Part One*, 50.

134. Jacques Derrida, *La dissemination*, 23/*Dissemination*, 15. On "formulae" and "schemata," see Hegel, *Enzyklopädie der philosophischen Wissenschaften im Grundrisse, Zweiter Teil: Naturphilosophie*, 212/*Hegel's Philosophy of Nature, Part Two of the Encyclopaedia of the Philosophical Sciences*, 39.

135. Hegel, *Phänomenologie des Geistes*, 366/*Hegel's Phenomenology of Spirit*, 338.

136. Hegel, *Grundlinien der Philosophie des Rechts*, 307/*Elements of the Philosophy of Right*, 302.

137. Hegel, *Grundlinien der Philosophie des Rechts*, 150–51/*Elements of the Philosophy of Right*, 151.

138. Timothy Bahti, *Allegories of History: Literary Historiography after Hegel*, 126.

139. Hegel, *Phänomenologie des Geistes*, 257/*Hegel's Phenomenology of Spirit*, 234.

140. And consider also the discussion of Isaac Newton, who stopped halfway, in Hegel, *Enzyklopädie der philosophischen Wissenschaften im Grundrisse*, 230/*Hegel's Philosophy of Nature, Part Two*, 71.

141. And see the illuminating discussion of time and futurity in Hegel, where, with and against Hegel, language points to an "excess of the future over the future" and where one is schooled, as Catherine Malabou has further written, in "the way the extraordinary and unexpected can only arise out of the prose of the well-known and the familiar" (Catherine Malabou, *The Future of Hegel: Plasticity, Temporality, and Dialectic*, 6, 190).

142. Hegel, *Phänomenologie des Geistes*, 489/*Hegel's Phenomenology of Spirit*, 453–54.

143. I learn here from the discussion of mourning in Hegel offered by Rebecca Comay in *Mourning Sickness: Hegel and the French Revolution*, in relation to repetition ("In its unappeasable hunger for originality, language falls into repetition, imitation, and self-citation" [113]), the body ("how to mourn a missing body, a body that has gone missing even to itself" [117]), and breath. "Toward the end of the *Phenomenology*, Hegel describes reconciliation as a sudden inspiration or 'inbreathing,'" Comay writes, "a fresh breath drawn by the consumptive" (142).

144. Werner Hamacher, *Pleroma—Reading in Hegel*, 38. And consider the reading of Hegel pursued by Anidjar in *The Jew, the Arab: A History of the Enemy*, 129–33.

145. Hegel, *Phänomenologie des Geistes*, 228/*Hegel's Phenomenology of Spirit*, 206.

146. See Hegel, *Enzyklopädie der philosophischen Wissenschaften im Grundrisse, Dritter Teil: Philosophie des Geistes*, 373/*Hegel's Philosophy of Mind*, 218. And consider the discussion offered in Haun Saussy, *The Problem of a Chinese Aesthetic*. Saussy shows that if China in Hegel is on the side of religion, origin, and simplicity ("China becomes Asia pure and simple and India the means of transition to West Asia and history" [159]), its reading in relation to history exacerbates the terms Hegel wishes to have installed and that he must keep repeating. China ought not to have belonged to history, but the exposition of this nonbelonging presupposes a belonging it has to have excluded. "So the East is history in the manner of nature, a history reducible to nature, history that does not yet know itself as independent of nature: the correlation bears instant interpretative fruit" (162). It is not only, as Saussy underlines, that the East is excluded from history in Hegel, but that it is incorporated into Europe, it is translated, as excluded, in order that it may become what it is: "a difference that history has to consolidate before it can pronounce on it" (183). If the Hegelian sentence "shows a history occurring before history, where it should not, by definition, occur" (184), this is to point to a confounding in reading that calls for more: for readings, translations, editions, if also university departments, and more, what may be called "the Orientalist absolute." "By not making sense, the East makes sense as an object for interpretation" (165).

147. Werner Hamacher, *Pleroma—Reading in Hegel*, 47.

148. Hegel, *Grundlinien der Philosophie des Rechts*, 308/*Elements of the Philosophy of Right*, 303.

149. Hegel, *Der Geist des Christentums und sein Schicksal*, 19/*The Spirit of Christianity and Its Fate*, 198.

150. Hegel, *Phänomenologie des Geistes*, 454/*Hegel's Phenomenology of Spirit*, 420.

151. Werner Hamacher, *Pleroma—Reading in Hegel*, 37.

152. Sinan Antoon, "Returning to the Wind: On Darwish's La Ta'tadhir 'Amma Fa'alta," 219.

153. Susanne Pinckney Stetkevych, *The Mantle Odes*, 14 passim. And see as well the discussion of the loss of and separation from the beloved as an event presupposed in the poem, giving place to it and its time, offered in Renate Jacobi, *Studien zur Poetik der Altarabischen Qaside*, 40.

154. Samera Esmeir, "Memories of Conquest: Witnessing Death in Tantura," 249, 248.

155. Nur al-Din al-Haj, *al-Ana al-ghina'i fi "Limadha tarakta al-hisana wahidan?,"* 58.

156. Kadhim Jihad, "Mahmoud Darwish fi majmu'atihi al-shi'iriyya al-ula wa qasa'idihi al-akhira," 88.

157. I learn here from the illuminating discussion of *Ahada 'ashara kawkaban* pursued in Ella Shohat, "Taboo Memories, Diasporic Visions: Columbus, Palestine, Arab-Jews"; and see also Jonathan Boyarin, *The Unconverted Self*; and, differently, Carl Schmitt, *Der Nomos der Erde*, 96–109/*The Nomos of the Earth*, 126–38.

158. Henry Staten, *Eros in Mourning*, 35.

159. Muhammad Siddiq, "Significant but Problematic Others," 487.

160. Shakir al-Nabulsi, *Majnun al-turab*, 420.

161. Darwish's reference here is to the philosopher Ibn Rushd (1126–98), the jurist and philologist Ibn Hazm al-Andalusi, the author of *Tawq al-hamama*, and, perhaps, to the translations of Greek philosophy into Arabic in eighth- through tenth-century Baghdad, and of Arabic into Latin and Hebrew in al-Andalus. A discussion of the former is presented in Dimitri Gutas, *Greek Thought, Arabic Culture.* On the translation movement in al-Andalus, see the essays contained in *The Introduction of Arabic Philosophy into Europe*, ed. Charles E. Butterworth and Blake Andrée Kessel. For a discussion of al-Andalus in relation to the exclusion of Arabic texts from the European curriculum, see Maria Rosa Menocal, *The Arabic Role in Medieval Literary History: A Forgotten Heritage.*

162. Ibn Hazm al-Andalusi, *Tawq al-hamama fi al-ilfa wa al-ullaf*, 204.

163. Fathi Rizq al-Khawalida, *Tahlil al-khitab al-shi'ri*, 95.

164. Marie-Hélène Avril-Hilal, "Les Andalousies de Mahmoud Darwich," 47.

165. Gil Anidjar, *"Our Place in al-Andalus": Kabbalah, Philosophy, Literature in Arab Jewish Letters*, 154.

166. Subhi Hadidi, "Madha yaf'al al-'ashiq min duna manfa?," 56.

167. Alessia Ricciardi, *The Ends of Mourning*, 84.

168. Mahmoud Darwish, "Hiwar ma' Mahmoud Darwish," 85.

169. Nouri Gana, "War, Poetry, Mourning: Darwish, Adunis, Iraq," 52.

170. Ferial Ghazoul, "Darwish's Mural," 45.

171. Thomas Keenan, *Fables of Responsibility: Aberrations and Predicaments in Ethics and Politics*, 66, 32.

172. Ahlam Yahya, *'Awdat al-hisan al-da'i': waqfa ma' al-sha'ir Mahmoud Darwish*, 252.

173. Judith Butler, *Excitable Speech*, 6–7.

174. Avital Ronell, "On the Misery of Theory without Poetry," 21.

175. I learn here from the discussion of the word *poiein* in Stathis Gourgouris, *Lessons in Secular Criticism*, 7 passim.

176. See Walter Benjamin, "Über den Begriff der Geschichte," 254–55/"On The Concept of History," 257, and, on interruption, "Was ist das epische Theater? (2)," 536/"What is Epic Theater," 151. On reading Darwish with Benjamin, consider Sinan Antoon, "Before the Ruins: When Mahmoud Darwish Met Walter Benjamin"; Judith Butler, *Parting Ways: Jewishness*

and the Critique of Zionism, 99–113 passim; and Amnon Raz-Krakotzkin, "'On the Right Side of the Barricades': Walter Benjamin, Gershom Scholem, and Zionism."

177. Abdul-Rahim al-Shaikh, "Palestine: The Nomadic Condition," 778.

178. Muhammad Bannis, "Mahmoud Darwish fi al-'qalaq al-shi'ri wa al wafa' al-insani," 299.

179. Mahmoud Darwish, *Hirat al-'a'id*, 108.

2. PHILOLOGIES

1. The text I cite throughout this chapter is a photocopy of the original edition, published in 1998 by Dar al-Ma'arif in Susa (Sousse), Tunisia. The original was published in Cairo in 1926 by Dar al-Kutub al-Misriyya.

2. The discussion I offer here learns from the reading pursued by Muhsin J. al-Musawi of the relation between Orientalism and Arabic thought in relation to the category "influence" and a new privileging of terms (*tamaddun* [civilization], *irtiqa'* [progress], and *'ilm* [knowledge]) (Muhsin J. al-Musawi, *al-Istishraq fi al-fikr al-'arabi*, 61–62).

3. See Muhsin Mahdi, *Ibn Khaldun's Philosophy of History*. And consider the discussion of logocentrism offered above, in chapter 1, in relation to Adunis, and the readings pursued in Brinkley Messick, *The Calligraphic State*; Timothy Mitchell, *Colonising Egypt*; and Nergis Ertürk, *Grammatology and Literary Modernity in Turkey*.

4. The reading I offer here learns from and hopes to contribute to the reflection on the restaging and reorganization of older categories and practices in the Arabic language in colonialism. I wish to underline in particular the discussion of *adab* offered in Timothy Mitchell, *Colonising Egypt*, 135–36; of the rewriting of the older, Arabic-Islamic tradition of *tabaqat* (generations) and of *adab* in relation to a privileging of "the sovereign individual subject" in Marilyn Booth's *May Her Likes Be Multiplied: Biography and Gender Politics in Egypt*, xxxvi, which is read in Booth's work in terms of a new understanding of "education" ("the widespread exhortation to build nations by building loyal little bodies and souls" [139]) and in relation to what "the rising elite saw as necessary to the formation of a state that would answer their needs" (44); and of "riyadat al-nafs" and its "reconfiguration" in relation to the national, colonial state and "the modern public sphere that emerged in Egypt during the 1920s and 1930s" and its relation to the "social body" in Wilson Chacko Jacob, *Working Out Egypt*, 14, 253, 77; the "displacement" of ethical and juridical modes of comportment in Michael Ezekiel Gasper, *The Power of Representation*, 59; the reading of *adab* in relation to "the modernist disciplinization of the body" in Omnia El Shakry, *The Great Social Laboratory*, 277; the reading offered by Shaden M. Tagelin in terms of the "replacement" of "religious faith" by "the 'theological' universal of language" (Shaden M. Tageldin, *Disarming Words*, 119) and her discussion of the "sudden" discrediting of imitation—and of the practice of *adab*—in relation to an opposition between "the modern ground of secular knowledge" and "the traditional ground of theological truth or

falsehood" ("Proxidistant Reading," 230, 262); the discussion of *adab* in relation to the category "world literature," in Michael Allan, "How *Adab* Became Literary"; and the compelling readings of *adab* pursued by Nauman Naqvi in "Acts of Askesis, Scenes of Poiesis"; and by Nergis Ertürk in *Grammatology and Literary Modernity in Turkey*, 31–69, and "Toward a Literary Communism: The 1926 Baku Turcological Congress," 192–93 passim. One may compare the reflection offered by Charles Hirschkind on "modes of sensory organization" (Charles Hirschkind, *The Ethical Soundscape: Casette Sermons and Islamic Counterpublics*, 97), in relation to the figure of the "private reader" ("As opposed to the private reader, whose stillness and solitude became privileged icons of a distinct kind of critical reasoning within the imaginary of the bourgeois public, it is the figure of the ethical listener—with all its dense sensory involvements—that founds and inhabits the counterpublic I describe here" [107]). And consider as well, and differently, the illuminating reading of *'ilm* (knowledge) in relation to its "reconfiguration" and "reorientation" as "science" in the Arabic nineteenth and twentieth centuries offered by Marwa Elshakry in *Reading Darwin in Arabic, 1860–1950*, 181, 297 passim. Elsewhere, I have tried to discuss the event of linguistic violence I study in this chapter in relation to the formation of a literary object in the Arabic language and the historical and temporal forms of understanding this formation privileges (Jeffrey Sacks, "Futures of Literature: Inhitat, Adab, Naqd").

5. Butrus al-Bustani, *Kitab muhit al-muhit*, 1:12.

6. Ibn Manzur, *Lisan al- 'arab*, 1:245. And see al-Fayruzabadi, *al-Qamus al-muhit*, 53.

7. *Muhit al-muhit* defines *qalib* as "what is emptied out of its contents, so that it may be a pattern for what is formed from it [li yakun mithalan li ma yusagh minha]" (Butrus al-Bustani, *Kitab muhit al-muhit*, 2:1747–48).

8. The reading I offer of the law here and throughout learns from the compelling discussion of Kafka and the law offered by Jacques Derrida in "Préjugés: Devant la loi"/"Before the Law." It is not, as Derrida makes clear, that *first* one is, and *then* one is called before the law, but that the law occasions a differentiating violence to which one is—already—solicited. Such anteriority does not mean that one may not contest the law or the juridical practice of the state but that one does so only insofar as one is already given place to in relation to the discriminating, dividing event of juridical violence installed through the force, and if however weak, of the law.

9. Selim Deringil, *The Well-Protected Domains*, 78. See also Carter V. Findely, *Bureaucratic Reform in the Ottoman Empire*, 146–47; and Butrus Abu-Manneh, "The Islamic Roots of the Gülhane Rescript." In the reading of the *tanzimat* I offer here I learn from discussions of sovereignty and the Ottoman state in historical and theoretical scholarship in Ottoman studies. An early reading is offered in Leslie P. Peirce, *The Imperial Harem: Women and Sovereignty in the Ottoman Empire*, which may be considered alongside the reading of the state institution in relation to seventeenth-century historical writing in Gabriel Piterberg, *An Ottoman Tragedy: History and Historiography at Play*. I have benefited as well from Rifa'at 'Ali Abou-El-Haj,

Formation of the Modern State: The Ottoman Empire, Sixteenth to Eighteenth Centuries; and Baki Tezcan, *The Second Ottoman Empire: Political and Social Transformation in the Early Modern World.* On the nineteenth-century reorganization of sovereignty—and in relation to the juridical reforms I gesture to here—I have learned in particular from Karen Barkey, *Empire of Difference: The Ottomans in Comparative Perspective*; and Christine M. Philliou, *Biography of an Empire: Governing Ottomans in an Age of Revolution.*

10. On capital in relation to language, see Timothy Mitchell, *Colonising Egypt*, 135; and Nergis Ertürk, *Grammatology and Literary Modernity in Turkey*, 5–14. The incorporation of the Ottoman Empire into the world economy is discussed in Reşat Kasaba, *The Ottoman Empire and the World Economy.* I have also learned from the work on political economy pursued in Beshara Doumani, *Rediscovering Palestine: Merchants and Peasants in Jabal Nablus, 1700–1900*; Bruce Masters, *The Origins of Western Economic Dominance in the Middle East*; and Leila Tarazi Fawaz, *Merchants and Migrants in Nineteenth-Century Beirut.* For a reading of the expansion of capital as producing, in the colonies, a colonial, political violence it is unable to resolve into a figure of social totality, see Ranajt Guha, *Dominance without Hegemony* and *History at the Limit of World History*, 92 passim. A discussion of "the juridical equality of all subjects" is offered in Ussama Makdisi, *The Culture of Sectarianism: Community, History, and Violence in Nineteenth-Century Ottoman Lebanon*, 10. I also learn from the discussion of the law in Talal Asad, "Conscripts of Western Civilization," *Formations of the Secular*, and *On Suicide Bombing*; from the readings pursued by Khaled Fahmy in *All the Pasha's Men*, "The Anatomy of Justice: Forensic Medicine and Criminal Law in Nineteenth Century Egypt," "The Police and the People in Nineteenth-Century Egypt," and "Justice, Law and Pain in Khedival Egypt"; and from Rudolph Peters, "'For His Correction and as a Deterrent Example for Others': Mehmed 'Ali's First Criminal Legislation (1829–1830)," "Administrators and Magistrates: The Development of a Secular Judiciary in Egypt, 1842–1871," and "Islamic and Secular Criminal Law in Nineteenth-Century Egypt: The Role and Function of the Qadi." I have benefited as well from the consideration of the privileging of the figure of the human being in relation to the 1883 penal code in Egypt, following its occupation by Britain in 1882, offered in Samera Esmeir, *Juridical Humanity: A Colonial History.* In what follows I read one legacy of this event, where the institution of the law occurs as "a juridical technology of colonial rule" (295) in relation to the institution of a literary object and a field of literature studies in Arabic. I retain the word *man* in what follows to point to a relation to Kant's third *Critique*, and to underscore the masculinist dimensions of the institution of literature studies and its persisting, divided—and dividing—paradigms. In two proximate contexts one may consider as well the reflection on the law in relation to the institution of national and religious categories offered in Joseph Massad, *Colonial Effects;* and Max Weiss, *In the Shadow of Sectarianism.*

11. Ussama Makdisi, *The Culture of Sectarianism*, 65.

12. The title page of the first edition of the first volume of *Da'irat al-ma'rif* provides a French translation, *Encyclopedie Arabe*, which it immediately translates into Arabic: "it is a general dictionary of all arts and affairs [wa huwa qamus 'am li kull fann wa matlab]" (Butrus al-Bustani, *Kitab da'irat al-ma'arif*, vol. 1).

13. Butrus al-Bustani, *Khutba fi adab al-'arab*, in *al-Jami'iyya al-suriyya li al-'ulum wa al-funun*, 117. References throughout are to this edition. *Al-Jami'iyya al-suriyya li al-'ulum wa al-funun* was edited by al-Bustani and published in Beirut in 1852 with contributions by al-Bustani, Eli Smith, Cornelius Van Dyck, Nasif al-Yaziji, and others. *Khutba fi adab al-'arab* was published as a separate text in Beirut in 1859. A canonical reading of al-Bustani is offered in Albert Hourani, *Arabic Thought in the Liberal Age*, to which I turn below. The reading I pursue of the trope of decline—*inhitat*—in Arabic letters in relation to the formation of a literary object also learns from Stephen Sheehi, *Foundations of Modern Arab Identity*; Jens Hanssen, *Fin-de-Siècle Beirut: The Making of an Ottoman Provincial Capital*; Joseph Massad, *Desiring Arabs*; Gabriel Piterberg, "The Tropes of Stagnation and Awakening in Nationalist Historical Consciousness: The Egyptian Case"; Mehmet Akif Kirecci, "Decline Discourse and Self-Orientalization in the Writings of Al-Tahtawi, Taha Husayn, and Ziya Gökalp"; and the discussion of decline in relation to the discourse on Alexandrian cosmopolitanism offered in Hala Halim, *Alexandrian Cosmopolitanism*. And see also the reading pursued in David Fieni, "French Decadence, Arab Awakenings: Figures of Decay in the Arab *Nahda*."

14. Butrus al-Bustani, *Khutba fi adab al-'arab*, 113.

15. Jens Hanssen, *Fin-de-Siècle Beirut: The Making of an Ottoman Provincial Capital*, 63. And consider as well Ussama Makdisi, "Ottoman Orientalism," 786.

16. A. L. Tibawi, "The American Missionaries in Beirut and Butrus al-Bustani," 166.

17. George Antonius, *The Arab Awakening*, 38.

18. Butrus al-Bustani, *Khutba fi adab al-'arab*, 115.

19. A. L. Tibawi, "The American Missionaries in Beirut and Butrus al-Bustani," 171.

20. Butrus al-Bustani, *Khutba fi adab al-'arab*, 108.

21. See Nasif al-Yaziji, *Kitab fasl al-khitab fi usul lughat al-a'rab* (Beirut, 1836), where *nahu* is defined in the following terms. "*Nahu* is knowledge through which one knows the condition of the endings of words from the point of view of their declension and structure. Its subject is speech, which consists in an utterance formed from two words or more. Its condition is that it give place to a complete meaning, after which the listener does not wait for anything else to complete the intended meaning [al-fa'ida al-maqsuda] of the sentence" (94). My intention is not to assimilate these texts—their content was the subject of heated debate and what Marwa Elshakry has called the "language wars" of the nineteenth century (Marwa Elshakry, "Knowledge in Motion: The Cultural Politics of Modern Science Translations in Arabic," 705)—but to underline that they remark a reorganization of language and of

the category *nahu* in relation to a new understanding and practice of form, which I elaborate through al-Bustani's *Khutba fi adab al-'arab*. The giving of sense in language is now to occur through this understanding and the restaging and appropriation of the categories and practices of language occasioned in what appears newly as a "past." For further discussion, consider Abdulrazzak Patel, "Language Reform and Controversy in the Nahda: Al-Shartuni's Position as a Grammarian in *Sahm*"; and Adrian Gully, "Arabic Linguistic Issues and Controversies of the Late Nineteenth and Early Twentieth Centuries."

22. Butrus al-Bustani, *Khutba fi adab al-'arab*, 110.

23. Albert Hourani, *Arabic Thought in the Liberal Age*, iv.

24. Ghali Shukri, *al-Nahda wa al-suqut fi al-fikr al-masri al-hadith*, 173.

25. Stephen Sheehi, *Foundations of Modern Arab Identity*, 15.

26. Consider also the brilliant reading of *Khutba fi adab al-'arab* Sheehi offers in relation to the paradoxes it sustains. "Consequently, Bustani's *nahdah* discourse articulates an Arab subject who perpetually recognizes a master of knowledge that precludes itself," "While in no uncertain terms the topos of the Abbasid refers to an Arab ideal, Bustani's narrative undermines the subjective referents it advances" ("Epistemography of the Modern Arab Subject," 73, 74). But Sheehi's reading solicits an understanding of coherency ("Bustani's *nahdah* discourse *articulates* [my emphasis] an Arab subject") and autonomy in language that it also places in question. "The ability to recognize knowledge as the sign of subjective presence supplies the necessary possibility for reform. But paradoxically, the Arab subject is only a curator, never an autonomous master" (73).

27. Stephen Sheehi, *Foundations of Modern Arab Identity*, 26. And compare the recent series of articles Sheehi has published, including "Arabic Literary-Scientific Journals: Precedence for Globalization and the Creation of Modernity," "A Social History of Early Arab Photography," "Towards a Critical Theory of al-Nahda," and "The Nahda After-Image, Or All Photography Expresses Social Relations." In the last of these, Sheehi underlines the relation of "the Nahda portrait" (408) to the violence of the colonial state and capital. Yet one wishes to ask whether the *nahda* portrait already temporally exceeds itself and the intelligibility it participated in naturalizing ("Through its production, exchange, circulation and deployment, photographic portraiture participated in the naturalisation of a signification system that had already made the subject intelligible within modernity's new social order" [402]). If, as Sheehi has compellingly argued, "the violence of the Nahda is tantamount to the ripping of communal identities and social organizations as much as economies" (408), one may underline that language is already more and less than the grounds said to have given place to it. Language already exceeds itself, compelling a reading of language as something other than an "ability," "articulation," "coherency," "vision," or "interiority." "Indeed, the al-Nahda literati were key organic intellectuals for the bourgeoisie, petite bourgeoisie, clerical and bureaucratic classes because they were *able* to *articulate* a *coherent vision* of their subjectivity *within* [emphases mine] a logic and language that matched the clarity of modernity's goal"

(404). And compare the discussion offered by Keith David Watenpaugh in terms of the "acceptance" of "the underlying logos of Western civilization" (*Being Modern in the Middle East*, 5) and the institution of historicism in the Arabic language ("Qastun's words also confirm the internalization of a specifically modern and middle-class view of history. Embracing a Hegelian notion that History is the unfolding of human freedom, this style of imagining the past derived from a general incorporation of modernist forms of history writing and narrative" [29]), an event that is, for Watenpaugh, "unprecedented" (45), pointing to a "fundamental cultural and political turn in the contemporary history of the Middle East" (3).

28. Butrus al-Bustani, *Khutba fi adab al-'arab*, 102.

29. Al-Bustani may here be responding to the missionary Eli Smith, who, compelling al-Bustani to appear as a remnant of his own past, wrote in a contribution to *al-Jami'iyya al-suriyya li al-'ulum wa al-funun* (Beirut, 1852), "As for your Arab race [jinsukum al-'arabi], your culture is a link that binds the ancient world, which was adorned with the Greek and Roman sciences, to the modern world, which is adorned with the sciences of the peoples of Europe and their civilization" ("Khutbat al-ra'is al-sanawiyya," 24). And compare the discussion offered by Fruma Zachs in terms of the category of the self and its "view" (*The Making of Syrian Identity*, 146).

30. On al-Bustani's response to the 'Urabi revolt, see Butrus Abu-Manneh, "The Christians between Ottomanism and Syrian Nationalism: The Ideas of Butrus al-Bustani," 299.

31. Butrus al-Bustani, *Khutba fi adab al-'arab*, 103.

32. Butrus al-Bustani, *Khitab fi al-hay'a al-ijtima'iyya wa al-muqabala bayna al-'awa'id al-'arabiyya wa al-afranjiyya*, 4.

33. Jens Hanssen, *Fin-de-Siècle Beirut*, 225.

34. Butrus al-Bustani, *Nafir Suriyya*, 31.

35. Leila Tarazi Fawwaz, *An Occasion for War: Civil Conflict in Lebanon and Damascus in 1860*, 106.

36. Butrus al-Bustani's *Khitab fi al-hay'a al-ijtima'iyya* takes as a starting point the division of humanity from animality to articulate what al-Bustani calls "the world [al-'alam]" (4). To speak of "human society" is to speak of its history, and to do so one must begin by dividing. "The basis of human society among the crude, neglected tribes was weak and simple, and that was because the needs of its members were few in number, and inferior in their value. So we see them wandering in the deserts, each on his own, in search of food and clothing from the bodies of the animals they hunt using simple tools that each made for himself from whatever appropriate material nature threw in front of him. In this crude state, there was not a great difference between the human being [al-insan] and the highest level of the animals [wa a'la tabaqa min al-hayawanat]" (1).

37. Butrus al-Bustani, *Nafir suriyya*, 64.

38. "*Al-ri'asa* is authority and sovereignty [al-siyada]. It has been applied recently to religious authority [al-sulta al-diniyya] as opposed to earthly authority [al-sulta al-dunyawiyya]" (Butrus al-Bustani, *Muhit al-muhit*, 1:736).

39. Butrus al-Bustani, *Nafir suriyya*, 57.

40. Butrus al-Bustani, *Khutba fi adab al-'arab*, 114.

41. Stephen Sheehi, *Foundations of Modern Arab Identity*, 69.

42. Butrus al-Bustani, *Nafir suriyya*, 31.

43. And consider that al-Bustani's *Khitab fi ta'lim al-nisa'* turns on the imparting of reading as a practice for the reorganization of language in logocentrism. "Women's need for this means is well known, because by means of letters and the power of sight she arrives at what she could not by means of the voice and the ear" (Butrus al-Bustani, *Khitab fi ta'ilm al-nisa'*, 49). To speak of reading as the pedagogy of *nahda* and *tanwir* al-Bustani engages a comparison that routes him to India, remarking the proliferation of a colonial and Orientalist idiom in discriminating division. "What should we say about the detestable, harsh, and barbaric custom in India with respect to the daughters of Eve? They bury women and burn them alive with the corpses of their husbands, as their children gather around the coals, not to put out the fire with their tears, but to give light to it with the lamp of their orphanhood. Were it not for British rule, you would see, every day, countless victims of this miserable race" (46). The reorganization of reading is articulated in relation to race and gender, and in the installation of a social body ("woman" is to become "a member worthy of a civilized community" [49])—a gesture in which "woman" remarks an emergence from and persistence within an excluding and incorporating economy. This gives place to an understanding of world as totality, where "woman" is to be given voice ("She shall no longer be considered solely a tool, without voice or opinion," "capable of being, in the world, an important member of the community" [50]), as it points to the world's shattered reorganization in colonialism.

44. Butrus al-Bustani, *Khutba fi adab al-'arab*, 101.

45. The reading I offer of al-Bustani learns from Ashis Nandy's underlining "the nexus between capitalism, imperialism and Christianity" (Ashis Nandy, *The Intimate Enemy*, 47), and the reflection on the reorganization of difference through the categories of the inside and the outside, the spiritual and the material, and the present and the past, underlined by Partha Chatterjee in *The Nation and Its Fragments* and *Nationalist Thought in the Colonial World*. Yet my interest here is to read the ways in which a particular, European idiom and practice, solicited in the juridical violence of the state, is generalized within the Arabic language, destroying more than one relation to time and compelling others. If, in the context Chatterjee underlines, difference is proliferated by the colonial state and in its interest ("That is to say, the notion of an undifferentiated body of public opinion that the government was supposed to treat impartially was only a theoretical idea; in practice, is was the duty of a colonial government to differentiate, and language was a simple and practical sign of difference" [Partha Chatterjee, *The Nation and Its Fragments*, 25]), I have wished to ask how a regime of difference, and differences, came to be proliferated in the Arabic language, installing more than one inside and outside, and in the fallout of which, as Chatterjee makes clear, categories of thought and language will have been articulated. The reading I offer here and below also learns and departs from, as I hope is clear, the work of Talal Asad, cited above.

46. Al-Shidyaq's gesturing to his own writing and language project as new is privileged in readings of his work. Consider the reading of al-Shidyaq and language offered in Muhammad Khalaf Allah, *Ahmad Faris al-Shidyaq wa ara'uhu al-lughawiyya wa al-adabiyya*, 95, and, for a fuller discussion, 92–142; and compare the discussion offered in Peter Gran, *Islamic Roots of Capitalism*, 153, and, differently, Luis 'Awad, *Tarikh al-fikr al-misri al-hadith*, 304. A relation between al-Shidyaq and older Arabic traditions, in relation to the understanding of the origin of language in the imitation of sound in Ibn Jinni's *al-Khasa'is*, is pursued in Muhammad 'Ali al-Zarkan, *al-Jawanib al-lughawiyya 'ind Ahmad Faris al-Shidyaq*, 65–107. For discussion of the reflection on the origin of language in Arabic, see Bernard Weiss, "Medieval Muslim Discussions of the Origin of Language"; and Sophia Vasalou, "'Their Intention Was Shown by Their Bodily Movements': Basran Mu'tazilites on the Institution of Language."

47. Fawwaz Trabulsi and 'Aziz al-Azmeh, introduction to Ahmad Faris al-Shidyaq, *al-Kitabat al-majhula li Ahmad Faris al-Shidyaq*, 8.

48. Nadia al-Baghdadi, "The Cultural Function of Fiction: From the Bible to Libertine Literature. Historical Criticism and Social Critique in Ahmad Faris al-Shidyaq," 390. And consider as well Nadia al-Baghdadi, "Print, Script, and the Limits of Free-Thinking in Arabic Letters of the 19th Century: The Case of al-Shidyaq." And compare the discussion of *al-Saq 'ala al-saq* offered by Sabry Hafez, where al-Shidyaq's text is said to remark the passing of an older order—the one, located in the side of death, is said to be grounded in "the hegemony of religious reason, whereas the second is grounded in logical, juridical reason" (Sabry Hafez, "Raqsh al-dhat la kitabatuha," 18)—and to stand at a point of division between "two different concepts of the self and two contradictory notions of the world, and therefore between two different periods of social development" (18).

49. Mohammed Bakir Alwan, "Ahmad Faris al-Shidyaq and the West," 132, 65.

50. And consider, alongside the corpus of Shidyaq scholarship I discuss here, Nadia Bou Ali's illuminating reading of al-Shidyaq's "mastery of the tongue," which "resists its [language's] transformation into a pedagogical subject" (Nadia Bou Ali, "Collecting the Nation: Lexicography and National Pedagogy in al-nahda al-'arabiyya," 47, 51).

51. Mohammed Bakir Alwan, "Ahmad Faris al-Shidyaq and the West," 34.

52. Throughout I read and translate the 1855 edition of *al-Saq 'ala al-saq*. I read the sentence I am translating here as it has been edited by Darwish Juwaidi in *Kitab al-saq 'ala al-saq*, 24.

53. Muhammad 'Ali al-Zarkan, *al-Jawanib al-lughawiyya 'ind Ahmad Faris al-Shidyaq*, 72–73. And consider also, in terms of the trope of decline in al-Shidyaq, the reading Geoffrey Roper offers of al-Shidyaq's participation in what he calls "a new culture based not only on a new means of transmitting texts, but also on a new approach to selecting, writing, and presenting them, aimed at a new kind of reader" (Geoffrey Roper, "Faris al-Shidyaq and the Transition from Scribal to Print Culture in the Middle East," 210).

This newness is said to have occasioned a simplification of language in relation to a new understanding of legibility and reading. "There is no doubt that he was steeped in the old classical norms and usages, and he also showed himself to be, in many of his writings, quite fond of obscurity and recondite verbiage. But he nevertheless realized that the new patterns of readership created by the print revolution necessitated a new, simpler, and more direct style, geared primarily to the communication of knowledge and ideas rather than to preserving the mystique of a literary elite" (219). The reading I offer does not wish to suggest that language was not "simplified" but that this event—and if it remarked "a new role for the author, and a new sense of self-awareness and autonomy for writers" (222)—occasioned a violent reorganization in language, a subordination of older understandings of language, which is repeated and displaced in al-Shidyaq. And compare Geoffrey Roper, "Ahmad Faris al-Shidyaq and the Libraries of Europe and the Ottoman Empire," especially 241, 243–44 passim.

54. And compare the discussion of "lexical obscurantism" in al-Shidyaq offered in Rebecca Carol Johnson, Richard Maxwell, and Katie Trumpener, "*The Arabian Nights*, Arab-European Literary Influence, and the Lineages of the Novel," 274.

55. And consider also the text-critical work al-Shidyaq offered in *Mumahakat al-ta'wil fi munaqidat al-injil*, where the historicity of the Gospels is to be demonstrated in relation to temporal coherence ("Everything that has been reported by these four [Matthew, Mark, Luke, and John] about Jesus, whether principles, lessons, miraculous stories, or states, is imaginary—neither certain nor determined [ghayr muhaqqaq wa la mu'ayyan]" [19]).

56. Marun 'Abbud, *Saqr Lubnan*, 111. And compare Bulus Mas'ad, *Faris al-Shidyaq*, 43.

57. Butrus al-Bustani, *Qissat As'ad al-Shidyaq*, 16.

58. Ussama Makdisi, *Artillery of Heaven*, 181, 197–98.

59. Butrus al-Bustani, *Qissat As'ad al-Shidyaq*, 42.

60. See Mohammed Bakir Alwan, "Ahmad Faris al-Shidyaq and the West," 132; Stephen Sheehi, *Foundations of Modern Arab Identity*, 123; and Kamran Rastegar, *Literary Modernity between the Middle East and Europe*, 103.

61. Geoffrey Roper, "Faris al-Shidyaq and the Transition from Scribal to Print Culture in the Middle East," 210.

62. Kamran Rastegar, *Literary Modernity between the Middle East and Europe*, 8. My reading of al-Shidyaq has benefited from Rastegar's translation of the epilogue (in *Literary Modernity*, 116–17), even as I offer a somewhat different rendering, to underline the attention to language and form I privilege in this chapter.

63. 'Imad al-Sulh, *Ahmad Faris al-Shidyaq: atharuhu wa 'asruhu*, 167.

64. Kamran Rastegar, *Literary Modernity between the Middle East and Europe*, 117, 103.

65. Mattityahu Peled, "al-Saq 'ala al-saq: A Generic Definition," 31.

66. Radwa 'Ashur, *al-Hadatha al-mumkina*, 13.

67. Jurji Zaydan, *Tarajim mashahir al-sharq*, 2:110.

68. ʻImad al-Sulh, *Ahmad Faris al-Shidyaq: atharuhu wa ʻasruhu*, 169. And consider also the reading of al-Shidyaq in relation to language and tradition offered by Mattityahu Peled, who reads the relation of *al-Saq ʻala al-saq* to the *maqama* through the installation of a break with the past. "The possibility of examining this 'unsuccessful' imitation as a work utterly unrelated to the *maqama* genre is not even mentioned by the writer [Peled is here pointing to and citing the literary historian Shawqi Dayf]" ("al-Saq ʻala al-saq: A Generic Definition," 36). And compare the discussion of al-Shidyaq's "modernization" of the *maqama* in Jaber ʻAsfur, *Zaman al-riwaya*, 99.

69. And compare the privileging of a "free" subject of language in Sulaiman Jubran, "The Function of Rhyming Prose in ʻal-Saq ʻala al-saq,'" 157.

70. Radwa ʻAshur, *al-Hadatha al-mumkina*, 36, 133.

71. *al-Kutub al-muqaddasa wa hiyya kutub al-ʻahd al-ʻatiq*, tr. Ahmad Faris al-Shidyaq, 235. And compare *Kitab al-ʻahd al-jadid li rabbina wa mukhlisina Yasuʻ al-masih*, tr. Butrus al-Bustani et. al., 254.

72. And see Eli Smith, *Kitab al-bab al-maftuh fi aʻmal al-ruh*, tr. Butrus al-Bustani, where he explains that "one who loves God" "does not only love the heavens, the seat of God's divinity, but also his speech [kalam, "words"], through which he announces his will" (220). This love is articulated in the subordination of scripture ("his speech") to God's will, and the incorporation of the former into the theologism of the latter. This gesture points to the gift of Christ's pain in giving place to love among "brothers." "The Christian must love intensely not only his creator but also those who share in his [the Christian's] nature," and this love "must be strong, because it is analogous to the love of Christ. A love that was not only through words, but from the depths of the heart, until it made him deny himself, to bear pain and death" (222). Smith continues to explain that just as Christ "gave himself in our place, we must give ourselves in place of our brothers" (223)—gesturing to the idiom that subtends the missionary project at stake in the texts I read here.

73. After completing this chapter, I read and learned from the stunning discussion of the body in al-Shidyaq offered in Tarek El-Ariss, *Trials of Arab Modernity* ("It is thus necessary to read al-Shidyaq's body in various environments and in relation to other bodies and objects, thereby treating it as a sign, a narrative, and a site of inscription for external stimuli and new meaning" [63]). El-Ariss underlines that the body in al-Shidyaq is a site of "collapse" (62) and points to an obsessive dimension of al-Shidyaq's language ("Through these affects, al-Shidyaq enacts a violent purging of the body from its ailment. His anger, which comes through in his obsessive return to the site of disgust and contradiction—namely food—rids al-Shidyaq from the ill and shakes off the ache with which he struggled throughout" [83]). Yet if al-Shidyaq is to be read as a subject "refusing" or "rejecting" an "epistemological model" (83) and "colonialism's homogenizing and hegemonic practices" (85), and through a privileging of that subject's modernity ("al-Shidyaq decenters modernity and civilization as fixed and coherent narratives and produces his thoroughly modern text" [78]), this would compel one to ask into the time of his text and its language, and the interrupted confounding of each.

74. Rahab 'Akawi, *al-Fariyaq: Ahmad Faris al-Shidyaq*, 110.

75. The first penal code in colonial Egypt was installed in 1829 and was republished in 1855 with the *Hatt-i Şerif-i Gülhane* appended to it. Its logic was proliferated in the penal code of 1883, modeled on the French Penal Code of 1810 (Samera Esmeir, *Juridical Humanity*, 39), one year after the British occupation of Egypt, and in relation to an understanding of "equality before the law" (39) and the category of the autonomous human being it solicits. Alongside Esmeir's *Juridical Humanity*, I learn here also from Khaled Fahmy, "The Anatomy of Justice: Forensic Medicine and Criminal Law in Nineteenth Century Egypt," "The Police and the People in Nineteenth-Century Egypt," and "Justice, Law and Pain in Khedival Egypt," where the 1862 "Decree for Replacing Flogging by Imprisonment [la'ihat tabdil al-darb bi al-habs]" is discussed in detail, and in relation to the figure of the criminal and its "mind" ("From now on punishment would be directed not to the body of the offender to restore the *status quo ante* or to cow the spectators into submitting to the will of the sovereign, but to the mind of the criminal with the intention of reforming him or her and redeeming his or her soul" [105]). And compare Fahmy's discussion of the historiography of the law in colonial Egypt, where, beginning in the late nineteenth and early twentieth century, "the legal system before the creation of the Mixed Courts in 1876" came to be dismissed "as despotic and inefficient" (86) ("As shown below, what was a complex and highly elaborate legal system was, therefore, suddenly dismissed as a system essentially characterized by a series of lacks and absences" [87]). A discussion of the 1829 code appears in Rudolph Peters, "'For His Correction and as a Deterrent Example for Others': Mehmed 'Ali's First Criminal Legislation (1829–1830)." On the 1855 code, see Gabriel Baer, "The Tanzimat in Egypt—The Penal Code," 38 n. 2 passim. And compare the discussion of the law in the Egyptian colonial state offered in Talal Asad, *Formations of the Secular*, 205–56.

76. Khaled Fahmy, "The Anatomy of Justice," 270, 245.

77. Samera Esmeir, *Juridical Humanity*, 11.

78. I point here to Sulayman al-Bustani, *Ilyadhat Humiros*; Ruhi al-Khalidi, *Tarikh 'ilm al-adab 'ind al-afranj wa al-'Arab, wa Victur Hugo*; Carlo Nallino, *Tarikh al-adab al-'arabiyya: min al-jahiliyya hatta 'asr Bani Umayya*; and Louis Massignon, *Muhadarat fi tarikh al-istilahat al-falsafiyya*. An illuminating reading of al-Khalidi is offered in Ferial J. Ghazoul, "Comparative Literature in the Arab World." On Nallino and Massignon—whose lectures were offered at the Egyptian University in 1910–11 and 1912–13, respectively—see the discussion in Abdelrashid Mahmoudi, *Taha Husain's Education*, 47–63. And see also the suggestive discussion of Zaydan in relation to Husayn and the discipline of Arabic literary history in Timothy Mitchell, *Colonising Egypt*, 168–70; and the bibliographical summary offered in Jan Brugman, *An Introduction to the History of Modern Arabic Literature in Egypt*, 327–32. I thank Pierre Cachia for pointing me to Nallino and suggesting his importance for reading Husayn, and Ferial Ghazoul for generously sharing a copy of "Comparative Literature in the Arab World." One may also consider the earlier reorganization of language in relation to

the pedagogical form of the lecture course in the lectures offered by Husayn al-Marsafi at the teacher's training college Dar al-'Ulum beginning in 1871. Here, the lecture course becomes what Muhammad Mandur has called a "tool" in relation to the pedagogical imparting of knowledge about language ("The writings of Aristotle were considered a means of gaining knowledge and logical thought, and more than that, they were considered throughout the middle ages the first and final source of all knowledge, logic, and philosophy. In the same way the 'Wasila' [*al-Wasila al-adabiyya ila al-'ulum al-'arabiyya*] of al-Shaikh Husayn al-Marsafi was considered a tool for learning the Arabic language and its literature, and for composing prose and poetry, in his age and in the generation that followed it" [Muhammad Mandur, *al-Naqd wa al-nuqqad al-mu'asirun*, 8]). In Mandur, al-Marsafi indexes, by analogy with Aristotle, a "middle ages" which is, like the period of Ottoman "decadence," to be left behind, if also strangely repeated, and this reading is mirrored in Brugman's discussion of *al-Wasila* in historicist terms ("Though al-Marsafi did not isolate himself from the literary achievements of his contemporaries, his modernity was only a thin veneer" [*An Introduction to the History of Modern Arabic Literature in Egypt*, 325]).

79. Samera Esmeir, *Juridical Humanity*, 25.

80. Abdeslam M. Maghraoui, *Liberalism without Democracy*, 38, 66.

81. Albert Hourani, *Arabic Thought in the Liberal Age*, vi.

82. See Ahmad Faris al-Shidyaq, *Kashf al-mukhabba 'an funun Urubba*, 324.

83. And consider also that A. L. Tibawi reports, "In 1837 the consultative council in Aleppo requested Ibrahim Pasha [the grandson of Mehmed 'Ali, viceroy of Egypt from 1805–1848] to give a printing press to the city and complained of lack of books for use by pupils" (*American Interests in Syria, 1800–1901*, 69). The complaint was referred to Mehmed 'Ali, and, after soliciting book lists—Tibawi underlines that "the *Rihla* of Rifa'a Tahtawi appears on all the lists" (70)—books printed at the Bulaq press in Egypt were sent. "A summary shows that some sixty titles altogether 1,596 copies were ordered, of which 622 were for Damascus and dependencies, 289 for Gaza, 231 for Tripoli, 216 for Latikia, 145 for Jaffa, and 93 for Aleppo" (71). For a discussion of the foundation of the Bulaq press, see Abu al-Futuh Rudwan, *Tarikh Matba'at Bulaq*, 43–50. Rudwan underlines that the press was founded in relation to Memed 'Ali's desire to create state institutions rather than out of a desire to publish juridical, educational, literary, or religious texts. And he also underscores that the principal institution in which Mehmed 'Ali invested the state—and the press—was the army (254). Yet Rudwan also explains that the first publication of the press was an Arabic-Italian dictionary, published in 1823, pointing to the fact of language, and to the relation of the Arabic language to others, in the translating and publication activities of the press (446). A compelling discussion of the formation of the Egyptian colonial state in relation to the army, and from which my discussion learns, appears in Khaled Fahmy, *All the Pasha's Men*. The classic study in English of the history of translation from the European languages into Arabic is Ibrahim Abu-Lughod, *The Arab Rediscovery of Europe*. And

see also Jak Tajir, *Harakat al-tarjama bi Misr khilal al-qarn al-tasi' 'ashar*; and Jamal al-Din al-Shayyal, *Tarikh al-tarjama wa al-haraka al-thaqafiyya fi 'asr Mehmed 'Ali*. And compare the discussion of "writers such as Taha Husyan" in terms of the "imposition" of "a Western value system" on "national culture" through translation (Richard Jacquemond, "Translation and Cultural Hegemony," 142).

84. One may consider here Husayn's dismissal of recent Arabic writing as decadent and in decline. He writes, for instance, in *Mustaqbal al-thaqafa fi Misr* (Cairo, 1938), that whereas Europe has progressed "in its Renaissance, making great strides on the path of advancement" "this Near East fell into decline, and excessively so, to the extent that it almost lost its rational character" (Taha Husayn, *Mustaqbal al-thaqafa fi Misr*, 27). Here Husayn repeats and domesticates the writing I have considered thus far (al-Bustani and al-Shidyaq) as well as others (e.g., Khayr al-Din al-Tunsi's *Aqwam al-masalik fi ma'arifat ahwal al-mamalik* [1867], Muhammad Abdu's *Risalat al-twahid* [1897], and Farah Antun's *Ibn Rushd wa falasatuhu* [1903]), whose work also shared, differently, in the privileging of the category of the historical and its differentiating force. For a reading of 'Abdu that points to a distinction between his work and that of Antun, while underlining a privileging of historicity in each, see Samira Haj, *Reconfiguring Islamic Tradition*, 67–108. And compare the discussion of 'Abdu offered in Aziz al-Azmeh, *Islams and Modernities*, 118–20 passim. For a discussion of the privileging of the category "history" and its remarking a new understanding of time in early-twentieth-century Egypt, consider also Yoav Di-Capua, *Gatekeepers of the Arab Past*. The relation to time I read here has been discussed by Reinhard Schulze as an event of determination in culture "mediated" through European concepts (Reinhard Schulze, "Mass Culture and Islamic Cultural Production in the Nineteenth-Century Middle East," 205). Rather than a "mediation," I consider language as a nonsimple site of translation in relation to colonial violence.

85. Sayyed al-Bahrawi, *al-Bahth 'an al-manhaj fi al-naqd al-'arabi al-hadith*, 39.

86. Readings of Husayn have underlined his "application of the research methods that he learned from French rationalism since Descartes, and Positivism, from Picoult to August Comte," to an Arabic content (Luis 'Awad, *Thaqafatina fi Muftaraq al-turuq*, 125). And compare Ahmad Buhasan, *al-Khitab al-naqdi 'ind Taha Husayn*; Miftah Tahar, *Taha Husain, sa critique littéraire et ses sources françaises*; and Abdelrashid Mahmoudi, *Taha Husain's Education*. This reading is also elaborated in the understanding of Husayn in *Fi al-shi'r al-jahili* as having applied a "European" method to a new object, literature, what has been called Husayn's "establishment of the study of Arabic literature in light of European methods of the study of literature" (Jaber 'Asfur, *al-Maraya al-mutajawira*, 245). And consider also, for readings pursued along these lines, M. M. Badawi, *Modern Arabic Literature and the West*, 172; Sabry Hafez, *The Genesis of Arabic Narrative Discourse*, 159; and Sa'ad al-Bazi'i, *Istiqbal al-akhar*, 97–100. These readings—insofar as they presuppose the availability and legibility of an object of

literature studies, the installation of which they wish to locate in Husayn—repeat the idiom installed in his text, and the relation it compels with the past. Such readings foreclose the violence and the event of lexical reorganization, which the institution of a literary object in the Arabic language, and in discreet textual instances, occasions.

87. See the section "From Theology to Literature" in Abdelrashid Mahmoudi, *Taha Husain's Education*, 18–38.

88. Abdelrashid Mahmoudi, *Taha Husain's Education*, 25.

89. Charles D. Smith, *Islam and the Search for Social Order in Modern Egypt*, 92.

90. The argument I have begun to offer and continue to elaborate here is indebted to and departs from Benedict Anderson's discussion of the transformation of "sacred languages" into the languages of nation-states (Benedict Anderson, *Imagined Communities: Reflections on the Origins and Spread of Nationalism*, 15). "In effect, ontological reality is apprehensible only through a single, privileged system of re-presentation: the truth language of Church Latin, Qur'anic Arabic, or Examination Chinese" (14). The designation of such languages as "sacred" solicits the thought of their secularization in relation to a withdrawal of religion, a reading that points to a colonial-theological understanding of time, and which gestures to the problems of reading I explore in this book. Rather than a transformation, I read what took place with language in the Arabic nineteenth century, and in Husayn, as an event of destruction in relation to the juridical violence of the state and the legacies of Orientalism and European philology, and in terms of a privileging of specific forms of life and ways of being. Alongside the work cited above (in the introduction to this book and in notes 2, 3, and 4 in this chapter), I learn here from Lisa Pollard, *Nurturing the Nation: The Family Politics of Modernizing, Colonizing, and Liberating Egypt*; Omnia El-Shakry, "The Arabic Freud: The Unconscious and the Modern Subject," "Youth as Peril and Promise," and "Schooled Mothers and Structured Play"; Benjamin Fortna, *The Imperial Classroom*; and Paul Sedra, *From Mission to Modernity: Evangelicals, Reformers and Education in Nineteenth-Century Egypt*. On Syria, Lebanon, and Palestine, I remain indebted to Jens Hanssen, *Fin-de-Siècle Beirut*; Ussama Makdisi, *The Culture of Sectarianism*; Stephen Sheehi, *Foundations of Modern Arab Identity*; Keith David Watenpaugh, *Being Modern in the Middle East*; Michelle Campos, *Ottoman Brothers: Muslims, Christians, and Jews in Early Twentieth-Century Palestine*; and Elizabeth M. Holt, "Narrative and the Reading Public in 1870's Beirut."

91. Faysal Darraj, "al-Shaykh al-taqlidi wa al-muthaqqaf al-hadith," 37. The essay has been reprinted in Faysal Darraj, *al-Hadatha al-mutaqahqira* and *Ma qabla al-dawla, ma ba'd al-hadatha*. I cite here the 1990 publication.

92. Pierre Cachia, *Taha Husayn: His Place in the Egyptian Literary Renaissance*, 131.

93. Jospeh Massad, *Desiring Arabs*, 20.

94. Avital Ronell, *The Test Drive* and "The Rhetoric of Testing," in *Stupidity*, 95–162.

95. Avital Ronell, *The Test Drive*, 102.

96. Samuel Weber, *Institution and Interpretation*, 159, 32. Alongside the work of Samuel Weber, Avital Ronell, Ranajit Guha, Omnia El Shakry, and Timothy Mitchell ("Objects of analysis do not occur as natural phenomena, but are partly formed by the discourse that describes them. The more natural the object appears, the less obvious this discursive manufacture will be" [*Rule of Experts: Egypt, Techno-Politics, Modernity*, 210]), I learn here from the discussion of the relation of writing procedures during the British Mandate in Gaza to the formation of distinct fields pursued by Ilana Feldman ("By providing grounds for determining documentary equivalency, the enforcement of uniformity in writing style contributes to the consolidation of a largely self-referential authoritative field" [Ilana Feldman, *Governing Gaza: Bureaucracy, Authority, and the Work of Rule*, 38]).

97. And see the reading of "history" in al-Tahtawi in Elliott Colla, *Conflicted Antiquities*, 124–31; and of "a more critical historical mind-set" in Juan R. Cole, "Rifa'a al-Tahtawi and the Revival of Practical Philosophy," 45; and the discussion of the "relocation" of "Arab history and literature within European time" in Shaden M. Tageldin, *Disarming Words*, 135, where this relocation is considered in relation to a sovereignty that will have to have been lost. "By 1834 language had already been written into the script of 'progress' toward a colonial 'modernity.' And so al-Tahtawi *must* [my emphasis] translate the sovereign Arabic speaking self into subalternity" (136).

98. Rifa' Rafi' al-Tahtawi, *Takhlis al-ibriz fi talkhis Bariz*, 273.

99. Rifa' Rafi' al-Tahtawi, *Takhlis al-ibriz fi talkhis Bariz*, 229. And see also Anouar Louca, *Voyagers et écrivains égyptiens en France*, 59.

100. Rifa' Rafi' al-Tahtawi, *Kitab manahij al-albab al-misriyya fi mabahij al-adab al-'asriyya*, 6.

101. And compare the reading offered by Juan R. Cole, where al-Tahtawi's *Kitab manahij al-albab al-misriyya* is read in relation to the ethical tradition in Arabic remarked in the word *adab*. "On the whole, however, al-Tahtawi's work clearly bears the imprint of the anthologizing method of *adab*" (Juan R. Cole, "Rifa'a al-Tahtawi and the Revival of Practical Philosophy," 33). Yet rather than read *adab* in al-Tahtawi in relation to "the reestablishment of direct contact with certain elements of the classical Islamic tradition" (30), and rather than read this tradition as holding a place behind al-Tahtawi's text ("al-Tahtawi indicates that the whole argument of the first chapter of the *Manahij* has behind it Miskawayh's division of virtue into intellectual and practical perfections" [41]), one may ask whether *Kitab manahij al-albab al-misriyya* translates the terms privileged in Miskawayh's *Tahdhib al-akhlaq*, in relation to a colonial, linguistic violence. To underline this violence is not to argue that al-Tahtawi "appropriated" concepts of "Western thought" (46), nor is it to argue for or against "the depth of the West's influence on him" (29), but it is to argue only that, to write of and in relation to *adab*, and to grant or withhold sanction in language ("The rapid influx of foreign technology, capital, and, to some extent, culture, which was characteristic of the years immediately prior to the writing of the *Manahij* was thus given classical Islamic sanction" [46]), is to do so—already—in relation to this violence.

102. Eve M. Troutt Powell, *A Different Shade of Colonialism*, 54. And consider as well the discussion of race offered by Samah Selim in "Languages of Civilization: Nation, Translation, and the Politics of Race in Colonial Egypt."

103. Anouar Louca, *Voyagers et écrivains égyptiens en France*, 73.

104. Rifa' Rafi' al-Tahtawi, *Kitab manahij al-albab al-misriyya fi mabahij al-adab al-'asriyya*, 350.

105. See Rifa' Rafi' al-Tahtawi, *Kitab manahij al-albab al-misriyya fi mabahij al-adab al-'asriyya*, 119. And consider as well Mitchell's discussion of *nahu* in *Colonising Egypt*, 146–50. I learn also from the discussion of "language reform" in the Arabic nineteenth century offered by Abdulrazzak Patel, who underlines in relation to a discussion of *nahu* that "until the *nahda*, commentaries on earlier grammars (i.e., by al-Ushmuni and al-Sabban on *Alfiyya* [the *Alfiyya* of Ibn Malik]) were used to teach Arabic grammar, while students were encouraged to memorize linguistic versifications/abridgements because this would develop in them the *aptitude* [my emphasis] to grasp the rules of grammar" ("Language Reform and Controversy in the Nahda," 535). And compare the discussion pursued by Adrian Gully in terms of "the need to adapt the rich features of the classical language to the requirements of the day" ("Arabic Linguistic Issues and Controversies of the Late Nineteenth and Early Twentieth Centuries," 111). Alongside the work of Khalil I. Seeman, *Linguistics in the Middle Ages*, the reading of the word *nahu* I offer learns as well from Jonathan Owens, "Models for Interpreting the Development of Medieval Arabic Grammatical Theory"; Kees Versteegh, *Arabic Grammar and Qur'anic Exegesis in Early Islam*; Rafael Talmon, *Arabic Grammar in Its Formative Age*; and Jaroslav Stetkevych, *The Modern Arabic Literary Language*. And see also, in relation to the citation of poetry in the grammatical tradition, Ramzi Ba'albaki, "The Historical Relevance of Poetry in the Arab Grammatical Tradition." An illuminating discussion of the "sciences [or knowledge] of language ['ulum al-lisan al-'arabi]," to which I turn below in relation to Ibn Khaldun, is offered in Wolfhart Heinrichs, "The Classification of the Sciences and the Consolidation of Philology in Classical Islam," and, differently, Muhsin Mahdi, *Alfarabi and the Foundation of Islamic Political Philosophy*, especially 65–78. And see also the work cited above (chapter 1, note 59), in relation to poetry, *shi'r*, and criticism, *naqd*, and that cited below (chapter 3, note 18), in relation to *adab* and *'ilm*. And compare, more generally, in relation to *'ilm*, Franz Rosenthal, *Knowledge Triumphant: The Concept of Knowledge in Medieval Islam*; and, in relation to institutions, George Makdisi, *The Rise of Colleges: Institutions of Learning in Islam and the West*.

106. Muhsin Mahdi, *Ibn Khaldun's Philosophy of History*, 114. And compare the reading of al-Tahtawi and language in relation to "the development of the Arabic language," in Mohammed Sawaie, "Rifa' Rafi' al-Tahtawi and His Contribution to the Lexical Development of Modern Literary Arabic," 395.

107. Ibn Khaldun, *al-Muqaddima*, in *Kitab al-'ibar*, 1:633.

108. Here I cite and slightly modify the translation offered in Khalil I. Seeman, *Linguistics in the Middle Ages*, 19.

109. I offer further discussion of Ibn Khaldun's writing on language below, p. 131-32. And compare as well the discussion of habitus offered in Saba Mahmood, *Politics of Piety: The Islamic Revival and the Feminist Subject*, 137. There habitus is read, following a certain thread of the work of Talal Asad, and drawing upon Michel Foucault, in relation to a particular understanding of Immanuel Kant ("The Kantian legacy, I would add, becomes particularly important in light of the tradition of Aristotalean ethics it displaces—a tradition in which morality was both realized through, and manifest in, outward behavioral forms" [25]), and through a hermeneutic conception of language and the subject. "Finally, in respect to agency, my arguments in this chapter show that the analytical payback in detaching the concept of agency from the trope of resistance lies in the series of questions such a move opens up in regard to issues of performativity, transgression, suffering, survival, and the articulation of the body *within* [my emphasis] different conceptions of the subject" (188). Mahmood underlines that the analysis she offers is to have been nonhermeneutic ("The analysis I have presented here should not be confused with a hermeneutical approach, one that focuses on the meanings that particular utterances, discourses, and practices convey. Rather, the framework I have suggested analyzes the *work* that discursive practices perform in making possible particular kinds of subjects" [188]), but the reading she offers displaces what it wishes to have avoided onto the interiority and temporal coherency of "difference" ("within different conceptions of the subject"). This difference is solicited as a ground ("Tradition, viewed in this way, is not a set of symbols and idioms that justify present practices, neither is at an unchanging set of cultural prescriptions that stand in contrast to what is changing, contemporary, or modern. Nor is it a historically fixed social structure. Rather, the past is the very ground through which the subjectivity and self-understanding of a tradition's adherents are constituted" [115]), which is called upon to secure the anthropologist's "view" of her or his object ("Tradition, viewed in this way, is not a set of symbols"). Already "the Kantian legacy," as it is discussed by Mahmood, comes to "tradition" later, it arrives from an outside to "constitute," and, as Asad makes clear, destroy "conceptions of the subject." And compare the readings Mahmood offers in "Religious Freedom, the Minority Question, and Geopolitics in the Middle East" and "Secularism, Hermeneutics, and Empire: The Politics of Islamic Reformation." And see also, differently, the discussion of habitus pursued in Pierre Bourdieu, *Logic of Practice*.

110. See Pierre Cachia, *Taha Husayn: His Place in the Egyptian Literary Renaissance*, 58; and the discussion of the university in 'Abd al-Mun'im al-Juma'i, *al-Jami'a al-misriyya al-qadima: nasha'tuha wa dawruha fi al-mujtama'*.

111. Sir William Jones, *The Moallakat, or Seven Arabian Poems, which were Suspended on the Temple at Mecca; With a Translation, a Preliminary Discourse, and Notes Critical, Philological, Explanatory*, 6.

112. al-Suyuti, *al-Itqan fi 'ulum al-Qur'an*, 301.

113. al-Zarkashi, *al-Burhan fi 'ulum al-Qur'an*, 1:294.

114. al-Shafi'i, *al-Risala*, 60.

115. Ibn Khaldun, *al-Muqaddima*, in *Kitab al-'ibar*, 1:633.

116. al-Jahiz, *al-Bayan wa al-tibyin*, 1:56.

117. Ibn Jinni, *al-Khasa'is*, 1:33.

118. Ibn Khaldun, *al-Muqaddima*, in *Kitab al-'ibar*, 1:633.

119. Ibn Khaldun, *al-Muqaddima*, in *Kitab al-'ibar*, 1:643.

120. Muhammad Abid al-Jabri, *al-Khitab al-'arabi al-mu'asir*, 194, 24.

121. A sustained critique of al-Jabri has been pursued by Jurj Tarabishi, and while I am not able in terms of the discussion I offer here to elaborate a close reading of Tarabishi, I do wish to underline that his "critique" presumes a figure of "organic unity" that repeats the privileging of the figure of the body remarked in al-Bustani, al-Shidyaq, and elsewhere ("Rather than relating the different manifestations of this reason in the fields of jurisprudence, theology, Sufism, and philosophy to the single organic structure [al-binya al-'udwiyya al-wahida] from which they arose, he relies upon the harsh, triple dismemberment of this reason into rhetorical, gnostic, and demonstrative" [Jurji Tarabishi, *Naqd naqd al-'aql al-'arabi: nizariyat al-'aql*, 19–20]).

122. Muhammad Abid al-Jabri, *Naqd al-'aql al-'arabi,* vol. 2, *Binyat al-'aql al-'arabi*, 110. And compare Wael Hallaq, "Was al-Shafi'i the Master Architect of Islamic Jurisprudence?".

123. Muhammad Abid al-Jabri, *Naqd al-'aql al-'arabi,* vol. 1, *Takwin al-'aql al-'arabi*, 105.

124. Muhammad Abid al-Jabri, *al-Khitab al-'arabi al-mu'asir*, 49.

125. And consider as well the use of the word *rawasib* in Muhammad Abid al-Jabri, *Naqd al-'aql al-'arabi,* vol. 2, *Binyat al-'aql al-'arabi*, 207.

126. Muhammad Abid al-Jabri, *al-Khitab al-'arabi al-mu'asir*, 37.

127. Muhammad Abid al-Jabri, *al-Khitab al-'arabi al-mu'asir*, 10, 9.

128. Muhammad Abid al-Jabri, *Naqd al-'aql al-'arabi,* vol. 1, *Takwin al-'aql al-'arabi*, 57.

129. Muhammad Abid al-Jabri, *al-Khitab al-'arabi al-mu'asir*, 194.

130. Muhammad Abid al-Jabri, *Naqd al-'aql al-'arabi,* vol. 2, *Binyat al-'aql al-'arabi*, 13.

131. Al-Jabri has edited and republished several of Ibn Rushd's works, among them *Tahafut al-tahafut.*

132. Muhammad Abid al-Jabri, *Naqd al-'aql al-'arabi,* vol. 2, *Binyat al-'aql al-'arabi*, 529.

133. Muhammad Nur, *Qarar al-niyaba*, 55–56. By September the matter had been raised in parliament (see Muhammad Nur, *Qarar al-niyaba*, 56). Further discussion of the responses to the publication of *Fi al-shi'r al-jahili* are outlined in Samih Kurayyam, *Ma'arik Taha Husayn*, 69–100.

134. Ibn Khaldun, *Kitab al-'ibar*, 2:42.

135. Ibn Khaldun, *Kitab al-'ibar*, 2:44.

136. Muhammad Nur, *Qarar al-niyaba*, 67–68.

137. I learn from and cite here the work of Vincente L. Rafael, *Contracting Colonialism*, 35.

138. 'Abd al-Mun'im al-Juma'i, *Taha Husayn wa al-jami'a al-misriyya*, 33.

139. Luis 'Awad, *Thaqafatuna fi muftaraq al-turuq*, 129.

140. Idwar al-Kharrat, "Akhir ayyam al-'amid," 91.

141. Taha Husayn, *al-Ayyam*, 81, 309/*The Days*, 57, 245. And compare the discussion offered by Fedwa Malti-Douglas of Husayn's staging, in *al-Ayyam*, of his relation to his teachers at al-Azhar (Fedwa Malti-Douglas, *Blindness and Autobiography: Al-Ayyam of Taha Husayn*, 68) through his negotiation of a relation between Egypt and Europe and his understanding of himself as an "individual" subject ("The hero also uses the appeal of the West to set himself apart from his Egyptian background and even to validate himself as an individual" [79]).

142. This moment in *al-Ayyam* has been read in historical terms and in relation to the emergence of a "literate public" in colonial Egypt (Jamal Mohammed Ahmed, *The Intellectual Origins of Egyptian Nationalism*, 19, 59). And compare Robert Tignor's discussion of the nonunderstanding of language over against which literacy is staged in historical scholarship ("*Kuttab* children were taught by religious *shaykhs* whose training varied greatly. Many were educated in al-Azhar, but their primary qualification was that they could read the Quran and recite it from memory. That the *shaykhs had no real understanding of what they read or recited* [my emphasis] was probably only recognized by the few who went beyond the *kuttab* level in their education" [Robert Tignor, *Modernization and British Colonial Rule in Egypt, 1882–1914*, 330]), and the reading of the "absence of a literate and appreciative public" in Matti Moosa, *The Origins of Modern Arabic Fiction*, ix). Moosa also explains that in nineteenth-century Egypt "the study of the Arabic language was not meant to develop or encourage creative writing or generate new themes and styles; it was seen as a means to understand and interpret the Quran and the Shari'a (Islamic law) [Moosa's gloss]") (2), a reading also mirrored in his discussion of *al-Ayyam*. "Husayn's account shows that learning in his time meant religion, grammar, philology, and traditional Arabic poetry and tales" (294).

143. Taha Husayn, *Mustaqbal al-thaqafa fi misr*, 31.

144. Taha Husayn, *al-Ayyam*, 346–47/277–78.

145. Taha Husayn, *Fi al-adab al-jahili*, 12.

146. Taha Husayn, *al-Ayyam*, 201/156.

147. Taha Husayn, *Fi al-adab al-jahili*, 12, 68.

148. Taha Husayn, *al-Ayyam*, 107/77.

149. Taha Husayn, *Fi al-adab al-jahili*, 56.

150. 'Abd al-Muhsin Taha Badr, *Tatawwur al-riwaya al-'arabiyya al-haditha fi Misr*, 304.

151. Taha Husayn, *Fi al-adab al-jahili*, 116.

152. And compare the illuminating reading of al-Bustani offered in Nadia Bou Ali, "Butrus al-Bustani and the Shipwreck of the Nation," 272 passim.

153. Werner Hamacher, "95 Theses on Philology," 32.

154. Friedrich Nietzsche, *Daybreak*, 5, cited in Hamacher, "95 Theses on Philology," 36 ("Philologie nämlich ist jene ehrwürdige Kunst, welche von

ihrem Vereher vor Allem Eins heischt, bei Seite gehn, sich Zeit lassen, still werden, langsam werden" [Friedrich Nietzsche, *Morgenröte*, 17]).

EXCURSUS

1. See *Entretiens avec Edmond Amran El Maleh*, 42.
2. Muhammad Barrada, "Une lecture dymanique de la mémoire," 33, 39.
3. *La peinture de Ahmed Cherkaoui*, ed. Mohamed Melehi; *Ahmed Cherkaoui: La passion du sign*, ed. Brahim Alaoui.
4. Edmond Amran El Maleh, "Les pierres blanches," 31-32.
5. Judith Butler, *Parting Ways: Judaism and the Critique of Zionism*, 51, 60.
6. Eduardo Cadava, "Lapsus Imaginis: The Image in Ruins," 39, 36.
7. Eduardo Cadava, "Trees, Hands, Stars, and Veils: The Portrait in Ruins," 23.
8. Edmond Amran El Maleh, "Les pierres blanches," 35.
9. Abdelkabir Khatibi, "L'envol des raciness," 17. The essay has been included in Abdelkabir Khatibi, *Maghreb pluriel*, 211–26. And compare, elsewhere, the discussion of calligraphy in Khatibi in relation to what he calls "Islamic metaphysics" (Abdelkabir Khatibi, *La blessure du nom propre*, 178 passim).
10. Gil Hochberg, *In Spite of Partition*, 33.
11. Bouazza Benachir, *Edmond Amran El Maleh: Cheminements d'une écriture*, 200, 201.
12. Lecia Rosenthal, *Mourning Modernism: Literature, Catastrophe, and the Politics of Consolation*, 117.

3. REPETITION

1. Elias Khoury, *al-Dhakira al-mafquda*, 17.
2. Throughout, I provide the transliteration of names offered in the English translation of *Bab al-shams*.
3. Elias Khoury, *Abwab al-madina*, 6/*Gates of the City*, 3.
4. Sonja Mejchar, "'Abwab al-Madina': madina la isma laha wa la dhakira," 85.
5. And compare Elise Salem, *Constructing Lebanon: A Century of Literary Narratives*, 110; and Nouri Gana, *Signifying Loss*, 167, and, more generally, 153–78.
6. Sami Suwaydan, *Abhath fi al-nass al-riwa'i al-'arabi*, 198. And consider further, as Suwaydan underlines, "In *al-Wujuh al-bayda'* [*White Faces*, Beirut, 1981] there is an insistence on pointing to its particular mode of narration. It does not cease narrating events, telling stories, and mentioning incidents, nor does it cease emphasizing its particular style of narration and storytelling, as if this were its real sphere of creativity" (195).
7. Sonja Mejchar, "'Abwab al-Madina': madina la isma laha wa la dhakira," 88.
8. Muhammad Barrada, *As'ila al-riwaya, as'ila al-naqd*, 146.

9. Fayyad Hibi, *al-Shaksiyya and ghayariyya fi al-riwaya al-lubnaniyya*, 142.

10. Sami Suwaydan, *Abhath fi al-nass al-riwa'i al-'arabi*, 226.

11. Heather Love, *Feeling Backward: Loss and the Politics of Queer History*, 147.

12. Ibn Jinni, *al-Luma' fi al-'arabiyya*, 73.

13. Ibn Hisham, *Sharh shudhur al-dhahab fi ma'arifat kalam al-'arab*, 45.

14. Ibn Jinni, *al-Luma' fi al-'arabiyya*, 71.

15. Ibn Hisham, *Sharh shudhur al-dhahab*, 170.

16. Elias Khoury, *Abwab al-madina*, 6/*Gates of the City*, 3.

17. Paul de Man, "Shelly Disfigured," 121.

18. "Under the name 'adab' one designates, roughly, the ensemble of secular sciences found alongside theology, philosophy, and jurisprudence [Sous le nom d'*adab* on désigne, en gros, l'ensemble des sciences profanes qui laissent de côté la théologie, la philosophie et la jurisprudence]. Poetry naturally constitutes one branch of *adab*. In all of the books of *adab* citations of verse occupy a fairly large place, and this confers on these writings an important value as anthologies, which justifies their mention here. What characterizes these works is their disorganized presentation of developments that bear upon a particular theme. Everything there is digression," Amjad Traboulsi writes. Further: "This *genre* [my emphasis] was born at the beginning of the third Hijra century, thanks to the vast erudition of a writer as much a master of his language as he was original, al-Jahiz" (*La critique poétique des Arabes*, 53). A recent essay surveying the field offers, through a discussion that underlines al-Jahiz, that "*adab*, therefore, is not synonymous with literary anthology; rather, literary anthology represents a type of *adab*" (Bilal Orfali, "A Sketch Map of Arabic Poetry Anthologies up to the Fall of Baghdad," 31). And compare the illuminating discussions of *adab* offered in Beatrice Gruendler, *Medieval Arabic Praise Poetry*, 5–9; Samer Ali, *Arabic Literary Salons in the Islamic Middle Ages*; and Muhsin J. al-Musawi, *The Islamic Context of the Thousand and One Nights*. And see as well the consideration of *adab* as a "skill" in Brinkley Messick, *The Calligraphic State*, 156; as an oral practice in relation to *'ilm* (knowledge) in Jonathan Berkey, *The Transmission of Knowledge in Medieval Cairo*, 24–26, 110, 157, 216; and the discussion offered by Berkey of *adab* and popular preaching in Mamluk Cairo in relation to an understanding of "suffering and death" (Jonathan Berkey, *Popular Preaching and Religious Authority in the Medieval Islamic Near East*, 49), "the social and political order" (68) and an understanding of world ("In a sense it was knowledge that held together not only the faith but the world" [70]). Such an understanding is further pursued in Michael Chamberlain, *Knowledge and Social Practice in Medieval Damascus*, where, through a stunning reading that dislodges language from later, colonial understandings ("The idea that books are singular products of individual wills, belonging to their authors as unmistakably as their personalities, is a modern one that would not have been understood in [medieval] Damascus" [141]), a reading of "the cultivation of 'ilm" (127, 129) and of *adab* as "a set of acquired dispositions" (150) is considered in relation to "the

social order" (133) and to practices of language. And consider also the illuminating reading of *adab* in relation to *zarf* offered in Khaled El-Rouayheb, *Before Homosexuality in the Arab-Islamic World, 1500–1800* ("Knowledge and appreciation of poetry was widely thought to be one of the hallmarks of the cultivated, refined person" [61]), and El-Rouayheb's discussion of the relation of *adab* to form, *sura* (pl. *suwar*) (103), pursued through a reading of 'Abd al-Ghani al-Nabulsi (d. 1731); and the reading of the aesthetic offered in Sinan Antoon, *The Poetics of the Obscene in Premodern Arabic Poetry: Ibn al-Hajjaj and Sukhf*, where the poetry of Ibn al-Hajjaj (941–1001) is read in relation to the poetic "distortion" and "inversion" of "the typical ideal images of perfect bodies in traditional poetry" (101). Antoon suggests that Ibn al-Hajjaj's writing at once reinforces a sociality and hierarchy of social and political relations (e.g., 71, 75, 132) and "violates" them ("Scatology in particular, more often than not, ends up, unconsciously if not consciously, violating other boundaries and hierarchies and manifesting anxieties about order and its human-made configurations" [133]), suggesting a reading of poetic practice in relation to social and political form. And compare the consideration of *zarf* offered in Sahar Amer, *Crossing Borders: Love between Women in Medieval French and Arabic Literatures*, 23–25, 144–46; and the reading of *adab* in Tarif Khalidi, *Arabic Historical Thought in the Classical Period*, where *adab* is increasingly located on the side of "critique" (87, 117, 128), the "transcending" of "traditional scripture" (121), and the "liberation" of history "from the cumbersome *isnad* [chain of transmitters]" ("The *khabar* [historical report], liberated from its cumbersome *isnad*, was free at last to roam the streets, picking up the sights and sounds of strata of society hitherto unrecorded" [122]), and where *adab* is opposed, in the figure of Ibn al-Muqaffa' (724–59), to "religion" (95) and its "dominance" ("In sum, the essays and epistles of Ibn al-Muqaffa' breathe a spirit distinctly, self-consciously at variance with the dominant culture of his age" [95]).

19. Saree Makdisi, *Romantic Imperialism*, 147.

20. Elias Khoury, *Dirasat fi naqd al-shi'r*, 125. The reading I offer here learns from the work of Ken Seigneurie, yet rather than read Khoury's relation to language and the past as a "reappropriation" (Ken Seigneurie, *Standing by the Ruins: Elegiac Humanism in Wartime and Postwar Lebanon*, 70), I underline the ways in which language—and the past—is given to be read as already devastated, as already in catastrophe. And compare the discussion of the trope of *nasib* and its "adaptation" offered by Hilary Kilpatrick through a discussion of the novelists Emile Habiby and Ahlam Mustaghanimi ("They show that elements of the cultural heritage, sensitively interpreted and adapted to concord with contemporary experience, still retain their significance" [Hilary Kilpatrick, "Literary Creativity and the Cultural Heritage: The *Atlal* in Modern Arabic Fiction," 43–44]).

21. Tejaswini Niranjana, *Siting Translation*, 45.

22. Elias Khoury, *Zaman al-ihtilal*, 52.

23. Elliott Colla, "The Image of Loss: Jalal Toufic's Filmic Beirut," 309.

24. Elias Khoury, *al-Dhakira al-mafquda*, 29.

25. Edward W. Said, *Orientalism*, 1.

26. Stathis Gourgouris, *Dream Nation*, 132.

27. Edward W. Said, *Beginnings: Intention and Method*, 179.

28. Elias Khoury, *Dirasat fi naqd al-shi'r*, 110.

29. Gretchen Head, "The Performative in Ilyas Khuri's *Bab al-Shams*," 149.

30. Stefan G. Meyer, *The Experimental Arabic Novel*, 132.

31. Paul de Man, "Anthropomorphism and Trope in the Lyric," 259.

32. Elise Salem, *Constructing Lebanon*, 191.

33. Paul de Man, "Shelly Disfigured," 94.

34. Paul de Man, "Autobiography as De-Facement," 67.

35. Paul de Man, "Autobiography as De-Facement," 72.

36. Paul de Man, "Intentional Structure of the Romantic Image," 6.

37. Elias Khoury, *Abwab al-madina*, 95/*Gates of the City*, 86.

38. Elias Khoury, *Abwab al-madina*, 7/*Gates of the City*, 4.

39. Radwa 'Ashur, *Sayyadu al-dhakira*, 67. And consider as well the discussion of pain offered in Fabio Caiani, "'My Name is Yalu': The Development of Metafiction in Ilyas Khuri's Work," 145.

40. The decisive legal document on the massacres at Sabra and Shatila is Sean MacBride, *Israel in Lebanon: Report of the International Commission to Inquire into Reported Violations of International Law by Israel during Its Invasion of Lebanon*. And see also, in relation to the events Khoury discusses here, Rosemary Sayigh, *Too Many Enemies*. And consider the illuminating reading pursued by Laleh Khalili, where the aporetical dimensions of forms of national commemoration are considered in relation to the violence imparted through the work of nongovernmental organizations and an appeal to rights in the staging of Palestinian victims of the 1982 massacres as "abject" (Laleh Khalili, *Heroes and Martyrs of Palestine: The Politics of National Commemoration*, 176, 207).

41. 'Aliya Mamduh Salih, *al-Bina' al-sardi fi riwayat Elias Khoury*, 194.

42. Ranjana Khanna, *Dark Continents: Psychoanalysis and Colonialism*, 30.

43. Samira Aghacy, "Elias Khoury's *The Journey of Little Gandhi*: Fiction and Ideology," 169.

44. Maher Jarrar, "*The Arabian Nights* and the Contemporary Arabic Novel," 309.

45. Elias Khoury, *Sinalkul*, 375.

46. Elias Khoury, *Tajribat al-bahth 'an ufuq*, 11–12.

47. Scholarship on the novel and its "origins" in the Arabic language points to an understanding of the novel form as remarking a break with tradition. Sayyed al-Bahrawi, summarizing this scholarship, has written, "Most of the studies which treat this issue agree that the novel is a literary genre which has come to us from the West following modern contact with it. This opinion is, scientifically, the more correct and precise one, because the other opinion, which argues that the novel is a continuation of classical Arabic narrative genres, does not understand the clear distinction between the artistry, and diversity, of those classical genres, and the artistic specificities of the novel as a defined literary genre (Sayyed al-Bahrawi, *Muhtawa al-shakl*

fi al-riwaya al-'arabiyya, 37). And consider as well the reading pursued in 'Abd al-Muhsin Taha Badr, where the the novel "in general" is understood as a domestic, European genre that remarks the falling away of a medieval past and its "forms of thought." "It is possible to summarize the form of thought that predominated in this society: social rigidity and conservative thought. One of the characteristics of this thought is that it sought refuge in idealism [al-mithaliyaa], the absolute [al-mutlaq], the general, [al-'am], and the abstract [al-mujarrad]" (Abd al-Muhsin Taha Badr, *Tatawwur al-riwaya al-'arabiyya al-haditha fi Misr*, 194). The novel, in Badr, and following the work of Ian Watt, remarks, in René Descartes and John Locke, a belief "in the power of the individual to discover reality with his senses" (195), which is said to occasion the withdrawal of the past. "Its method is the study of human experience through the intermediary of the researcher in which he hypothesizes that he is liberated from the previous burdens and inherited rules" (195), Badr writes. The absence of this liberation in colonial Egypt points, in Badr, to "impediments" (211, 215) faced by the "development of the artistic novel" (205) there. Historical difference prevents the repetition, in colonial Egypt, of what is taken to have been a European, normative mode of economic and cultural development. "It was *natural* [my emphasis] that a decisive and radical change not take place in Egyptian society, for its *general nature* was *still* agricultural, and the middle class was not able to change the form of the society, and it was therefore not able *to develop its culture or its arts* in an essential way" (210; emphases mine). This reading is redoubled in the discussion of Taha Husayn in the work of Faysal Darraj, and may be compared to readings of the novel in Arabic that underline its newness. Consider Yahya Haqqi, *Fajr al-qissa al-misriyya*, 16–17; Shakir Mustafa, *al-Qissa fi Suriyya*, 44; Muhammad Rushda Hasan, *Athar al-maqama fi nash'at al-qissa al-misriyya*, 79–82; and Sayyed al-Bahrawi, *Muhtawa al-shakl fi al-riwaya al-'arabiyya*, 67, 61–114. And compare Muhsin J. al-Musawi, *al-Riwaya al-'arabiyya, al-nasha't wa al-tahawwul*; Mary N. Layoun, *Travels of a Genre: The Modern Novel and Ideology*, especially 60–62; and Roger Allen, *The Arabic Novel: An Historical and Critical Introduction*, 11–51.

48. H. A. R. Gibb, "The Egyptian Novel" ("Zaynab broke away decisively in language, style, subject, and treatment from anything that had gone before in Arabic literature" [8]). And compare Hilary Kilpatrick, *The Modern Egyptian Novel*, 20; Matti Moosa, *The Origins of Modern Arabic Fiction*, 262; Roger Allen, *The Arabic Novel: An Historical and Critical Introduction*, 33–37; Muhammad Siddiq, *Arab Culture and the Novel*, 36, and the reading of the "Arabic novel" and it "origins" at 25–26; and Elliott Colla, "How *Zaynab* Became the First Arabic Novel."

49. See Radwa 'Ashur, *al-Hadatha al-mumkina: al-Shidyaq wa al-Saq 'ala al-saq, al-riwaya al-ula fi al-adab al-'arabi al-hadith* (A Possible Modernity: al-Shidyaq and *al-Saq 'ala al-saq*, the First Novel in Modern Arabic Literature). And compare the reading of *al-Saq 'ala al-saq* as "the first autobiographical text [awwal nass sirdhati] in our modern Arabic literature" in Sabry Hafez, "Raqsh al-dhat la kitabatuha," 19. If, and as Roger Allen has written, an understanding of generic temporal delimitation and

the designation of origins has been placed in question in the field of Arabic literature studies ("In this retrospective context, nothing illustrates the problems associated with such a developmental model better than the way in which Muhammad Husayn Haykal's novel, *Zaynab*, has been evaluated. The ascription of 'firstness' to such a work and the total confusion in placing its antecedents into some sort of narrative categories or developmental sequence provide an excellent illustration of the consequences of the unbalanced picture presented by the failure of the scholarly community to come to terms with the nature of generic change as it was affected by attitudes to modernity and pre-modernity during the 19th century" [Roger Allen, "Rewriting Literary History," 253–54]), the desire to point to a stark newness in language, and in relation to what called itself *nahda* and *tanwir*, persists. As Allen also underlines in a consideration of "the continuing presence of the '*maqamah* spirit' in cultural life," and in relation to Ahmad Faris al-Shidyaq, "If his *maqamat* are to be viewed as a continuation of that tradition, then it is al-Shidyaq, with his *Al-Saq 'ala al-saq*, who moves Arabic narrative in *entirely new* [my emphasis] directions" (259).

50. Matti Moosa, *The Origins of Modern Arabic Fiction*, xii, 253. And compare the discussion in 'Abd al-Rahman Yaghi, *Fi al-juhud al-riwa'iyya: Min Salim al-Bustani ila Najib Mahfuz*, 23–51; Sharon Halevi and Fruma Zachs, "'Asma' (1873): The Early Arabic Novel"; and Stephen Sheehi, *Foundations of Modern Arab Identity*, 76–106.

51. Shaden M. Tageldin, *Disarming Words*, 29, 159.

52. *Hadith 'Isa ibn Hisham* was published serially between 1898 and 1902. On its publication history, see Roger Allen, *A Period of Time: A Study and Translation of Hadith 'Isa ibn Hisham by Muhammad al-Muwaylihi*, 1–97. A discussion of *Hadith 'Isa ibn Hisham* in relation to its having been designated the "first" Arabic novel is offered on p. 96. Consider as well that in the reading offered by Allen *Hadith 'Isa ibn Hisham* points to the end of an older era exemplified in the prose form of the *maqama*. "It was al-Muwaylihi who continued the trend started by al-Shidyaq by using certain aspects of the form, and in particular the style, as a means of treating the social and cultural problems of the day and of expressing the author's own views on what he saw during his travels, whether in the Orient or in Europe. In so doing, al-Muwaylihi delivered the *coup de grace* to the *maqama* genre. (20). A discussion of *Hadith 'Isa ibn Hisham* as "the first narrative text in modern Arabic literature" appears in Sayyed al-Bahrawi, *Muhtawa al-shakl*, 61. And compare the discussion of the time of language in *Hadith 'Isa ibn Hisham* in Kamran Rastegar, *Literary Modernity between the Middle East and Europe*, 95 passim. I have elsewhere tried to offer a discussion of al-Muwaylihi in relation to the ways in which the reading of *Hadith 'Isa ibn Hisham*, in the work of Faysal Darraj and Sayyed al-Bahrawi, occurs through a staging of its language in relation to time (Jeffrey Sacks, "Futures of Literature: Inhitat, Adab, Naqd"). Darraj's reading of al-Muwaylihi appears in *Nizariyat al-riwaya wa al-riwaya al-'arabiyya*, 165–82, and it may be

compared to his discussion of the category of the novel as an event of language that belongs to a secular, historical time which "does not know the sacred" ("Wada' al-riwaya al-'arabiyya fi haql thaqafi ghayr riwa'i," 94), and in relation to what he calls its "handicapped birth [wilada mu'awwaqa]" in the Arabic language (Faysal Darraj, *al-Riwaya wa ta'wil al-tarikh*). In a parallel gesture, al-Bahrawi's reading, in *Muhtawa al-shakl fi al-riwaya al-'arabiyya*, turns on an understanding of al-Muwaylihi's text as sharing in "the new period of transition to the modern Arabic language—the language of the newspaper and of literature—which was free of rhetorical artifice" (67). The *maqama*, and the past to which it metonymically gestures, is compelled to appear on the side of death, it is a "dead art that had lost its connection to the people" (107).

53. Elliott Colla, "How *Zaynab* Became the First Arabic Novel," 217.

54. A compelling discussion of the discourse on the "origin" of the novel form in Arabic has been pursued by Samah Selim in *The Novel and the Rural Imaginary in Egypt* (discussed in the introduction to this book, note 17) and in a series of compelling articles. "I suggest that both the mechanics of representation in discrete narrative texts and the formal organization of these texts into literary canons construct a cultural discourse through which power is strategically instituted and wielded in the social world" (Samah Selim, "The Narrative Craft: Realism and Fiction in the Arabic Canon," 110), and this strategic wielding of power points to the generalization of "the textual institution of authorship" (117) in relation to an "autonomous self" and the "social body" ("In its effort to forge its own destiny, the autonomous self is made to contain and resolve the existential contradiction produced by the new social order, this emerging as a kind of 'mirror' of the social body as a whole" [113]). The privileging of Haykal's *Zaynab* as starkly new works to dismiss and appropriate earlier and contemporary writing as belonging to the past or to an insufficiently educated present ("Most literary historians however, tend to dismiss this prolific fictional production prior to *Zaynab* as a series of imperfect experiments in an evolving process of adaptation and assimilation of an imported genre" [114]), to point to the repeated installation of a series of historical categories. These categories are privileged, differently, in al-Bustani, al-Tahtawi, and others, for example, the lectures presented by Muhammad 'Abdu in Beirut in 1885, and which were published in Cairo in 1897, where language is compelled to appear in terms of a harsh division between the present and the past in relation to what is repudiated newly as *taqlid* [imitation] ("[Islam] drew men's hearts from their attachment to what their fathers had done and what their sons had inherited, and pointed to the stupidity and foolishness of those who rely upon others who have come before" [Muhammad 'Abdu, *Risalat al-tawhid*, *al-A'mal al-kamila*, 3:443]). As Selim also underlines, "The anti-colonial struggle also involved a struggle to liberate Egyptian sensibility from the chains of social convention and blind imitation of what was now seen as an aging and decrepit literary canon. One of the most important strategies by which this new Egyptian man would create his world afresh in his own image was literature—particularly narrative literature, unfettered by the shackles of a

burdensome and largely irrelevant classical and medieval tradition" (121). And see as well the reading pursued by Selim in "Fiction and Colonial Identities: Arsène Lupin in Arabic," where "the steady institutionalization of legal reforms and medico-forensic innovation" and "the way personhood was constructed and managed by the state and its bureaucracies in the Egypt of the British occupation" (198) is discussed in relation to the "autonomous self" in language. The institution of the self through the "bio-juridical system" (198) Selim elaborates mirrors the institution of a reflection on the novel in Arabic in relation to its origins, where translation "functions as a rhetorical and *social* medium of shifting genre poetics in specific historical moments of reception" (209–10). Learning from this work, I argue that in Khoury novelistic writing discombobulates the lines of paternity and generation called upon to authorize reading practices, confounding both the understanding of language in relation to what are said to have been its "origins" and the time or sequence of its "reception" in history.

55. See Edward W. Said, "After Mahfouz." The work of Mahfouz to which Said alludes includes Mahfouz's trilogy, *Bayn al-qasrayn* (1956), *Qasr al-shawq* (1957), and *al-Sukariyya* (1957), and other, late writings. Yet a close reading of these texts would show that they do not sustain the "stateliness" (Edward W. Said, "After Mahfouz," 322) to which Said appeals in staging Khoury, Kanafani, and Habiby over against Mahfouz. "Finally, of course, Khoury's work embodies the actuality of Lebanon's predicament, so unlike Egypt's majestic stability as delivered in Mahfouz's fiction" (325). If Said reads Khoury's text as coming "after" Mahfouz, one may ask whether this relation questions the distinction between Khoury and Mahfouz Said also wishes to draw. And compare the reading of Mahfouz pursued by Idwar al-Kharrat in "Min a'la namadhij al-hissasiyya al-qadima" and the discussion of Mahfouz in relation to later, post-1960s novelistic writing in Egypt in terms of "inheritance" in Samia Mehrez, *Egyptian Writers between History and Fiction*, 9. And consider also the reading of Mahfouz's *Awlad haritna* (1959) pursued by Ayman A. El-Desouky, where Mahfouz's language points to "a radical form of historical consciousness, of modernity's experience of time, as a counter-vision to religious and state histories" ("Heterologies of Revolutionary Action," 433). I point to El-Desouky's reading to underline that if in Mahfouz—and if also in Husayn's *Fi al-shi'r al-jahili* and Ali 'Abd al-Raziq's *al-Islam wa usul al-hukm* (1925), each of which El-Desouky gestures to—"new forms of historical consciousness" (431) are indexed, these forms are given in relation to the juridical violence of the state and its relation to language. Such consciousness, and if it is one, would remark that violence and participate in it, even as one would wish to underline its differentiated occurrence in relation to Husayn, 'Abd al-Raziq, and Mahfouz. The reading I offer of Khoury also learns from the insight that "the Arabic novel in Egypt is thoroughly implicated in cultural and philosophical concerns that, strictly speaking, cannot always be subsumed under literary or aesthetic categories" (Muhammad Siddiq, *Arab Culture and the Novel*, 32), even as I would not wish to suggest that "literary or aesthetic categories" will ever have been divorced from "cultural and philosophical concerns" but that

those categories are already cultural, philosophical, and, as I have tried to underline, polemical. Siddiq has also recalled, in a reading that is consonant with El-Desouky's in certain ways, and through a discussion of Mahfouz's *Awlad haritna*, that there is a relation of inheritance between the Arabic novel as a form and "the secularizing legacies of the *nahda*" (23) in language. Siddiq writes that "he [Mahfouz or even "the Arab novelist"] inherits the mantle of the Arab/Islamic reformer of the late nineteenth and early twentieth century," where "the Arabic novel often appear[s] to carry on the cultural work left unfinished by the Arab Awakening (*nahda*) [interpolation in the original]" (15). The reading I offer learns from these interventions to ask how language, in Khoury, reiterates a relation to the loss and destruction of the giving of sense in the Arabic nineteenth century. I argue that language, in Khoury, points neither to a "historical consciousness" (El-Desouky) nor to a "secular" form of writing ("Nor is it an accident that his [Mahfouz's] literary talent found its fullest realization in the novel, perhaps the most quintessentially secular and, therefore, most hospitable to philosophical interests and pursuits of all literary genres" [Muhammad Siddiq, *Arab Culture and the Novel*, 15]) but that it occasions more than one iteration of loss—I argue that it *is* iterations of loss—that gesture to, as they repeat in advance, more than one event of linguistic violence that will never simply have preceded it.

56. Elias Khoury, *al-Dhakira al-mafquda*, 107.

57. And consider also that the institutional writing of the history of the Arabic novel is intimately tied to, and repeats, the principal rhetorical and temporal understandings privileged in the *nahda*. As Selim has further underlined, "The story of the *Nahdah* is closely entwined with the history of the Arabic novel, which is for the most part conceived to have begun with the translation, adaptation and imitation of the European novel toward the end of the nineteenth century" (Samah Selim, "The People's Entertainments: Translation, Popular Fiction, and the Nahda in Egypt," 37). Selim's reading points—and perhaps uniquely—to a relation between *nahda* and *tanwir* ("In either case, the region's 'enlightenment' [*tanwir*] is understood to have been initiated, for better or worse, by the colonial project" [36]), to underscore a division within what she calls "the *Nahdah* as a whole" (37). "My project, rather, is to try to understand how the dominant genealogical methodology in Arabic literary history has arrived at a modern novelistic cannon that represents the fruits of a *particular* version of modernity, a particular *Nahdah* to the exclusion of all others" (38). This particular *nahda* points to "the hegemony of the European-liberal concept of the subject, with its related institutions of authorship and copyright in the literary domain" (45) in relation to "the disciplinary project of a middle class in the process of constituting itself as a national bourgeoisie" (38). Language, here, is understood as as a transparent medium and translation "as the mechanism through which Arab societies achieved enlightenment and modernity" (38). In the second *nahda*, which Selim reads through the practice of literary translation in the late nineteenth and early twentieth century, language is dislodged from a relation to older Arabic and contemporary European literary and linguistic categories. "Like the oral epic and folktale, popular translations act as more

or less freely circulating narratives, largely unbound from the Romantic conventions of authorship that the *Nahdah* appropriated and celebrated" (53), and "the majority of these printed texts were fictions, unbound from both the classical Arabic literary and language canons and the high conventions of the European genre that they appropriated and carnivalized" (52). Through the reading I offer here, and without erasing the differences, I wish to underline a generalized linguistic violence, with respect to which "other" *nahdas* ("a particular *Nahda* to the exclusion of all others") may not be said to be or to have been absolutely distinct or "unbound." And compare, differently, and in relation to the category of the "nation," the reading offered in Ziad Fahmy, *Ordinary Egyptians*.

58. The reading I offer hopes to contribute to the reconsideration of "the Arabic novel" under way in the work of several scholars (Samah Selim, Kamran Rastegar, Najat Rahman, Sonja Mejchar, Shaden Tageldin, Tarek El-Ariss, Mara Naaman, and others), by displacing a "monolithic historiography" and a "linear, Hegelian historiography" (Hosam Aboul-Ela, *Other South: Faulkner, Coloniality, and the Mariátegui Tradition*, 151, 34) through a close attention to language—and languages—in relation to the appropriating force imparted in literary critical institutions.

59. Elias Khoury, *Dirasat fi naqd al-shi'r*, 12.

60. For a discussion of the relation of *Alf layla wa layla* to *adab* and *zarf*, see Muhsin J. al-Musawi, *The Islamic Context of the Thousand and One Nights*, 3, 33 passim; and Samer Ali, *Arabic Literary Salons*, 52. A suggestive reading of Khoury's *Rihlat Ghandi al-Saghir* (The Journey of Little Ghandi) (Beirut, 1989) in relation to *Alf Layla wa Layla* is offered in Sabah Ghandour, "History, Religion, and the Construction of Subjectivity in Elias Khoury's *Rihlat Ghandi al-Saghir*" ("Are we then reading stories that in their form and their delineation of incidents are similar to the stories told by Shahrazad to King Shahrayar?" [190]). And consider also the discussion of *Bab al-shams* pursued in Maher Jarrar, "*The Arabian Nights* and the Contemporary Arabic Novel," 308–10.

61. Ferial J. Ghazoul, *Nocturnal Poetics*, 2.

62. Abdelfattah Kilito, *L'oeil et l'aiguille: Essais sur "les mille et un nuits"*, 13.

63. Elias Khoury, *Tajribat al-bahth 'an ufuq*, 10.

64. Marc Nichanian, "Mourning and Reconciliation," 204, 198. And consider as well, in relation to the reconstruction of the city of Beirut following the Lebanese Civil War, Saree Makdisi, "Laying Claim to Beirut."

65. Elias Khoury, "Su'al al-nakba," 51–52.

66. Marc Nichanian, "On the Archive III: The Secret; or, Borges at Yale," 20, 30, 18. And see also Marc Nichanian, *Mourning Philology*.

67. Marc Nichanian, "Catastrophic Mourning," 113.

68. Nasrin Qader, *Narratives of Catastrophe: Boris Diop, ben Jelloun, Khatibi*, 159.

69. Paul de Man, "Anthropomorphism and Trope in the Lyric," 245.

70. Paul de Man, "Aesthetic Formalization," 272.

71. Cynthia Chase, *Decomposing Figures*, 73.

72. David Lloyd, "The Memory of Hunger," 220, 226.

73. Eduardo Cadava, *Emerson and the Climates of History*, 132.

74. Edward W. Said, "After Mahfouz," 322.

75. Elias Khoury, *Zaman al-ihtilal*, 32.

76. Yumna al-'Id, *Fan al-riwaya al-'arabiyya: bayna khususiyyat al-hikaya wa tamayyuz al-khitab*, 159.

77. See Avital Ronell, *Dictations: On Haunted Writing*, x passim. And see also the discussion of "auto-bio-thanatography" in Jacques Derrida, *Psyché: Inventions de l'autre, Tome 1*, 270/*Psyche: Inventions of the Other*, vol. 1, 260, and *The Post Card*; and Philippe Lacoue-Labarthe, "The Echo of the Subject."

78. Elias Khoury, "al-Akhta' . . . al-addad," 152.

79. Emile Habiby, *al-Waqa'i' al-ghariba*, 13/*The Secret Life of Saeed the Pessoptimist*, 3. Throughout, I provide the transliteration of names offered in the English translation of this text.

80. Emile Habiby, *al-Waqa'i' al-ghariba*, 15/*The Secret Life of Saeed the Pessoptimist*, 4.

81. Elias Khoury, "Min ajli nahda thalitha," 30.

82. Elias Khoury, *al-Dhakira al-mafquda*, 159.

83. Yumna al-'Id, *Fan al-riwaya al-'arabiyya: bayna khususiyyat al-hikaya wa tamayyuz al-khitab*, 157.

84. Emile Habiby, *al-Waqa'i' al-ghariba*, 16/*The Secret Life of Saeed the Pessoptimist*, 6.

85. Emile Habiby, *al-Waqa'i' al-ghariba*, 22/*The Secret Life of Saeed the Pessoptimist*, 12.

86. Emile Habiby, *al-Waqa'i' al-ghariba*, 79/*The Secret Life of Saeed the Pessoptimist*, 62.

87. David Lloyd, "The Memory of Hunger," 216.

88. Emile Habiby, *al-Waqa'i' al-ghariba*, 30/*The Secret Life of Saeed the Pessoptimist*, 19.

89. Elias Khoury, "al-Akhta' . . . al-addad," 154.

90. Elias Khoury, "al-Akhta' . . . al-addad," 154.

91. Jabra Ibrahim Jabra, *al-Bahth 'an Walid Mas'ud*, 14.

92. Jabra Ibrahim Jabra, *al-Bahth 'an Walid Mas'ud*, 268.

93. Jabra Ibrahim Jabra, *al-Bahth 'an Walid Mas'ud*, 11.

94. Elias Khoury, "al-Akhta' . . . al-addad," 155.

95. Dina al-Kassim, *On Pain of Speech: Fantasies of the First Order and the Literary Rant*, 33.

96. Elias Khoury, "al-Batal al-filastini fi qissas Ghassan Kanafani," 110.

97. Elias Khoury, "al-Akhta' . . . al-addad," 153.

98. Elias Khoury, "Shi'iriyyat al-muthanna," 135.

99. Elias Khoury, "Hikayat al-diwan al-akhir li Mahmoud Darwish," 36.

100. Mahmoud Darwish, "Mahmoud Darwish ... la ahad yasil," 36.

101. Elias Khoury, "Hikayat al-diwan al-akhir li Mahmoud Darwish," 35.

102. Elias Khoury, "Shi'iriyyat al-muthanna," 138.

103. Elias Khoury, "Hikayat al-diwan al-akhir li Mahmoud Darwish," 35.

104. Edward W. Said, *Beginnings: Intention and Method*, 236.

105. Elias Khoury, "al-Akhta' . . . al-addad," 157. The passage I cite here from *Arabesques* appears in Anton Shammas, *Arabeskot*, 203/*Arabesques*, 226.

106. Alessia Ricciardi, *The Ends of Mourning: Psychoanalysis, Literature, Film*, 4, 157.

107. Abdelfattah Kilito, *L'oeil et l'aiguille: Essais sur "les mille et un nuits"*, 35.

108. Mu'mina Bashir al-'Awf, *Fi al-riwaya al-'arabiyya al-mu'asira*, 161.

109. Ferial J. Ghazoul, *Nocturnal Poetics*, 98.

110. Frantz Fanon, *Les damnés de la terre*, 90/*The Wretched of the Earth*, 94. I have tried elsewhere (Jeffrey Sacks, "For Decolonization") to offer a reading of the historicist, vitalist privilege in Fanon ("The living expression of the nation is the moving consciousness of the whole of the people. It is the coherent, enlightened action of men and women" [193/204]), and which is also pointed to in several of the passages I cite in this paragraph.

111. Jalal Toufic, *Over-Sensitivity*, 71. And consider also the readings Toufic pursues in *Forthcoming*.

112. Rei Terada, "Seeing Is Reading," 173.

4. LITERATURE

1. Alongside the Hebrew and English, I read throughout the Arabic translation of *Iya* offered in *Nuzur al-kharif*.

2. The illuminating title of Nancy Berg's *Exile from Exile: Israeli Writers from Iraq* points to the aporetical event of "return" I underline here. Yet one would not wish to read *Iya* as remarking an end ("The first novella of *Otot Stav*, 'Iyah,' revisits the end of the Jewish community in Iraq" [141]) but as confounding the institution of the end, and of the end of a relation to a place and to the Arabic language, compelled in the Zionist ideology and remarked in the institution of the state of Israel in 1948. If anything, and if minimally, the relation of language to more than one past, and of Ballas's Hebrew-language writing to Arabic, interrupts the desire to read Ballas in relation to rigidly differentiated languages and historical periods. And consider also the discussion of the disappearance and death of "the last generation of Jewish writers of literary Arabic" in Lital Levy, "Historicizing the Concept of Arab Jews in the Mashriq," 452. A reading of the category of the end in scholarly writing on Arab Jewish letters, and from which I also learn, is offered in Gil Anidjar, *"Our Place in al-Andalus": Kabbalah, Philosophy, Literature in Arab Jewish Letters*, 1–9 passim. The juridical context of the departure of the Iraqi Jewish community, which mirrors the logic of the Israeli state and the division of language and languages it compels, is discussed in detail in Abbas Shiblak, *Iraqi Jews: A History of Mass Exodus*. These legacies are juridically remarked in the Law of Denaturalization "Passed by the Iraqi chamber of Deputies on 2 March 1950 and by the Iraqi Senate on 4 March 1950, as Law No. 1 of 1950" (Abbas Shiblak, *Iraqi Jews*, 171). Article 1 of the law reads: "The Council of Ministers is empowered to divest any Iraqi Jew who, of his own free will and choice, desires to leave Iraq for good of

his Iraqi nationality after he has signed a special form in the presence of an official appointed by the Minister of the Interior" (171). And see also Nancy Berg, *Exile within Exile*, 22–27. As Shiblak underlines, the Law of Denaturalization points to an extension of colonial-juridical and Orientalist legacies also marked in the Balfour Declaration of 1917, the report of the Peel Commission of 1937, and the Partition Plan of 1947. On the convergence of colonial-Orientalist legacies in the texts I have underlined here, I learn as well from Moshe Behar, "Palestine, Arabized Jews, and the Elusive Consequences of Jewish and Arab National Formations." We have been taught to read the Orientalist dimensions of Zionism in Edward W. Said, *The Question of Palestine*, Ella Shohat, "Sephardim in Israel: Zionism from the Standpoint of its Jewish Victims," and Amnon Raz-Krakotzkin, "The Zionist Return to the West and the Mizrahi Jewish Perspective" ("From the outset, Zionist discourse was premised upon the adoption of orientalist attitudes, and Orientalism was essential to the nationalization of the Jewish collectivity and the ways in which the nation was imagined. While modern Jewish discourse produced expressions of ambivalence and resistance, Zionism was based on the explicit denial of the ambivalence" [166]). Remarking a persistence with older, European, Christian legacies, these attitudes occasioned—as Edward W. Said, Amnon Raz-Krakotzkin, Ella Shohat, Ammiel Alcalay, Gil Anidjar, Gil Hochberg, Gabriel Piterberg, Ariella Azoulay, and others have argued—the institution of more than one line of division between and within Jews and Arabs, and Arabic and Hebrew, and which *Iya* interrupts and confounds.

3. On the negation of exile in the Zionist ideology, see Amnon Raz-Krakotzkin, "The Zionist Return to the West and the Mizrahi Jewish Perspective," 167 passim, "A National-Colonial Theology—Religion, Orientalism, and the Construction of the Secular in Zionist Discourse," and *Exil et souveraineté: Judaïsme, sionisme et pensée binationale*; and Gabriel Piterberg, *The Returns of Zionism: Myths, Politics, and Scholarship in Israel.*

4. Yitzhak Laor, *Anu kotvim otakh moledet*, 8. Laor's intervention may be compared with that of Benjamin Harshav, who in his discussion of what he calls "the new Hebrew society" explains that "there was no culture in Eretz-Israel into which the immigrants could or would assimilate. In this vacuum, they established their own, secular polysystem, and created a *Hebrew frame language* to absorb it" (Benjamin Harshav, *Language in Time of Revolution*, 142). Harshav further writes, in a discussion of the Second Aliya (1904–14), "To adapt to physical labor in a forsaken province of the backward and despotic Ottoman Empire, in that desolate and hot land, amid the hostile Arabs, was difficult and required a sharp break with the Diaspora: the separation of languages [Yiddish from Hebrew] served that purpose" (110). Quite unlike the understanding of language and of the relation to the past Harshav describes ("Deliberately cut off from the world of their parents, from mother's tenderness, from grandmother's tales, from the customs and superstitions of generations, from the language and the food of their childhood, and, *in fact* [my emphasis], from the disgusting life of the shtetl and its dead-end existence—they tried to create a new world based on the self-education of the individual: to eat the strange and bitter olives, to work the land with a *turiya* (a hoe), and

to speak Hebrew" [137]), in Ballas, as *Iya* makes clear, language already takes place in iteration, and it already occurs, in Hebrew, through a relation to the Arabic language and the legacies remarked in the Arabic nineteenth century. And consider as well, in relation to the context discussed in Harshav, and the Orientalist dimensions of the modern Hebrew literary institution pointed to in the scholarship cited above, the illuminating reading of Hayim Nahman Bialik (1873–1934) offered by Sami Shalom Chetrit ("he depicts the country [Palestine] as a desolate and moribund place, which only the miraculous touch of the European Jew (the Ashkenazi Zionist) can restore to life, both physically and spiritually" [Sami Shalom Chetrit, "Revisting Bialik," 9 passim]). I learn here also from the illuminating reading offered in Gil Hochberg, "A Poetics of Haunting: From Yizhar's Hirbeh to Yehoshua's Ruins to Koren's Crypts." The iterative dimensions of idiom pointed to in Ballas are engaged, differently, in Ammiel Alcalay, "Exploding Identities: Notes on Ethnicity and Literary History" and *After Jews and Arabs*; Gil Anidjar, *Semites*, 67–83; Gil Hochberg, *In Spite of Partition*; and Nancy Berg, *Exile from Exile*.

5. Hanan Hever, *Sifrut nikhtevet mi kan*, 8. And see also Hannan Hever, *Producing the Modern Hebrew Canon*.

6. Ammiel Alcalay, *After Jews and Arabs*, 243.

7. Hanan Hever, *Producing the Modern Hebrew Canon*, 172.

8. Readings of Ballas have related his work to modern Hebrew and Arabic writing in Israel, in Ibrahim Taha, "Duality and Acceptance: The Image of the Outsider in the Literary Work of Shimon Ballas"; Reuven Snir, "Till Spring Comes: Arabic and Hebrew Literary Debates among Iraqi-Jews in Israel"; and Hanan Hever, *Producing the Modern Hebrew Canon*, 160–74. Other readings have dismissed entirely the linguistic complexity of Ballas's writing (consider, e.g., Gershon Shaked, *Modern Hebrew Fiction*, 184–85, and compare Ronen Zeidel, "A Question of Language and Audience: On the Possibility of 'Iraqi Novels' in Hebrew," 232–33). Yael Halevi-Wise reads Ballas's *Ve hu akher* (1991) to underline that it "joins *Mizrahi* writing's general tendency to memorialize in order to reconstruct identity and reassert loss of status" (Yael Halevi-Wise, "Ethics and Aesthetics of Memory," 58). And see the critique of this reading offered in Yerach Gover, *Zionism: The Limits of Moral Discourse*, 126–31. A reading of Ballas in terms of his "integration" into "the history of Jewish writing" is pursued in Lital Levy, "Reorienting Literary History: The View from the East." Levy writes that the discussion she offers wishes to place in question "the Eurocentrism of Hebrew literary historiography, with an eye to exploring the relationship between Ashkenazim, Sephardim and Arab Jews in Jewish literature produced from the nineteenth century onward" (130). The "integration" she elaborates ("Rather, I call for a more comprehensive history of Jewish writing that integrates non-European writers and seeks connections across regional, cultural, and linguistic boundaries" [130]), is to redress the occlusion of non-Ashkenazi writing from discourses on Hebrew and Jewish literatures. "More to the point is that the entire cultural-literary context from which Arab Jewish and other non-Ashkenazi writers emerged has been occluded from Hebrew literary discourse (as well as studies of modern Jewish Culture more generally)"

(130). And compare the discussion of Dahud ben Sleyman Semah offered by Levy in "'From Baghdad to Bialik with Love': A Reappropriation of Modern Hebrew Poetry, 1933," where "lines of lineage and paternity are blurred" (141), even as the interiority of Hebrew literary history is maintained ("Semah's poem is an ingenious performance of literary erudition and stylistic virtuosity *in* [my emphasis] a Hebrew poetic tradition long identified with Middle Eastern Jewry" [146–47]), and, further, Lital Levy, "Jewish Writers in the Arab East: Literature, History, and the Politics of Enlightenment, 1863–1914." In a way that learns and breaks from Levy's intervention, the reading I offer of Ballas—and if also of El Maleh—considers this writing in relation to the destruction in language in the Arabic nineteenth century, and which I discussed above, in chapter 2. Rather than read these texts as already taking place within the interior of "modern Jewish cultural production" (Lital Levy, "Reorienting Literary History," 130)—although they are neither simply nor solely exterior to it—I read each in its relation to the Arabic language, to consider these texts as neither inside nor outside of Jewish or Hebrew—or Arabic—literature(s) but as confounding the terms called upon to read language in relation to literary institutions and the state form.

9. And compare the discussion of "cultural cosmopolitanism" in Joel Beinin, *The Dispersion of Egyptian Jewry: Cutlure, Politics, and the Formation of a Modern Diaspora*, 85 passim; and, more generally, and in relation to a critique of Orientalism, the intervention offered by Hala Halim in *Alexandrian Cosmopolitanism: An Archive*; and, differently, Deborah Starr, *Remembering Cosmopolitan Egypt: Literature, Culture, and Empire.*

10. I transliterate here the Arabic translation of Maha Suleiman offered in Shimon Ballas, *Nuzur al-kharif*, 87.

11. Shimon Ballas, "al-Hadir al-gha'ib fi al-thaqafa al-ukhra," 222.

12. And consider also the discussion of language offered by Ballas in an interview conducted with Ammiel Alcalay. "The whole project of a nationalist conception, of Zionist ideology, of the Jewish point of view, the bonds between Jews and the diaspora in Israel, all of this is quite marginal for me and doesn't play a major role, it's not part of my cultural world. I am not in dialogue with the nationalistic or Zionist point of view, nor am I in dialogue with Hebrew literature. I am not conducting a dialogue with them. If anything, I am in dialogue with language itself. On the one hand, I am trying to fend off, avoid, or neutralize ideological connections or associations within the language. On the other hand, I think I am probably trying to bring my Hebrew closer and closer to Arabic. This isn't done through syntax, but maybe through some sense of structure or way of approaching things. It is very abstract and I don't do it in a way that is completely conscious either. That's the problem, and it's extremely difficult to describe or quantify" (Shimon Ballas, "At Home in Exile," 68). In this chapter I try to linger with this difficulty, to ask how it compels a reading of Ballas in relation to the Arabic language.

13. Peggy Kamuf, *The Division of Literature: Or, The University in Deconstruction*, 38.

14. Ibrahim Taha, "Duality and Acceptance," 84.

15. Husayn's relation to Ballas is discussed by Reuven Snir in terms of the category "inspiration" ("Educated at the Alliance School, he mastered Arabic and French, the latter serving as his window to world literature. He even attributes his membership in the Communist Party, when he was sixteen, as being triggered by reading *The Iron Heel* by Jack London (1876–1916) in French. *Yet* [my emphasis] Arabic literature, especially authored by Jubran Khalil Jubran (1883–1931) and Taha Husayn (1889–1973), proved to be his major inspiration" [Reuven Snir, "Till Spring Comes: Arabic and Hebrew Literary Debates among Iraqi-Jews in Israel," 114–15]). Differently, I read the citation of Husayn's name in the interview I am considering here—"al-Hadir al-gha'ib fi al-thaqafa al-ukhra" ("The Present Absentee in the Other Culture")—as remarking a bereaved, unfinished relation to the Arabic language. And I consider this bereavement in relation to the categories of reading privileged in the fallout of the First World War, an event that haunts *Iya* from its first word to its last.

16. Taha Husayn, *Du'a' al-karawan*, 86/*The Call of the Curlew*, 68.

17. Taha Husayn, *Du'a' al-karawan*, 151/*The Call of the Curlew*, 121.

18. The Arabic appears in *Nuzur al-kharif*, 94.

19. The Arabic appears in *Nuzur al-kharif*, 98.

20. Jacques Derrida, *Psyché: Inventions de l'autre, Tome 1*, 254/*Psyche: Inventions of the Other*, vol. 1, 244.

21. Walter Benjamin, "Die Aufgabe des Übersetzers," 50/"The Task of the Translator," 70.

22. Jacques Derrida, *Psyché: Inventions de l'autre*, 218/*Psyche: Inventions of the Other*, 207.

23. Walter Benjamin, "Die Aufgabe des Übersetzers," 56/"The Task of the Translator," 72.

24. Jacques Derrida, *Psyché: Inventions de l'autre*, 280/*Psyche: Inventions of the Other*, 271.

25. Jacques Derrida, *Psyché: Inventions de l'autre*, 218/*Psyche: Inventions of the Other*, 207.

26. The Hebrew text with an English translation is provided in *JPS Hebrew-English Tanakh*, 2nd ed.

27. Jacques Derrida, "Circonfession," 123–24/"Circumfession," 129–30.

28. The reading I pursue here follows the illuminating discussion of these passages in "Circonfession" and *La carte postale* in Hélène Cixous, *Portrait of Jacques Derrida as a Young Jewish Saint*, especially 3–24. And consider as well: "That's the key: this *like* or *as if*. I am *as if* I were another. He is as if, like (as if he were) another" (53). I learn here also from the discussion of Derrida's initials ("*Déjà* is a crypt of his own signature") offered in Gayatri Chakravorty Spivak, "Glas Piece: A Compte Rendu," and the reading pursued by Sarah Kofman in relation to a wounding in *Lectures de Derrida*, 146, which teaches us to consider an excess in the reading of the name, and of words, that I pursue here. The reading I offer of the name "Paul-Moïse"

in relation to its homonymic proliferation also learns from Elissa Marder's recalling us to read "bits of words" in Derrida. "Furthermore, as he demonstrates at great length in *Glas*, 'Fors,' and 'Cartouches,' the *mors* resists conceptualization because it operates on language not merely though words but through bits of words" (Elissa Marder, *The Mother in the Age of Mechanical Reproduction*, 240).

29. Jacques Derrida, *L'animal que donc je suis*, 133/*The Animal That Therefore I Am*, 95.

30. Jacques Derrida, *Donner la mort*, 115–16/*The Gift of Death*, 83.

31. Jacques Derrida, *Marges de la philosophie*, 188/*Margins of Philosophy*, 158.

32. Jacques Derrida, *L'animal que donc je suis*, 53/*The Animal That Therefore I Am*, 31.

33. Jacques Derrida, *Marges de la philosophie*, 254/*Margins of Philosophy*, 213. And consider as well the discussion of the particularity of European, philosophical language in Dana Hollander, *Exemplarity and Chosenness: Rosenzweig and Derrida on the Nation of Philosophy*, 87 passim; and, in terms of the category "Christianity," Gil Anidjar, *Blood: A Critique of Christianity*. On language, translation, and violence ("Can one feign speaking a language?"), and on the cultural particularity of languages ("Philosophical language belongs to a system of language(s)"), see the reading of Emmanuel Levinas pursued by Derrida in "Violence at métaphysique: Essai sur la pensée d'Emmanuel Levinas," 133, 167/"Violence and Metaphysics: An Essay on the Thought of Emmanuel Levinas," 89, 113 passim.

34. Henry Staten, *Wittgenstein and Derrida*, 54, 119. My reading of form remains deeply indebted to Staten's intervention—in Western metaphysics, or in philosophy, form, Staten argues, and through a reading of Derrida on Kant and Aristotle, remains "conceivable only on the model of the form of an entity," form is "the guardrail of unity and self-identity, both in what is known and in the act of mind by which it is known" (12)—as I also remain indebted to the reading of Derrida, history, origin, and time pursued by Paola Marrati, *Genesis and Trace: Derrida Reading Husserl and Heidegger*, especially 87–113; and to the provocative reading of Derrida in relation to the category "atheism" offered by Martin Hägglund ("This experience of such mourning is the experience of radical atheism" [Martin Hägglund, *Radical Atheism: Derrida and the Time of Life*, 163]).

35. Jacques Derrida, *De la grammatologie*, 226/*Of Grammatology*, 157.

36. Jacques Derrida, *Parages*, 59/46.

37. Jacques Derrida, *La dissemination*, 384/*Dissemination*, 316.

38. Ranjana Khanna, *Algeria Cuts: Women and Representation, 1830 to the Present*, 46. And consider also the discussion offered by Gil Anidjar of "the trace of a number of so-called identities (African, Algerian, Arab Jew, Hispano-Moor, and more recently, Franco-Maghrebian, and later 'animal' in 'l'animal que donc je suis')," in relation to the placing in question of the category "being" in the writing of "je suis" in Derrida (Gil Anidjar, *The Jew, the Arab*, 44). The reading I offer learns from Anidjar's recalling us to read the confounding of being in relation to the name and to "a number of

so-called identities." "It seems necessary therefore to return to the issue of following and pursuing, 'je suis,' as an alternative to being, 'je suis,' as an otherwise than identity" (45).

39. Jacques Derrida, *De la grammatologie*, 150/*Of Grammatology*, 102.

40. I press the English translation of this passage here somewhat ("En tant qu'il *met en jeu* la présence du présent et la vie du vivant, le mouvement du langage n'a pas seulement, on s'en doute, un rapport d'analogie avec l'auto-affection 'sexuelle.' Il se confonde avec elle en totalité même si cette totalité est fortement articulée et différenciée. Vouloir les distinguir, tel est le voeu logocentrique par excellence" [*De la grammatologie*, 237]).

41. Jacques Derrida, *Marges de la philosophie*, 381/*Margins of Philosophy*, 321.

42. On aesthetics and ethnology, see Jacques Derrida, *De la grammatologie*, 294/*Of Grammatology*, 206.

43. Walter Benjamin, "Die Aufgabe des Übersetzers," 51/"The Task of the Translator," 71.

44. Eduardo Cadava, "Nadar's Photographopolis," 65.

45. Paola Marrati, *Genesis and Trace: Derrida Reading Husserl and Heidegger*, 130, 122.

46. Michael Naas, *Miracle and Machine: Jacques Derrida and the Two Sources of Religion, Science, and the Media*, 270.

47. Henry Staten, *Wittgenstein and Derrida*, 91.

48. Reuven Snir, *'Araviyut, yahdut, tsiyonut: ma'avak zehuyot bi yetsirtam shel yehuday 'Irak*, 331.

49. The Arabic appears in *Nuzur al-kharif*, 105.

50. Eduardo Cadava, *Words of Light*, 110.

51. Peter Fenves, *The Messianic Reduction: Walter Benjamin and the Shape of Time*, 131, 88, 135.

52. The Arabic appears in *Nuzur al-kharif*, 102.

53. This passage is read by Ibrahim Taha in terms of a privileging of identity. "At the end of the first novella in *Otot Stav*, Ephriam gives a copy of the Koran to Zakiyya, an act that symbolizes his understanding and identification with her solemn feeling and her return to her Moslem family, her original identity" (Ibrahim Taha, "Duality and Acceptance," 83–84). The giving of the Qur'an, Taha writes, is a "dead end from which there is no turning back," and which mirrors what is said to be the coming "end" of the Iraqi Jewish community. And compare the reading of this passage offered by Orit Bashkin in *New Babylonians: A History of Jews in Modern Iraq*, in terms of "an artifact that binds them [Iya and Farumi] culturally: the Qur'an" (225).

54. al-Zamakhshari, *al-Kashshaf*, 4:180.

55. Nasr Hamid Abu Zayd, *Mafhum al-nass: dirasa fi 'ulum al-Qur'an*, 223.

56. Consider also the elaborations offered in Abu Zayd, *al-Itijah al-'aqli fi al-tafsir: dirasa fi qadiyat al-majaz 'ind al-mu'tazila*, and in relation to the term *history*, *al-Nass wa al-sulta wa al-haqiqa: iradat al-ma'rifa wa iradat al-haymana*.

57. Nasr Hamid Abu Zayd, *Mafhum al-nass,* 82. And see as well the elaborations of "critique" in Nasr Hamid Abu Zayd, *Naqd al-khitab al-dini.*

58. And compare the reading of Abu Zayd offered by Charles Hirschkind, where the privileging of the category "history" points to Abu Zayd's participation in a "modernist" form of argumentation (Charles Hirschkind, "Heresy or Hermeneutics: The Case of Nasr Hamid Abu Zayd," 475). Yet if Hirschkind reads Abu Zayd as sharing in "Enlightenment assumptions" (464) about "our modern concept of history" (469), this points to what Hirschkind calls Abu Zayd's writing "within" a "conceptual terrain" (471) in which some share and others—as if they had simply refused or declined such a sharing and the historical violence to which it points—do not. Hirschkind's reading locates Abu Zayd in particular kinds of ways—he is modernist, Lockean (471), and a scholar who is "supposedly working within the same [Islamic] tradition of moral inquiry" [473])—and this designation allows Hirschkind to shield the interiority of what he calls "tradition" and its "horizon" ("More importantly, now we can see that it is imperative for a religious thinker working *within* such a tradition to pose the possibility of God or the divine—even as a necessary act of faith—in order to set the *horizon within which* reasoning may occur" [474; emphases mine]).

59. Nasr Hamid Abu Zayd, *Mafhum al-nass,* 12.

60. And see also al-Suyuti, who explains that there is a difference of opinion "regarding the first of what was revealed of the Qur'an [fi awwal ma nazala min al-Qur'an]" (al-Suyuti, *al-Itqan fi 'ulum al-Qur'an*, 73). The first opinion, which he explains is "the correct one" (73), is "*Iqra' bi ismi rabbika*" (Qur'an 96:1), the verse cited and referenced by Abu Zayd in the discussion he offers in *Mafhum al-nass*, and which I am reading here. The second is "*Ya ayyuha al-mudaththir* [O thou shrouded in thy mantle]" (Qur'an 74:1). The third is *Surat al-fatiha* (Qur'an 1:1–7). Further discussion and detail are offered in al-Zarkashi, *al-Burhan fi 'ulum al-Qur'an*, 207–10.

61. Nasr Hamid Abu Zayd, *Mafhum al-nass,* 139.

62. Avital Ronell, *Loser Sons: Politics and Authority*, 22.

BIBLIOGRAPHY

Aarsleff, Hans. *From Locke to Saussure: Essays on the Study of Language and Intellectual History.* Minneapolis: University of Minnesota Press, 1982.

'Abbas, Ihsan. *Itijahat al-shi'r al-'arabi al-mu'asir.* 'Amman: Dar al-Shuruq, 2001.

———. *Tarikh al-naqd al-adabi 'ind al-'arab: naqd al-shi'r min al-qarn al-thani hatta al-qarn al-thamin al-hijri.* 'Amman: Dar al-Shuruq, 1993 [1971].

'Abbud, Marun. *Saqr Lubnan: bahth fi al-nahda al-adabiyya al-haditha wa rajuluha al-awwal Ahmad Faris al-Shidyaq.* Beirut: Dar al-Makshuf, 1950.

'Abd al-Raziq, 'Ali. *al-Islam wa usul al-hukm.* Ed. Muhammad 'Imara. Beirut: al-Mu'assasa al-'Arabiyya li al-Dirasat wa al-Nashr, 2000 [1925].

'Abdu, Muhammad. *al-A'mal al-kamila li al-Imam Muhammad 'Abdu.* 7 vols. Ed. Muhammad 'Imara. Beirut: al-Mu'assasa al-'Arabiyya li al-Dirasat wa al-Nashr, 1972–74.

Abou-El-Haj, Rifa'at. *Formation of the Modern State: The Ottoman Empire, Sixteenth to Eighteenth Centuries.* Syracuse: Syracuse University Press, 2005 [1991].

Aboul-Ela, Hosam. *Other South: Faulkner, Coloniality, and the Mariátegui Tradition.* Pittsburgh: University of Pittsburgh Press, 2007.

Abraham, Nicolas, and Maria Torok. "Mourning *or* Melancholia: Introjection *versus* Incorporation." In *The Shell and the Kernel,* vol. 1, ed. and tr. Nicholas T. Rand, 125–38. Chicago: University of Chicago Press, 1994.

———. *The Wolfman's Magic Word: A Cryptonomy.* Tr. Nicholas Rand. Minneapolis: University of Minnesota Press, 1986.

Abu Dib, Kamal. *Jamaliyyat al-tajawur, aw, tashabuk al-fada'at al-ibda'iyya.* Beirut: Dar al-'Ilm li al-Malayin, 1997.

Abu El-Haj, Nadia. *Facts on the Ground: Archaeological Practice and*

Territorial Self-Fashioning in Israeli Society. Chicago: University of Chicago Press, 2002.

Abu-Lughod, Ibrahim. *The Arab Rediscovery of Europe: A Study in Cultural Encounters*. Introd. Rashid Khalidi. London: Saqi, 2011 [1963].

Abu-Manneh, Butrus. "The Christians between Ottomanism and Syrian Nationalism: The Ideas of Butrus al-Bustani." *International Journal of Middle East Studies* 11 (1980): 287–304.

———. "The Islamic Roots of the Gülhane Rescript." *Die Welt des Islams* 43.2 (November 1994): 173–203.

Abu Zayd, Nasr Hamid. *al-Itijah al-'aqli fi al-tafsir: dirasa fi qadiyat al-majaz 'ind al-mu'tazila*. Beirut: Dar al-Tanwir, 1982.

———. *Mafhum al-nass: dirasa fi 'ulum al-Qur'an*. Beirut: al-Markaz al-Thaqafi al-'Arabi, 1998.

———. *Naqd al-khitab al-dini*. Cairo: Sina li al-Nashr, 1994.

———. *al-Nass wa al-sulta wa al-haqiqa: iradat al-ma'rifa wa iradat al-haymana*. Beirut: Al-Markaz al-Thaqafi al-'Arabi, 2000.

Adorno, Theodor. *Ästhetische Theorie*. Frankfurt am Main: Suhrkamp, 1970. Tr. Robert Hullot-Kentor as *Aesthetic Theory*. Minneapolis: University of Minnesota Press, 1997.

———. *Minima Moralia: Reflexionen aus dem beschädigten Leben*. Frankfurt am Main: Suhrkamp, 1969 [1951]. Tr. E. F. N. Jephcott as *Minima Moralia: Reflections from Damaged Life*. London: Verso, 1974.

———. *Negative Dialektik*. Frankfurt am Main: Suhrkamp, 2003 [1966]. Tr. E. B. Ashton as *Negative Dialectics*. New York: Continuum, 1973.

———. "Rede über Lyrik und Gesellschaft." In *Noten zur Literatur, Gesammelte Schriften*, vol. 2. Ed. Rolf Tiedemann, 49–68. Frankfurt am Main: Suhrkamp, 1974. Tr. Shierry Weber Nicholsen as "On Lyric Poetry and Society." In *Notes to Literature*, 1:37–54. New York: Columbia University Press, 1991.

Adorno, Theodor, and Max Horkheimer. *Dialektik der Aufklärung: Philosophische Fragmente*. Frankfurt am Main: Fischer, 1969. Tr. E. F. N. Jephcott as *Dialectic of Enlightenment: Philosphical Fragments*. Stanford: Stanford University Press, 2002.

Adunis ('Ali Ahmed Sa'id). *Diwan al-shi 'r al-'arabi*. 3 vols. Beirut: al-Maktaba al-'Asriyya, 1964–68.

———. *Fatiha li nihayat al-qarn*. Beirut: Dar al-Nahar, 1998 [1980].

———. *al-Kitab: ams, al-makan, al-an*. 3 vols. Beirut: Dar al-Saqi, 1995–2002.

———. *Kitab al-hisar*. Beirut: Dar al-Adab, 1996 [1985].

———. *Muqaddima li al-shi'r al-'arabi*. Beirut: Dar al-'Awda, 1971.

———. *al-Thabit wa al-mutahawwil: bahth fi al-ibda' wa al-ittiba' 'ind al-'arab*. 4 vols. Beirut: Dar al-Saqi, 1994 [3 vols., 1974–78].

———. *Zaman al-shi'r*. Beiruit: Dar al-'Awda, 1996 [1972].

Agamben, Giorgio. *The Time That Remains: A Commentary on the Letter to the Romans*. Tr. Patricia Dailey. Stanford: Stanford University Press, 2005.

Aghacy, Samira. "Elias Khoury's 'The Journey of Little Gandhi': Fiction and Ideology." *International Journal of Middle East Studies* 28 (1996): 163–76.

Ahmed, Jamal Mohammed. *The Intellectual Origins of Egyptian Nationalism*. London: Oxford University Press, 1960.

'Akawi, Rahab. *al-Fariyaq: Ahmad Faris al-Shidyaq*. Beirut: Dar al-Fikr al-'Arabi, 2003.

Alaoui, Brahim, ed. *Ahmed Cherkaoui: La passion du sign*. Paris: Institut du Monde Arabe, 1996.

Alcalay, Ammiel. *a little history*. Ed. Fred Dewey. Los Angeles: re:public/UpSet Press, 2012.

———. *After Jews and Arabs: Remaking Levantine Culture*. Minneapolis: University of Minnesota Press, 1993.

———. "Exploding Identities: Notes on Ethnicity and Literary History." In *Jews and Other Differences*, ed. Jonathan Boyarin and Daniel Boyarin, 330–44. Minneapolis: University of Minnesota Press, 1997.

———. *Keys to the Garden: New Israeli Writing*. Ed. Ammiel Alcalay. San Francisco: City Lights, 1996.

Ali, Samer M. *Arabic Literary Salons in the Islamic Middle Ages: Poetry, Public Performance, and the Presentation of the Past*. Notre Dame: University of Notre Dame Press, 2010.

Allan, Michael. "How *Adab* Became Literary: Formalism, Orientalism and the Institutions of World Literature." *Journal of Arabic Literature* 43 (2012): 172–96.

Allen, Roger. *The Arabic Novel: An Historical and Critical Introduction*. 2nd ed. Syracuse: Syracuse University Press, 1995 [1982].

———. *A Period of Time: A Study and Translation of Hadith 'Isa ibn Hisham by Muhammad al-Muwaylihi*. Reading: Ithaca Press, 1992 [1974].

———. "Rewriting Literary History: The Case of the Arabic Novel." *Journal of Arabic Literature* 38.3 (2007): 247–60.

Alwan, Mohammed Bakir. "Ahmad Faris al-Shidyaq and the West." Ph.D. dissertation, Indiana University, 1970.

Amer, Sahar. *Crossing Borders: Love between Women in Medieval French and Arabic Literatures*. Philadelphia: University of Pennsylvania Press, 2008.

Anderson, Benedict. *Imagined Communities: Reflections on the Origins and Spread of Nationalism*. London: Verso, 2003 [1983].

Anidjar, Gil. *Blood: A Critique of Christianity*. New York: Columbia University Press, 2014.

———. *The Jew, the Arab: A History of the Enemy*. Stanford: Stanford University Press, 2003.

———. *"Our Place in al-Andalus": Kabbalah, Philosophy, Literature in Arab Jewish Letters*. Stanford: Stanford University Press, 2002.

———. *Semites: Race, Religion, Literature*. Stanford: Stanford University Press, 2007.

Antonius, George. *The Arab Awakening*. Saftey Harbor, FL: Simon Publications, 2001 [1939].

Antoon, Sinan. "Before the Ruins: When Mahmoud Darwish Met Walter Benjamin." The Legacy of Mahmoud Darwish. University of California, Los Angeles. 5 November 2009. Lecture.

———. "Mahmoud Darwish's Allegorical Critique of Oslo." *Journal of Palestine Studies* 31.2 (Winter 2002): 66–77.

———. *The Poetics of the Obscene in Premodern Arabic Poetry: Ibn al-Hajjaj and Sukhf*. New York: Palgrave Macmillan, 2014.

———. "Returning to the Wind: On Darwish's La Ta'tadhir 'Amma Fa'alta." In *Mahmoud Darwish: Exile's Poet*, ed. Najat Rahman and Hala Khamis Nassar, 215–38. Northampton, MA: Interlink, 2007.

Antun, Farah. *Ibn Rushd wa falasafatuhu*. Beirut: Dar al-Farabi, 2007 [1903].

Apter, Emily. *Against World Literature: On the Politics of Untranslatability*. London: Verso, 2013.

———. *The Translation Zone: A New Comparative Literature*. Princeton: Princeton University Press, 2006.

Arberry, A. J. *The Koran Interpreted*. New York: Oxford University Press, 1964.

———. *The Seven Odes*. London: Allen and Unwin, 1957.

Arendt, Hannah. *The Origins of Totalitarianism*. New York: Harcourt Brace & Company, 1979 [1948].

Aristotle. *Kitab Aristutalis fi al-shi'r*. Tr. Abu Bishr Matta ibn Yunus. Ed. Shukri Muhammad 'Ayyad. Cairo: Dar al-Katib al-'Arabi, 1967.

———. *On Poetics*. Tr. Seth Benardete and Michael Davis. South Bend, IN: St. Augustine's Press, 2002.

Asad, Talal. "Conscripts of Western Civilization." In *Dialectical Anthropology: Essays in Honor of Stanley Diamond*, ed. Christine Gailey, 333–51. Gainesville: University Press of Florida, 1992.

———. *Formations of the Secular: Christianity, Islam, Modernity*. Stanford: Stanford University Press, 2003.

———. *Genealogies of Religion: Discipline and Reasons of Power in Christianity and Islam*. Baltimore: Johns Hopkins University Press, 1993.

———. *On Suicide Bombing*. New York: Columbia University Press, 2007.

'Asfur, Jaber. *al-Maraya al-mutajawira: dirasa fi naqd Taha Husayn*. Cairo: al-Hay'a al-Misriyya al-'Ama li al-Kitab, 1983.

———. *Zaman al-riwaya*. Dimashq: Dar al-Mada, 1999.

'Ashmawi, Sayyed. *al-Fellahun wa al-sulta: 'ala daw' al-harakat al-fellahiyya al-misriyya, 1919–1999*. Cairo: Mirit li al-Nashr wa al-Ma'lumat, 2001.

'Ashur, Radwa. *al-Hadatha al-mumkina: al-Shidyaq wa al-Saq 'ala al-saq, al-riwaya al-ula fi al-adab al-'arabi al-hadith*. Cairo: Dar al-Shuruq, 2009.

———. *Sayyadu al-dhakira: fi al-naqd al-tatbiqi*. al-Dar al-Bayda': al-Markaz al-Thaqafi al-'Arabi, 2001.

Auerbach, Erich. "Figura." Tr. Jane O. Newman in *Time, History, Literature: Selected Essays of Erich Auerbach*, ed. James I. Porter, 65–113. Princeton: Princeton University Press, 2014.

Austin, J. L. *How to Do Things with Words*. Ed. J. O. Urmson and Marina Sbisa. Cambridge, MA: Harvard University Press, 1975.

Avril-Hilal, Marie-Hélène. "Les Andalousies de Mahmoud Darwich." In *Poétique et Politique: La poésie de Mahmoud Darwich*, ed. Sobhi Boustani and Marie-Hélène Avril-Hilal, 29–50. Pessac: Presses Universitaires de Bourdeaux, 2010.

'Awad, Luis. *al-Huriyya wa naqd al-huriyya*. Cairo: al-Hay'a al-'Ama li al-Ta'lif wa al-Nashr, 1971.

———. *Tarikh al-fikr al-misri al-hadith*. Cairo: Dar al-Hilal, 1994.

———. *Thaqafatuna fi muftaraq al-turuq*. Beirut: Dar al-Adab, 1983.

al-'Awf, Mu'mina Bashir. *Fi al-riwaya al-'arabiyya al-mu'asira*. Beirut: Dar al-Mashriq, 2008.

al-Azmeh, Aziz. *Islams and Modernities*. 3rd ed. London: Verso, 2009.

Azoulay, Ariella. *The Civil Contract of Photography*. New York: Zone Books, 2012.

———. "Declaring the State of Israel: Declaring a State of War." *Critical Inquiry* 37.2 (Winter 2011): 265–85.

———. *From Palestine to Israel: A Photographic Record of Destruction and State Formation, 1947–1950*. Tr. Charles S. Kamen. London: Pluto, 2011.

Ba'albaki, Ramzi. "The Historical Relevance of Poetry in the Arab Grammatical Tradition." In *Poetry and History: The Value of Poetry in*

Reconstructing Arab History, ed. Ramzi Baalbaki, Saleh Said Agha, and Tarif Khalidi, 95–120. Beirut: American University of Beirut Press, 2011.

Badawi, M. M. *A Critical Introduction to Modern Arabic Poetry.* New York: Cambridge University Press, 1975.

———. *Modern Arabic Literature and the West.* London: Ithaca Press, 1985.

Badr, ʻAbd al-Muhsin Taha. *Tatawwur al-riwaya al-ʻarabiyya al-haditha fi Misr (1870–1938).* Cairo: Dar al-Maʻarif, 1992.

Baer, Gabriel. "The Tanzimat in Egypt—The Penal Code." *Bulletin of the School of Oriental and African Studies* 26.1 (1963): 29–49.

———. "The Transition from Traditional to Western Criminal Law in Turkey and Egypt." *Studia Islamica* 45 (1977): 139–58.

al-Baghdadi, Nadia. "The Cultural Function of Fiction: From the Bible to Libertine Literature. Historical Criticism and Social Critique in Ahmad Faris al-Shidyaq." *Arabica* 46 (1999): 375–401.

———. "Print, Script, and the Limits of Free-Thinking in Arabic Letters of the 19th Century: The Case of al-Shidyaq." *al-Abhath* 48–49 (2000): 99–122.

al-Bahrawi, Sayyed. *al-Bahth ʻan al-manhaj fi al-naqd al-ʻarabi al-hadith.* Cairo: Dar al-Sharqiyyat, 1993.

———. *Muhtawa al-shakl fi al-riwaya al-ʻarabiyya: al-nusus al-misriyya al-ula.* Cairo: al-Hay'a al-Misriyya al-ʻAma li al-Kitab, 1996.

Bahti, Timothy. *Allegories of History: Literary Historiography after Hegel.* Baltimore: Johns Hopkins University Press, 1992.

Ballas, Shimon. "At Home in Exile: An Interview with Shimon Ballas by Ammiel Alcalay." In *Keys to the Garden: New Israeli Writing,* ed. Ammiel Alcalay, 62–69. San Francisco: City Lights, 1996.

———. "al-Hadir al-gha'ib fi al-thaqafa al-ukhra." Interview with Muhammad Hamza Ghanayim. *al-Karmel* 60 (Summer 1999): 211–30.

———. *Be guf rishon.* Bnei Brak: Ha Kibbutz Ha Miuchad, 2009.

———. *Iya.* In *Otot stav,* 9–50. Tel Aviv: Zmora-Bitan, 1992. Tr. Susan Einbinder as *Iya.* In *Keys to the Garden: New Israeli Writing,* ed. Ammiel Alcalay, 69–99. San Francisco: City Lights, 1996.

———. *Ha maʻabara.* Tel Aviv: Am Oved, 1964.

———. *Nuzur al-kharif.* Tr. M. Suleiman. Köln: Manshurat al-Jamal, 1997.

———. *Ve hu akher.* Bnei Brak: Ha Kibutz Ha Miukhad, 2005 [1991]. Tr. Ammiel Alcalay and Oz Shelach as *Outcast.* San Francisco: City Lights: 2007.

Bamyeh, Mohammed A. *The Social Origins of Islam: Mind, Economy, Discourse.* Minneapolis: University of Minnesota Press, 1999.

Bannis, Muhammad. "Mahmoud Darwish fi al-ʻqalaq al-shiʻri wa al wafa' al-insani." In *Mahmoud Darwish: al-mukhtalif al-haqiqi*, 295–300. 'Amman: Dar al-Shuruq, 1999.

———. *al-Shi'r al-'arabi al-hadith: binyatuhu wa ibdalatuha*. 4 vols. al-Dar al-Bayda': Dar Tubqal li al-Nashr, 1989–91.

Barakat, Selim. *Taysh al-yaqut*. Beirut: Dar al-Nahar, 1996.

Barkey, Karen. *Empire of Difference: The Ottomans in Comparative Perspective*. New York: Cambridge University Press, 2008.

Baron, Beth. *The Women's Awakening in Egypt: Culture, Society, and the Press*. New Haven: Yale University Press, 1994.

Barrada, Muhammad. *As'ila al-riwaya, as'ila al-naqd*. al-Dar al-Bayda': al-Rabita, 1996.

———. "Une lecture dynamique de la mémoire." *Horizons Maghrebins—Le droit a la memoire: Presences d'Edmond Amran El Maleh* 27 (December 1994–January 1995): 33–40.

Bashkin, Orit. *New Babylonians: A History of Jews in Modern Iraq*. Stanford: Stanford University Press, 2012.

Baydun, 'Abbas. "al-Mukhtalif al-haqiqi." In *Mahmoud Darwish: al-mukhtalif al-haqiqi*, 247–49. 'Amman: Dar al-Shuruq, 1999.

al-Bazi'i, Sa'ad. *Istiqbal al-akhar: al-gharb wa al-naqd al-'arabi al-hadith*. al-Dar al-Bayda': al-Markaz al-Thaqafi al 'Arabi, 2004.

Behar, Moshe. "Palestine, Arabized Jews, and the Elusive Consequences of Jewish and Arab National Formations." *Nationalism and Ethnic Politics* 13.4 (2007): 581–611.

Behdad, Ali. *Belated Travelers: Orientalism in the Age of Colonial Dissolution*. Durham: Duke University Press, 1993.

Behrens, Klaus. *Friedrich Schlegel's Geschichtsphilosophie (1794–1808)*. Tübingen: Max Niemeyer, 1984.

Beinin, Joel. *The Dispersion of Egyptian Jewry: Cutlure, Politics, and the Formation of a Modern Diaspora*. Berkeley: University of California Press, 1998.

———. "Writing Class: Workers and Modern Egyptian Colloquial Poetry (Zajal)." *Poetics Today* 15.2 (Summer, 1994): 191–215.

Benachir, Bouazza. *Edmond Amran El Maleh: Cheminements d'une écriture*. Paris: Hartmann, 1997.

Benjamin, Walter. "Die Aufgabe des Übersetzers." In *Illuminationen*, 50–62. Frankfurt am Main: Suhrkamp, 1977. Tr. Harry Zohn as "The Task of the Translator." In *Illuminations*, 69–82. New York: Schocken Books, 2007.

———. *Der Begriff der Kunstkritik in der deutschen Romantik*. In *Gesammelte Schriften*, vol. 1, ed. Rolf Tiedemann and Hermann Schweppenhäuser, 11–122. Frankfurt am Main: Suhrkamp, 1974.

———. "Über den Begriff der Geschichte." In *Illuminationen*, 251–61. Frankfurt am Main: Suhrkamp, 1977. Tr. Harry Zohn as "Theses on the Philosophy of History." In *Illuminations*, 253–64. New York: Schocken Books, 2007.

———. *Ursprung des deutschen Trauerspiels*. In *Gesammelte Schriften*, vol. 1, ed. Rolf Tiedemann and Hermann Schweppenhäuser, 203–430. Frankfurt am Main: Suhrkamp, 1974. Tr. John Osbourne as *The Origin of German Tragic Drama*. London: Verso, 2003.

———. "Was ist das epische Theater (2)." In *Gesammelte Schriften*, vol. 2, ed. Rolf Tiedemann and Hermann Schweppenhäuser, 532–39. Frankfurt am Main: Suhrkamp, 1977. Tr. Harry Zohn as "What Is Epic Theater?" In *Illuminations*, 147–54. New York: Schocken Books, 2007.

Benslama, Fethi. *Psychoanalysis and the Challenge of Islam*. Tr. Robert Bononno. Minneapolis: University of Minnesota Press, 2009.

Berg, Nancy. *Exile from Exile: Israeli Writers from Iraq*. Albany: State University of New York Press, 1996.

Berkey, Jonathan. *Popular Preaching and Religious Authority in the Medieval Islamic Near East*. Seattle: University of Washington Press, 2001.

———. *The Transmission of Knowledge in Medieval Cairo: A Social History of Islamic Education*. Princeton: Princeton University Press, 1992.

Biddick, Kathleen. *The Typological Imaginary: Circumcision, Technology, History*. Philadelphia: University of Pennsylvania Press, 2003.

Blumenberg, Hans. *The Genesis of the Copernican World*. Tr. Robert Wallace. Cambridge, MA: MIT Press, 2000.

———. *The Legitimacy of the Modern Age*. Tr. Robert Wallace. Cambridge, MA: MIT Press, 1985.

Booth, Marilyn. *May Her Likes Be Multiplied: Biography and Gender Politics in Egypt*. Berkeley: University of California Press, 2001.

Bou Ali, Nadia. "Butrus al-Bustani and the Shipwreck of the Nation." *Middle Eastern Literatures* 16.3 (2013): 266–81.

———. "Collecting the Nation: Lexicography and National Pedagogy in al-nahda al-ʿarabiyya." In *Archives, Museums and Collecting Practices in the Arab World*, ed. Sonja Mejchar-Attasi and John Pedro Schwartz, 33–56. London: Ashgate, 2012.

Bourdieu, Pierre. *The Logic of Practice*. Tr. Richard Nice. Stanford: Stanford University Press, 1990.

Boyarin, Daniel. *Border Lines: The Partition of Judaeo-Christianity*. Philadelphia: University of Pennsylvania Press, 2004.

———. *Unheroic Conduct: The Rise of Heterosexuality and the Invention of the Jewish Man*. Berkeley: University of California Press, 1997.

Boyarin, Jonathan. *The Unconverted Self: Jews, Indians, and the Identity of Christian Europe*. Chicago: University of Chicago Press, 2009.

Brown, Nathan J. *Peasant Politics in Modern Egypt: The Struggle against the State*. New Haven: Yale University Press, 1990.

Brugman, Jan. *An Introduction to the History of Modern Arabic Literature in Egypt*. Leiden: Brill, 1984.

Buhasan, Ahmad. *al-Khitab al-naqdi 'ind Taha Husayn*. Beirut: Dar al-Tanwir li al-Tiba'a wa al-Nashr, 1985.

al-Bustani, Butrus. *Khitab fi al-hay'a al-ijtima'iyya wa al-muqabala bayna al-'awa'id al-'arabiyya wa al-afranjiyya*. Jouneh: Jami'at al-Ruh al-Quds, 1999 [1869].

———. *Khitab fi ta'lim al-nisa'*. In *al-Jama'iyya al-suriyya li al-'ulum wa al-funun, 1847–1852*, 45–53. Beirut: Dar al-Hamra', 1990 [1849].

———. *Khutba fi adab al-'arab*. In *al-Jama'iyya al-suriyya li al-'ulum wa al-Funun, 1847–1852*, 101–17. Beirut: Dar al-Hamra', 1990 [1859].

———. *Kitab al-'ahd al-jadid li rabbina wa mukhlisina Yasu' al-masih*. Tr. Butrus al-Bustani et. al. Beirut: n.p., 1867.

———. *Kitab da'irat al-ma'arif*. 6 vols. Beirut: Matba'at al-Ma'arif, 1876–82.

———. *Kitab misbah al-talib fi bahth al-matalib: Mutawwalun fi al-sarf wa al-nahu wa 'ilm al-'arud wa al qawafi*. Beirut: n.p., 1854.

———. *Kitab muhit al-muhit*. 2 vols. Beirut: Matba'at al-Ma'arif, 1867–70.

———. *Nafir Suriyya*. Beirut: Dar al-Fikr li al-Abhath wa al-Nashr, 1990 [1860–61].

———. *Qissat As'ad al-Shidyaq*. Beirut: Dar al-Hamra', 1992 [1860].

al-Bustani, Sulayman. *Ilyadhat Humiros*. 2 vols. Beirut: Dar Ihya' al-Turath al-'Arabi, 1976 [1902].

Butler, Judith. *Antigone's Claim*. New York: Columbia University Press, 2000.

———. *Excitable Speech: A Politics of the Performative*. New York: Routledge, 1997.

———. *Giving an Account of Oneself*. New York: Fordham University Press, 2004.

———. *Parting Ways: Jewishness and the Critique of Zionism*. New York: Columbia University Press, 2012.

———. *The Psychic Life of Power: Theories in Subjection*. Stanford: Stanford University Press, 1997.

———. *Subjects of Desire: Hegelian Reflections in Twentieth-Century France*. New York: Columbia University Press, 1999 [1987].

Butterworth, Charles E., and Blake Andrée Kessel, eds. *The Introduction of Arabic Philosophy into Europe*. Brill: Leiden, 1997.

Cachia, Pierre. *Taha Husayn: His Place in the Egyptian Literary Renaissance*. Piscataway, NJ: Gorgias, 2005.

Cadava, Eduardo. *Emerson and the Climates of History*. Stanford: Stanford University Press, 1997.

———. "Lapsus Imaginis: The Image in Ruins." *October* 96 (Spring 2001): 35–60.

———. "Nadar's Photographopolis." *Grey Room* 48 (Summer 2012): 56–77.

———. "Trees, Hands, Stars, and Veils: The Portrait in Ruins." In Fazal Sheikh, *Portraits*, 5–43. Göttingen: Steidl, 2011.

———. *Words of Light: Theses on the Photography of History*. Princeton: Princeton University Press, 1997.

Caiani, Fabio. "'My Name is Yalu': The Development of Metafiction in Ilyas Khuri's Work." *Middle Eastern Literatures* 10.2 (August 2007): 137–55.

Campos, Michelle. *Ottoman Brothers: Muslims, Christians, and Jews in Early Twentieth-Century Palestine*. Stanford: Stanford University Press, 2011.

Caruth, Cathy. *Empirical Truths and Critical Fictions: Locke, Wordsworth, Kant, Freud*. Baltimore: Johns Hopkins University Press, 2009 [1991].

Certeau, Michel de. *The Writing of History*. Tr. Tom Conley. New York: Columbia University Press, 1988.

Chakrabarty, Dipesh. *Habitations of Modernity: Essays in the Wake of Subaltern Studies*. Chicago: University of Chicago Press, 2002.

———. *Provincializing Europe: Postcolonial Thought and Historical Difference*. Princeton: Princeton University Press, 1999.

Chamberlain, Michael. *Knowledge and Social Practice in Medieval Damascus, 1190–1350*. New York: Cambridge University Press, 1994.

Chase, Cynthia. *Decomposing Figures: Rhetorical Readings in the Romantic Tradition*. Baltimore: Johns Hopkins University Press, 1986.

Chatterjee, Partha. *Lineages of Political Society: Studies in Postcolonial Democracy*. New York: Columbia University Press, 2011.

———. *The Nation and Its Fragments: Colonial and Postcolonial Histories*. Princeton: Princeton University Press, 1993.

———. *Nationalist Thought and the Colonial World: A Derivative Discourse*. Minneapolis: University of Minnesota Press, 1993 [1986].

———. *The Politics of the Governed: Reflections on Popular Politics in Most of the World*. New York: Columbia University Press, 2004.

Cheah, Pheng. *Spectral Nationality: Passages of Freedom from Kant to Postcolonial Literatures of Liberation*. New York: Columbia University Press, 2003.

Chetrit, Sami Shalom. *Petikha*. Tel Aviv: Eked, 1988.

———. "Revisiting Bialik: A Radical Mizrahi Reading of the Jewish National Poet." *Comparative Literature* 62.1 (2010): 1–21.

Chow, Rey. *The Age of the World Target: Self-Referentiality in War, Theory, and Comparative Work*. Durham: Duke University Press, 2006.

Cixous, Hélène. *Portrait of Jacques Derrida as a Young Jewish Saint*. Tr. Beverley Bei Brahic. New York: Columbia University Press, 2004.

Cohn, Bernard. *Colonialism and Its Forms of Knowledge*. Princeton: Princeton University Press, 1996.

Cole, Juan R. *Colonialism and Revolution in the Middle East: Social and Cultural Origins of Egypt's 'Urabi Movement*. Princeton: Princeton University Press, 1993.

———. "Rifa'a al-Tahtawi and the Revival of Practical Philosphy." *Muslim World* 70 (1980): 29–46.

Colla, Elliott. *Conflicted Antiquities: Egyptology, Egyptomania, Egyptian Modernity*. Durham: Duke University Press, 2007.

———. "How *Zaynab* Became the First Arabic Novel." *History Compass* 6 (2008): 214–25.

———. "The Image of Loss: Jalal Toufic's Filmic Beirut." *Visual Anthropology* 10 (1998): 305–17.

Comay, Rebecca. *Mourning Sickness: Hegel and the French Revolution*. Stanford: Stanford University Press, 2010.

Cooper, Frederick. *Colonialism in Question: Theory, Knowledge, History*. Berkeley: University of California Press, 2005.

Cuno, Kenneth M. *The Pasha's Peasants: Land, Society, and Economy in Lower Egypt, 1740–1858*. New York: Cambridge University Press, 1992

Darraj, Faysal. *al-Hadatha al-mutaqahqira: Taha Husayn wa Adunis*. Ramallah: Muwatin, 2005.

———. *Ma qabl al-dawla, ma ba'd al-hadatha*. 'Amman: Azmina li al-Nashr wa al-Tawzi', 2011.

———. *Nizariyat al-riwaya wa al-riwaya al-'arabiyya*. al-Dar al-Bayda': al-Markaz al-Thaqafi al-'Arabi, 1999.

———. *al-Riwaya wa ta'wil al-tarikh*. Beirut: al-Markaz al-Thaqafi al-'Arabi, 2004.

———. "al-Shaykh al-taqlidi wa al-muthaqqaf al-hadith." In *Taha Husayn: al-'aqlaniyya, al-dimuqratiyya, al-hadatha*, ed. 'Abd al-Rahman Munif, Faysal Darraj, Sa'd Allah wa al-Nus, and Jaber 'Asfur. Damascus: Mu'assasat 'Ibal, 1990.

———. "Wada' al-riwaya al-'arabiyya fi haql thaqafi ghayr riwa'i." *al-Tariq* 2 (March–April 1998): 93–110.

Darwich, Mahmoud. *La Palestine comme métaphore*. Tr. from Arabic Elias Sanbar and from Hebrew Simone Bitton. Paris: Actes Sud, 1997.

Darwish, Mahmoud. *'Abirun fi kalam 'abir*. Beirut: Dar al-'Awda, 1994.

———. *Ahada 'ashara kawkaban*. Beirut: Dar al-Jadid, 1992.

———. *Ara ma urid*. Beirut: Dar al-Jadid, 1993.

———. *Athar al-farasha*. Beirut: Riyad al-Rayyes, 2008.

———. *Dhakira li al-nisyan*. Beirut: Riyad al-Rayyes, 2007.

———. *Fi hadrat al-ghiyab*. Beirut: Riyad al-Rayyes, 2006.

———. *Hirat al-'a'id*. Beirut: Riyad al-Rayyes, 2007.

———. *Hisar li mada'ih al-bahr*. Beirut: Dar al-'Awda, 1984.

———. "Hiwar ma' Mahmoud Darwish." Interview by 'Abdu Wazin. In *Mahmoud Darwish: al-gharib yaq' 'ala nafsihi*, 57-154. Beirut: Riyad al-Rayyes, 2006.

———. *Hiyya ughniyya, hiyya ughniyya*. Beirut: Dar al-Kalima, 1986.

———. *Jidariyya*. Beirut: Riyad al-Rayyes, 2000.

———. *Ka zahr al-lawz aw ab'ad*. Beirut: Riyad al-Rayyes, 2005.

———. *La ta'tadhir 'amma fa'alta*. Beirut: Riyad al-Rayyes, 2004.

———. *Limadha tarakta al-hisana wahidan?* Beirut: Riyad al-Rayyes, 1995. Tr. J. Sacks as *Why Did You Leave the Horse Alone?* New York: Archipelago, 2006.

———. "Mahmoud Darwish ... La ahad yasil." Interview by Ghassan Zaqtan, Husayn al-Barghuthi, Hasan Khadr, and Zakariyya Muhammad. In *Mahmoud Darwish: al-mukhtalif al-haqiqi*, 14–46. 'Amman: Dar al-Shuruq, 1999.

———. *Sarir al-ghariba*. Beirut: Riyad al-Rayyes, 1999.

———. *Ward aqall*. al-Dar al-Bayda': Dar Tubqal li al-Nashr, 1986.

———. *Yawmiyyat al-huzn al-'adi*. Beirut: Dar al-'Awda, 1978 [1973].

———. *Yawmiyyat al-huzn al-'adi*. Beirut: Riyad al-Rayyes, 2007 [1973].

Darwish, Mahmoud, and Samih al-Qasim. *al-Rasa'il*. Beirut: Dar al-'Awda, 1990.

Davis, Kathleen. *Periodization and Sovereignty: How Ideas of Feudalism and Secularization Govern the Politics of Time*. Philadelphia: University of Pennsylvania Press, 2008.

Davis, Rochelle. *Palestinian Village Histories: Geographies of the Displaced*. Stanford: Stanford University Press, 2010.

de Man, Paul. "Aesthetic Formalization: Kleist's *Über das Marionettentheater*." In *The Rhetoric of Romanticism*, 263–90.

———. *Aesthetic Ideology*. Ed. Andrzej Warminski. Minneapolis: University of Minnesota Press, 1996.

———. "Autobiography as De-Facement." In *The Rhetoric of Romanticism*, 67–81.

———. "Anthropomorphism and Trope in the Lyric." In *The Rhetoric of Romanticism*, 239–62.

———. "Hypogram and Inscription." In *The Resistance to Theory*, 27–53.

———. "Intentional Structure of the Romantic Image." In *The Rhetoric of Romanticism*, 1–17.

———. "Kant and Schiller." In *Aesthetic Ideology*, 129–62.

———. "Kant's Materialism." In *Aesthetic Ideology*, 119–28.

———. "Phenomenality and Materiality in Kant." In *Aesthetic Ideology*, 70–90.

———. *The Resistance to Theory*. Foreword Wlad Godzich. Minneapolis: University of Minnesota Press, 1986.

———. "The Resistance to Theory." In *The Resistance to Theory*, 3–20.

———. "The Return to Philology." In *The Resistance to Theory*, 21–26.

———. *The Rhetoric of Romanticism*. New York: Columbia University Press, 1984.

———. "The Rhetoric of Temporality." In *Blindness and Insight: Essays in the Rhetoric of Contemporary Criticism*, introd. Wlad Godzich, 187–228. Minneapolis: University of Minnesota Press, 1983 [1971].

———. "Shelly Disfigured." In *The Rhetoric of Romanticism*, 93–123.

Deringil, Selim. *The Well-Protected Domains: Ideology and the Legitimation of Power in the Ottoman Empire, 1876–1909*. London: I. B. Taurus, 2011 [1998].

Derrida, Jacques. *L'animal que donc je suis*. Ed. Marie-Louise Mallet. Paris: Galilée, 2006. Tr. David Wills as *The Animal That Therefore I Am*. New York: Fordham University Press, 2008.

———. *La carte postal: De Socrate à Freud et au-delà*. Paris: Flammarion, 1980. Tr. Alan Bass as *The Post Card: From Socrates to Freud and Beyond*. Chicago: University of Chicago Press, 1987.

———. "Circonfession." In Jacques Derrida and Geoffrey Bennington, *Jacques Derrida*. Paris: Seuil, 1991. Tr. Geoffrey Bennington as "Circumfession." In *Jacques Derrida*. Chicago: University of Chicago Press, 1993.

———. *De la grammatologie*. Paris: Minuit, 1967. Tr. Gayatri Chakravorty Spivak as *Of Grammatology*. Baltimore: Johns Hopkins University Press, 1998 [1977].

———. *La dissemination*. Paris: Seuil, 1972. Tr. Barbara Johnson as *Dissemination*. Chicago: University of Chicago Press, 1981.

———. *Donner la mort*. Paris: Galilée, 1999. Tr. David Wills as *The Gift of Death*. 2nd ed. Chicago: University of Chicago Press, 2008.

———. "Fors." In Nicolas Abraham and Maria Torok, *Cryptonymie: Le verbier de l'homme aux loups*, 7–73. Paris: Flammarion, 1976. Tr. Barbara Johnson as "Fors." In Nicolas Abraham and Maria Torok, *The Wolfman's Magic Word: A Cryptonomy*, xi–xlvii. Minneapolis: University of Minnesota Press, 1986.

———. *Glas*. Paris: Galilée, 1974. Tr. John P. Leavey and Richard Rand as *Glas*. Lincoln: University of Nebraska Press, 1986.

———. *Marges de la philosophie*. Paris: Minuit, 1972. Tr. Alan Bass as *Margins of Philosophy*. Chicago: University of Chicago Press, 1982.

———. *Mémoires pour Paul de Man*. Paris: Galilée, 1988. Tr. Cecile Lindsay, Jonathan Culler, Eduardo Cadava, and Peggy Kamuf as *Memoires for Paul de Man*. New York: Columbia University Press, 1989 [1986].

———. *Parages*. Paris: Galilée, 2003. Tr. Tom Conley, James Hulbert, John P. Leavey, and Avital Ronell as *Parages*. Ed. John P. Leavey. Stanford: Stanford University Press, 2011.

———. *Politiques de l'amitié*. Paris: Galilée, 1994. Tr. George Collins as *Politics of Friendship*. London: Verso, 1997.

———. "Préjugés: Devant la loi." In *La Faculté de Juger*, 87–139. Paris: Minuit, 1985. Tr. Avital Ronell as "Before the Law." In *Acts of Literature*, ed. Derek Attridge, 181–220. New York: Routledge, 1992.

———. *Psyché: Inventions de l'autre, Tome 1*. Paris: Galilée, 1998. Tr. and ed. Peggy Kamuf and Elizabeth Rottenberg as *Psyche: Inventions of the Other*, vol. 1. Stanford: Stanford University Press, 2007.

———. *Schibboleth: Pour Paul Celan*. Paris: Galilée, 1986. Tr. Joshua Wilner as "Shibboleth: For Paul Celan." In *Sovereignties in Question: The Poetics of Paul Celan*, ed. Thomas Dutoit and Outi Pasanen, 1–64. New York: Fordham University Press, 2005.

———. *Spectres de Marx: L'état de la dette, le travail de deuil at la nouvelle Internationale*. Paris: Galilée, 1993. Tr. Peggy Kamuf as *Specters of Marx: The State of the Debt, the Work of Mourning, and the New International*. New York: Routledge, 1994.

———. *La vérité en peinture*. Paris: Flammarion, 1978. Tr. Geoff Bennington and Ian McLeod as *The Truth in Painting*. Chicago: University of Chicago Press, 1987.

———. "Violence at métaphysique: Essai sur la pensée d'Emmanuel Levinas." In *L'écriture et la difference*, 117–228. Paris: Seuil, 1967. Tr. Alan Bass as "Violence and Metaphysics: An Essay on the Thought of Emmanuel Levinas." In *Writing and Difference*, 79–153. Chicago: University of Chicago Press, 1978.

De Vries, Hent. *Philosophy and the Turn to Religion*. Baltimore: Johns Hopkins University Press, 1999.

———. *Religion and Violence: Philosophical Perspectives from Kant to Derrida.* Baltimore: Johns Hopkins University Press, 2001.

DeYoung, Terri. *Placing the Poet: Badr Shakir al-Sayyab and Postcolonial Iraq.* Albany: State University of New York Press, 1998.

Di-Capua, Yoav. *Gatekeepers of the Arab Past: Historians and History Writing in Twentieth-Century Egypt.* Berkeley: University of California Press, 2009.

Djaït, Hichem. *La grande discorde: Religion et politique dans l'Islam des origins.* Paris: Gallimard, 1990.

Donner, Fred. *Narratives of Islamic Origins: The Beginnings of Islamic Historical Writing.* Princeton: Darwin Press, 1998.

Doumani, Beshara. *Rediscovering Palestine: Merchants and Peasants in Jabal Nablus, 1700–1900.* Berkeley: University of California Press, 1995.

Dyer, Rebecca. "Poetry and the Politics of Mourning: Mahmoud Darwish's Genre-Transforming Tribute to Edward W. Said." *PMLA* 122.5 (October 2007): 1447–62.

El-Ariss, Tarek. *Trials of Arab Modernity: Literary Affects and the New Political.* New York: Fordham University Press, 2013.

El-Desouky, Ayman A. "Heterologies of Revolutionary Action: On Historical Consciousness and the Sacred in Mahfouz's *Children of the Alley.*" *Journal of Postcolonial Writing* 47.4 (2011): 428–39.

Elinson, Alexander E. *Looking Back at al-Andalus: The Poetics of Loss and Nostalgia in Medieval Arabic and Hebrew Literature.* Leiden: Brill, 2009.

El Maleh, Edmond Amran. *Entretiens avec Edmond Amran El Maleh.* Paris: La Pensée Sauvage, 2005.

———. *Jean Genet: Le captif amoureux et autres essais.* Paris: La Pensée Sauvage, 1988.

———. *Lettres à moi-même.* Casablanca: Fennec, 2010.

———. *Mille ans, un jour.* Paris: La Pensée Sauvage, 1986.

———. "Les pierres blanches" (French with English translation). In *Ahmed Cherkaoui: La passion du signe*, 31–63. Paris: Institut du Monde Arabe, 1996.

Elshakry, Marwa. "The Gospel of Science and American Evangelism in Late Ottoman Beirut." *Past & Present* 196 (August 2007): 173–214.

———. "Knowledge in Motion: The Cultural Politics of Modern Science Translations in Arabic." *Isis* 99.4 (December 2008): 701–30.

———. *Reading Darwin in Arabic, 1860–1950.* Chicago: University of Chicago Press, 2013.

El Shakry, Omnia. "The Arabic Freud: The Unconscious and the Modern Subject." *Modern Intellectual History* 11.1 (2014): 89–118.

———. *The Great Social Laboratory: Subjects of Knowledge in Colonial and Postcolonial Egypt.* Stanford: Stanford University Press, 2007.

———. "Schooled Mothers and Structured Play: Child Rearing in Turn-of-the-Century Egypt." In *Remaking Women: Feminism and Modernity in the Middle East*, ed. Lila Abu-Lughod, 126–70. Princeton: Princeton University Press, 1998.

———. "Youth as Peril and Promise: The Emergence of Adolescent Psychology in Postwar Egypt." *International Journal of Middle East Studies* 43 (2011): 591–610.

Eng, David L, and David Kazanjian, eds. *Loss: The Politics of Mourning.* Berkeley: University of California Press, 2003.

Ertürk, Nergis. *Grammatology and Literary Modernity in Turkey.* New York: Oxford University Press, 2011.

———. "Toward a Literary Communism: The 1926 Baku Turcological Congress." *boundary 2* 40.2 (2013): 183–213.

Esmeir, Samera. *Juridical Humanity: A Colonial History.* Stanford: Stanford University Press, 2011.

———. "Memories of Conquest: Witnessing Death in Tanturah." In *Nakba: Palestine, 1948, and the Claims of Memory*, ed. Ahmad M. Sa'di and Lila Abu-Lughod, 229–52. New York: Columbia University Press, 2007.

Fadl, Salah. *Asalib al-shi'iriyya al-mu'asira.* Beirut: Dar al-Adab, 1995.

Fahmy, Khaled. *All the Pasha's Men: Mehmed Ali, His Army, and the Making of Modern Egypt.* Cairo: American University in Cairo Press, 2002 [1998].

———. "The Anatomy of Justice: Forensic Medicine and Criminal Law in Nineteenth-Century Egypt." *Islamic Law and Society* 6.2 (1999): 224–71.

———. "Justice, Law and Pain in Khedival Egypt." In *Standing Trial: Law and the Person in the Modern Middle East*, 85–115. London: I. B. Taurus, 2004.

———. "The Police and the People in Nineteenth-Century Egypt." *Die Welt des Islams* 39.3 (1999): 340–77.

Fahmy, Khaled, and Rudolph Peters. "The Legal History of Ottoman Egypt." *Islamic Law and Society* 6.2 (1999): 129–35.

Fahmy, Ziad. *Ordinary Egyptians: Creating the Modern Nation through Popular Culture.* Stanford: Stanford University Press, 2011.

Fakhr al-Din, Jawdat. *Shakl al-qasida al-'arabiyya fi al-naqd al-'arabi hatta al-qarn al-thamin al-hijri.* Beirut: Dar al-Harf al-'Arabi, 2004.

Fanon, Frantz. *Le damnés de la terre.* Paris: Découverte, 2002. Tr. Constance Farrington as *The Wretched of the Earth.* New York: Grove Press, 1961.

Fawaz, Leila Tarazi. *An Occasion for War: Civil Conflict in Lebanon and Damascus in 1860.* Berkeley: University of California Press, 1994.

———. *Merchants and Migrants in Nineteenth-Century Beirut*. Cambridge, MA: Harvard University Press, 1983.

al-Fayruzabadi, Majd al-Din Muhammad ibn Ya'qub. *al-Qamus al-muhit*. Beirut: Dar al-Katib al- 'Arabi, 2010.

Feldman, Ilana. *Governing Gaza: Bureaucracy, Authority, and the Work of Rule, 1917–1967*. Durham: Duke University Press, 2008.

Fenves, Peter. *A Peculiar Fate: Metaphysics and World History in Kant*. Ithaca: Cornell University Press, 1991.

———. "Taking Stock of the Kantian Sublime." *Eighteenth-Century Studies* 28.1 (Autumn 1994): 65–82.

———. *The Messianic Reduction: Walter Benjamin and the Shape of Time*. Stanford: Stanford University Press, 2011.

Fieni, David. "French Decadence, Arab Awakenings: Figures of Decay in the Arab *Nahda*." *boundary 2* 39.2 (Summer 2012): 143–60.

Findley, Carter V. *Bureaucratic Reform in the Ottoman Empire: The Sublime Porte, 1789–1922*. Princeton: Princeton University Press, 1980.

Fortna, Benjamin. *Imperial Classroom: Islam, the State and Education in the Late Ottoman Empire*. New York: Oxford University Press, 2002.

Foucault, Michel. *The Order of Things*. New York: Vintage, 1994.

Freud, Sigmund. "Trauer und Melancholie." In *Gesammelte Werke*, 10:428–46. London: Imago, 1945. Tr. James Strachey as "Mourning and Melancholy." In *The Standard Edition of the Complete Psychological Works of Sigmund Freud*, 14:243–58. London: Hogarth, 1957.

Funkenstein, Amos. *Perceptions of Jewish History*. Berkeley: University of California Press, 1993.

———. *Theology and the Scientific Imagination from the Middle Ages to the Seventeenth Century*. Princeton: Princeton University Press, 1989.

Furani, Khaled. *Silencing the Sea: Secular Rhythms in Palestinian Poetry*. Stanford: Stanford University Press, 2012.

Gadamer, Hans-Georg. *Truth and Method*. 2nd rev. ed. Tr. Joel Weinsheimer and Donald G. Marshall. New York: Continuum, 1996.

Gana, Nouri. *Signifying Loss: Toward a Poetics of Narrative Mourning*. Lanham, MD: Bucknell University Press, 2011.

———. "War, Poetry, Mourning: Darwish, Adunis, Iraq." *Public Culture* 22.1 (2010): 33–65.

Gasché, Rudolph. *The Idea of Form: Rethinking Kant's Aesthetics*. Stanford: Stanford University Press, 2003.

Gasper, Michael Ezekiel. *The Power of Representation: Publics, Peasants, and Islam in Egypt*. Stanford: Stanford University Press, 2009.

Gendzier, Irene L. *The Practical Visions of Ya'qub Sanu'*. Harvard Middle

Eastern Monograph Series. Cambridge, MA: Harvard University Press, 1966.

Genet, Jean. *Un captif amoureux*. Paris: Gallimard, 1986. Tr. Barbara Bray as *Prisoner of Love*. Hanover, NH: Wesleyan University Press, 1992.

Ghandour, Sabah. "History, Religion, and the Construction of Subjectivity in Elias Khoury's *Rihlat Ghandi al-Saghir*." In *Tradition, Modernity, and Postmodernity in Arabic Literature: Essays in Honor of Professor Issa J. Boullata*, ed. Kamal Abdel-Malek and Wael Hallaq, 186–202. Leiden: Brill, 2002.

al-Ghazali, Abu Hamid Muhammad. *Tahafut al-falasifa*. Beirut: Dar al-Shuruq, 1990.

Ghazoul, Ferial J. "Comparative Literature in the Arab World." *Comparative Critical Studies* 3.1–2 (2006): 113–24.

———. "Darwish's Mural." *Interventions: International Journal of Postcolonial Studies* 14.1 (2012): 37–54.

———. *Nocturnal Poetics: The Arabian Nights in Comparative Context*. Cairo: American University in Cairo Press, 1996.

al-Ghitani, Jamal, ed. *Najib Mahfuz yatadhakkar*. Beirut: Dar al-Masira, 1980.

Gibb, H. A. R. "The Egyptian Novel." *Bulletin of the School of Oriental Studies* 7.1 (1933): 1–22.

Godzich, Wlad. *The Culture of Literacy*. Cambridge, MA: Harvard University Press, 1994.

Goldberg, David Theo. *The Racial State*. Malden, MA: Blackwell, 2002.

Gourgouris, Stathis. *Dream Nation: Enlightenment, Colonization, and the Institution of Modern Greece*. Stanford: Stanford University Press, 1996.

———. *Lessons in Secular Criticism*. New York: Fordham University Press, 2013.

Gover, Yerach. *Zionism: The Limits of Moral Discourse in Israeli Hebrew Fiction*. Minneapolis: University of Minnesota Press, 1994.

Gran, Peter. *Islamic Roots of Capitalism: Egypt, 1760–1840*. Syracuse: Syracuse University Press, 1998 [1979].

Gruendler, Beatrice. *Medieval Arabic Praise Poetry: Ibn al-Rumi and the Patron's Redemption*. London: Routledge Curzon, 2003.

Guha, Ranajit. *Dominance without Hegemony: History and Power in Colonial India*. Cambridge, MA: Harvard University Press, 1997.

———. *Elementary Aspects of Peasant Insurgency in Colonial India*. Durham: Duke University Press, 1999 [1983].

———. *History at the Limit of World History*. New York: Columbia University Press, 2002.

———. "The Prose of Counter Insurgency." In *Selected Subaltern Studies,* ed. Ranajit Guha and Gayatri Chakravorty Spivak, 45–84. New York: Oxford University Press, 1988.

———. *A Rule of Property for Bengal.* Durham: Duke University Press, 1996 [1963].

Gully, Adrian. "Arabic Linguistic Issues and Controversies of the Late Nineteenth and Early Twentieth Centuries." *Journal of Semitic Studies* 42.1 (Spring 1997): 75–120.

Gutas, Dimitri. *Greek Thought, Arabic Culture: The Graeco-Arabic Translation Movement in Baghdad and Early Abbasid Society.* New York: Routledge, 1998.

Habiby, Emile. *Khurafiyyat Saraya bint al-Ghul.* Haifa: Dar 'Arabesque, 1991.

———. *al-Waqa'i' al-ghariba fi ikhtifa' Sa'id abi Nahs al-mutasha'il.* Beirut: Dar Ibn Khaldun, 1989 [1974]. Tr. Salma Khadra Jayyusi and Trevor LeGassick as *The Secret Life of Saeed the Pessoptimist.* London: Zed, 1985.

Haddad, Qasim. "Fi shurfat Mahmoud Darwish." *al-Karmel* 90 (Spring 2009): 118–22.

Hadidi, Subhi. "Madha yaf'al al-'ashiq min duna manfa?" In *Mahmoud Darwish: al-mukhtalif al-haqiqi,* 47–73. 'Amman: Dar al-Shuruq, 1999.

———. "Mahmoud Darwish fi 'khutbat al-hindi al-ahmar': istratijiyyat al-ta'bir wa tamthilat al-ma'na." *al-Karmel* 90 (Spring 2009): 37–53.

Hafez, Sabry. *The Genesis of Arabic Narrative Discourse.* London: Saqi, 1993.

———. "Raqsh al-dhat la kitabatuha: Tahawwulat al-istratijiyyat al-nassiyya fi al-sira al-dhatiyya." *Alif: Journal of Comparative Poetics* 22 (2002): 7–33.

Hägglund, Martin. *Radical Atheism: Derrida and the Time of Life.* Stanford: Stanford University Press, 2008.

al-Haj, Nur al-Din. *al-Ana al-ghina'i fi "Limadha tarakta al-hisana wahidan?"* Safaqis, Tunisia: Dar al-Amal li al-Nashr wa al-Tawzi', 2008.

Haj, Samira. *Reconfiguring Islamic Tradition: Reform, Rationality, and Modernity.* Stanford: Stanford University Press, 2009.

al-Hakim, Tawfiq. *Yawmiyyat na'ib fi al-aryaf.* Cairo: Dar Misr li al-Tiba'a, n.d. [1937].

Halevi, Leor. *Muhammad's Grave: Death Rites and the Making of Islamic Society.* New York: Columbia University Press, 2007.

Halevi, Sharon, and Fruma Zachs. "'Asma' (1873): The Early Arabic Novel as a Social Compass." *Studies in the Novel* 39.4 (Winter 2007): 416–30.

Halevi-Wise, Yael. "Ethics and Aesthetics of Memory in Contemporary Mizrahi Literature." *Journal of Israeli History: Politics, Society, Culture* 20.1 (2001): 49–66.

Halim, Hala. *Alexandrian Cosmopolitanism: An Archive*. New York: Fordham University Press, 2013.

Hallaq, Wael. *A History of Islamic Legal Theories: An Introduction to Sunni Usul al-Fiqh*. New York: Cambridge University Press, 1997.

———. *The Origins and Evolution of Islamic Law*. New York: Cambridge University Press, 2005.

———. "Was al-Shafi'i the Master Architect of Islamic Jurisprudence?" *International Journal of Middle East Studies* 25 (1993): 587–605.

Hamacher, Werner. *Für die Philologie*. Engeler: Solothurn, 2009.

———. *Pleroma—Reading in Hegel*. Tr. Nicholas Walker and Simon Jarvis. Stanford: Stanford University Press, 1998.

———. *Premises: Essays on Philosophy and Literature from Kant to Celan*. Tr. Peter Fenves. Stanford: Stanford University Press, 1996.

———. "95 Theses on Philology." Tr. Catherine Diehl. *Diacritics* 39.1 (Spring 2009): 25–44.

Hamilton, John T. *Security: Politics, Humanity, and the Philology of Care*. Princeton: Princeton University Press, 2013.

———. *Soliciting Darkness: Pindar, Obscurity, and the Classical Tradition*. Cambridge, MA: Harvard University Press, 2003.

Hanna, Nelly. *In Praise of Books: A Cultural History of Cairo's Middle Class, Sixteenth to the Eighteenth Century*. Syracuse: Syracuse University Press, 2003.

Hanssen, Jens. *Fin-de-Siècle Beirut: The Making of an Ottoman Provincial Capital*. New York: Oxford University Press, 2005.

Haqqi, Yahya. *Fajr al-qissa al-misriyya*. Cairo: al-Hay'a al-Misriyya al-'Ama li al-Kitab, 1975.

———. *Qindil Umm Hashim*. Damascus: Dar al-Mada, 2004 [1943].

Harlow, Barbara. *Resistance Literature*. London: Methuen, 1987.

Harshav, Benjamin. *Language in Time of Revolution*. Stanford: Stanford University Press, 1999.

Hasan, Muhammad Rushda. *Athar al-maqama fi nash'at al-qissa al-misriyya al-haditha*. Cairo: al-Hay'a al-Misriyya al-'Ama li al-Kitab, 1974.

Haverkamp, Anselm. *Leaves of Mourning: Hölderlin's Late Work—With an Essay on Keats and Melancholy*. Tr. Vernon Chadwick. Albany: State University of New York Press, 1996.

Haykal, Muhammad Husayn. *Zaynab: manazir wa akhlaq rifiyya*. Cairo: Dar al-Ma'arif, 2004.

Head, Gretchen. "The Performative in Ilyas Khuri's Bab al-Shams." *Journal of Arabic Literature* 42 (2011): 148–82.

Hegel, Georg Wilhelm Friedrich. *Enzyklopädie der philosophischen Wissenschaften im Grundrisse, Dritter Teil: Philosophie des Geistes*. Ed. Friedhelm Nicolin and Otto Pöggeler. Hamburg: Felix Meiner, 1991. Tr. William Wallace as *Hegel's Philosophy of Mind*. Oxford: Clarendon Press, 1971.

———. *Enzyklopädie der philosophischen Wissenschaften im Grundrisse, Erster Teil: Die Wissenschaft der Logik*. Ed. Friedhelm Nicolin and Otto Pöggeler. Hamburg: Felix Meiner, 1991. Tr. T. F. Geraets, W. A. Suchting, and H. S. Harris as *The Encyclopaedia Logic, Part One of the Encyclopaedia of the Philosophical Sciences*. Indianapolis: Hackett, 1991.

———. *Enzyklopädie der philosophischen Wissenschaften im Grundrisse, Zweiter Teil: Naturphilosophie*. Ed. Friedhelm Nicolin and Otto Pöggeler. Hamburg: Felix Meiner, 1991. Tr. A. V. Miller as *Hegel's Philosophy of Nature, Part Two of the Encyclopaedia of the Philosophical Sciences*. Oxford: Clarendon Press, 2004.

———. *Der Geist des Christentums und sein Schicksal*. Gütersloh: Gütersloher Verlagshaus, 1970. Tr. T. M. Knox as *The Spirit of Christianity and Its Fate* in *Early Theological Writings*. Philadelphia: University of Pennsylvania Press, 1975.

———. *Grundlinien der Philosophie des Rechts*. Ed. Hermann Klenner. Berlin: Akademie Verlag, 1981. Tr. H. S. Nisbet as *Elements of the Philosophy of Right*. Cambridge: Cambridge University Press, 1991.

———. *Phänomenologie des Geistes*. Ed. Hans-Friedrich Wessels and Heinrich Clairmont. Hamburg: Felix Meiner, 1988. Tr. A. V. Miller as *Hegel's Phenomenology of Spirit*. New York: Oxford University Press, 1977.

———. *Vorlesungen über die Ästhetik*. 3 vols. Frankfurt am Main: Suhrkamp, 1986. Tr. T. M. Knox as *Hegel's Aesthetics: Lectures on Fine Art*. 2 vols. Oxford: Clarendon Press, 1998.

Heidegger, Martin. *Was Heißt Denken?* Tübingen: Max Niemeyer, 1997 [1954]. Tr. J. Glenn Gray as *What Is Called Thinking?* New York: HarperCollins, 1976.

Heinrichs, Wolfhart. *Arabische Dichtung und Greichische Poetik*. Beirut: Orient Institute, 1969.

———. "Authority in Arabic Poetry." In *La notion d'autorité au Moyen Age*, ed. Janine Sourdel-Thomine, 263–72. Paris: Presses Universitaires de France, 1982.

———. "The Classification of the Sciences and the Consolidation of Philology in Classical Islam." In *Centres of Learning: Learning and Location in Pre-Modern Europe and the Near East*, ed. Jan Willem Drijvers and Alasdair MacDonald, 119–39. Leiden: Brill, 1995.

———. "An Evaluation of 'Sariqa.'" *Quaderni di Studi Arabi* 5–6 (1987–88): 357–68.

———. "Literary Theory: The Problem of Its Efficiency." In *Arabic Poetry: Theory and Development*, ed. G. E. von Grunebaum, 19–69. Wiesbaden: Otto Harrassowitz, 1973.

———. "On the Genesis of the haqiqa-majaz Dichotomy." *Studia Islamica* 59 (1984): 111–40.

Heller-Roazen, Daniel. *Echolalias: On the Forgetting of Language*. New York: Zone Books, 2005.

Herder, Johann Gottfried. *Treatise on the Origin of Language*. In *Herder: Philosophical Writings*, ed. Michael N. Forster, 65–163. New York: Cambridge University Press, 2002.

Heschel, Susannah. *Abraham Geiger and the Jewish Jesus*. Chicago: University of Chicago Press, 1998.

———. "Revolt of the Colonized: Abraham Geiger's Wissenschaft des Judentums as a Challenge to Christian Hegemony in the Academy." *New German Critique* 77 (Spring–Summer 1999): 61–85.

Hess, Jonathan. *Germans, Jews, and the Claims of Modernity*. New Haven: Yale University Press, 2002.

Hever, Hanan. *Producing the Modern Hebrew Canon: Nation Building and Minority Discourse*. New York: New York University Press, 2002.

———. *Sifrut nikhtevet mi kan*. Tel Aviv: Yediyot Ahronot, 1999.

Hibi, Fayyad. *al-Shaksiyya and ghayariyya fi al-riwaya al-lubnaniyya fi zill al-harb al-ahliyya (1975–1990): Elias Khoury namudhajan*. 'Amman: Azmina li al-Nashr wa al-Tawzi', 2007.

Hirschkind, Charles. *The Ethical Soundscape: Cassette Sermons and Islamic Counterpublics*. New York: Columbia University Press, 2006.

———. "Heresy or Hermeneutics: The Case of Nasr Hamid Abu Zayd." *American Journal of Islamic Social Sciences* 12.4 (1995): 463–77.

Hirschler, Konrad. *The Written Word in Medieval Arabic Lands: A Social and Cultural History of Reading Practices*. Edinburgh: Edinburgh University Press, 2012.

Hochberg, Gil. *In Spite of Partition: Jews, Arabs, and the Limits of Separatist Imagination*. Princeton: Princeton University Press, 2007.

———. "A Poetics of Haunting: From Yizhar's Hirbeh to Yehoshua's Ruins to Koren's Crypts." *Jewish Social Studies* 18.3 (Spring–Summer 2012): 55–69.

Hollander, Dana. *Exemplarity and Chosenness: Rosenzweig and Derrida on the Nation of Philosophy*. Stanford: Stanford University Press, 2008.

Holt, Elizabeth M. "Narrative and the Reading Public in 1870's Beirut." *Journal of Arabic Literature* 40.1 (2009): 37–70.

Hourani, Albert. *Arabic Thought in the Liberal Age, 1798–1939*. New York: Cambridge University Press, 1983 [1962].

———. "The Changing Face of the Fertile Crescent in the XVIIIth Century." *Studia Islamica* 8 (1957): 89–122.

Husayn, Taha. *al-Ayyam*. Cairo: Markaz al-Ahram li al-Tarjama wa al-Nashr, 1992 [1926–27/1929]. Tr. E. H. Paxton, H. Wayment, and K. Cragg as *The Days*. Cairo: American University in Cairo Press, 1997.

———. *Du'a' al-karawan*. Cairo: Dar al-Ma'arif, 1978 [1934]. Tr. A. B. As-Safi as *The Call of the Curlew*. Leiden: Brill, 1980.

———. *Falsafat Ibn Khaldun al-ijtima'iyya*. Tr. Muhammad 'Inan. Cairo: Matba'at al-I'timad, 1925.

———. *Fi al-adab al-jahili*. Cairo: Dar al-Ma'arif, n.d [1927].

———. *Fi al-shi'r al-jahili*. Susa, Tunis: Dar al-Ma'arif, 1998 [1926].

———. *Hadith al-arbi'a'*. In *al-Majmu'a al-kamila li mu'allifat al-duktur Taha Husayn*, vol. 2.

———. *Khisam wa naqd*. In *al-Majmu'a al-kamila li mu'allifat al-duktur Taha Husayn*, vol. 11.

———. *al-Majmu'a al-kamila li mu'allifat al-duktur Taha Husayn*. 16 vols. Beirut: Dar al-Kitab al-Lubnani, 1973–83.

———. *Mustaqbal al-thaqafa fi Misr*. Cairo: al-Hay'a al-Misriyya al-'Ama li al-Kitab, 1993 [1938].

———. *Qadat al-fikr*. Cairo: Dar al-Ma'arif, 1964 [1925].

Ibn Hazm, 'Ali ibn Hamad al-Andalusi. *Tawq al-hamama fi al-ilfa wa al-ullaf*. Ed. Ihsan 'Abbas. Tunis: Dar al-Ma'arif li al-Tiba'a wa al-Nashr, 1992.

Ibn Hisham, Jamal al-Din 'Abd Allah al-Ansari. *Sharh shudhur al-dhahab fi ma'arifat kalam al-'arab*. Beirut: Dar al-Kutub al-'Ilmiyya, 1996.

Ibn Jinni, Abu al-Fath 'Uthman al-Muwsuli. *al-Khasa'is*. Ed. Muhammad 'Ali al-Najjar. Beirut: Dar al-Huda, 1952.

———. *al-Luma' fi al-'arabiyya*. Beirut: Maktabat al-Nahda al-'Arabiyya, 1985.

Ibn Khafaja, Abu Ishaq Ibrahim ibn al-Andalusi. *Diwan Ibn Khafaja*. Ed. al-Sayyed Mustafa Ghazi. Alexandria: Mansha'at al-Ma'arif, 1960.

Ibn Khaldun, Abd al-Rahman ibn Muhammad al-Khadrami. *Tarikh ibn Khaldun: kitab al-'ibar wa diwan al-mubtada' wa al-khabar fi ayam al-'Arab wa al-'ajam wa al-barbar*. 7 vols. Beirut: Dar al-Kutub al-'Ilmiyya, 1992.

Ibn Manzur, Jamal al-Din Abi al-Fadl Muhammad Mukarram al-Ifriqi. *Lisan al-'arab*. 12 vols. Beirut: Dar al-Kutub al-'Ilmiyya, 2003.

Ibn Rashiq, Abu 'Ali Hasan al-Qayrawani al-Azdi. *al-'Umda fi mahasin al-shi'r wa adabihi wa naqdihi*. Beirut: Dar al-Jil, 1981.

Ibn Rushd, Abu al-Walid Muhammad ibn Ahmad. *Tahafut al-tahafut*. Ed. and introd. Muhammad 'Abid al-Jabri. Beirut: Markaz Dirasat al-Wihda al-'Arabiyya, 2001 [1998].

al-'Id, Yumna. *Fan al-riwaya al-'arabiyya: bayna khususiyyat al-hikaya wa tamayyuz al-khitab*. Beirut: Dar al-Adab, 1998.

Izutsu, Toshihiko. *Ethico-Religious Concepts in the Qur'an*. Montreal and Kingston: McGill-Queen's University Press, 2002 [1959].

Jabès, Edmond. *Le livre des questions*. 2 vols. Paris: Gallimard, 1963–73. Tr. Rosemarie Waldrop as *The Book of Questions*. 2 vols. Hanover, NH: Wesleyan University Press, 1972–83.

Jabra, Jabra Ibrahim. *al-Bahth 'an Walid Mas'ud*. Beirut: Dar al-Adab, 1990.

al-Jabri, Muhammad Abid. *al-Khitab al-'arabi al-mu'asir*. Beirut: Markaz Dirasat al-Wihda al-'Arabiyya, 1994.

———. *Nahnu wa al-turath*. Beirut: Dar al-Tali'a, 1980.

———. *Naqd al-'aql al-'arabi*, vol. 2, *Binyat al-'aql al-'arabi*. Beirut: Markaz Dirasat al-Wihda al-'Arabiyya, 1996.

———. *Naqd al-'aql al-'arabi*, vol. 1, *Takwin al-'aql al-'arabi*. Beirut: Markaz Dirasat al-Wihda al-'Arabiyya, 1994.

Jacob, Wilson Chacko. *Working Out Egypt: Effendi Masculinity and Subject Formation in Colonial Modernity, 1870–1940*. Durham: Duke University Press, 2011.

Jacobi, Renate. *Studien zur Poetik der Altarabischen Qaside*. Wiesbaden: Franz Steiner, 1971.

Jacobs, Carol. *In the Language of Walter Benjamin*. Baltimore: Johns Hopkins University Press, 1999.

Jacquemond, Richard. "Translation and Cultural Hegemony: The Case of French-Arabic Translation." In *Rethinking Translation: Discourse, Subjectivity, Ideology*, ed. Lawrence Venuti, 139–58. New York: Routledge, 1992.

al-Jahiz, Abu 'Uthman 'Amru ibn Bahr. *al-Bayan wa al-tibyin*. Ed. Darwish Juwaidi. Beirut: al-Maktaba al-'Asriyya, 2003.

Jarrar, Maher. "*The Arabian Nights* and the Contemporary Arabic Novel." In *The Arabian Nights in Historical Context: Between East and West*, ed. Saree Makdisi and Felicity Nussbaum, 297–315. New York: Oxford University Press, 2008.

Jayyusi, Salma Khadra. *Trends and Movements in Modern Arabic Poetry*. 2 vols. Leiden: Brill 1977.

JPS Hebrew-English Tanakh. 2nd ed. Philadelphia: Jewish Publication Society, 2000.

Jihad, Kadhim. "Mahmoud Darwish fi majmu'atihi al-shi'iriyya al-ula wa qasa'idihi al-akhira." *al-Karmel* 90 (Spring 2009): 75–103.

Johnson, Rebecca Carol, Richard Maxwell, and Katie Trumpener. "*The Arabian Nights*, Arab-European Literary Influence, and the Lineages of the Novel." *Modern Language Quarterly* 68.2 (June 2007): 243–79.

Jones, A. "The History of the Text of the Qur'an after the Death of Muhammad." In *Arabic Literature to the End of the Umayyad Period*, ed. A. F. L. Beeston, T. M. Johnstone, R. B. Serjeant, and G. R. Smith, 235–45. Cambridge: Cambridge University Press, 1983.

Jones, Sir William. *The Moallakat, or Seven Arabian Poems, which were Suspended on the Temple at Mecca; With a Translation, a Preliminary Discourse, and Notes Critical, Philological, Explanatory.* London: J. Nichols, 1782.

Jubran, Sulaiman. "The Function of Rhyming Prose in 'al-Saq 'ala al-saq.'" *Journal of Arabic Literature* 20.2 (September 1989): 148–58.

Judy, Ronald A. T. *(Dis)forming the American Canon: African-Arabic Slave Narratives and the Vernacular.* Minneapolis: University of Minnesota Press, 1993.

al-Juma'i, 'Abd al-Mun'im. *al-Jami'a al-misriyya al-qadima: nasha'tuha wa dawruha fi al-mujtama', 1908–1925*. Cairo: Dar al-Kitab al-Jami'i, 1980.

———. *Taha Husayn wa al-jami'a al-misriyya.* Cairo: Dar al-Kitab al-Jami'i, 1981.

Kadhim, Hussein. *The Poetics of Anti-Colonialism in the Arabic Qasidah.* Leiden: Brill, 2004.

Kamuf, Peggy. *The Division of Literature: Or, The University in Deconstruction.* Chicago: University of Chicago Press, 1997.

Kanafani, Ghassan. *al-Adab al-filastini al-muqawim taht al-ithtilal, 1948–1968.* Beirut: Mu'assasat al-Abhath al-'Arabiyya, 1987 [1968].

———. *Adab al-muqawama fi Filastin al-muhtalla, 1948–1966.* Beirut: Mu'assasat al-Abhath al-'Arabiyya, 1987 [1966].

———. *'A'id ila Haifa.* In *al-Athar al-Kamila: al-Riwayat*, 337–416. Beirut: Dar al-Tali'a, 1972.

———. *Rijal fi al-shams.* In *al-Athar al-Kamila: al-Riwayat*, 29–152. Beirut: Dar al-Tali'a, 1972.

Kant, Immanuel. *Anthropologie in pragmatischer Hinsicht.* Ed. Reinhard Brandt. Hamburg: Felix Meiner, 2000. Tr. Robert B. Louden as *Anthropology from a Pragmatic Point of View.* New York: Cambridge University Press, 2006.

———. *Kritik der reinen Vernunft.* Ed. Jens Timmermann. Hamburg: Felix Meiner, 1998. Tr. Norman Kemp Smith as *Critique of Pure Reason.* New York: St. Martin's, 1929.

———. *Kritik der Urteilskraft*. Ed. Heiner F. Klemme. Hamburg: Felix Meiner, 2009. Tr. Werner S. Pluhar as *Critique of Judgment*. Indianapolis: Hackett, 1987.

———. *Die Religion innerhalb der Grenzen der bloßen Vernunft*. Ed. Bettina Stangneth. Hamburg: Felix Meiner, 2003. Tr. and ed. Allen W. Wood and George di Giovanni as *Religion within the Bounds of Mere Reason*, in *Religion and Rational Theology*, 40–215. New York: Cambridge University Press, 1996.

Kantorowicz, Ernst H. *The King's Two Bodies: A Study in Medieval Political Theology*. Princeton: Princeton University Press, 1997 [1957].

Kasaba, Reşat. *The Ottoman Empire and the World Economy: The Nineteenth Century*. Albany: State University of New York Press, 1988.

Kassab, Elizabeth. *Contemporary Arab Thought: Cultural Critique in Comparative Perspective*. New York: Columbia University Press, 2010.

al-Kassim, Dina. *On Pain of Speech: Fantasies of the First Order and the Literary Rant*. Berkeley: University of California Press, 2012.

Keenan, Thomas. *Fables of Responsibility: Aberrations and Predicaments in Ethics and Politics*. Stanford: Stanford University Press, 1997.

Khalaf Allah, Muhammad. *Ahmad Faris al-Shidyaq wa ara'uhu al-lughawiyya wa al-adabiyya*. Cairo: Jami'at al-Duwal al-'Arabiyya, Ma'had al-Dirasat al-'Arabiyya al-'Aliya, 1955.

Khalidi, Rashid. *The Iron Cage: The Story of the Palestinian Struggle for Statehood*. Boston: Beacon Press, 2006.

al-Khalidi, Ruhi. *Tarikh 'ilm al-adab 'ind al-afranj wa al- 'Arab, wa Victur Hugo*. Cairo: Maktabat al-Hilal, 1904.

Khalidi, Tarif. *Arabic Historical Thought in the Classical Period*. New York: Cambridge University Press, 1994.

Khalidi, Walid. *All That Remains: The Palestinian Villages Occupied and Depopulated by Israel in 1948*. Beirut: Institute for Palestine Studies, 1992.

Khalili, Laleh. *Heroes and Martyrs of Palestine: The Politics of National Commemoration*. New York: Cambridge University Press, 2007.

Khanna, Ranjana. *Algeria Cuts: Women and Representation, 1830 to the Present*. Stanford: Stanford University Press, 2008.

———. *Dark Continents: Psychoanalysis and Colonialism*. Durham: Duke University Press, 2003.

al-Kharrat, Idwar. "Akhir Ayyam al-'Amid." In *al-Hissasiyya al-jadida: maqalat fi al-zahira al-qissasiyya*, 88–94. Beirut: Dar al-Adab, 1993.

———. "Min a'la namadhij al-hissasiyya al-qadima: al-qadariyya wa al-anmat al-ra'isiyya fi 'alim Najib Mahfuz." In *al-Hissasiyya al-jadida*, 37–58. Beirut: Dar al-Adab, 1993.

Khatibi, Abdelkabir. *La blessure du nom propre*. Paris: Denoël, 1974.

———. "L'envol des raciness" (French with English translation). In *Ahmed Cherkaoui: La passion du signe*, 15–23. Paris: Institut du Monde Arabe, 1996.

———. *Maghreb pluriel*. Paris: Denoël, 1983.

al-Khawalida, Fathi Rizq. *Tahlil al-khitab al-shi'ri: thuna'iyyat al-itisaq wa al-insijam fi diwan "Ahada 'ashara kawkaban."* 'Amman: Azmina li al-Nashr wa al-Tawzi', 2006.

Khoury, Elias. *Abwab al-madina*. Beirut: Dar al-Adab, 1981. Tr. Paula Haydar as *Gates of the City*. Minneapolis: University of Minnesota Press, 1993.

———. "al-Akhta' . . . al-addad." *al-Tariq* 3 (May–June 1996): 152–57.

———. *Bab al-shams*. Beirut: Dar al-Adab, 1998. Tr. Humphry Davies as *Gate of the Sun*. New York: Archipelago, 2006.

———. "al-Batal al-filastini fi qissas Ghassan Kanafani." In *Ghassan Kanafani: insanan, adiban, wa munadilan*, ed. Ihsan 'Abbas, Fadl al-Naqib, and Elias Khoury, 85–130. Beirut: al-Ittihad al-'Am li al-Kuttab wa al-Sahafiyyin al-Filastiniyyin, 1974.

———. *al-Dhakira al-mafquda*. Beirut: Dar al-Adab, 1990.

———. *Dirasat fi naqd al-shi'r*. Beirut: Mu'assasat al-Abhath al-'Arabiyya, 1979.

———. "Hikayat al-diwan al-akhir li Mahmoud Darwish." *al-Karmel* 90 (Spring 2009): 23–36.

———. *al-Jabal al-saghir*. Beirut: Dar al-Adab, 1977.

———. *Ka'annaha na'ima*. Beirut: Dar al-Adab, 2007.

———. *Mamlakat al-ghuraba'*. Beirut: Dar al-Adab, 1993.

———. "Min ajli nahda thalitha." *al-Tariq* 1 (January–February 2002): 28 39.

———. *Rihlat Ghandi al-saghir*. Beirut: Dar al-Adab, 1989.

———. "Rita wa shi'riyyat al-muthanna." *al-Tariq* (March–April 2001): 126–41.

———. *Sinalkul*. Beirut: Dar al-Adab, 2012.

———. "Su'al al-nakba: al-sira' bayna al-hadir wa al-ta'wil, Idward Sa'id wa Mas'alat Filastin." *al-Karmel* 78 (Winter 2004): 46–55.

———. *Tajribat al-bahth 'an ufuq: muqaddima li dirasat al-riwaya al-'arabiyya ba'd al-hazima*. Beirut: Munazzamat al-Tahrir al-Filastiniyya, Markaz al-Abhath, 1974.

———. *al-Wujuh al-bayda'*. Beirut: Mu'assasat al-Abhath al-'Arabiyya, 1986 [1981].

———. *Yalu*. Beirut: Dar al-Adab, 2002.

———. *Zaman al-ihtilal*. Beirut: Mu'assasat al-Abhath al-'Arabiyya, 1985.

Khuri-Makdisi, Ilham. *The Eastern Mediterranean and the Making of Global Radicalism, 1860–1914*. Berkeley: University of Calfornia Press, 2010.

Kilito, Abdelfattah. *L'oeil et l'aiguille: Essais sur "les mille et un nuits."* Paris: Decouverte, 1992.

———. *Les séances: Récites et codes culturels chez Hamadhani et Hariri*. Paris: Sindbad, 1983.

Kilpatrick, Hilary. "Literary Creativity and the Cultural Heritage: The *Atlal* in Modern Arabic Fiction." In *Tradition, Modernity, and Postmodernity in Arabic Literature*, ed. Kamal Abdel-Malek and Wael Hallaq, 28–44. Leiden: Brill, 2000.

———. *The Modern Egyptian Novel: A Study in Social Criticism*. London: Ithaca Press, 1974.

Kirecci, Mehmet Akif. "Decline Discourse and Self-Orientalization in the Writings of Al-Tahtawi, Taha Husayn, and Ziya Gökalp: A Comparative Study of Modernization in Egypt and Turkey." Ph.D. dissertation. University of Pennsylvania, 2007.

Kittler, Friedrich. *Discourse Networks 1800/1900*. Tr. Michael Metteer, with Chris Cullens. Stanford: Stanford University Press, 1990.

Kofman, Sarah. *Lectures de Derrida*. Paris: Galilée, 1984.

Koselleck, Reinhart. *Futures Past: On the Semantics of Historical Time*. Tr. Keith Tribe. Cambridge, MA: MIT Press, 1985.

Kurayyam, Samih. *Ma'arik Taha Husayn*. Beirut: Dar al-Qalam, 1977.

Lacoue-Labarthe-Philippe. "The Echo of the Subject." In *Typography: Mimesis, Philosophy, Politics*, ed. Christopher Fynsk, 139–207. Stanford: Stanford University Press, 1998.

Lacoue-Labarthe, Philippe, and Jean-Luc Nancy. *L'absolu littéraire: Théorie de la littérature du romantisme allemande*. Paris: Seuil, 1978. Tr. Philip Barnard and Cheryl Lester as *The Literary Absolute: The Theory of Literature in German Romanticism*. Albany: State University of New York Press, 1988.

Laor, Yitzhak. *Anu kotvim otakh moledet*. Tel Aviv: Ha Kibbutz Ha Miuchad, 1995.

Larkin, Margaret. *The Theology of Meaning: 'Abd al-Qahir al-Jurjani's Theory of Discourse*. New Haven: American Oriental Society, 1995.

Laroui, Abdallah. *The Crisis of the Arab Intellectual: Traditionalism or Historicism?* Tr. Diarmid Cammell. Berkeley: University of California Press, 1976.

———. *L'idéologie arab contemporaine*. Paris: Maspero, 1977.

Layoun, Mary N. "Between Here and There: National Community from the

Inside Out and the Outside In—Palestine 1982." In *Wedded to the Land: Gender, Boundaries, and Nationalism in Crisis*, 127–62. Durham: Duke University Press, 2001.

———. *Travels of a Genre: The Modern Novel and Ideology.* Princeton: Princeton University Press, 1990.

Lennon, Brian. *In Babel's Shadow: Multilingual Literatures, Monolingual States.* Minneapolis: University of Minnesota Press, 2010.

Levy, Lital. "'From Baghdad to Bialik with Love': A Reappropriation of Modern Hebrew Poetry, 1933." *Comparative Literature Studies* 42.3 (2005): 125–54.

———. "Historicizing the Concept of Arab Jews in the Mashriq." *Jewish Quarterly Review* 98.4 (Fall 2008): 452–69.

———. "Jewish Writers in the Arab East: Literature, History, and the Politics of Enlightenment, 1863–1914." Ph.D. dissertation, University of California, Berkeley, 2007.

———. "Reorienting Literary History: The View from the East." *Prooftexts* 29.2 (Spring 2009): 127–72.

Lloyd, David. *Anomalous States: Irish Writing and the Post-Colonial Moment.* Durham: Duke University Press, 1993.

———. "The Indigent Sublime: Specters of Irish Hunger." *Representations* 92.1 (Fall 2005): 152–85.

———. "The Memory of Hunger." In *Loss: The Politics of Mourning*, ed. David L. Eng and David Kazanjian, 205–28. Berkeley: University of California Press, 2003.

Lockman, Zachary. *Comrades and Enemies: Arab and Jewish Workers in Palestine, 1906–1948.* Berkeley: University of California Press, 1996.

———. "Imagining the Working Class: Culture, Nationalism, and Class Formation in Egypt, 1899–1914." *Poetics Today* 15.2 (Summer 1994): 157–90.

Louca, Anouar. *Voyagers et écrivains égyptiens en France aux XIX siècle.* Paris: Didier, 1970.

Love, Heather. *Feeling Backward: Loss and the Politics of Queer History.* Cambridge, MA: Harvard University Press, 2007.

Lowry, Joseph E. *Early Islamic Legal Theory: The Risala of Muhammad ibn Idris al-Shafi'i.* Leiden: Brill, 2007.

Lyotard, Jean-François. *Lessons on the Analytic of the Sublime.* Tr. Elizabeth Rottenberg. Stanford: Stanford University Press, 1994.

MacBride, Sean. *Israel in Lebanon: Report of the International Commission to Inquire into Reported Violations of International Law by Israel during Its Invasion of Lebanon.* London: Ithaca, 1983.

Maghraoui, Abdeslam M. *Liberalism without Democracy: Nationhood and Citizenship in Egypt, 1922–1936*. Durham: Duke University Press, 2006.

Mahdi, Muhsin. *Alfarabi and the Foundation of Islamic Political Philosophy*. Foreword Charles E. Butterworth. Chicago: University of Chicago Press, 2001.

———. *Ibn Khaldun's Philosophy of History*. Chicago: University of Chicago Press, 1964 [1957].

Mahfuz, Najib. *Awlad haritna*. Beirut: Dar al-Adab, 1986 [1959].

———. *Bayn al-qasrayn*. Cairo: Maktabat Misr, n.d. [1956].

———. *Qasr al-shawq*. Cairo: Maktabat Misr, n.d. [1957].

———. *al-Sukariyya*. Cairo: Maktabat Misr, n.d. [1957].

Mahmood, Saba. *Politics of Piety: The Islamic Revival and the Feminist Subject*. Princeton: Princeton University Press, 2005.

———. "Religious Freedom, the Minority Question, and Geopolitics in the Middle East." *Comparative Studies in Society and History* 54.2 (2012): 418–46.

———. "Secularism, Hermeneutics, and Empire: The Politics of Islamic Reformation." *Public Culture* 18.2 (2006): 323–47.

Mahmoudi, Abdelrashid. *Taha Husain's Education: From the Azhar to the Sorbonne*. Richmond, Surrey: Curzon, 1998.

Makdisi, George. *The Rise of Colleges: Institutions of Learning in Islam and the West*. Edinburgh: Edinburgh University Press, 1981.

Makdisi, Saree. "Laying Claim to Beirut: Urban Narrative and Spatial Identity in the Age of Solidere." *Critical Inquiry* 23.3 (Spring 1997): 660–705.

———. *Romantic Imperialism: Universal Empire and the Culture of Modernity*. New York: Cambridge University Press, 1998.

Makdisi, Ussama. *Artillery of Heaven: American Missionaries and the Failed Conversion of the Middle East*. Ithaca: Cornell University Press, 2008.

———. *The Culture of Sectarianism: Community, History, and Violence in Nineteenth-Century Ottoman Lebanon*. Berkeley: University of California Press, 2000.

———. "Ottoman Orientalism." *American Historical Review* 107.3 (June 2002): 768–96.

Malabou, Catherine. *The Future of Hegel: Plasticity, Temporality, and Dialectic*. Tr. Lisabeth During. London: Routledge, 2005.

Malti-Douglas, Fedwa. *Blindness and Autobiography: Al-Ayyam of Taha Husayn*. Princeton: Princeton University Press, 1988.

Mandur, Muhammad. *al-Naqd wa al-nuqqad al-mu'asirun*. Cairo: Nahdat Misr, 1997.

Marchand, Suzanne L. *German Orientalism in the Age of Empire: Religion, Race and Scholarship*. Cambridge: Cambridge University Press, 2009.

Marder, Elissa. *The Mother in the Age of Mechanical Reproduction: Psychoanalysis, Photography, Deconstruction*. New York: Fordham University Press, 2012.

Marrati, Paola. *Genesis and Trace: Derrida Reading Husserl and Heidegger*. Tr. Simon Sparks. Stanford: Stanford University Press, 2005.

al-Marsafi, Husayn. *Risalat al-kalim al-thamin*. Beirut: Dar al-Tali'a, 1982 [1881].

———. *al-Wasila al-adabiyya ila al-'ulum al-'arabiyya*. 2 vols. Cairo: al-Hay'a al-Misriyya al-'Amma li al-Kitab, 1982 [1872–75].

Marx, Karl, and Friedrich Engels. *Manifest der Kommunistischen Partei*. Philipp Reclam: Stuttgart, 1999 [1848]. *The Communist Manifesto*. Tr. Samuel Moore. London: Verso, 1998.

Masalha, Nur. *Expulsion of the Palestinians: The Concept of "Transfer" in Zionist Political Thought, 1882–1948*. Beirut: Institute for Palestine Studies, 1992.

Mas'ad, Bulus. *Faris al-Shidyaq*. Cairo: Matba'at al-Ikha', 1934.

Massad, Joseph. *Colonial Effects: The Making of National Identity in Jordan*. New York: Columbia University Press, 2001.

———. *Desiring Arabs*. Chicago: University of Chicago Press, 2007.

———. *The Persistence of the Palestinian Question*. New York: Routledge, 2006.

Massignon, Louis. *Muhadarat fi tarikh al-istilahat al-falsafiyya*. Cairo: al-Ma'had al 'Ilmi al-Faransi li al-Athar al-Sharqiyya, 1983.

Masters, Bruce. *The Origins of Western Economic Dominance in the Middle East: Mercantilism and the Islamic Economy in Aleppo, 1600–1750*. New York: New York University Press, 1987.

Masuzawa, Tomoko. *The Invention of World Religions, Or, How European Universalism Was Preserved in the Language of Pluralism*. Chicago: University of Chicago Press, 2005.

al-Mazini, Ibrahim 'Abd al-Qader. *Ibrahim al-katib*. Beirut: Dar al-Mada, 2004 [1931].

Mbembe, Achille. *On the Postcolony*. Berkeley: University of California Press, 2001.

Mehrez, Samia. *Egyptian Writers between History and Fiction: Essays on Naguib Mahfouz, Sonallah Ibrahim, and Gamal al-Ghitani*. Cairo: American University in Cairo Press, 1994.

Mejchar, Sonja. "'Abwab al-madina': madina la isma laha wa la dhakira." *al-Tariq* (January–February 2001): 83–90.

Melas, Natalie. *All the Difference in the World: Postcoloniality and the Ends of Comparison*. Stanford: Stanford University Press, 2007.

Melehi, Mohamed, ed. *La peinture de Ahmed Cherkaoui*. Casablanca: Shoof Publications, 1976.

Menocal, Maria Rosa. *The Arabic Role in Medieval Literary History: A Forgotten Heritage*. Philadelphia: University of Pennsylvania Press, 2004 [1987].

Messick, Brinkley. *The Calligraphic State: Textual Domination and History in a Muslim Society*. Berkeley: University of California Press, 1993.

Meyer, Stefan G. *The Experimental Arabic Novel: Postcolonial Literary Modernsim in the Levant*. Albany: State University of New York Press, 2001.

Miskawayh, Ahmad ibn Muhammad. *Tahdhib al-akhlaq*. Beirut: Dar Maktabat al-Hayat, 1961.

Mitchell, Timothy. *Colonising Egypt*. Berkeley: University of California Press, 1991 [1988].

———. "The Limits of the State: Beyond Statist Approaches and Their Critics." *American Political Science Review* 85.1 (March 1991): 77–96.

———. *Rule of Experts: Egypt, Techno-Politics, Modernity*. Berkeley: University of California Press, 2002.

Moosa, Matti. *The Origins of Modern Arabic Fiction*. Boulder: Lynne Reiner, 1997.

Moreh, Shmuel. *Modern Arabic Poetry, 1800–1970*. Leiden: Brill, 1976.

Mufti, Aamir R. *Enlightenment in the Colony: The Jewish Question and the Crisis of Postcolonial Culture*. Princeton: Princeton University Press, 2007.

———. "Global Comparativism." *Critical Inquiry* 31.2 (Winter 2005): 472–89.

———. "Orientalism and the Institution of World Literatures." *Critical Inquiry* 36.3 (Spring 2010): 458–93.

al-Musawi, Muhsin J. *Arabic Poetry: Trajectories of Modernity and Tradition*. London: Routledge, 2006.

———. "Arabic Rhetoric." In *Oxford Encyclopaedia of Rhetoric,* ed. Thomas O. Sloane, 29–33. Oxford: Oxford University Press, 2001.

———. *The Islamic Context of the Thousand and One Nights*. New York: Columbia University Press, 2009.

———. *al-Istishraq fi al-fikr al-'arabi*. Beirut: al-Mu'assasa al-'Arabiyya li al-Dirasa wa al-Nashr, 1993.

———. *al-Riwaya al-'arabiyya: al-nasha'at wa al-tahawwul*. Beirut: Dar al-Adab, 1988.

Mustafa, Shakir. *al-Qissa fi Suriyya hatta al-harb al-'alamiyya al-thaniyya*. Cairo: Ma'had al-Buhuth wa al-Dirasat al-'Arabiyya, 1958.

al-Mutawwi, Muhammad al-Hadi. *Ahmad Faris al-Shidyaq, 1801–1887: hayatuhu wa atharuhu wa ara'uhu fi al-nahda al-'arabiyya al-haditha*. Beirut: Dar al-Gharb al-Islami, 1989.

Muthu, Sankar. *Enlightenment against Empire*. Princeton: Princeton University Press, 2003.

al-Muwaylihi, Muhammad. *Hadith 'Isa Ibn Hisham*. In *al-A'mal al-kamila*, vol. 1, ed. Roger Allen. Cairo: al-Majlis al-a'la li al-thaqafa, 2002.

Myers, David N. *Re-Inventing the Jewish Past: European Jewish Intellectuals and the Zionist Return to History*. New York: Oxford University Press, 1995.

Naas, Michael. *Miracle and Machine: Jacques Derrida and the Two Sources of Religion, Science, and the Media*. New York: Fordham University Press, 2012.

al-Nabulsi, Shakir. *Majnun al-turab: dirasa fi shi'r wa fikr Mahmoud Darwish*. Beirut: al-Mu'assasa al-'Arabiyya li al-Dirasa wa al-Nashr, 1987.

Nallino, Carlo. *Tarikh al-adab al-'arabiyya: min al-jahiliyya hatta 'asr Bani Umayya*. Cairo: Dar al-Ma'arif, 1970.

Nancy, Jean-Luc. *Le poids d'une pensée*. Grenoble: Presses Universitaires de Grenoble, 1991.

Nandy, Ashis. *The Intimate Enemy: Loss and Recovery of Self under Colonialism*. Delhi: Oxford University Press, 1983.

al-Naqqash, Raja'. *Mahmoud Darwish: sha'ir al-ard al-muhtalla*. Beirut: Mu'assasat al-Abhath al-'Arabiyya, 1972.

Naqvi, Nauman. "Acts of Askesis, Scenes of Poiesis: The Dramatic Phenomenology of Another Violence in a Muslim Painter-Poet." *diacritics* 40.2 (2012): 50–71.

Nasir, Amjad. "Mahmoud Darwish wa qasidat al-nathr." *al-Karmel* 90 (Spring 2009): 111–17.

The New Oxford Annotated Bible. Ed. Herbert G. May and Bruce M. Metzger. New York: Oxford University Press, 1971.

Newmark, Kevin. *Irony on Occasion: From Schlegel to Kierkegaard to Derrida and de Man*. New York: Fordham University Press, 2012.

Nichanian, Marc. "Catastrophic Mourning." Tr. Jeff Fort. In *Loss: The Politics of Mourning*, ed. David L. Eng and David Kazanjian, 99–124. Berkeley: University of California Press, 2003.

———. *Mourning Philology: Art and Religion at the Margins of the Ottoman Empire*. Tr. G. M. Goshgarian and Jeff Fort. New York: Fordham University Press, 2014.

———. "Mourning and Reconciliation." Tr. Catherine Coquio. In *Living Together: Jacques Derrida's Communities of Violence and Peace*, ed. Elisabeth Weber, 191–210. New York: Fordham University Press, 2013.

———. "On the Archive III: The Secret; or, Borges at Yale." Tr. Gil Anidjar. *boundary 2* 40.3 (2013): 1–38.

Nietzsche, Friedrich. *Morgenröte*. In *Kritische Studienausgabe*, vol. 3, ed. Giorgio Colli and Mazzino Montinari, 9–332. Berlin: Walter de Gruyter, 1999. Tr. R. J. Hollingdale as *Daybreak*. New York: Cambridge University Press, 1997.

Niranjana, Tejaswini. *Siting Translation: History, Post-Structuralism, and the Colonial Context*. Berkeley: University of California Press, 1992.

Nur, Muhammad. *Qarar al-niyaba*. In *Muhakamat Taha Husayn*, ed. and introd. Khayri Shalabi, 55-99. Alexandria: Dar al-Mustaqbal, 1994 [1927].

Nüsse, Heinrich. *Die Sprachtheorie Friedrich Schlegels*. Heidelberg: Carl Winter Universitatsverlag, 1962.

Olender, Maurice. *The Languages of Paradise: Race, Religion, and Philology in the Nineteenth Century*. Tr. Arthur Goldhammer. Cambridge, MA: Harvard University Press, 2008 [1992].

Orfali, Bilal. "A Sketch Map of Arabic Poetry Anthologies up the Fall of Baghdad." *Journal of Arabic Literature* 43 (2012): 29–59.

Owens, Jonathan. "Models for Interpreting the Development of Medieval Arabic Grammatical Theory." *Journal of the American Oriental Society* 111.2 (April–June 1991): 225–38.

Pape, Ilan. *The Ethnic Cleansing of Palestine*. Oxford: Oneworld, 2007.

Patel, Abdulrazzak. "Language Reform and Controversy in the Nahda: Al-Shartuni's Position as a Grammarian in *Sahm*." *Journal of Semitic Studies* 55.2 (Autumn 2010): 509–38.

Peirce, Leslie P. *The Imperial Harem: Women and Sovereignty in the Ottoman Empire*. New York: Oxford University Press, 1993.

Peled, Mattityahu. "al-Saq 'ala al-saq: A Generic Definition." *Arabica* 32.1 (March 1985): 31–46.

Peters, Rudolph. "Administrators and Magistrates: The Development of a Secular Judiciary in Egypt, 1842–1871." *Die Welt des Islams* 39.3 (November 1999): 378–97.

———. "'For His Correction and as a Deterrent Example for Others':

Mehmed 'Ali's First Criminal Legislation (1829–1830)." *Islamic Law and Society* 6.2 (1999): 164–92.

———. "Islamic and Secular Criminal Law in Nineteenth-Century Egypt: The Role and Function of the Qadi." *Islamic Law and Society* 4.1 (1997): 70–90.

Philliou, Christine M. *Biography of an Empire: Governing Ottomans in an Age of Revolution*. Berkeley: University of California Press, 2011.

Piterberg, Gabriel. *An Ottoman Tragedy: History and Historiography at Play*. Berkeley: University of California Press, 2003.

———. *The Returns of Zionism: Myths, Politics, and Scholarship in Israel*. London: Verso, 2008.

———. "The Tropes of Stagnation and Awakening in Nationalist Historical Consciousness: The Egyptian Case." In *Rethinking Nationalism in the Arab Middle East*, ed. James Jankowski and Israel Gershoni, 42–61. New York: Columbia University Press, 1997.

Pollard, Lisa. *Nurturing the Nation: The Family Politics of Modernizing, Colonizing, and Liberating Egypt, 1805–1923*. Berkeley: University of California Press, 2005.

Powell, Eve M. Troutt. *A Different Shade of Colonialism: Egypt, Great Britain, and the Mastery of the Sudan*. Berkeley: University of California Press, 2003.

Qader, Nasrin. *Narratives of Catastrophe: Boris Diop, ben Jelloun, Khatibi*. New York: Fordham University Press, 2009.

Rafael, Vincente L. *Contracting Colonialism: Translation and Christain Conversion in Tagalog Society under Early Spanish Rule*. Durham: Duke University Press, 2005 [1988].

Rahman, Najat. *Literary Disinheritance: The Writing of Home in the Work of Mahmoud Darwish and Assia Djebar*. Lanham, MD: Lexington Books, 2008.

Rastegar, Kamran. *Literary Modernity between the Middle East and Europe: Textual Transactions in Nineteenth-Century Arabic, Persian, and English Literatures*. New York: Routledge, 2010 [2007].

Raz-Krakotzkin, Amnon. *The Censor, the Editor, and the Text: The Catholic Church and the Shaping of the Jewish Canon in the Sixteenth Century*. Tr. Jackie Feldman. Philadelphia: University of Pennsylvania Press, 2007.

———. *Exil et souveraineté: Judaïsme, sionisme et pensée binationale*. Tr. Catherine Neuve-Eglise. Paris: La Fabrique, 2007.

———. "Galut be toch ribonut: le bikoret 'Shlilat ha galut' ba tarbut ha israelit" (Part I). *Theory and Criticism* (Fall 1993): 23–55.

———. "Galut be toch ribonut: le bikoret 'Shlilat ha galut' ba tarbut ha israelit" (Part II). *Theory and Criticism* (Fall 1994): 113–32.

———. "Jewish Memory between Exile and History." *Jewish Quarterly Review* 97.4 (Fall 2007): 530–43.

———. "A National Colonial Theology: Religion, Orientalism, and the Construction of the Secular in Zionist Discourse." *Tel Aviver Jahrbuch fur deutsche Geschichte* 30 (2002): 312–26.

———. "'On the Right Side of the Barricades': Walter Benjamin, Gershom Scholem, and Zionism." *Comparative Literature* 65.3 (2013): 363–81.

———. "The Zionist Return to the West and the Mizrahi Jewish Perspective." In *Orientalism and the Jews*, ed. Ivan Davidson Kalmar and Derek J. Pinslar, 161–81. Waltham, MA: Brandeis University Press, 2005.

Redfield, Marc. "De Man, Schiller, and the Politics of Reception." In *The Politics of Aesthetics: Nationalism, Gender, Romanticism*, 95–124. Stanford: Stanford University Press, 2003.

———. *Phantom Formations: Aesthetic Ideology and the Bildungsroman*. Ithaca: Cornell University Press, 1995.

———. *The Rhetoric of Terror: Reflections on 9/11 and the War on Terror*. New York: Fordham University Press, 2009.

Ricciardi, Alessia. *The Ends of Mourning: Psychoanalysis, Literature, Film*. Stanford: Stanford University Press, 2003.

Rickels, Laurence. *Aberrations of Mourning: Writing on German Crypts*. Minneapolis: University of Minnesota Press, 2011 [1988].

Robbins, Jill. *Prodigal Son/Elder Brother: Interpretation and Alterity in Augustine, Petrarch, Kafka, Levinas*. Chicago: University of Chicago Press, 1991.

Ronell, Avital. *Crack Wars: Literature, Addiction, Mania*. Lincoln: University of Nebraska Press, 1992.

———. *Dictations: On Haunted Writing*. Lincoln: University of Nebraska Press, 1993 [1986].

———. *Loser Sons: Politics and Authority*. Urbana: University of Illinois Press, 2012.

———. "On the Misery of Theory without Poetry: Heidegger's Reading of Hölderlin's 'Andenken.'" *PMLA* 120.1 (January 2005): 16–32.

———. *Stupidity*. Urbana: University of Illinois Press, 2002.

———. *The Telephone Book: Technology—Schizophrenia—Electric Speech*. Lincoln: University of Nebraska Press, 1989.

———. *The Test Drive*. Urbana: University of Illinois Press, 2005.

Roper, Geoffrey. "Ahmad Faris al-Shidyaq and the Libraries of Europe and the Ottoman Empire." *Libraries & Culture* 33.3 (Summer 1998): 233–48.

———. "Faris al-Shidyaq and the Transition from Scribal to Print Culture in the Middle East." In *The Book in the Islamic World: The Written Word and Communication in the Middle East*, ed. George N. Atiyeh, 209–31. Albany: State University of New York Press, 1995.

Rosenthal, Lecia. *Mourning Modernism: Literature, Catastrophe, and the Politics of Consolation*. New York: Fordham University Press, 2011.

Rosenthal, Franz. *Knowledge Triumphant: The Concept of Knowledge in Medieval Islam*. Leiden: Brill, 1970.

Rottenberg, Elizabeth. *Inheriting the Future: Legacies of Kant, Freud, and Flaubert*. Stanford: Stanford University Press, 2005.

Rudwan, Abu al-Futuh. *Tarikh matba'at Bulaq*. Cairo: al-Matba'a al-Amiriyya, 1953.

Sacks, Jeffrey. "For Decolonization." *Arab Studies Journal* 17.1 (Spring 2009): 110–28.

———. "Futures of Literature: Inhitat, Adab, Naqd." *diacritics* 37.4 (Winter 2007): 32–55.

———. "Untranslatability, or, Mourning Translation (Darwish with Schmitt and Agamben)." *MLN: Modern Language Notes* 126.5 (December 2011): 1083–1122.

Sa'di, Ahmad H., and Lila Abu-Lughod, eds. *Nakba: Palestine, 1948, and the Claims of Memory*. New York: Columbia University Press, 2007.

Said, Edward W. *After the Last Sky: Palestinian Lives*. New York: Columbia University Press, 1999 [1986].

———. "After Mahfouz." In *Reflections on Exile and Other Essays*, 317–26. Cambridge, MA: Harvard University Press, 2000.

———. *Beginnings: Intention and Method*. New York: Columbia University Press, 1985 [1975].

———. *Culture and Imperialism*. New York: Vintage, 1993.

———. *On Late Style: Music and Literature against the Grain*. New York: Vintage, 2006.

———. "On Mahmoud Darwish." *Grand Street* 12.48 (1994): 112–15.

———. *Orientalism*. New York: Vintage, 1978.

———. *The Question of Palestine*. New York: Vintage, 1979.

———. "The Return to Philology." In *Humanism and Democratic Criticism*, 57–84. New York: Columbia University Press, 2004.

———. *The World, the Text, and the Critic*. Cambridge, MA: Harvard University Press, 1983.

Sajdi, Dana. *The Barber of Damascus: Nouveau Literacy in the Eighteenth-Century Levant*. Stanford: Stanford University Press, 2013.

Salem, Elise. *Constructing Lebanon: A Century of Literary Narratives*. Gainesville: University Press of Florida, 2003.

Salih, 'Aliya Mamduh. *al-Bina' al-sardi fi riwayat Elias Khoury.* 'Amman: Azmina li al-Nashr wa al-Tawzi', 2005.

Salim, Hilmi. *al-Thaqafa taht al-hisar.* Cairo: Dar Shuhdi, 1984.

Saussy, Haun. *The Problem of a Chinese Aesthetic.* Stanford: Stanford University Press, 1995.

Sawaie, Mohammed. "Rifa' Rafi' al-Tahtawi and His Contribution to the Lexical Development of Modern Literary Arabic." *International Journal of Middle East Studies* 32 (2000): 395–410.

Sayigh, Rosemary. *The Palestinians: From Peasants to Revolutionaries.* London: Zed, 2007 [1979].

———. *Too Many Enemies: The Palestinian Experience in Lebanon.* London: Zed, 1994.

Schelling, Friedrich. "Das älteste Systemprogramm des Deutschen Idealismus." In *Briefe und Dokumente,* ed. Horst Fuhrmans. Bonn: H. Bouvier, 1961. Tr. H. S. Harris as "The Earliest System-Program of German Idealism," in H. S. Harris, *Hegel's Development toward the Sunlight, 1770–1801.* Oxford: Clarendon Press, 1972.

Schlegel, Friedrich. *Friedrich Schlegel's Lucinde and the Fragments.* Tr. Peter Firchow. Minneapolis: University of Minnesota Press, 1971.

———. *Kritische Friedrich Schlegel Ausgabe.* 35 vols. Ed. Ernst Behler. Paderborn: Verlag Ferdinand Schöningh.

———. *Lessings Geist aus seinen Schriften.* In *Kritische Schriften,* ed. Wolfdietrich Rasch. Munich: Carl Hanser Verlag, 1970.

———. *On the Language and Wisdom of the Indians.* Tr. E. J. Millington in *The Aesthetic and Miscellaneous Works of Frederick von Schlegel.* London: Henry G. Bohn, 1849.

Schmitt, Carl. *Der Nomos der Erde.* Berlin: Duncker & Humblot, 1997 [1950]. Tr. G. L. Ulmen as *The Nomos of the Earth.* New York: Telos, 2006.

———. *Politische Theologie: Vier Kapitel zur Lehre von der Souveränität.* Berlin: Duncker & Humblot, 2004 [1922]. Tr. George Schwab as *Political Theology: Four Chapters on the Concept of Sovereignty.* Chicago: University of Chicago Press, 2005 [1985].

Schulze, Reinhard. "Mass Culture and Islamic Cultural Production in the Nineteenth-Century Middle East." In *Mass Culture, Popular Culture, and Social Life in the Middle East,* ed. Georg Stauth and Sami Zubaida, 189–222. Boulder: Westview Press, 1987.

Schwab, Raymond. *The Oriental Renaissance.* Introd. Edward W. Said. Tr. Gene Patterson-Black and Victor Reinking. New York: Columbia University Press, 1984.

Scott, David. *Conscripts of Modernity: The Tragedy of Colonial Enlightenment.* Durham: Duke University Press, 2004.

———. *Refashioning Futures: Criticism after Postcoloniality.* Princeton: Princeton University Press, 1999.

Sedra, Paul. *From Mission to Modernity: Evangelicals, Reformers and Education in Nineteenth-Century Egypt.* London: I. B. Tauris, 2011.

Seeman, Khalil I. *Linguistics in the Middle Ages: Phonetic Studies in Early Islam.* Leiden: Brill, 1968.

Seigneurie, Ken. *Standing by the Ruins: Elegiac Humanism in Wartime and Postwar Lebanon.* New York: Fordham University Press, 2011.

Seikaly, Sherene. "Return to the Present." In *Living Together: Jacques Derrida's Communities of Violence and Peace*, ed. Elisabeth Weber, 227–39. New York: Fordham University Press, 2013.

Selim, Samah. "Fiction and Colonial Identities: Arsène Lupin in Arabic." *Middle Eastern Literatures* 13.2 (August 2010): 191–210.

———. "Languages of Civilization: Nation, Translation and the Politics of Race in Colonial Egypt." *Translator* 15.1 (2009): 139–156.

———. "The Narrative Craft: Realism and Fiction in the Arabic Canon." *Edebiyat* 14.1–2 (2003): 109–28.

———. *The Novel and the Rural Imaginary in Egypt, 1880–1985.* New York: Routledge, 2004.

———. "The People's Entertainments: Translation, Popular Fiction, and the Nahda in Egypt." In *Other Renaissances: A New Approach to World Literature,* ed. Brenda Deen Schildgen, Gang Zhou, and Sander L. Gilman, 35–58. New York: Palgrave Macmillan, 2006.

Sells, Michael. "Sound, Spirit, and Gender in Surat al-Qadr." *Journal of the American Oriental Society* 111.2 (April–June 1991): 239–59.

Serfaty, Abraham. *Ecrits de prison sur la Palestine.* Paris: Arcantere, 1992.

al-Shafi'i, Muhammad ibn Idris. *al-Risala.* Ed. 'Abd al-Latif al-Humaym and Mahir Yasin al-Fahl. Beirut: Dar al-Kutub al-'Ilmiyya, 2005.

———. *al-Shafi'i's Risala: Treatise on the Foundations of Islamic Jurisprudence.* Tr. and introd. Majid Khadduri. Baltimore: Johns Hopkins University Press, 1961.

Shafir, Gershon. *Land, Labor, and the Origins of the Israeli-Palestinian Conflict, 1882–1914.* Berkeley: University of California Press, 1996.

al-Shaikh, Abdul-Rahim. "Palestine: The Nomadic Condition." *Third Text* 23.6 (November 2009): 763–78.

Shaked, Gershon. *Modern Hebrew Fiction.* Ed. Emily Miller Budick. Tr. Yael Lotan. Bloomington: Indiana University Press, 2002.

Shammas, Anton. *Arabeskot.* Tel Aviv: Am Oved, 1986. Tr. Vivan Eden as *Arabesques.* Berkeley: University of California Press, 2001.

al-Shayyal, Jamal al-Din. *Tarikh al-tarjama wa al-haraka al-thaqafiyya fi 'asr Mehmed 'Ali*. Cairo: Dar al-Fikr al-'Arabi, 1951.

Sheehan, Jonathan. *The Enlightenment Bible: Translation, Scholarship, Culture*. Princeton: Princeton University Press, 2005.

Sheehi, Stephen. "Arabic Literary-Scientific Journals: Precedence for Globalization and the Creation of Modernity." *Comparative Studies of South Asia, Africa, and the Middle East* 25.2 (2005): 438–48.

———. "Epistemography of the Modern Arab Subject: al-Mu'allim Butrus al-Bustani's *Khutbah fi adab al-'arab*." *Public* 16 (Fall 1997): 65–85.

———. *Foundations of Modern Arab Identity*. Gainesville: University Press of Florida, 2004.

———. "The Nahda After-Image, Or All Photography Expresses Social Relations." *Third Text* 26.4 (2012): 401–14.

———. "A Social History of Early Arab Photography, Or a Prolegomenon to an Archaeology of the Lebanese Imago." *International Journal of Middle East Studies* 39 (2007): 177–208.

———. "Towards a Critical Theory of al-Nahdah: Epistemology, Ideology and Capital." *Journal of Arabic Literature* 43 (2012): 269–98.

Shiblak, Abbas. *Iraqi Jews: A History of Mass Exodus*. London: Saqi, 2005 [1986].

al-Shidyaq, Ahmad Faris. *al-Jasus 'ala al-qamus*. Istanbul: Matba'at al-Jawa'ib, 1881.

———. *Kanz al-ragha'ib fi muntakhibat al-Jawa'ib*. 7 vols. Istanbul: Matba'at al-jawa'ib, 1871–81.

———. *Kitab ghunyat al-talib wa munyat al-raghib: durus fi al-sarf wa al-nahu wa huruf al-ma'ani*. Susa, Tunis: Dar al-Ma'arif li al-Tiba'a wa al-Nashr, 1992 [1871].

———. *Kitab al-saq 'ala al-saq fi ma huwwa al-Fariyaq*. Ed. Darwish Juwaidi. Beirut: al-Dar al-Namudhajiyya li al-Dirasa wa al-Nashr, 2006.

———. *Kitab al-saq 'ala al-saq fi ma huwwa al-Fariyaq, aw ayam wa shuhur wa a'wam fi 'ajam al-'Arab wa al-a'jam*. Paris: Benjamin Duprat, 1855.

———. *al-Kitabat al-majhula li Ahmad Faris al-Shidyaq*. Ed. Fawwaz Traboulsi and Aziz al-Azmeh. Beirut: Riyad al-Rayyes, 1995.

———. *al-Kutub al-muqaddasa wa hiyya kutub al-'ahd al-'atiq qad turjimat hadithan min al-lugha al-'ibraniyya al-asliyya wa kutub al-'ahd al-jadid li rabbina Yasu' al-masih qad turjimat hadithan min al-lugha al-yunaniyya al-asliyya ila al-'arabiyya*. London: William Watts, 1857.

———. *Mumahakat al-ta'wil fi munaqidat al-Injil*. Ed. Muhammad Ahmad 'Amayira. 'Amman: Dar Wa'il li al-Nashr, 2003.

———. *Sirr al-layalil fi al-qalb wa al-ibdali*. Ed. and introd. Muhammad al-Hadi bin al-Tahir al-Mutawwi. Beirut: Dar al-Gharb al-Islami, 2006 [1867].

———. *al-Wasita fi ma'arifat ahwal Malta wa Kashf al-mukhabba 'an funun Urubba*. Ed. Qasim Wahb. Beirut: al-Mu'assassa al-'Arabiyya li al-Dirasat wa al-Nashr, 2004.

Shohat, Ella. "The Invention of the Mizrahim." *Journal of Palestine Studies* 29.1 (Autumn 1999): 5–20.

———. *Israeli Cinema: East/West and the Politics of Representation*. London: I. B. Taurus, 2010 [1989].

———. "Kulumbus, Filastin, wa al-Yahud al-'arab: nahwa muqaraba 'ala'iqiyya li huwiyat al-majmu'." Tr. Subhi Hadidi. *al-Karmel* 52 (Summer 1997): 38–52.

———. "Sephardim in Israel: Zionism from the Standpoint of Its Jewish Victims." *Social Text* 19–20 (Autumn 1988): 1–35.

———. *Taboo Memories, Diasporic Voices*. Durham: Duke University Press, 2006.

Shukri, Ghali. *al-Nahda wa al-suqut fi al-fikr al-masri al-hadith*. Cairo: al-Hay'a al-Misriyya al-'Ama li al-Kitab, 1992.

Siddiq, Muhammad. *Arab Culture and the Novel: Genre, Identity, and Agency in Egyptian Fiction*. New York: Routledge, 2010 [2007].

———. "Significant but Problematic Others: Negotiating 'Israelis' in the Works of Mahmoud Darwish." *Comparative Literature Studies* 47.4 (2010): 487–503.

Slyomovics, Susan. *The Object of Memory: Arab and Jew Narrate the Palestinian Village*. Philadelphia: University of Pennsylvania Press, 1998.

Smith, Charles D. *Islam and the Search for Social Order in Modern Egypt: A Biography of Muhammad Husayn Haykal*. Albany: State University of New York Press, 1983.

Smith, Eli. "Khutbat al-ra'is al-sanawiyya." In *al-Jami'iyya al-suriyya li al-'ulum wa al-funun, 1847–1852*, 23–25. Beirut: Dar al-Hamra', 1990.

———. *Kitab al-bab al-maftuh fi a'mal al-ruh*. Tr. Butrus al-Bustani. Beirut: Matba'at Beirut al-Injiliyya, 1843.

Snir, Reuven. *'Araviyut, yahdut, tsiyonut: ma'avak zehuyot bi yetsirtam shel yehuday 'Irak*. Jerusalem: Ben Zvi Institute, 2005.

———. "Till Spring Comes: Arabic and Hebrew Literary Debates among Iraqi-Jews in Israel." *Shofar: An Interdisciplinary Journal of Jewish Studies* 24.2 (Winter 2006): 92–123.

Spivak, Gayatri Chakravorty. *An Aesthetic Education in the Era of Globalization*. Cambridge, MA: Harvard University Press, 2012.

———. *A Critique of Postcolonial Reason.* Cambridge, MA: Harvard University Press, 1999.

———. *Death of a Discipline.* New York: Columbia University Press, 2004.

———. "Glas Piece: A Compte Rendu." *Diacritics* 7.3 (Autumn 1977): 22–43.

Starr, Deborah. *Remembering Cosmopolitan Egypt: Literature, Culture, and Empire.* New York: Routledge, 2009.

Staten, Henry. *Eros in Mourning: From Homer to Lacan.* Baltimore: Johns Hopkins University Press, 1995.

———. *Wittgenstein and Derrida.* Lincoln: University of Nebraska Press, 1986 [1984].

Stetkevych, Jaroslav. *The Modern Arabic Literary Language: Lexical and Stylistic Developments.* Washington, DC: Georgetown University Press, 2006 [1970].

———. *The Zephyrs of Najd: The Poetics of Nostalgia in the Classical Arabic Nasib.* Chicago: University of Chicago Press, 1993.

Stetkevych, Susanne Pinckney. "Abu Tammam and the Arabic Critical tradition." In *Abu Tammam and the Poetics of the 'Abbasid Age*, 3–106. Leiden: Brill, 1991.

———. *The Mantle Odes: Arabic Praise Poems to the Prophet Muhammad.* Bloomington: Indiana University Press, 2010.

———. *The Mute Immortals Speak: Pre-Islamic Poetry and the Poetics of Ritual.* Ithaca: Cornell University Press, 1993.

Stoler, Ann Laura. *Race and the Education of Desire: Foucault's History of Sexuality and the Colonial Order of Things.* Durham: Duke University Press, 1995.

al-Sulh, 'Imad. *Ahmad Faris al-Shidyaq: atharuhu wa 'asruhu.* Beirut: Dar al-Nahar li al-Nashr, 1980.

Suwaydan, Sami. *Abhath fi al-nass al-riwa'i al-'arabi.* Beirut: Mu'assasat al-Abhath al-'Arabiyya, 1986.

al-Suyuti, Jalal al-Din 'Abd al-Rahman. *al-Itqan fi 'ulum al-Qur'an.* Beirut: Dar al-Katib al-'Arabi, 2007.

Swedenburg, Ted. *Memories of Revolt: The 1936–1939 Rebellion and the Palestinian National Past.* Fayetteville: University of Arkansas Press, 2003.

Tageldin, Shaden. *Disarming Words: Empire and the Seductions of Translation in Egypt.* Berkeley: University of California Press, 2011.

———. "Proxidistant Reading: Toward a Critical Pedagogy of the Nahda in U.S. Comparative Literary Stuidies." *Journal of Arabic Literature* 43 (2012): 227–68.

Taha, Ibrahim. "Duality and Acceptance: The Image of the Outsider in the Literary Work of Shimon Ballas." *Hebrew Studies* 38 (1997): 63–87.

Tahar, Miftah. *Taha Husain, sa critique littéraire et ses sources françaises.* Tunis: Maison Arabe du Livre, 1976.

al-Tahtawi, Rifa' Rafi'. *Kitab manahij al-albab al-misriyya fi mabahij al-adab al-'asriyya.* Cairo: Matba'at Sharikat al-Ragha'ib, 1912 [1867].

———. *Kitab al-tuhfa al-maktabiyya li taqrib al-lugha al-'arabiyya.* Cairo: n.p., 1868.

———. *Takhlis al-ibriz fi talkhis Bariz aw al-diwan al-nafis bi iywan Baris.* Tarablus: al-Dar al-'Arabiyya li al-Kitab, 1991 [1834].

Tajir, Jak. *Harakat al-tarjama bi Misr khilal al-qarn al-tasi' 'ashar.* Cairo: Dar al-Ma'arif, n.d.

Talmon, Rafael. *Arabic Grammar in Its Formative Age.* Leiden: Brill, 1997.

Tamari, Salim, ed. *Jerusalem 1948: The Arab Neighborhoods and Their Fate in the War.* Beirut: Institute for Palestine Studies, 1999.

Tarabishi, Jurj. *Nizariyat al-'aql: naqd naqd al-'aql al-'arabi.* Beirut: Dar al-Saqi, 1996.

Taubes, Jacob. *Die Politische Theologie des Paulus.* Ed. Aleida Assman and Jan Assman. Munich: Wilhelm Fink, 2003. Tr. Dana Hollander as *The Political Theology of Paul.* Stanford: Stanford University Press, 2004.

Terada, Rei. *Looking Away: Phenomenality and Dissatisfaction, Kant to Adorno.* Cambridge, MA: Harvard University Press, 2009.

———. "Seeing Is Reading." In *Legacies of Paul de Man,* ed. Marc Redfield, 162–77. New York: Fordham University Press, 2007.

Tezcan, Baki. *The Second Ottoman Empire: Political and Social Transformation in the Early Modern World.* New York: Cambridge University Press, 2012.

Thompson, Elizabeth. *Colonial Citizens: Republican Rights, Paternal Privilege, and Gender in French Syria and Lebanon.* New York: Columbia University Press, 2000.

Tibawi, A. L. *American Interests in Syria, 1800–1901.* Oxford: Clarendon Press, 1966.

———. "The American Missionaries in Beirut and Butrus al-Bustani." *St. Antony's Papers* 16.3 (1963): 137–82.

al-Tibrizi, Abu Zakariyya Yahya ibn 'Ali. *Sharh al-qasa'id al-'ashar.* Beirut: Dar al-Kutub al-'Ilmiyya, 1985.

Tignor, Robert. *Modernization and British Colonial Rule in Egypt, 1882–1914.* Princeton: Princeton University Press, 1966.

Torok, Maria. "The Illness of Mourning and the Fantasy of the Exquisite Corpse." In Nicolas Abraham and Maria Torok, *The Shell and the*

Kernel, vol. 1, ed. and tr. Nicholas T. Rand, 107–24. Chicago: University of Chicago Press, 1994.

Toufic, Jalal. *Forthcoming*. Berkeley: Atelos, 2000.

———. *Over-Sensitivity*. Los Angeles: Sun & Moon Press, 1996.

Traboulsi, Amjad. *La critique poétique des Arabes*. Damascus: n.p., 1955.

Traboulsi, Fawwaz. *Guernica/Beirut: al-fann wa al-hayat bayna jidariyya li Picasso wa madina 'arabiyya fi al-harb*. Beirut: al-Mu'assasa al-'Arabiyya li al-Dirasa wa al-Nashr, 1987.

al-Tunsi, Khayr al-Din. *Aqwam al-masalik fi ma'rifat ahwal al-mamalik*. Beirut: al-Mu'assasa al-Jami'iyya li al-Dirasat wa al-Nashr wa al-Tawzi', 1985 [1867].

Uthman, I'tidal. "al-Nass: nahwa qira'a naqdiyya ibda'iyya li ard Mahmoud Darwish." In *Ida'at al-nass: qira'at fi al-shi'r al-'arabi al-hadith*, 95–143. Cairo: al-Hay'a al-Misriyya al-'Ama li al-Kitab, 1998 [1988].

Van Gelder, G. J. H. *Beyond the Line: Classical Arabic Literary Critics on the Coherence and Unity of the Poem*. Leiden: Brill, 1982.

Vasalou, Sophia. "'Their Intention Was Shown by Their Bodily Movements': Basran Mu'tazilites on the Institution of Language." *Journal of the History of Philosophy* 47.2 (April 2009): 201–21.

Versteegh, Kees. *Arabic Grammar and Qur'anic Exegesis in Early Islam*. Leiden: Brill, 1993.

Vico, Giambattista. *New Science*. Tr. David Marsh. New York: Penguin, 2001.

Watenpaugh, Keith David. *Being Modern in the Middle East: Revolution, Nationalism, Colonialism, and the Arab Middle Class*. Princeton: Princeton University Press, 2006.

Watt, W. Montgomery, and Richard Bell. *Introduction to the Qur'an*. Edinburgh: Edinburgh University Press, 1970.

Wazin, 'Abdu. "Qira'a fi a'mal Mahmoud Darwish al-jadida." In 'Abdu Wazin, *Mahmoud Darwish: al-gharib yaq' 'ala nafsihi*, 9–55. Beirut: Riyad al-Rayyes, 2006.

Weber, Samuel. *Benjamin's—abilities*. Cambridge, MA: Harvard University Press, 2008.

———. *Institution and Interpretation*. Stanford: Stanford University Press, 2001 [1983].

———. *Targets of Opportunity: On the Militarization of Thinking*. New York: Fordham University Press, 2005.

Weiss, Bernard. "Medieval Muslim Discussions of the Origin of Language." *Zeitschrift der Deutschen Morgenländischen Gesellschaft* 124.1 (1974): 33–41.

———. *The Spirit of Islamic Law*. Athens: University of Georgia Press, 2006 [1998].

Weiss, Max. *In the Shadow of Sectarianism: Law, Shi'ism, and the Making of Modern Lebanon*. Cambridge, MA: Harvard University Press, 2010.

Wolf, Friedrich August. *Prolegomena to Homer*. Tr. and ed. Anthony Grafton, Glenn W. Most, and James E. G. Zetzel. Princeton: Princeton University Press, 1985.

Xavier, François. *Mahmoud Darwich et la nouvelle Andalousie*. Paris: Esquilles, 2002.

Yaghi, 'Abd al-Rahman. *Fi al-juhud al-riwa'iyya: Min Salim al-Bustani ila Najib Mahfuz*. Beirut: Dar al-Farabi, 1999.

Yahya, Ahlam. *'Awdat al-hisan al-da'i': waqfa ma' al-sha'ir Mahmoud Darwish*. Damascus: Dar al-Ninwa, 2003.

Yerushalmi, Yosef Hayim. *Freud's Moses: Judaism Terminable and Interminable*. New Haven: Yale University Press, 1991.

———. *Zakhor: Jewish History and Jewish Memory*. Seattle: University of Washington Press, 1982.

al-Yaziji, Nasif. *Kitab fasl al-khitab fi usul lughat al-a'rab*. Beirut: n.p., 1836.

Yuval, Israel Jacob. *Two Nations in Your Womb: Perceptions of Jews and Christians in Late Antiquity and the Middle Ages*. Tr. Barbara Harshav and Jonathan Chipman. Berkeley: University of California Press, 2006.

Zachs, Fruma. *The Making of Syrian Identity: Intellectuals and Merchants in Nineteenth-Century Beirut*. Leiden: Brill, 2005.

al-Zamakhshari, Abu al-Qasim Mahmud ibn 'Umar. *al-Kashshaf 'an haqa'iq ghawamid al-tanzil wa 'uyun al-aqawil fi wujuh al-ta'wil*. Beirut: Dar al-Kitab al-'Arabi, 2008.

Zaqtan, Ghassan. "Madha katabta ayyuha al-sha'ir fi al-harb?" In *Mahmoud Darwish: al-mukhtalif al-haqiqi*, 254–60. 'Amman: Dar al-Shuruq, 1999.

al-Zarkan, Muhammad 'Ali. *al-Jawanib al-lughawiyya 'ind Ahmad Faris al-Shidyaq*. Damascus: Dar al-Fikr, 1988.

al-Zarkashi, Badr al-Din Muhammad Ibn Abd Allah. *al-Burhan fi 'ulum al-Qur'an*. Ed. Muhammad Abu al-Fadl Ibrahim. Cairo: Dar Ihya' al-Kutub al-'Arabiyya, 1957.

al-Zawzani, al-Husayn ibn Ahmad. *Sharh al-mu'allaqat al-sab'*. Beirut: Dar al-Ma'rifa, 2003.

Zaydan, Jurji. *al-Falsafa al-lughawiyya*. Cairo: Dar al-Hilal, 1969 [1886].

———. *al-Lugha al-'arabiyya, ka'in hayy*. Cairo: Dar al-Hilal, n.d. [1904].

———. *Tarajim mashahir al-sharq fi al-qarn al-tas' 'ashar*. Beirut: Dar Maktabat al-Hayat, 1970 [1903].

———. *Tarikh adab al-lugha al-'arabiyya*. 4 vols. Cairo: Dar al-Hilal, n.d. [1914].

Zeidel, Ronen. "A Question of Language and Audience: On the Possibility of 'Iraqi Novels' in Hebrew." *Hebrew Studies* 50 (2009): 229–43.

INDEX